Islamic Economics Series – 17

Islam and the Economic Challenge

M. UMER CHAPRA

I0806576

The Islamic Foundation
and
The International Institute of Islamic Thought

Islam and the Economic Challenge

Published by:
THE ISLAMIC FOUNDATION,
Markfield Coference Centre, Ratby Lane,
Markfield, Leicestershire LE67 9SY,
United Kingdom

Quran House, P.O. Box 30611, Nairobi, Kenya

P.M.B. 3193, Kano, Nigeria

and
The International Institute of Islamic Thought,
555 Grove Street, Herndon, VA 22070, USA

Copyright © The Islamic Foundation 1992/1412 H.
Copyright © The International Institute of Islamic Thought
2nd Impression 2016/1437 H.

All rights reserved. No part of this publication may be reproduced, stored in a retrieval system or transmitted in any form or by any means, electronic, mechanical, photocopying, recording or otherwise, without the prior permission of the copyright owner.

Views expressed by different authors of books and studies represent their personal views and do not necessarily represent the views of the Islamic Foundation or the International Institute of Islamic Thought.

British Library Cataloguing in Publication Data

Chapra, Muhammad Umer
Islam and the Economic Challenge.
(Islamic Economics Series; No. 17)
1. Title II. Series
330.12

ISBN 978-0-86037-217-2 *paperback*

Cover design by Mustapha Aksay

To

my parents

رَّبِّ ٱرۡحَمۡهُمَا كَمَا رَبَّيَانِى صَغِيرًا

O my Lord! Bestow Your mercy on them, even
as they affectionately reared me in childhood

(Qur'an, 17: 24)

بسم الله الرحمن الرحيم

Contents

Foreword

The collapse of socialism and its centrally-planned economies in the former Soviet Union and Eastern Europe has raised a host of critical questions for all concerned with the ideological future of mankind. Does this represent the final demise of the socialist system and the unequivocal victory of the Western doctrine of economic and political liberalism, as is being claimed by some of the enthusiasts of Western capitalism, heralding the 'end of history', or does it constitute yet another phase in the never-ending ebb and flow of history? Does the fall of socialism of itself vindicate capitalism? If socialism has collapsed under the weight of its contradictions and inequalities does that necessarily mean that capitalism has overcome its own historical contradictions, injustices and failures? If the rise of socialism was owed, at least in part, to certain perceived failures of capitalism, how can its collapse mean that those failures (which prompted the search for alternatives) were illusory? Euphoria at the fall of a false god aside, the critical questions that still perplex the mind and conscience of man crave cogent answers.

Islam and the Economic Challenge represents a timely effort to reflect on these questions, and to suggest that the search for appropriate answers need not be confined to the Western experience, that it can profitably be widened to other religio-cultural horizons. It may open up radical new opportunities for mankind if questing minds will sincerely and objectively examine the merit of the submission of Muslim intellectuals that more satisfying and befitting answers to the economic questions of our time can be found in the Islamic approach to them.

Mankind has experimented, under the leadership of the West, with four major economic ideologies during the last three hundred years: capitalism, socialism, nationalist-fascism and the welfare state. All of them were based on the fundamentally and characteristically Western premise that religion and morality are not relevant to the solution of man's economic problems, that economic affairs are better settled by reference to the laws of economic behaviour and not in respect of any social code of moral conduct. Capitalism built its house on the principle of unfettered private enterprise, the profit motive and the mechanism of the market. Socialism sought millennium through public enterprise, social motivation, and a centrally-planned command economy. Fascism represented a distinct blend of the two resulting in a state capitalism geared to political aggrandisement and military adventurism. The welfare state is founded on a system of mixed economy, a form of capitalism blended with a measured socialist compassion. Despite note-worthy achievements in certain specific fields, these major ideologies on the economic stage have failed to resolve the major economic problems of mankind. Fascism was the first to fall into the dustbin of history. The latest fallen god is socialism. It would be the height of folly to assume that, by elimination, capitalism and the welfare state have been vindicated.

The economic crisis of our times remains as deep and distressing as ever and can be ignored only at the gravest peril. There is an urgent need for objective analysis of the entire economic landscape with a view to finding a fresh approach which seeks the objectives of efficiency and equity *simultaneously* and for *all* human beings.

Dr. Muhammad Umer Chapra's pioneering work *Islam and the Economic Challenge* represents one such effort. Dr. Chapra is a professional economist, educated at the universities of Karachi and Minnesota. He brings to the task wide experience of teaching and research in economics. He has been associated with a number of prestigious academic and research institutions like the Institute of Development Economics and the Central Institute of Islamic Research, Pakistan. He has taught at the Universities of Wisconsin, Plattville and Kentucky, Lexington, U.S.A. For the past twenty-six years he has served as Senior Economic Adviser at the Saudi Arabian Monetary Agency. This has given him a unique opportunity to drink deep at the wells of both theoretical knowledge and practical application of economics. He has also had abundant exposure to the Western as well as the Islamic perspectives on economics and society.

For the last fifteen years, he has been deeply involved in the development of an Islamic approach to economics. His earlier work, *Towards a Just Monetary System* (The Islamic Foundation, Leicester, 1985), won wide acclaim in the academic community of the Muslim world, and brought its author two prestigious awards – the Islamic Development Bank Award for distinguished service to Islamic Economics (1990), and the King Faisal International Prize for Islamic Studies (1990). Dr. Chapra is thus eminently qualified to address the more fundamental issue of the economic system for our times.

Islam and the Economic Challenge is the result of a decade of research and reflection. In this masterly treatise he examines with sophistication and academic rigour the three major economic systems of the Western world, and comes up with a realistic balance sheet of their achievements and failures. He also spells out the Islamic approach to the economy and its problems, and puts forward concrete suggestions for restructuring the Muslim economies and pursuing new paths towards strategic developmental planning. In broad terms, his recipe for the Muslim world comprises development planning together with the application of a socially-accepted moral filter for the market mechanism, more broadly-based motivation for economic effort and fundamental structural reforms to establish a supporting framework.

Dr. Chapra has dealt with the subject as a trained social scientist and objective Islamic scholar. His grasp of the contemporary economic systems and their problems is thorough and incisive; his presentation of the Islamic economic order is precise and convincing. His balanced critique of the Western systems as well as that of the contemporary Muslim society is presented in a style that is scholarly yet simple, clear and prescriptive. *Islam and the Economic Challenge* is not merely a treatise in theory, it is of immense relevance to the policy makers, not merely in the Muslim world, but in the world as a whole.

I foresee *Islam and the Economic Challenge* becoming a standard work on contemporary economic systems, and a catalyst for promoting the Islamic approach to the solution of the economic problems of the contemporary Muslim world.

Dr. Chapra's unique contribution lies in the realism of his

thought and approach. He identifies the problem with clarity; he discusses the prevalent approaches with professional distance, acknowledging the achievements of different experiments without reservation, and analysing their failures without exaggeration; at the same time he expounds the Islamic alternative with a quiet precision, without apology or affectation.

Dr. Chapra has clearly demonstrated that well-being cannot be attained through the pursuit of material possessions alone, and that efficiency and equity can become operational concepts only if they are redefined in the context of their linkage to moral values and socio-economic structures. His is a plea for the rediscovery of man as the centre-piece of economic thinking and effort. He uses the tools of economic analysis as effectively as can be done by a good Western economist, but his real contribution lies in a highly thoughtful effort to build a new house for economics where it is not torn from its moral foundation, and where economic effort can take place within a socio-economic framework that ensures efficient allocation and equitable distribution simultaneously, and not merely for a particular segment of society, of humanity, but for all. He strives to lift economics to the next stage of its evolution when, drawing upon its moral springs as well as vast empirical experiences spread over several centuries, it may be capable of playing an effective role towards general human fulfilment and not merely material excess for the privileged. If economics is to become a real blessing for man, a tool for his well-being, the missing dimension needs to be restored. *Islam and the Economic Challenge* is a step towards such an economics of tomorrow.

Leicester **Khurshid Ahmad**
3 January 1992
27 Jumādā al-Thānī 1412

Preface

The ongoing revival of Islam in almost all Muslim countries has created the need for a clear, integrated picture of the programme that Islam has to offer to realise the kind of well-being that it envisages, and to counter the different problems now facing mankind, particularly in the economic field. Of special interest is a strategy that would help reduce to manageable limits the macroeconomic and external imbalances that most countries are now experiencing around the world, and would yet enable them to attain full employment, remove poverty, fulfil needs, and minimise inequalities of income and wealth. Can the Muslim countries formulate such a strategy within the framework of the secularist worldview of capitalism, socialism and the welfare state? Can Islam help them realise their goals? If so, what kind of a policy package do Islamic teachings imply? This book is an effort to answer these and other related questions.

The first draft of the manuscript was circulated to a dozen scholars in the field of Islamic and conventional economics. These include Dr. M. Anas Zarqa, Dr. M. Nejatullah Siddiqi, Dr. Munawar Iqbal and Dr. M. Fahim Khan in Saudi Arabia, Prof. Kenneth Boulding, Prof. Everett Hagen, Prof. Frank Vogel, and Dr. Zubair Iqbal in the United States, Prof. Rodney Wilson and Prof. John Presley in the United Kingdom, Prof. Volker Nienhaus in Germany, and Prof. Khurshid Ahmad in Pakistan. I am grateful to all of them for the precious time they have spared to read the manuscript carefully and to give me the benefit of their valuable comments and suggestions. I have revised the manuscript substantially in the light of these. Consequently, even though the main thesis of the original remains intact, the final product reflects in many places their rich insights.

I have benefited most especially from the penetrating critique of Dr. Zarqa, Dr. Siddiqi, Dr. Munawar Iqbal, and Prof. Boulding, indeed far more than it is possible for me to acknowledge. The first three, being resident in Saudi Arabia, also spared a substantial part of their valuable time for discussions with me on a number of crucial issues. These discussions not only improved my personal understanding of the subject, but also helped to strengthen the logic of the Islamic strategy.

Thus, if readers find this book worthwhile, a substantial part of the credit goes to the scholars listed above. None of them has, however, seen the final draft. Any errors that still remain should hence be attributed to me alone, particularly as I was unable to carry out all their suggestions for fear of making the book too technical and bulky. The views expressed in this book are mine and do not necessarily reflect the views of the institution where I work.

My debt to the classical and current literature on Islamic economics is so great that even the great number of footnote references to specific sources cannot discharge it. Moreover, there has been such an exponential growth in the current literature, that comprehensive referencing is not even possible, particularly in a book that covers the three prevalent systems as well as Islam. I have hence been highly selective and, in the process, may have left out some references which others consider to be important. Transliteration marks have been put only where necessary to avoid overburdening the book with such marks. I have used certain Arabic words and expressions essential for understanding the Islamic message, in preference to English translations which would not allow the reader to get out of the culturally conditioned connotations of these terms, something that is necessary to do.

I am indebted also to many others who have indirectly participated in the writing and publication of this book. Prominent among them are my wife and children who have been a source of great inspiration and moral support. My brothers Abdul Raḥman and Muhammad have also provided continuous encouragement. I have also benefited significantly from the translations of the Qur'ān by Abdullah Yusuf Ali, T. B. Irving and Muhammad Asad, even though I have not reproduced their translations. Translations from the *fiqh, ḥadīth* and other Arabic literature are my own. However, my daughter Sumayyah has helped generously in solving some of the difficult problems of translation. Credit is also due to Dr. M. M. Ahsan and other brothers at the Islamic Foundation for their help and cooperation in preparing and checking the manuscript, and for seeing it through the press. I am also indebted to Mr. Mobin Ahmad for the research and secretarial assistance he has so efficiently rendered to me during the writing of this book. May God reward them all generously for their contribution.

Riyadh, Saudi Arabia **M. Umer Chapra**
11 Jumādā al-Ākhirah 1411
28 December 1990

Postscript

The Soviet economic system has collapsed since the manuscript of this book was finalised and the Swedish Social Democratic Party has also lost its majority in the parliament after being in power for more than 50 years. These developments further reinforce the central thesis of this book and, in particular, the analysis of Chapters 2 and 3 on socialism and the welfare state.

9 Rabī' al-Awwal 1412
18 September 1991

Introduction

> The very objective of the *Sharī'ah* is to promote the welfare of the people, which lies in safeguarding their faith, their life, their intellect, their posterity and their wealth. Whatever ensures the safeguarding of these five serves public interest and is desirable.
>
> al-Ghazālī[1]

> The basis of the *Sharī'ah* is wisdom and welfare of the people in this world as well as the Hereafter. This welfare lies in complete justice, mercy, well-being and wisdom. Anything that departs from justice to oppression, from mercy to harshness, from welfare to misery and from wisdom to folly, has nothing to do with the *Sharī'ah*.
>
> Ibn al-Qayyim[2]

THE CHALLENGE

Human well-being has been the professed objective of all societies. There is, however, a difference of opinion on what constitutes well-being and how it may be realised. Even though material conditions are not the only constituents of well-being, the modern, secularist perspective, with its emphasis primarily on those conditions, seems to believe that well-being could be ensured if certain material goals were realised. These goals include: elimination of poverty, fulfilment of the basic material needs of all individuals,[3] availability to everyone of an opportunity to earn an honest living, and equitable distribution of income and wealth. However, no country around the world, irrespective of whether it is rich or poor, has been able to realise even these material goals.

The centrally-planned economies, which had claimed to be able to secure these material goals, have not only failed to do so but are also facing a serious economic crisis which has, beyond doubt, assured the system's failure. A corresponding euphoria among the market economy countries has urged the superiority of the market system more vehemently than ever. However, even though the performance of the market economy countries has certainly been better, they too have failed to realise the desired material goals. Their failure is made all the more conspicuous by their economic instability and macroeconomic imbalances, reflected in frequent economic fluctuations, high rates of inflation and unemployment, excessive budgetary and balance of payments deficits, and volatility in the foreign exchange, commodity and stock markets. The developing countries are further plagued by difficult debt-servicing problems, threatening not only their future development but also the health and survival of the international financial system.

In addition to these problems, practically all countries around the world are experiencing a scale of depletion of non-renewable natural resources and environmental pollution which is endangering life on earth. There is a rising level of stress, tension and strife in human affairs, accompanied by an increase in all the symptoms of anomie, such as frustration, crime, alcoholism, drug addiction, divorce, child battering, mental illness and suicide, all indicating lack of inner contentment in the life of individuals.

Muslim countries, the main focus of this book, are not an exception. They too are in a state of turmoil, like the rest of the world. Poverty and inequalities have become more marked: while even the basic needs of a considerable proportion of the population remain unsatisfied, the rich and upper middle classes live in great affluence. The existence of poverty alongside affluence tends to corrode the fabric of brotherhood and social solidarity and serves as one of the prime causes of crime and violence, social unrest and political instability. Most of these countries are also beset with extremely difficult macroeconomic imbalances. This failing on the part of Muslim countries is all the more serious because Islam places an uncompromising emphasis on human dignity, brotherhood and socio-economic justice, which will remain empty slogans until all the essential elements of well-being are secured.

EFFICIENCY AND EQUITY?

Why is it that no country around the world has been able to realise even the material elements of human well-being? Can scarcity of resources be held responsible for the failure? Most economists would tend to answer negatively, because they do not consider resources to be scarce in an absolute sense. Resources are only scarce relatively to the claims on them. Most economists would tend to agree that, in spite of the relative scarcity of resources, it is possible to realise material goals and to minimise instability and imbalances if the available resources are used 'efficiently' and 'equitably'.[4] It is this possibility that poses a challenge to humanity – to use the available resources in such an 'efficient' and 'equitable' way that the universally-accepted goals for material well-being are actualised and the instability and imbalances are minimised. This brings into focus a host of difficult questions related to the meaning of 'efficiency' and 'equity' and how they can be realised.

'Efficiency' and 'equity' have been defined in different ways. Within the framework of this study, the most appropriate definitions seem to be those that are in harmony with the universally-accepted material goals. An economy may be said to have attained optimum efficiency if it has been able to employ the total potential of available human and material resources in such a way that the maximum feasible quantity of need-satisfying goods and services is produced with a reasonable degree of economic stability and a sustainable rate of future growth. The test of such efficiency lies in the inability to attain a socially more acceptable result without creating prolonged macroeconomic imbalances, and without unduly depleting non-renewable resources or damaging the environment to an extent that life on earth becomes endangered. An economy may be said to have attained optimum equity if the goods and services produced are distributed in such a way that the needs of all individuals are adequately satisfied and there is an equitable distribution of income and wealth, without adversely affecting the motivation for work, saving, investment and enterprise. Since it is basically economic systems which address the question of realising efficiency and equity, the most rational approach would be to adopt an economic system that would help realise both.

The Three Questions

To allocate resources efficiently and to distribute them equitably, every economic system must answer the three well-known fundamental economic questions of what, how, and for whom to produce: how much of which alternative goods and services shall be produced, who will produce them with what combination of resources and in what technological manner, and who will enjoy to what extent the goods and services produced.[5] The answers to these questions determine not only the allocation of resources in an economy but also their distribution between individuals and between the present (consumption) and the future (saving and investment). Allocation and distribution cover a major part of economics, and ultimately determine whether the needs of all individuals are fulfilled, whether all other desired socio-economic goals are realised, and whether there is sufficient motivation for a people to put in the best performance for their realisation. The crucial test for an economic system lies not in its professed goals but rather in their realisation.

The Role of Worldview and Strategy

All three questions, though apparently straightforward, are value-laden and cannot be answered in a vacuum. It is necessary to have a worldview or underlying philosophy *(weltanschauung)* and strategy. Every society or system is dominated by its own worldview which is based on a set of implicit or explicit assumptions about the origin of the universe and the nature of human life. This worldview controls, in the words of Arthur Lovejoy, "the nature of man's reflections on almost any subject".[6] Differences in views about human nature lead to differences in conclusions about the meaning and purpose of human life, the ultimate ownership and objective of the limited resources at the disposal of human beings, the relationship of human beings towards each other (their rights and responsibilities) and their environment, and the criteria for efficiency and equity. Such a worldview performs the same function for an economic system as the foundation does for a building: even though the supporting foundation is invariably invisible and unmentioned, it continues to play a determining role.

The system's strategy is a logical outcome of this worldview. To be complete and effective in enabling the system to realise its goals, the strategy must consist of a number of indispensable elements. It must have a filter mechanism through which all claims may be passed by either the 'invisible' or the 'visible' hand to maintain a balance between resources and the claims on them and to realise optimum efficiency and equity. It must provide a mechanism to motivate individuals to put in their best performance in their own interest and in the interest of society. It must also have an effective way of bringing about socio-economic restructuring to enable a prompt transfer of resources from one use to another until the most efficient and equitable allocation and distribution have been attained.

Unless the worldview and the strategy of a system are in harmony with its professed goals, the goals cannot be actualised.[7] To grow a mango tree, you need a mango seed; a lemon seed, no matter how good, will not do.[8] Systems which reflect an inherent inconsistency between their goals and their worldview and strategy are unable to bring about the fundamental adjustments in the life-styles and the structure and organisation of their economies. They are therefore crisis-prone. People living in such systems cannot but be the victims of false promises – promises that cannot be fulfilled, no matter how many minor adjustments are made. Such minor adjustments do not penetrate to the root of the problem. They address merely the symptoms of the inconsistency but fail to achieve consistency between the worldview and strategy and the goals. The problems therefore reappear in a different form, more serious, and more aggravated each time.

THE PREVAILING SYSTEMS

There have been several explanations of the universe and of the nature and meaning of human life. These explanations have led to different ways of life and different economic systems, each based explicitly or implicitly on its own worldview and each providing a different strategy for solving the economic problem. Three economic systems are dominant in the present-day world – capitalism, socialism and their joint offspring, the secularist welfare state. Each of these has undergone significant revisions relative to the original version because of various problems faced over the years, and the changes introduced to solve them. The systems in their present form are thus far from what they were originally. Nevertheless, in spite of the various 'revisions' in the systems, the enormous wealth that the countries following these systems have created, and the relative abundance of their resources, these countries have failed in varying degrees to realise the goals they aspire for. Many of them are also facing serious macroeconomic imbalances. Their problems have in fact increased continually. Social unrest and crime have also risen and they are in general facing a crisis situation.

Their problems, as will be shown in this book, are not contingent events, external to the systems. They are rather a natural and fairly predictable consequence of the inherent structural defects in the systems themselves. These defects result from the conflict in their goals, which are rooted in their moral and religious past, and their worldview and strategy, which are an outgrowth of secularism and reflect a discord with their religious traditions. Hence, the existing systems, which themselves need, in the words of Burtt, "to rethink a correct philosophy of man",[9] cannot provide a model which may be emulated by Muslim countries to realise their goals with resources that are relatively much smaller and would take decades to reach anywhere near those of the countries following these systems.

THE ISLAMIC ALTERNATIVE

Islam envisages an economic system fundamentally different from the prevailing systems. It has its roots in the *Sharī'ah* (Islamic teachings) from which it derives its worldview as well as its goals and strategy. The goals of Islam *(maqāṣid al-Sharī'ah),* unlike those of the predominantly secularist systems of the present-day world, are not primarily materialist. They are rather based on its own concepts of human well-being *(falāḥ)* and good life *(ḥayāt ṭayyibah)* which give utmost importance to brotherhood and socio-economic justice and require a balanced satisfaction of both the material and the spiritual needs of *all* human beings.[10] This is because of the belief that all human beings are equal in being God's vicegerents on earth and His dependents, and cannot feel inner happiness and tranquillity until the real well-being of all has been attained through the satisfaction of both spiritual and material needs.

The *Maqāṣid Al-Sharī'ah*

The *maqāṣid al-Sharī'ah* (referred to hereafter as the *maqāṣid*) include everything that is needed to realise *falāḥ* and *ḥayāt ṭayyibah* within the constraints of the *Sharī'ah*. Ghazālī, as the quotation given at the beginning of this Introduction indicates, incorporates in the *maqāṣid* everything that is considered necessary to preserve and enrich faith, life, intellect, posterity and wealth.

Ghazālī wisely puts faith at the head of the list of *maqāṣid* because, within the Islamic perspective, faith is the most important ingredient for human well-being. It puts human relations on a proper foundation, enabling human beings to interact with each other in a balanced and mutually caring manner to help ensure the well-being of all. It also provides a moral filter for allocation and distribution of resources in accordance with the dictates of brotherhood and socio-economic justice, and a motivating system that gives biting power to the goals of need-fulfilment and equitable distribution of income and wealth. Without injecting the dimension of faith into all human decisions, irrespective of whether they take place in the household, the corporate boardroom, the market, or the politburo, it may not be possible to realise efficiency and equity in the allocation and distribution of resources, to minimise macroeconomic imbalances and economic instability, or to overcome crime, strife, tensions and the different symptoms of anomie.

Efficiency and equity cannot even be defined without resort to a moral filter.[11] As Frank Knight has rightly argued, the most important principle of physical science is that matter can neither be created nor destroyed. Total output will thus always be equal to total input in physical terms. The correct definition of efficiency would hence be the ratio, not between total 'output' and total 'input' but between *useful* output and total output or input.[12] This means that a measure of 'usefulness' is needed to measure efficiency. As will be argued in this book, individual preferences and prices cannot by themselves provide such a measure if the objective is the well-being of all. It is necessary to complement these by a socially-agreed moral filter. If it is difficult to define efficiency without moral criteria, then it is even more difficult to define equity without these.

Ghazālī places wealth at the end of the list because it is not an end in itself. It is only a means, though an important and indispensable one, for realising human well-being. Wealth cannot help realise this objective unless it is allocated efficiently and distributed equitably. This requires, as indicated above, the satisfaction of certain moral criteria in the pursuit of wealth and the operation of markets or the politburo. If wealth becomes an end in itself, it leads to inequities, imbalances and environmental excesses, which ultimately reduce the well-being of most members of the present and the future generations.

The three goals in the middle (life, intellect and posterity) relate to the human being himself, whose well-being is the primary objective of the *Sharī'ah*. The firm direction that a moral commitment to the enrichment of these three can provide to the allocation and distribution of resources, cannot come from prices and markets alone in a secularist environment. It is the life, intellect and posterity of all human beings that are to be preserved and enriched and not just of the rich and the highly placed. Everything that is necessary for enriching these three for all must be considered a 'need' and everything possible done to ensure its fulfilment – adequate nutrition, clothing, proper upbringing and education for spiritual and intellectual development, housing, a healthy spiritual and physical environment (with reduced tensions, crime and pollution), medical facilities, comfortable transport, enough leisure to meet all essential family and social obligations, and an opportunity to earn an honest living. Allocation and distribution of resources must take a course that helps fulfil these and other needs that are considered essential. The fulfilment of all these needs would make all members of both the present and the future generations tranquil, comfortable, healthy and efficient, and able to contribute richly towards the realisation and perpetuation of *falāḥ* and *ḥayāt ṭayyibah.* Any allocation and distribution of resources that does not help realise *falāḥ* and *ḥayāt ṭayyibah* does not, in accordance with the quotation of Ibn al-Qayyim given above, reflect wisdom, and cannot be considered either efficient or equitable.

The Wide Gulf

Unfortunately, because of a number of historical factors, two of which are the decadence of Muslims and their consequent subjugation by imperialist forces, both capitalist and socialist, there is a wide gulf between the *Sharī'ah* and the actual practice in Muslim countries. The Muslim society does not reflect the spiritual lustre of Islam and, in fact, among a vast majority of the society, there is not even an awareness of the necessary characteristics required of the Muslim or of the Islamic society. The dominant ideology in Muslim countries is not Islam but rather secularism along with a mixture of feudalism, capitalism and socialism. The Islamic economic system does not prevail in any part of the Muslim world. The Muslim countries have been trying to solve their economic problems through policies developed within the secularist perspective of the prevailing systems. Their problems have become aggravated and they have moved farther and farther from the realisation of the *maqāṣid.* Despite a rise in gross domestic product, poverty has not declined; rather, it has risen. Inequalities of income and wealth have also worsened, and the basic needs of their people remain unsatisfied. The public sector budgetary deficits have risen, as have balance of payments deficits and external debt, and the threat of inflation persists. Malaysia's Prime Minister, Mahathir Muhammad, observed that ideas for ending Third World poverty were running out. "The search for solutions in our negotiations with the developed economies has practically ground to a halt." The Third World officials "faced a daunting task in finding new ideas to pull poor countries out of mounting indebtedness".[13] Why is this so, and can Islamisation (reconstruction of the economies of Muslim countries in the light of Islamic teachings) be helpful?

ABOUT THIS BOOK

This book is an attempt to answer this question. It consists of two parts. The first part covers the unsuccessful systems – systems that the Muslim countries must avoid if they wish to actualise their socio-economic goals. The first three chapters of this part analyse the worldview and strategy of the prevalent systems, not just for the sake of criticism, but to identify the reasons for, and the nature and implications of, the conflict between their goals and their worldview and strategy. This will enable readers to appreciate why this lack of harmony has frustrated, and will continue to frustrate, the efforts of countries following these systems to realise simultaneously both efficiency and equity in the allocation of their scarce resources. It will also enable them to follow the discussion in Chapter 4 of why the formulation of policies within the perspective of the prevailing systems has led to inconsistencies in the economic policies pursued by developing countries, and has aggravated their problems by not only accentuating macroeconomic and external imbalances but also frustrating their goal of realising equity.

The second part, consisting of seven chapters, discusses the Islamic response. The first of these chapters, Chapter 5, indicates the worldview and strategy of Islam and the inherent consistency of these with the *maqāṣid*. Chapter 6, through an account of the malaise in the Muslim world, lays the groundwork for a discussion of five different policy dimensions that the Muslim countries need to adopt, in the light of Islamic teachings, to realise the *maqāṣid* without prolonged imbalances. Each of these policy dimensions is addressed in a separate chapter. Chapter 7 discusses the ways of invigorating the human factor, which is generally recognised to be very important, but which acquires a crucial significance in a system that makes human beings the pivot of all socio-economic reform and efforts to realise both efficiency and equity. Chapter 8 discusses the different ways of reducing concentration of wealth, necessary to realise socio-economic justice to which Islam gives maximum importance in its value system. Chapters 9 and 10 indicate the kinds of economic and financial restructuring that are needed to realise the socio-economic goals of Islam. Chapter 11 goes briefly into the strategic policy planning, which is necessary to implement effectively the policy implications of Islamic teachings.

The concluding chapter sums up the discussion running through all eleven chapters. This should enable the reader to review the gist of the whole analysis. Since this book is basically a discussion of the economic problem, it does not cover the spiritual aspects of *falāḥ* and *ḥayāt ṭayyibah* except to the extent to which they are directly related to the economic problem.

It may seem preposterous to discuss the problems of all Muslim countries in a single book. There are high-income, middle-income and low-income countries in different stages of economic development and facing different problems. However, while that is true, the quintessence of their problems is much the same, the differences being only in magnitude.[14] They are all faced with relative scarcity of resources. Nevertheless, being Muslim countries, it is their incontrovertible moral obligation to realise the *maqāṣid* without creating prolonged imbalances. Hence they can all benefit from the discussion, though in varying degrees. The book is mainly addressed, however, to the poorer and middle-income countries whose problems are more acute.

Notes and References (Introduction)

1 Al-Ghazālī, *al-Mustasfā* (1937), vol. 1, pp. 139–40.

2 Ibn Qayyim al-Jawziyyah, *I'lām al-Muwaqqi'īn* (1955), vol. 3, p. 14.

3 For determining material human needs, one must first determine what really contributes to the survival, comfort and development of human beings. This may be difficult, but not impossible, to do. Keynes' observation on this subject may be useful. He stated that even though "the needs of human beings may seem to be insatiable", . . . "they fall into two classes – those needs which are absolute in the sense that we feel them whatever the situation of our fellow human beings may be, and those which are relative ones in the sense that their satisfaction lifts us above, makes us feel superior to, our fellows. Needs of the second class, those which satisfy the desire for superiority, may indeed be insatiable; for the higher the general level, the higher still are they. But this is not so true of the absolute needs." (J. M. Keynes, *The Collected Writings of John Maynard Keynes*, vol. IX, Essays in Persuasion, the essay on "Economic Possibilities for our Grandchildren", 1972, p. 326.) This classification implies

that needs which are absolute, originate within the individual himself and are necessitated by the human condition. Their fulfilment is necessary for human survival, comfort and development. In contrast with this, needs which are relative are, as Galbraith puts it, "contrived for him". (Galbraith, *The Affluent Society*, p. 152.) They include all status symbols and all goods and services which do not add to his well-being. The former may be called *needs* while the latter may be called *wants*. The desire for want satisfaction is created artificially by means of advertising and social pressures to conform.

If poverty is defined as the inability of a person to fulfil his and his dependents' material needs out of his or her own resources, then elimination of poverty and need satisfaction are not synonymous terms. Needs may be fulfilled by means of assistance from other individuals, organisations and the state. The preferable objective would be to enable everyone to fulfil needs through his or her own effort. This may not always be possible to accomplish because of the individual's physical or mental inability and the difficulty of finding suitable employment. Nevertheless, it is the obligation of a society to do its utmost to remove poverty.

4 Muhammad Baqir al-Sadr has rightly stated the Islamic position on this subject by saying that poverty and deprivation are due to inequitable distribution and the absence of a morally-defined framework of human relationships between the rich and the poor (Muhammad Baqir al-Sadr, *Iqtiṣādunā* (1981), p. 343).

5 For a clear presentation of the position of conventional economists on the subject, see Milton Rose Friedman, *Free to Choose* (1980), pp. 9-37; and P. A. Samuelson, *Economics* (1980), pp. 15–18.

6 Arthur Lovejoy, *The Great Chain of Being* (1960), p. 7.

7 For an elaboration of this thesis, see, with respect to capitalism, Edward S. Greenberg, *Serving the Few: Corporate Capitalism and the Bias of Government Policy* (1974); and with respect to the secularist welfare state, Claus Offe, *Contradictions of the Welfare State*, ed., John Keane (1984).

8 This analogy of mango and lemon seeds has been borrowed from Sayyid Abul A'la Mawdudi, *Islāmī Riyāsat* (1982), p. 695.

9 Edwin A. Burtt, *The Metaphysical Foundations of Modern Science* (1955), p. 27.

10 The word *falāḥ* (well-being) is used in the Qur'ān at least forty times in different conjugational forms. The call for *falāḥ* is also made from the minaret five times a day and each time the phrase, "come for *falāḥ*", is repeated twice. According to Islam, spiritual uplift is an essential ingredient of human well-being and any effort to realise it otherwise is bound to fail.

The expression of *ḥayāt ṭayyibah* comes from the following verse of the Qur'ān: "All those, male or female, who do righteous deeds and are believers, We will most certainly grant to them *ḥayāt ṭayyibah*, and also reward them (in the Hereafter) in accordance with the best of what they did" (16: 97).

11 See M. Anas Zarqa, "Capital Allocation, Efficiency and Growth in an

Interest-free Islamic Economy'', November 1982, p. 49; and ''Islamic Economics: An Approach to Human Welfare'', in K. Ahmad, *Studies in Islamic Economics* (1980), pp. 3–18. See also Benjamin Ward, *What is Wrong with Economics?* (1972), p. 211.

12 Frank H. Knight, ''Social Economic Organisation'', reprinted from his *The Economic Organisation*, pp. 3–30, in W. Breit, *et al.*, *Readings in Microeconomics* (1986), p. 4. I am grateful to Dr. Anas Zarqa, who drew my attention to this argument.

13 *Arab News*, 2 March 1988.

14 It would be pertinent to quote here Gottfried Haberler, who says: ''I believe in what some development economists call 'monoeconomics'; that is to say, the same principles apply to developing and developed countries alike. From the adoption of monoeconomics, however, it does not follow that policy prescriptions should be the same for all countries.'' (Gottfried Haberler, ''Liberal and Illiberal Development Policy'', in Gerald M. Meier, ed., *Pioneers in Development*, Second Series (1987), p. 53.

PART I

THE UNSUCCESSFUL SYSTEMS

فَأَعْرِضْ عَن مَّن تَوَلَّىٰ عَن ذِكْرِنَا
وَلَمْ يُرِدْ إِلَّا ٱلْحَيَوٰةَ ٱلدُّنْيَا

Therefore, turn away from those who do not remember Us and care for no more than the life of this world (Qur'an, 53: 29)

إِنَّ هَٰٓؤُلَآءِ يُحِبُّونَ ٱلْعَاجِلَةَ
وَيَذَرُونَ وَرَآءَهُمْ يَوْمًا ثَقِيلًا

Indeed, they love this fleeting life and pay no attention to the Hard Day (Qur'an, 76: 27)

CHAPTER 1

The Limits of Capitalism

> Poverty in the midst of plenty
> and joyless affluence are but
> symptoms of a profound disorder.
>
> Tibor Scitovsky[1]

Capitalism, in its classical *laissez-faire* sense, does not exist anywhere. It has been modified over the centuries. Governments have intervened extensively to correct some of its deficiencies and to offset, at least partly, some of its adverse effects on equity. Nevertheless, it continues to exercise a charismatic appeal as a model. This appeal has gained further strength from the failure of socialism, the disenchantment with a large government role in the economy, and the backlash against the welfare state. Calls have been intensified in recent years from both intellectual and political platforms for liberalism, or a return, as nearly as possible, to the classical model with 'minimum' government intervention. This call is at present tending to dominate the thinking and economic policies of not only the Western industrial countries but also a substantial part of the Third World and the now-liberalising Communist countries. It is hence desirable to understand the logic of the system, the factors that led to the development of its worldview and strategy, and to see whether it is logically possible for this system to realise efficiency, which is taken for granted as its hallmark, and equity, which many economists now recognise, it cannot realise. Some of the modifications that had become a part of the conventional wisdom as a result of the system's failures, but which are now being challenged, will be discussed partly in this Chapter but mainly in Chapter 3 on the Welfare State.

Capitalism may be said to have the following five distinguishing features: (a) it considers accelerated wealth expansion and maximum production and 'want' satisfaction in accordance with individual preferences to be of primary importance in human well-being; (b) it deems unhindered individual freedom to pursue pecuniary self-interest and to own and manage private property to be necessary for individual initiative; (c) it assumes individual initiative along with decentralised decision-making in freely operating competitive markets to be sufficient conditions for realising optimum efficiency in the allocation of resources; (d) it does not recognise the necessity of a significant role for government or collective value judgements in either allocative efficiency or distributive equity; and (e) it claims that serving of self-interest by all individuals will also automatically serve the collective social interest.

THE LOGIC OF THE SYSTEM: THE CLAIMED SYMMETRY

The crucial feature in the entire logic of the market system is the claimed symmetry between public and private interests. It is assumed that individuals, in their capacity as sovereign consumers, act rationally and maximise their utility by buying at the lowest price the goods and services that occupy a higher place on their preference scales. Their preferences are reflected in the market place through their demand or willingness to pay the market price. Individuals, in their capacity as producers, also act rationally and respond 'passively' to this demand by producing at the lowest cost whatever will help them maximise their profits. The free interaction of utility-maximising consumers and profit-maximising producers under perfectly competitive market conditions determines the market clearing prices for goods and services. These prices (and costs, which are also prices) serve as an impartial, value-neutral filter mechanism and lead to the production of that configuration of goods and services which is in maximum harmony with consumer preferences. These prices also automatically determine the transfer of resources from one use to another, thus contributing to their most efficient utilisation without anyone's conscious effort or intervention.

Since the resultant configuration of goods and services is a reflection of consumer preferences, it is the most 'efficient' – it is not possible to improve upon it. Since this configuration also determines the incomes earned by the respective factors of production on the basis of their contribution to output and revenue, the resultant income distribution is also 'equitable'.[2] At the point of equilibrium, consumer satisfactions (utilities) are maximised, supplier costs are minimised, and factor earnings (including wages and profits) are maximised. The market system, it is thus concluded, determines not only the most 'efficient' use of resources but also the most 'equitable' distribution of income in a rational and impartial manner without value judgements. It also automatically brings about a harmony between private and public interests. Questions about whether this configuration satisfies basic human needs and whether the distribution is equitable are improper because such questions cannot be answered without collective value judgements which, unlike market clearing prices, cannot be established impartially. Questions about differentials in wealth holdings are similarly improper because the wealth of individuals represents the savings resulting from the market value of their contributions to output and their abstinence from consumption. Hence there is no need for government intervention except to the extent to which it is necessary to ensure competition and orderly markets and to offset market failure in the supply of public goods.

Every competitive equilibrium is considered to be a Pareto optimum – it is not possible to make anyone better off without making someone else worse off – which must be accepted as both 'efficient' and 'equitable'. Thus the terms 'efficiency' and 'equity', as defined within this framework, do not have a direct relationship with the objectives of removing poverty, fulfilling needs, and reducing inequalities of income and wealth. It is assumed that these objectives will also be realised as a 'necessary' concomitant of 'efficiency' and 'equity' brought about by the competitive equilibrium. Any outside intervention to change the status quo must necessarily lead to results which are less 'efficient' and 'equitable'. The only acceptable way to change the status quo would be within the framework of Pareto optimality – to make some people 'better off' without making anyone 'worse off'.

But history and experience belie the claimed symmetry between private and social interest. The system has failed to realise equity. The 'invisible' hand of market forces, guided primarily by 'self-interest' has led, in the words of Dalton, to "an inhumane, squalid and unjust society of rampant commercialism, social division, and conflict between employer and employee, landlord and tenant, and ruler and ruled."[3] The reason is that the logic of capitalism is based on a number of assumptions about preconditions which are unrealistic and which have not been and cannot be satisfied under normal conditions. As Brittan has rightly indicated: "The full set of assumptions, side conditions and constraints required for the pursuit of market gain to yield beneficial results can never be fully written down. Many of the most important rules are not formulated explicitly until a special problem arises."[4] Since the secularist thrust of capitalism's worldview has played the most decisive role in its failure to harmonise individual and social interest, it is important to look at the historical factors which have led to the development of this worldview.

THE THRUST TOWARD SECULARISM

The Enlightenment Worldview

The worldview of capitalism was greatly influenced by the 'Enlightenment' movement stretching over approximately two centuries, from the early 17th century to the beginning of the 19th. The Enlightenment, a term often used interchangeably with the 'Age of Reason', was in its extreme form "a repudiation, and in some respects an antithesis, of much of Christian belief."[5] It is beyond the scope of this book to go into the many reasons for this anti-religious posture. One of them, certainly, was corruption and despotism in the Church. There was "so much laxity of morals among the clergy that a thousand testimonies could be adduced to prove it."[6] This anti-clerical sentiment, unfortunately, also shook confidence in revealed religion so that everything that the Church stood for came to be regarded as "quite untenable".[7] Voltaire's "crush the infamous thing" rang through the Enlightenment period.[8] Durant in fact asserts that "The Church might have sustained the supernatural sanctions provided by the Hebraic Scriptures and the Christian tradition if her personnel had led lives of decency and devotion."[9]

The leading Enlightenment thinkers crowned human reason as the absolute sovereign of human affairs in place of faith and intuition. Knowledge was to be derived from only sense perceptions. Great confidence was placed in the power of reason alone to establish ultimate metaphysical truths. The classic sequence of Locke – Berkeley – Hume – Kant acquired respectability among the elite and played an important role in arousing general scepticism about God, immortality of the human soul, moral values, life after death, and other religious notions. Hume described such beliefs as "sophistry and illusion".[10] Such remarks helped create a favourable climate for the acceptance of the Newtonian worldview which reduced God to the position of a "clock-maker", who had to exist to set the "Newtonian world machine" in motion and to guarantee its uninterrupted running, but who did not interfere with its operations. This was stated by Voltaire in the oft-quoted aphorism: "If god did not exist, it would be necessary to invent him."[11]

This mechanical concept of the universe led to a mechanical explanation of even the human soul.[12] Man, like the physical universe around him, began to be treated as the chance product of a blind, purposeless nature operating through accidental variations in a self-designed and self-propelled evolution. He was at the mercy of brute forces that "unknowingly happen to throw him into being".[13] It did not matter whether the assumptions on which the new worldview was based were 'scientifically' valid or not. In the name of science, they were taken to be *a priori* well-grounded.

The hold of religion, which provides the sanction for morality and human brotherhood and which, therefore, constitutes the foundation of life, thus became continually weaker. If the existence of God is doubtful, or carries no significance for human life, then there is no question of continuity of life after death or of accountability before the Supreme Being. If indeed there were some ultimate purpose in life, it was, according to Descartes, impossible for us to know. Human purpose became a concept that was "scientifically useless"[14] and gradually disappeared from social thought.[15] Accordingly, Bertrand

Russell concluded that "all the labours of the ages, all the devotion, all the inspirations, all the noonday brightness of human genius are destined to extinction in the vast death of the solar system, and the whole temple of Man's achievement must invariably be buried beneath the debris of a universe in ruins."[16] If there is no ultimate purpose in life, there is no question of transcendental values to live for.[17] Everything is permitted. The only foundation for values, as Sartre epitomised, is human freedom and no external justification is needed for the values that anyone chooses to adopt.[18] Social Darwinism further reinforced this idea and its concepts of 'struggle for existence' and 'survival of the fittest' took root.

Materialism and Determinism

The Enlightenment repudiation of religious ideas engendered, in the social sciences, the attempt to explain individual and social behaviour by analogy with the principles of Newtonian physics. Human actions were also, as La Mettrie observed, wholly due to physical or chemical causes and processes.[19] Positivism, which denied the existence or intelligibility of forces or substances that could not be established by experiment and observation, took hold as a movement. It exalted reason and science without realising their limitations. This effort to explain the functions of human beings in mechanical terms tended to make the social sciences materialist and determinist.[20]

Materialism, a logical consequence of the denial of God, holds that matter is the primordial or fundamental constituent of the universe, which is not governed by intelligence, purpose or final causes. Everything is to be explained in terms of material entities or processes. Human feelings and values began to be described as illusions for which the world of fact gave no warrant.[21] Accordingly, wealth, bodily satisfactions, and sensuous pleasures were either the only, or the greatest, values one could seek or attain. Materialism thus provided the foundation for the commercial culture which has gone from strength to strength over the years and has multiplied wants far beyond the ability of available resources to satisfy.

Determinism was also a natural outcome of the denial of a

conscious human soul. It implied that all the facts in the physical universe, and hence also in human history, are absolutely dependent upon and conditioned by their physical, social or psychical causes. Locke considered the human mind to be a "tabula rasa" which had no inner nature of its own and which served as raw material for the external social and economic forces to shape and design. Marx, Freud, Watson and Skinner, all emphasised that human beings are conditioned by their environment, by factors outside their conscious control. Human behaviour was thus explained as being determined by mechanical and automatic responses to external stimuli as in animals (Watson and Skinner), by unconscious mental states beyond their conscious control (Freud), or by social and economic conflict (Marx). Besides ignoring the distinctiveness and complexity of the human self, determinism led to a repudiation of moral responsibility for individual behaviour. This was in sharp contrast with the religious view that human beings are responsible, and hence accountable before God, for their acts.

The Unsuccessful Protest

This mechanical view of the universe and man did not go unchallenged. The Romantic and Idealist philosophers like Rousseau, Kant and Bergson, and a much larger number of religious scholars, raised a series of protests and emphasised not only the limitations of reason but also the role of emotion and intuition in knowledge, with the objective of restoring to man his enviable status in the cosmic scheme. They expressed a great contempt for the Enlightenment. Wordsworth called Voltaire's *Candide* "that dull product of a scoffer's pen". In the view of the Romantics, the Enlightenment philosophers were guilty of holding a worldview that was mechanistic and unfeeling and therefore unrealistic and inhuman. But the Romantics' efforts were unable to counter successfully the tide of secularism that was gaining ground in the Western world. While the early thinkers of the Enlightenment like Descartes, Spinoza, Leibniz and Locke carried neither their rationalism nor their opposition to revealed religion to radical extremes, the philosophers in the second half of the eighteenth century like Voltaire, Hume and

Holbach were different. They were not only more radical, they were also hostile.

Consequently, the Enlightenment movement, which had started with a few intellectuals, continued to penetrate in the generations that followed until a major part of the intellectual elite and a substantial part of even the masses became consciously or unconsciously engulfed in it. E. F. Schumacher has accordingly observed that "these nineteenth century ideas are firmly lodged in the minds of practically everybody in the western world today, whether educated or uneducated."[22] Crane Brinton also observes that "Westerners, and specially Americans, are still spiritual children of the Enlightenment."[23]

In spite of this popularity of the Enlightenment movement, faith in God and the hope that it arouses remained deeply rooted in the hearts of men and the institutions of society and did not surrender easily to the verdict of the rationalists. Complete atheism was as rare during the Enlightenment as it is today.[24] What did happen, however, was that the thrust of Enlightenment ideas undermined the role of religion as a collective force in society. Its place was taken by secularism, which reduces religion to a matter of individual preference. Moral values lost their collective sanction and collective value judgements became an anathema.[25] Ethics courses are seldom mandatory in academic institutions, and as options they do not attract students who "prefer to take courses that they believe will yield instant payoffs when they step into the real world. Business Ethics does not qualify."[26]

Loss of the Moral Filter

Since the socio-economic importance of religion essentially lies in the collective sanction it provides to moral values, thereby ensuring their unchallenged acceptance as a basis for socio-economic and political decisions, the loss of the religious sanction for values was a great tragedy. Society became deprived of the socially-agreed filter mechanism. Self-interest, prices and profits replaced it as the primary criteria for allocating and distributing resources and for equating aggregate demand and supply. Even though the individual conscience ingrained in the inner consciousness of the human self may still be there to serve as a filter mechanism at the individual level, it is not sufficient to perform the function of a socially-agreed filter mechanism which is needed to create a harmony between individual self-interest and social interest.

Given the reluctance to use the filter mechanism provided by morally-sanctioned value judgements, and the weakening of the feeling of social obligation that religion intensifies, it is not possible to realise the dream of a society where all human beings are brothers created by the One God, and where scarce resources are used not only to fulfil the needs of all but also to create an equitable distribution of income and wealth. Toynbee and Durant have rightly concluded, after their extensive study of history, that moral uplift and social solidarity are not possible without the moral sanction that religions provide. Toynbee asserts that, "religions tend to quicken rather than destroy the sense of social obligation in their votaries" and that "the brotherhood of Man presupposes the fatherhood of God – a truth which involves the converse proposition that, if the divine father of the human family is left out of the reckoning, there is no possibility of forging any alternative bond of purely human texture which will avail by itself to hold mankind together."[27] Will and Ariel Durant have also observed forcefully that "there is no significant example in history, before our time, of a society successfully maintaining moral life without the aid of religion."[28]

Utilitarianism

In the absence of the "collective conscience" of society which morally-sanctioned values provide, how were 'right' and 'wrong', 'desirable' and 'undesirable' or 'just' and 'unjust' to be determined? Jeremy Bentham (1748–1832), himself an atheist, tried unsuccessfully to provide the philosophical basis for the answer. The hedonist approach of utilitarianism was to take the place of moral values – it was assumed that what gives 'pleasure' is 'good' and what causes 'pain' is 'bad', thus 'good' and 'bad' or 'right' and 'wrong' were to be determined by the measurable criteria of 'pleasure' and 'pain'.[29] The principle of utility was assumed to be as reliable as arithmetic, provided that all non-arithmetical considerations were left out. As Bentham put it in a letter to the Reverend John Forster in 1779, utility provided "an oracle which, if properly consulted, would afford the only true solution that could be given to every question of right and wrong."[30] A good man was accordingly one who strove to maximise his utility and the good society was one that sought to maximise the sum total of all utility. The pursuit by every individual of his pleasure would lead to the "greatest happiness of the greatest number" because, it was assumed, there was a perfect harmony between public and private interests. The individual could, according to Bentham, pursue his own self interest and any talk of "rights of men" was "plain nonsense" in the Benthamite logic.[31]

Since the question of what contributes to individual and social 'happiness', which is only a psychological state of the mind, was not adequately addressed, the utility principle has remained spongy and nonoperational. It is not possible to measure and aggregate the happiness of millions of people for purposes of comparing the aggregate utility of alternative policies.[32] It is not even possible to reach a socially satisfactory consensus where the interests of all participants are conflicting, where everyone pursues his own self-interest without caring for, or being aware of, the impact of his actions on others, and where people in positions of power and influence can tilt the balance in their favour. Rawls's principle of the 'veil of ignorance', whereby every participant expresses his preference without having any knowledge of his own social and economic position, the market value of his own talent, and other key factors of importance to him in decision making, is no more than wishful thinking and cannot be of any practical use in deriving 'just' principles for social organisation.[33] Hence one can only conclude that utilitarianism is incapable of creating any kind of normative knowledge about general well-being and justice. It must rather generate an infinite number of questions without ever supplying definite answers. Moreover, even if utilitarianism was able to construct normative knowledge, it could not, as religion can, be able to motivate individuals to abide by its social imperatives. Hence, even within the Western world there were protests against it. These have now led to total disenchantment with the concept of 'objectivity' in the derivation of moral principles.[34]

Utilitarianism has nevertheless had a dominating influence on Western philosophy over the last two centuries,[35] thus exercising a significant sway over the Western way of life, and through the West, on the rest of the world. It, and other intellectual traditions like pragmatism, which followed its footsteps, tended to strip moral values of their absolute character and made them relative and subjective, dependent on their 'usefulness' and 'cash value' for the individuals. Given such an attitude there can be no commitment to specific principles and hence an accepted code of moral behaviour because different people may hold conflicting views about the outcome or 'cash value' of a particular principle, and because "most men", admits Bertrand Russell, "are more interested in their own welfare than in that of other people."[36]

Utilitarianism reinforced by materialism, provided the logical rationale for single-minded pursuit of wealth and bodily pleasures. It projected consumption as the highest purpose of economic life, the supreme source of Benthamite 'happiness', the ultimate justification of all human effort and toil. It identified the maximising of earnings and want satisfaction with supreme virtue. Everything done by the individual toward this end was justified – it would serve his self-interest and ultimately the interest of all. This philosophy has contributed in a major way to moral decline, which may have been considerably less if religious beliefs and moral values had continued to play the role of a socially-accepted filter mechanism. Alexander Solzhenitsyn observed in his Harvard address of 1978:

> Two hundred or even fifty years ago, it would have seemed quite impossible, in America, that an individual could be granted boundless freedom with no purpose, simply for the satisfaction of his whims. Subsequently, however, all such limitations were eroded everywhere in the West; a total emancipation occurred from the moral heritage of Christian centuries with their great reserves of mercy and sacrifice.[37]

THE SOURING OF THE STRATEGY

Some Untenable Concepts

The introduction of these ideas into economics gave rise to a number of concepts which have served, consciously or unconsciously, as the foundation of the discipline and shaped the strategy of capitalism.

Laws of Economics

The first of these was the belief, based on the mechanical view of the universe, that knowledge in the social sciences is not different from knowledge in the physical sciences and that human behaviour can, in principle, be predicted and controlled in the same manner as the physical universe. Smith borrowed from Newtonian physics the outlook that social and economic life, like the physical universe, was incomparable beauty, order and harmony and that "human society, when we contemplate it in a certain abstract and philosophical light, appears like an immense machine whose regular and harmonious movements produce a thousand agreeable effects."[38] Economists have since been "greatly under the influence of a majestic image of the Laws of Physics and have sometimes been led to hope for a set of Laws of Economic Motion as forceful as Newton's laws."[39]

Rational Economic Man

The second of these concepts was that of the rational 'economic man', which has served as the kingpin of modern economics. Self-interest was the only well-spring of his action. All his behaviour conformed to what Jevons called "the mechanics of utility and self interest."[40] His "one and only one social responsibility", according to Friedman, "is to increase his profit".[41] Pure theory equated rationality with self-interested action. In fact, Edgeworth had proudly declared that "the first principle of economics is that every agent is activated only by self-interest".[42] Almost all modern economic models have been built on this principle.

However, the pursuit of unfettered self-interest had a social and religious stigma attached to it. Unless this stigma had been removed, the doctrine of free markets could not have got the social blessing it needed to be considered seriously in a Christian society in which individual and social conscience were not yet dead. How was this stigma to be removed? It was done by showing it to be a constructive force for collective welfare. The role of unfettered self-interest was made equivalent in human society to that of the force of gravity in nature. Just as gravitation produces a coordinated movement among the planetary bodies, so self-interest acts to organise constructively the movements of human bodies in society.[43] Adam Smith argued that if everyone pursued his self-interest, the 'invisible hand' of market forces would, through the restraint imposed by competition, promote the interest of the whole society, thus bringing about a harmony between private interests and public good.[44] Unfettered self-interest would therefore serve the ends of society. Adam Smith's great contribution to economic thought was thus the sanctity he accorded to self-interest, turning thereby the eyes away from the moral intentions and social obligations of individuals to the 'unintended' consequences or the final social outcome of their actions.

Most scholars would not quarrel with the commitment of pure theory to the assumption that economic behaviour is generally rational, but little room was left for differences of opinion on what constitutes rationality. Pecuniary self-interest and internal consistency were considered to be the sole determinants of rationality. Pecuniary self-interest became identified with unlimited wealth acquisition and maximum want satisfaction. Consistency also began to be seen in relation to self-interest. No room was left in the account for a person's values, objectives in life, social obligations and other non-pecuniary motivations. Since these factors could not be quantified, they did not fit into the epistemology of capitalism and classical economics.

Positivism

The third concept was the umbrella of sanctity provided to 'positive economics' which was by definition considered to be "independent of any particular ethical position or normative judgements."[45] Accordingly, value judgements became an anathema and economics drifted away from ethics. The rank and file of the discipline fell docilely into line. The 'Pareto optimum', identified with 'economic efficiency', became a favourite child of welfare economics. If a million persons felt themselves to be better off but there was one person who felt he was worse off as a result of a proposed policy, then the economist was compelled to suspend value judgement about the desirability of that policy measure. As Harvey Leibenstein has put it, "where universal consent does not exist then welfare economists simply are unable to declare whether there has been an increase in welfare in the cases in which some people feel better off and others feel worse off."[46] This is another way of saying that the 'Pareto optimum' grants a veto power to anyone opposed to change. This has led to the near-paralysis of policy making, "to inaction, to nonchoice, to drifting", particularly in pluralist societies where every group tries to serve its own interest.[47]

Say's Law

The fourth concept was Say's Law, which was an important by-product of the application of the laws of Newtonian physics to economics. It was asserted that, just like the universe, the economy will run perfectly if left to itself. Production would create its own demand and there would be no overproduction or unemployment. Any tendency on the part of the economy to create overproduction or unemployment would be automatically corrected. 'Economic laws' were all powerful and brooked no interference. The government could do nothing and should hence abstain from intervening. Market forces would themselves create an 'order' and 'harmony', and 'efficiency' and 'equity', and any effort on the part of the government to intervene in the self-adjusting market could not but lead to distortions and inefficiency. The mechanical concept of the universe and of man thus gave rise to a blind faith in the efficacy of market forces.

Social Darwinism

The sanctity accorded to self-interest and positive economics played an important role in undermining the long-standing moral commitment to socio-economic justice and equitable distribution of income and wealth. It freed economists from any sense of social or moral obligation and exonerated them from blame for the inadequacies and injustices of the system. It became their task to describe and analyse, but not to pass moral judgement or be socially concerned. It thus became 'unscientific' to state that in general an impoverished and starving man receiving a dollar would derive a greater satisfaction from the use of that dollar than would an average millionaire, on the grounds that such a statement requires an interpersonal comparison and interpersonal comparisons are incommensurable; it is not possible to enter into the mind of an individual and register its imageries or to measure the qualitative character of the psychic responses that occur there.[48] It was perhaps because of this undermining of commitment to socio-economic justice that Thomas Malthus (1766–1834), the English economist, was able to summon up sufficient courage to assert in a Christian society that: "A man who is born into a world already possessed, if he cannot get substance from his parents on whom he has a just demand, and if the society does not want his labour, has no claim of right to the smallest portion of food, and, in fact, has no business to be where he is. At Natures' mighty feast there is no vacant cover for him. She tells him to be gone, and will quickly execute her own orders."[49]

Social Darwinism, having entered by this route into economics, condoned poverty and unemployment by offering a new kind of rationality which did not trouble itself over moral or equity considerations and which allowed the rich to pacify their sense of guilt.[50] The poor and the unemployed were held to be lazy, shiftless, improvident, or unenterprising – traits that could be overcome only by the spur of need or the punishment of misery. Tampering with the verdict of the free market by providing them with what they did not deserve would sabotage the only mechanism available for proportioning reward to merit. Truly productive and enterprising people would be penalised in order to provide for the drones, and the inevitable outcome would be reduced productivity and less for all. If the syllogisms of economics failed to drive the point home, the authority of theologians was invoked to show that poverty was a punishment for wickedness, and wealth, a reward for virtue. The case thus seemed overwhelming – at least to prosperous merchants and manufacturers – that the poor must be left to private charity if not to their own devices. Such ideas were expressed with varying degrees of eloquence by a large number of writers from Daniel Defoe (1704), Bernard Mandeville (1714) and Arthur Young (1771) through Herbert Spencer (1850) and Dicey (1905) down to Calvin Coolidge.[51]

Capitalism thus became a system which gave the highest value to unfettered freedom to enable the individual to pursue his self-interest and to maximise his wealth and want satisfaction. Since the 'laws' of the market economy, like the laws of physics, were objectively valid, their success or failure ought not to be judged by the deprivation and misery of those who were left behind in the struggle for survival. Social Darwinism taught that unrestrained competition between individuals in a free market would be the best guarantee of general welfare. It would keep self-interest within bounds, minimise costs and prices, and thus ensure maximum efficiency and health of the system. Consequently, there was no need for value judgements or for government intervention. Only if the state did not interfere, only if the private entrepreneur was left free to pursue his economic goals, would optimum welfare be attained and the interest of the nation adequately safeguarded. Everyone was the best judge of his own interest and, if left alone, could not only better himself but also, in the long run, better everyone else.

The Sour Fruits

There is no doubt that the market system led to a long period of prosperity in the Western market-oriented economies. High rates of economic growth were generally realised and there was a vast expansion in wealth. With the triumph of the market, the political system ceased to intervene in social relations and, in Polanyi's phrase, the society became virtually "an adjunct of the market".[52] However, this unprecedented prosperity did not lead to the removal of poverty or the fulfilment of everyone's needs. Inequalities of income and wealth have in fact increased. There has also been a substantial degree of economic instability and unemployment which have added further to the miseries of the poor. This indicates that both efficiency and equity have remained elusive in spite of the rapid development and the enormous growth in wealth.

The practical consequences have been repugnant to the innate sense of justice in human nature. Hence, the basic concepts of capitalism have not gone unchallenged in the past or the present. Many literary figures, including Thomas Carlyle (*Past and Present,* 1843), Ruskin (*Unto this Last,* 1862) and Charles Dickens (*Hard Times,* 1854–55) in England, and Henry George (*Progress and Poverty,* 1879) in America, ridiculed the dominant doctrine of *laissez-faire* with its emphasis on self-interest. Thomas Carlyle called economics a "dismal science" and rejected the idea that free and uncontrolled private interests will work in harmony and further the public welfare.[53] Henry George condemned the resulting contrast between wealth and poverty and wrote: "So long as all the increased wealth which modern progress brings goes but to build great fortunes, to increase luxury and make sharper the contrast between the House of Have and the House of Want, progress is not real and cannot be permanent."[54]

However, such criticisms from writers who were enormously popular in their own day, were unable to change the tide of economic thought. They were left behind as towering, but nevertheless merely 'historic', figures.[55] There are several modern critics of capitalism who also bemoan its sour fruits. Their views have been starkly epitomised by Hyman Minsky in the statement that "capitalist societies are inequitable and inefficient."[56]

The reason behind capitalism's failure to actualise the socially-desired goals is the conflict between the goals of society and the worldview and strategy of capitalism. The goals were humanitarian, based on a moral foundation; the worldview and the strategy were social Darwinist. The claimed harmony between private and public interests was based on certain assumptions about background conditions which were false and so unrealistic that they could never have become true. Since these background conditions are not generally spelled out clearly in economic literature, it is not normally realised how their absence is bound to frustrate the realisation of both 'efficiency' and 'equity' in the allocation of scarce resources, defined in relation to the humanitarian goals of society and not social Darwinism.

THE 'INEFFICIENT' ALLOCATION

What to Produce

The claim that the market system leads to an 'efficient' use of scarce resources is true only in the social Darwinist sense. It does lead to the production of that configuration of goods and services which is in conformity with the preferences of 'rational' consumers – consumers pursuing their self-interest in a value-free society. Such a configuration could be congruent to that of a need-based economy if, and only if, certain assumptions tacitly made by the market system about background conditions are true. These assumptions are however false and unrealistic.

Unrealistic Assumptions

Individual Preferences Reflect Social Priorities

Firstly, it is assumed that even without being guided by collective value judgements, the sovereign consumer confines his claims on scarce resources to only need-satisfaction, such that there is no conflict between the preferences of 'rational' consumers and social priorities in the use of resources. This assumption has proved to be false for at least three reasons.

(i) There is no reason why in the absence of moral values, the 'sovereign consumer' would apply brakes to his wants as long as he has the wherewithal to purchase. It is rational to expect only that he will buy whatever fits into his preference scale irrespective of the effect this may have on the availability of resources for the need satisfaction of the poor. Given the social Darwinist outlook to which he has become indoctrinated in a secularist society, he will feel no qualms about the inability of the poor to satisfy their needs. He will not blame his own excessive demands for the lack of need fulfilment of the poor. He will rather blame their misery on them, on their sloth and inefficiency.

(ii) Differentiation between 'need' and 'want' or 'necessary' and 'unnecessary' is not possible without a socially-agreed filter mechanism which the epistemology of capitalism disdains. In the absence of such values and a complementary role for the state to determine what the society can or cannot afford within the framework of its resources and the goal of universal need fulfilment, there is no mechanism by which a rich person would know, even if he cared to, whether his pursuit of maximum want satisfaction would deprive others of need-satisfying goods.

(iii) In the pursuit of profit maximisation, businesses subject the sovereign consumer to a battery of sales promotion campaigns through mail and news media. They appeal to the consumer's vanity, sexual appetite and envy, either overtly or covertly. He is made to believe that his sense of self-actualisation and social-esteem are dependent on the frequency and value of his purchases. His judgements are thus distorted, particularly so if he has the money to buy and is not committed to any moral criteria relating to consumption.[57] A vast array of unwarranted wants is thus generated through an unending competition for status symbols. "All forms of consumer persuasion affirm that", asserts Galbraith, "the consumption of goods is the greatest source of pleasure, the highest measure of human achievement."[58] This leads to a tremendous amount of 'wasteful' production. It is hence disingenuous to talk of consumer sovereignty when the consumer is deprived of rational, independent choice. His wants are made infinite as compared with 'real' human needs which recede ever further into the background.[59] While this helps producers maximise profits, it puts a tremendous pressure on scarce resources and reduces the ability of society to satisfy needs. This race for ostentatious consumption is further exacerbated by the excessive expansion of consumer credit by the banking system. Whereas, in the words of Daniel Bell, "previously one had to save in order to buy, . . . with credit cards one could indulge in instant gratification – the creation of new wants and new ways of gratifying those wants."[60] Even without the satisfaction of all needs, the process has given rise to deficits, monetary expansion, inflation, external imbalance and burdensome foreign debt. A number of scholars have criticised this process of accentuating envy and jealousy in society.

> However laudable this criticism may be, it has no prospect of being effective in the absence of a filter mechanism which only agreed collective values provide, and a motivating system, which moral accountability ensures, and a thorough reform of the economic and financial systems.

Equal Distribution

Secondly, it is assumed that there exists an equal or fair distribution of income and wealth in the economy. Given the absence of a filter mechanism and the indiscriminate pursuit of want satisfaction, only an equal distribution of income and wealth would give everyone an equal weight in influencing the decision-making process of the market. However, incomes are not equally distributed and it is not even possible to realise this, given the steep inequalities in inherited wealth combined with unequal access to credit facilities and education, and the differences in talents, physical stamina, family background, and personal ambition. The prevalent inequalities allow the upper strata of income groups, who get a share of national income and credit significantly greater in proportion to their numerical size, to divert scarce national resources, by the sheer weight of their votes, into products which are socially less desirable. Given their enormous personal wealth, the price mechanism does not make any significant dent in their demand for prestige symbols and wasteful consumption. Of itself, the price system is not even concerned with how many votes any individual has and how he uses them: it is concerned with the aggregate of votes in favour of any particular good or service. Hence the configuration of goods and services produced by the market system in a secularist society cannot be in conformity with the wishes of the majority of consumers. Thus, to bring about a socially desired allocation of resources, capitalism puts a far greater burden on the price mechanism than it is capable of carrying. The result is, as Tawney has rightly indicated, "a part of the goods which are annually produced, and which are called wealth is, strictly speaking, waste because it consists of articles which though reckoned as part of the income of the nation, either should not have been produced until other articles had been produced in sufficient abundance or should not have been produced at all.''[61] As a result of this wasteful production, the GNP, which is the aggregate of the money value rather than the inherent economic value of what has been produced, rises, but without necessarily increasing the real well-being of the people. The GNP is thus a poor measure of the real well-being of all the people in a country.

Prices Reflect Urgency of Wants

Thirdly, it is assumed that the urgency of wants of different consumers can be compared by the use of prices because each unit of currency represents a ballot. The willingness on the part of two individuals to spend an equal amount of money is assumed to indicate wants of equal urgency. This premise is questionable. Even though the urgency for milk is the same for children irrespective of whether they are poor or rich, the amount of dollar votes that a poor family is able to cast for milk is not the same as those which a rich family is able to cast for status symbols. Hence the system of balloting through dollar votes leads to a lower than optimum quantity of milk production because of resources being diverted to the production of status symbols. Arthur Okun hence rightly observes that markets ''award prizes that allow the big winners to feed their pets better than the losers can feed their children.''[62] The result also leads incidentally to a relatively higher price for milk, which hurts the poor families, and a relatively lower price for status symbols, which benefits the rich families.[63]

Perfect Competition

Fourthly, it is assumed that the market operates under conditions of perfect competition, which is said to prevail if there are: many buyers, many sellers, no barriers to entry, and perfect information about the present and the future. These conditions are not satisfied anywhere. A perfectly competitive market has remained an unrealised dream and is likely to remain so, particularly because of the tendency of capitalism to promote big business and concentration of wealth and power (to be discussed later). The innumerable imperfections that exist in the market thwart the efficient operation of market forces and produce deviations from ideally competitive marginal-cost pricing, thus leading to prices that do not reflect real costs or benefits. Consequently prices of certain goods or services tend to be out of tune with opportunity costs, and payments to resource owners tend to be far above or below the value of their contribution to real output. Moreover, in an individualistic society, where most operators in the market are 'economic men' whose only motivating force is self-interest, whose time horizon is short, and whose social perspective is generally narrow and limited, long-term costs as well as social costs and benefits tend to be disregarded by them in their accounting, even though these costs or benefits are extremely important from the point of view of continued social welfare. The claimed self-correcting tendencies of the price system which tend to reduce the divergence between private and social interests usually take such an extremely long time that faith in this self-correcting tendency is not meaningful.

Distortion of Priorities

Since "no real world market is likely to be even approximately satisfactory in all the background conditions", there is a considerable distortion in the expression of priorities in the market place.[64] As the 'socially desired' priorities do not, and cannot, get expressed in the market-place, there is, with flagrant inequalities of income and wealth and in the absence of agreed values, a built-in tendency on the part of market forces to lead to an 'inefficient' and 'inequitable' use of resources. Even the essential needs of the poor remain unfulfilled while the rich are able to have scarce resources diverted to the satisfaction of even 'inessential' wants through sheer weight of enormous purchasing power. No wonder Samuelson has pointed out that "*laissez-faire* perfect competition could lead to starving cripples; to malnourished children who grow up to produce malnourished children; to perpetuation of Lorenz curves of great inequality of incomes and wealth for generations or for ever." He further adds that "Adam Smith . . . had no right to assert that an Invisible Hand successfully channels individuals who selfishly seek their own interest into promoting the 'public interest' . . . Smith has proved nothing of this kind nor has any economist since 1776.''[65] It is Galbraith's contention in *The Affluent Society* that the prevailing pattern of resource allocation in the U.S. is biased in favour of the satisfaction of artificially-induced consumer wants so that basic needs are grossly neglected. Included among these are education, housing, medical care and public utilities which are essential for individual and social well-being and for future progress.[66]

Can anything be done to enable the votes cast in the market place to reflect social priorities? Conventional economics with its utilitarian philosophy, irrespective of whether it has social Darwinist or Welfare State orientation, has no answer. Given a secularist interpretation of the universe with no Divine Guidance for human beings, reliance on the 'free' play of market forces is probably the only and the most logical strategy for allocation of resources. In the absence of Divine Guidance, it is but rational to deny anyone the authority to make value judgements. This is because if individual human beings or a group are given the authority to make value judgements for all, then their own individual circumstances, likes and dislikes, and vested interests will become automatically reflected in their judgements.

Once collective value judgements are out, it is but natural for the rational economic man to be left with no other goal but to serve his self-interest by maximising his utility. The nature and quality of this utility or its distribution among the members of society do not matter because these involve value judgements about 'what is' and 'what ought to be' and economists are not supposed to make value judgements. Satisfaction of a maximum amount of wants hence becomes the primary objective of the economic system and the entire machinery of production gets directly or indirectly directed toward this goal, irrespective of whether the satisfaction of such wants is 'necessary' for fulfilling human needs and realising human well-being. This multiplication of wants becomes rationalised because it not only serves business interests but also promotes economic growth. Hence, reducing wants themselves to a manageable limit through a mechanism other than the price system is considered to be inappropriate. Such rationalisation naturally appears extremely logical to every social scientist, particularly when the tacit assumptions about background conditions on which it is based do not get the emphasis they deserve. Since the assumptions were false, the results that the system has produced have been unacceptable.

The question of "what to produce" cannot hence be answered by market forces alone if the desire is to satisfy the essential needs of all individuals in society. The market does not satisfy the background conditions in any of the present-day capitalist or welfare states. The market, as aptly pointed out by Schumacher, institutionalises individualism and non-responsibility. Neither the buyer nor the seller is responsible for anything but himself.[67] Moreover, "capitalism 'socializes' private priorities and is institutionally opposed to any redistribution of the relative shares of wealth."[68] With the help of only prices and 'some' government intervention, the system is unable either to motivate individuals to restrain their claims on resources primarily for need fulfilment or to bring about structural adjustments in the production system to assure a sufficient supply of need-satisfying goods and services.

How to Produce

The Criteria

Production of any good or service requires the combined effort of management, labour, capital and technology. However, since production takes place in a human society with the help of human effort and scarce resources, the production system should reflect a number of characteristics if it is to be characterised as both 'efficient' and 'equitable'. Firstly in addition to producing need-satisfying goods and services, as indicated earlier, it should be able to motivate both management and labour to render the best in terms of their mental and physical potential to maximise productivity and minimise wastage and costs. The costs to be minimised should not be just private costs; social costs should also receive significant importance. Moreover, the costs to both the present and the future generations as well as the costs due to lack of need fulfilment, moral degeneration and social disintegration should be taken into account. Secondly, the production system should promote human dignity and brotherhood. These would be realised if: (i) both management and workers receive a 'just' reward for their contribution to output; (ii) cooperation rather than conflict is promoted between them; (iii) monotony and drudgery of work are minimised; (iv) opportunities for employment and self-employment are maximised; and (v) concentrations of wealth and power are reduced. Any system that fails to motivate both management and workers to render their best, or leads to unemployment, inequitable rewards and concentration of wealth and power, is undesirable.

The Preconditions

It is argued that capitalism is the most conducive to productive efficiency. Under it the entrepreneur is the society's agent to determine how goods and services are to be produced. Private property and the pursuit of profit motivate him to play an effective role. Prices serve as his signalling device. While the motive to maximise profits provides him with the necessary incentive to do his best, the constraints imposed by competition in a perfectly competitive market, where he is a price taker rather than a price maker, prevent exploitation and safeguard the interests of society. Competition forces him to minimise his costs, eliminate waste, and seek the lowest factor costs, thus enabling him to maximise his profits at the point where his marginal cost becomes equal to the price of the product. Hence, it is argued, competition keeps the producer, driven by self-interest, from overcharging and serves as a stick that enforces order and fair play, thus serving the consumers' interest and thereby of the society as a whole. It acts as a self-regulating mechanism of the economy and eliminates wastage, exploitation, and excessive profits without any government intervention.

There can be no doubt that private property and profit motive are necessary to motivate people towards greater efficiency and improved quality. This is now being increasingly recognised even by the socialist countries – Soviet Russia, Eastern Europe and China. Some of the socialist countries of the Third World like India are also increasingly turning to privatisation for greater efficiency after a long but sad experience with grossly mismanaged government enterprises.

There are however certain preconditions which must be fulfilled to ensure that private ownership of property and profit motive operate for the good of the society. These are healthy competition, adherence to socially-agreed norms, and government vigilance.

Healthy competition is absolutely imperative not only for inducing greater effort and efficiency but also for keeping self-interest within constraint. Competition tends to be healthy if it takes root in the desire of competitors to excel each other in quality, service and efficiency rather than in the principle of survival of the fittest. Competition becomes unhealthy if it breeds and reinforces the psychology of economic man, fosters unscrupulousness and unfair practices, which are incompatible with the spirit of human brotherhood and cooperation. However, the pervasiveness of social Darwinism almost compels every firm to try to eliminate its competitors or, failing that, to collude with them. Elimination, or the threat of it, adds to tension, insecurity, stress and social unrest, which take a heavy toll in human welfare. Collusion creates monopoly or oligopoly and generates a favourable climate for exploitation. Both elimination or collusion tend to become endemic if the system supports and pampers large enterprises and suffocates or discourages small and medium businesses.

Competition cannot be effective and healthy unless there is a large number of firms, such that none of them is able to influence prices and all of them adhere to certain principles and values, not merely as a matter of personal preferences, but rather as a social and moral obligation. Unless a society is collectively charged by a set of moral values and accountability before God, the urge to maximise profits may lead to unfair business practices and disregard of market externalities and social costs. There may also be duplication and mutual cancellation of efforts in the form of advertising and competitive research and development. Indirect costs to society may in this case outweigh the gains to individual producers or consumers from greater profit or cheaper products.

Government regulation cannot take the place of the moral imperative, but is nevertheless indispensable to give expression to socially-acceptable standards of quality and behaviour for the purpose of safeguarding public interest. If, however, the supremacy of moral values is not recognised collectively, more and more regulations may have to be enacted and enforced, at a prohibitive economic cost. The system may still not operate in an orderly and healthy manner because of the effort to evade regulations or to bribe the regulators.

Preconditions Unfulfilled

The Western capitalist system, while recognising the role of private enterprise and profit motive, has not fulfilled the conditions required to enable them to serve the general public interest. Competition has been on the decline. Collective value judgements are not recognised as a force of importance and government regulation is also now out of favour after a long period of excessive dependence on it to offset the moral vacuum. "Competition, which was the predominant form of market relations in 19th century Britain, has ceased to occupy that position, not only in Britain but everywhere else in the capitalist world."[69]

Big business has become prominent in all industrial countries through a process of expansion which has continued nearly uninterrupted for more than a century. Today the typical economic unit in the capitalist world is not the small firm producing a negligible fraction of a homogeneous output for an anonymous market as visualised by Adam Smith, but a large-scale enterprise producing a significant share of the output of an industry, or even several industries, and able to control its prices, the volume of its products, and the types and amounts of its investments. Several hundred giant companies "play a preponderant role in the United States, Canada, Japan, and the nations of Western Europe."[70] These giant corporations account for a relatively large share of economic activity in manufacturing, mining, transportation, utilities, banking and insurance, and in certain branches of commerce in these countries. Even in the agricultural sector the move is towards the consolidation of farm lands into fewer hands. According to Norm White, "government policies that favour big operations and cause more and more medium-sized farmers to go down the tube will eventually result in a few huge conglomerates owning most of the land and controlling the food supply.''[71] Such a vast corporate growth has far-reaching effects.

Firstly, by virtue of their enormous size and resources, these giant corporations wield considerable social and political influence in their countries. Their activities have consequences that are public in character and as pervasive as those of many governments. Corporations account for about 80 per cent of all economic activity in the United States though they comprise only 10 per cent of all business firms. However, even the activity of the remaining 90 per cent of business firms is determined in various ways by these large corporations. They dominate the American economy, whether measured in terms of capital, production, investment, new products, consumer impact, or employment.[72] No more than 200 of these corporations control most economic activity in the United States. The prodigious and unprecedented market power allows this small set of corporations to pervade, influence and shape almost every aspect of social life in the United States. They even influence government decisions by insisting that the ''government meet their demands even if these demands run counter to those of citizens expressed through their polyarchal controls.''[73]

Moreover, the giant corporation itself is also not a democratic institution. Control over the policies of these corporations virtually rests in the hands of a few families, the controlling stock in most corporations being held by a few people.[74] One per cent of all tax filers in 1960 owned 48 per cent of all stock held by individuals.[75] Since most shareholders do not participate in board meetings the phrase 'shareholder democracy' is a misnomer. ''In approximately 150 companies on the current Fortune 500 lists, controlling ownership rests in the hands of an individual or of the members of a single family.''[76] Hence there is concentration of power in the hands of a small elite in the major sector of the economy, giving them immense power to make basic product, price and investment decisions that affect the entire nation and, in fact, the world.[77]

Secondly, small businessmen, farmers and artisans have increasingly lost their independence and bargaining power. In the United States, the proportion of the population dependent on wages and salaries has risen steeply over the last two centuries from 20 per cent in 1780 to 84 per cent in 1970. Accordingly the proportion of those who are self-employed or those who work as managers and officers has declined from 80 per cent to 16 per cent over this period.[78] Disregarding short-term variations, the long-term trend seems to be decidedly in favour of bigger businesses and farms. Leveraged buy-outs through the issue of junk bonds have further accelerated this trend. The socio-political environment has become dominated by the chief executives and directors of giant conglomerates, leading to a greater concentration of wealth and power in society. In Marxist terminology, this implies that wage-slavery and hence alienation have substantially increased.

Thirdly, large corporations are able to escape from competitive market restraints.[79] This is accomplished in such a skillful and covert manner that it is difficult to detect. In fact, many observers believe that the pricing patterns among the leading firms show a lack of competitiveness.[80]

Fourthly, the large size places a limit on the entry of new firms. Huge resources are required for entry and these are difficult to muster because of the greater initial risk to which a new firm is exposed. Only the rich who have an access to vast resources of their own and also of the banking system can plan an entry.

Fifthly, there has been a separation of ownership and control. Most large corporations are managed by professional managers rather than stockholders. These managers exercise substantial control over the affairs of the corporation such that, even though in theory they are employees hired to manage someone else's property, in practice they regard themselves as the sole authority and the stockholders as simply one of the several constituencies to which they must report at periodic intervals.[81] Most of these professional managers are drawn from the upper strata of society and, as Andrew Hacker has indicated, the democratic social climate is "not reflected in the upper echelons of the large European corporations, and there were even signs that the inequality of selection was increasing rather than decreasing."[82] Wealth and connections are of utmost importance in getting management position in a large corporation. They are the tickets of admission to the inner echelons of power. Mills indicated the prevalence of the same state of affairs in the U.S. by saying: "The corporation is the source of wealth, and the basis of the continued power and privilege of wealth. All the men and the families of great wealth are now identified with large corporations in which their property is seated.''[83]

If all this had stemmed merely from the search for greater efficiency then one might have condoned corporate expansion into vast conglomerates. However, according to many observers, ''the optimum size of the efficient firm is substantially smaller than many people believe.''[84] The structures of most large corporations are really the equivalent of a congeries of semi-independent companies which could have easily operated with equal, or even greater, efficiency as separate companies with an independent identity.[85] Moreover, ''concentration is enhanced by the heavily interlocked nature of large business firms. Nominal competitors, for instance, usually have directors sitting on each other's board of directors, raising the suspicion that competition is not the essence of their relationship. Interlock is further enhanced by the trust activities of banks, by trade associations, by the practice of price leadership and, occasionally, by outright collusion and conspiracy.''[86] If profit is an indicator of efficiency, then research has shown profit rates in industries having a large number of smaller firms to be just as high as in those in which a few big companies dominate a market.[87] Largeness does not therefore necessarily contribute to greater efficiency even in the capitalist sense.

The banking system, as will be seen later, has provided impetus and lifeblood to the process of expansion of firms through leveraged buy-outs of competitors, and vertical as well as horizontal expansion. Banks prefer to finance a few large businesses compared with innumerable small ones. This has now become true even in the farming sector traditionally assumed to be the stronghold of the family farms. In the United States, the number of operating farms has dropped by about two-thirds and the trend is accelerating. This is largely because of banks. ''Over 60 per cent of the country's colossal farm debt (about the same size as the respective foreign debt of Brazil and Mexico combined) is owed by just 19 per cent of U.S. farmers . . . The chips are stacked particularly high against the small to medium-sized commercial farmer.''[88]

Corporate expansion has also been helped by the tendency of

most corporations to turn over only about half of their earnings to stockholders as dividends and plough the rest into the purchase of new capital equipment and the expansion of operations. Although there is nothing basically wrong in ploughing back profits, the way it is done intensifies management autonomy; corporate executives can get access to resources that enable them to move the firm into fields of their choosing. Some observers have accordingly argued that all earnings should be paid out to the stockholders and that a corporation desiring capital funds should be required to approach the investing public each time it wishes to embark on a new venture. Such a procedure would oblige the management to make a persuasive case to a constituency outside its own boardroom.[89] It would also lead to greater democratic participation in the use of scarce resources for investments.

Corporate expansion has also accentuated the problem of unemployment. The major underlying reasons for this are the ability of large corporations to have easy access to credit and their built-in bias towards capital-intensive production methods. The need to keep interest rates low during the Second World War and the two decades immediately after it to help reduce the cost of servicing the public sector debt and to accelerate post-war rehabilitation and growth, promoted not only corporate expansion but also capital-intensive techniques of production. While initially this promoted higher growth, it has now contributed immensely to the unemployment problem.

Although theoretically the postulate is still true that private ownership of means of production, combined with healthy competition, contributes to greater efficiency in the use of resources, in practice capitalism has fostered large conglomerates, most of which are unnecessary, greater concentration of power, and unemployment. The result is, as Berle has succinctly expressed it: "The capital is there and so is capitalism. The waning factor is the capitalist."[90] Thus the two central pillars of capitalism have been shaken – the ultimate power of the consumer and the creative drive of the entrepreneur. The individual (both as consumer and entrepreneur) has become "increasingly subordinate to the goals of the producing organisation."[91]

This development is not something external to the system which could therefore have been avoided. It is a natural outcome of the system's structure, particularly a system operating on the crutches of value neutrality and an interest-based banking system. Regulatory agencies have not been as helpful as expected because they have also tended "to become the instruments, even the puppets, of the industries that they are supposed to regulate."[92]

Much of the landmark legislation has not only served to assist the corporation, but was, in fact, conceived, formulated and drafted by leading businessmen.[93] Thus Galbraith has been led to conclude that "the power in the modern economy lies with the great organisations and increasingly less with the supposedly sovereign consumer and citizen."[94] In the process, the realisation of socio-economic goals has suffered. The only way the hold of corporations could be reduced would be by democratising them. This could be done by reducing their size to an optimum level, increasing their number, substantially raising the proportion of equity in their capital structure, and introducing widespread ownership of shares. However, as will be discussed later, without a reform and restructuring of the financial system along the lines given by Islam, this revolutionary change is not feasible. As indicated earlier, the corporate buy-outs, the issue of junk bonds and the bias of the banking system towards large businesses have in fact set the trend in the opposite direction under capitalism.

THE 'INEQUITABLE' DISTRIBUTION

Income distribution is the *summum bonum* of all economic activity. Factors of production participate in economic activity precisely for the sake of getting a 'fair' share in the total output, just like the farmer, all of whose toil and investment are in the hope of getting a rich harvest. Accordingly, the structure of a 'good' society will be determined not merely by the 'efficiency' of its allocative machinery, but also the 'fairness' of its distributive machinery. It has already been shown that capitalism has failed to answer the questions of what and how to produce in a way that would lead to an efficient allocation of resources. It remains now to be shown that capitalism has not and cannot bring about even an equitable distribution of resources.

Rationalising the Status Quo

Distribution has not received as much attention in conventional Western economics as allocation has. This is because it is assumed that the attainment of 'efficiency' in the allocation of resources will automatically bring about a distribution which is in conformity with the contribution made by the marginal product of each factor of production to total revenue. Any income which, it is argued, does not reflect the above principle of economics, cannot be sustained in the long-run. Since wealth also represents incomes saved over the years, the existing distribution of wealth is also considered to be in conformity with the laws of economics and, accordingly, 'fair'. Conventional economists have hence "devoted some of their most ingenious intellectual efforts to explain to each other why they had so little to say."[95] Samuelson has accordingly recognised that, "the theory of distribution is still in an unsettled state."[96] Why, one may ask, is this the case in such an important area of economics?

While the marginal productivity theory tried to rationalise the share of each factor of production in total output, the concept of Pareto optimality confirmed the 'undesirability' of any effort to change the existing distribution. It was argued that any redistribution would make the rich somewhat worse off even though it would make the poor substantially better off. Redistribution would take the economy away from the point of 'bliss' as indicated by the Pareto optimum. Hence economists, who have been wary of interpersonal utility comparisons, could not 'scientifically' make a statement that a more equal pattern of income distribution is preferable to a less equal one.[97] The prevailing income distribution was taken for granted to be the result of a system, a mechanism and a process – 'the iron law of nature' – and accordingly 'fair'.

Efforts to change the prevailing distribution in accordance with some utopian standard would not only fail but also be undesirable. There was thus a justification, combined with a degree of determinism, in economic ideas about the prevailing income distribution. Wide disparities of income became "accepted as natural and unavoidable; anything like economic or social equality was lacking even as a distant goal. Even philanthropy could only increase misery."[98] This made capitalism "outrageously unjust",[99] but this was also rationalised on the grounds that the self-seeking of the individual which had led to this situation, was "a necessary and beneficent social force".[100] Even the eminent American sociologist and Yale University professor, William Sumner, proclaimed that "the millionaires are a product of natural selection . . . the naturally selected agents of society for certain work. They get high wages and live in luxury, but the bargain is a good one for society."[101] Their high incomes contributed to savings, encouraged entrepreneurship and promoted economic growth. There was no realisation of what Robert Owen felt that "the poor and unemployed were not responsible for their poverty and material insecurity but were the victims of impersonal markets and machines."[102]

The Emphasis on Growth

With redistribution ruled out as an important way to raise the standard of living of the poor, the major alternative was economic growth. As Pareto put it: "A decrease in the inequality of incomes cannot come about . . . except when total income increases more rapidly than the population."[103] Pareto's contention was that redistribution was impossible and that incomes could be improved only by an increase in the product. Accordingly, both liberals and conservatives in Western societies have relied on economic growth to avoid making distributive judgements. Thurow summarises this trend of thinking fairly in the statement: "If the country just has more growth, then it will have more good jobs and high incomes for everyone, and it won't have to worry about the distribution of those jobs or incomes. Individuals will be happy with their new higher incomes regardless of their relative status, and society won't have to address the divisive issue of equity. In any case the distribution of economic resources will automatically become more equal in the process of economic growth."[104]

Economic growth thus received undue emphasis and became the primary tool for reducing inequalities. However, even though the high rate of growth raised the consumption level of the poor, it did not help them fulfil all their needs. Since income disparities between the rich and the poor have risen, the consumption gap between them has also widened. According to Kolko, "the consumption gap between income classes will remain very great as long as income distribution remains inequitable."[105] Higher growth gave a greater boost to the income of the rich because all the capitalist institutions which promote inequalities have continued unhampered. Moreover, growth has not been steady and continuous. It has been interrupted by recessions and unemployment, which, though bad for all, are particularly severe in their impact on the poor.

Although the need for growth cannot be denied, undue emphasis on it has created a number of problems which will be reviewed later. It has accentuated budgetary and balance of payments deficits, inflation and stagflation, and debt-servicing burden. It has also led to accelerated depletion of scarce natural resources, and intensified air and water pollution, which have led to a number of ecological hazards that are threatening human, animal and plant life.

There is no doubt that some other weapons have also been used for reducing income disparities. These are progressive taxation, transfer payments and subsidies. Since these are among the tools of the welfare state, they will be discussed in greater detail in the third chapter. It is sufficient to state here that progressive taxation has not made a significant impact. A preponderant majority of the population, as already indicated, depends mainly on wages and salaries for its incomes, and since wages and salaries are subject to withholding, the earnings of a preponderant proportion of the population get fully taxed, while in the case of profits and other incomes there is scope for tax avoidance or evasion and of thus not being taxed fully. Transfer payments have no doubt helped reduce poverty to the extent to which they have gone to the poor. Subsidies, have however tended to benefit the rich more than the poor.

The Sceptical View

Even in capitalist countries a sceptical view has always been taken of the distribution adequacy of the competitive market mechanism.[106] The role of 'market failure', the inability of a market economy to attain certain desired outcomes in resources use, has also been increasingly recognised. It is admitted that perfect competition does not prevail, and monopoly, unequal opportunity, unwarranted access to large financial resources, rigging and restrictions on entry to an industry, a region, or an occupation, have a great role to play in the prevailing inequalities of income and wealth. It is realised that the normative framework of society and the structure of the economy and all its institutions are indissolubly bound up with inequality. It is also admitted that the main reason for glaring inequalities of income is not the individuals' differing abilities; while abilities seem to be distributed along a normal curve, incomes are highly skewed in distribution.[107] Hence individuals' differing abilities do not explain the prevailing inequalities of income.

One of the most important reasons for income inequalities is rather the absence of a broad-based distribution of businesses and means of production. The banking system has played a crucial role in this. Credit is made available mainly to big businesses. Galbraith has aptly emphasised that: "The large corporation of the planning system, when it must borrow, is a favoured client of the banks, insurance companies and investment banks."[108] He further states that "those who least need to borrow and those who are most favoured as borrowers are in the planning system. Those who most rely on borrowed funds or are least favoured at the banks are in the market system."[109] The easy availability of credit to big businesses makes it possible for them to expand without a significant increase in equity. Businesses have thus tended to become bigger and bigger on the basis of a narrow equity base. Debt has grown faster than equity and has led to the concentration of income-earning assets in a few hands, reducing a preponderant portion of the population to the position of wage and salary earners with fixed incomes. Marx realised this but the solution he proposed, abolition of private ownership of means of production, was not realistic. It has created more problems than it has solved.

Large-scale businesses and their mentors, the banks, have become so powerful in the capitalist system that it is doubtful if capitalism can ever succeed in bringing about an equitable distribution of income by means of the cosmetic changes that it is accustomed to making. Vested interests in big business and big finance have become so strong both economically and politically that it may not be possible to dislodge them to introduce the radical changes necessary for better results. David Rockefeller once shocked bankers by pointing out that according to a poll, three out of five students believed that big business has taken the reins of government away from the Congress and Administration. The results of this poll were corroborated by a University of Michigan survey which revealed that 59 per cent of all Americans thought that "the Government is run by a few big interests looking out for themselves."[110] Thus, the need for a radical change in the structure of the economy and its institutions to reduce income and wealth inequalities is widely felt. Such a change is not possible, however, without commitment to moral values, a financial system that helps reduce rather than accentuate inequalities, and a state that plays a positive role in realising socially-agreed goals. The end of *laissez-faire* and the rise of the welfare state, to be discussed later, have not succeeded in doing this.

THE END OF *LAISSEZ-FAIRE*

Two events served to wash the ground away completely from under *laissez-faire* capitalism, particularly its principle of government non-intervention in the economy. These were the Great Depression of the 1930s and the socialist onslaught. They gave rise to the Keynesian revolution and the welfare state. Hence *laissez-faire* capitalism, as it was formulated by Adam Smith, is now dead as had been forecast even by a number of non-Marxist scholars, like Schumpeter and Toynbee. There have nevertheless been some economists, like Milton Friedman and Friedrich Hayek, who have continued to support it, though in a somewhat modified form. The circle of such economists has, however, widened considerably in the 1980s. The enthusiasm for a substantial degree of state intervention that had come to prevail after the Great Depression has subsided as a result of the inefficiencies of government machinery, the unmanageable budgetary deficits, and the resultant backlash against the welfare state.

The Great Depression which had settled on the world in the 1930s demolished the long-standing faith in Say's Law. The economy did not correct itself automatically. Keynes was appalled at the *laissez-faire* attitudes of the British and most other governments in the face of this economic crisis. While his classical predecessors had found the economic organisation of nineteenth-century capitalism to be "natural, reasonable, eternal and simplicity itself" (it was so portrayed by the general equilibrium theory), Keynes wrote in the *Economic Consequences of the Peace* that, on the contrary, it was "unusual, unstable, complicated, unreliable, temporary".[111]

The Thorny Path of Reform: Beginning of the Welfare State

The essence of Keynes's General Theory is not the discussion of the liquidity preference, or the consumption and the saving-investment functions, but the repudiation of the classical concept prevailing since Adam Smith that full employment was automatically assured.[112] Keynes argued that free-market economies cannot be expected to maintain full employment and prosperity at all times. Such economies can slump into lengthy depressions and indeed remain depressed for very protracted periods. The belief that given time, a depressed free-market economy would always rebound to prosperity in the long-run was, to Keynes, based on erroneous economics. Nobody had the patience to wait for the long-run because "in the long-run we may all be dead".[113] Hence there came the Keynesian proposal of an important role for the government in removing demand deficiency through deficit financing to correct the depression. Thus, while the traumatic depression of the 1930s killed *laissez-faire* capitalism in practice, Keynes destroyed its theoretical rationale. This, along with the socialist onslaught, served as the basis of the welfare state.

Lack of Priorities

It must, however, be emphasised that Keynes dealt with only one aspect of the welfare state – that of achieving full employment. For this purpose he prescribed a greater role for the government in the overall management of effective demand through fiscal policy. Since this Keynesian prescription has helped in correcting inflationary and deflationary gaps and thereby reducing the amplitude of business cycles, it has bred confidence, rightly or wrongly, that a deep and prolonged depression of the 1930s type is a thing of the past and will not recur.

Keynes however offered no advice on the criteria for allocating public sector spending – the priorities to be served. The principal remedy in his prescription was to maintain aggregate demand at full employment level. Governments could do this by increasing or reducing spending on any expenditure head – defence and physical infrastructure, or education, health, and welfare. Keynes was not concerned with the question of priorities. From his point of view the prevailing capitalist system failed only in its solution of the unemployment problem; it solved appropriately the problem of resource allocation and income distribution. Keynes hence specified only a small modification in the capitalist system to maintain full employment. He did not believe in the need for changing other features of capitalism which did not interfere with the achievement of full employment.[114]

Economic Problems

Deficit financing, which was proposed by Keynes as a compensatory measure for tightening recessions or depressions, has also been used by most governments to generate high rates of economic growth and to finance their social welfare spending as well as their defence buildup. This expansion in public sector deficits in most countries was not accompanied by an offsetting decline in private sector consumption. Rather, the worldwide cult of consumerism, persuasive advertising, and credit expansion led to a rapid rise in private sector spending. This rise was not something that could have been avoided. It was a natural and predictable outcome of the absence of agreed priorities in a materialist environment where maximum consumption was the most cherished goal of life and where no group in society was willing to make any sacrifice for the well-being of others. The expansion in spending by both the public and the private sectors contributed to two decades (fifties and sixties) of prosperity in the West. However, the continuous overloading of the economy with claims, which the system had directly encouraged and sanctioned and which it could not possibly satisfy within the constraint of scarce resources, has created strains and led to a number of very serious problems.

One of these has been the accelerating rate of inflation brought about by excessive monetary expansion. From the beginning of the eighteenth century until the eve of World War II, a span of more than two centuries, there was an overall rise of only 33 per cent in prices. However, during the decade of the 1940s, prices nearly doubled. This may be explained away as a result of the War and hence condoned. But during the three decades from 1950–1989, they rose by more than six times.[115] It is not possible to condone this rapid rise because it is now widely recognised that it has had adverse effects on both efficiency and equity. Although initially it led to a rise in output and employment, it ultimately led to stagflation – rising prices and rising wages going hand in hand with declining demand, lower production, higher unemployment and excess production capacity. Rates of growth in most industrial countries have been low and unemployment has been relatively high. Under these circumstances, managing aggregate demand in the Keynesian fashion has become difficult. It fans inflation further without helping on the growth and the employment fronts; a stable price scenario is now widely considered to be necessary for stimulating real growth and reducing unemployment.

Although the rate of inflation declined substantially in the 1980s, a number of economists feel that this may be a temporary respite and there is a great possibility that inflation may become a serious problem once again, particularly if the large budgetary deficits of the United States continue to persist.[116] This may receive a further boost if Soviet Russia and Eastern Europe resort to extensive borrowing in the world financial markets to solve their economic problems, and other industrial countries also maintain a high level of spending to attain higher growth rates and lower unemployment.

A second problem is the high degree of volatility created in the foreign exchange, stock and commodity markets by the excessive liquidity in the financial markets. Capitalist markets have become, according to the Brady Commission Report, intolerably and dangerously volatile and nothing much can be done about it.[117] Extremely volatile markets are inevitable when there are huge budgetary deficits, dramatically unstable interest rates and exchange rates, and erratic movements in short-term funds across national frontiers. Some other reasons for the instability of capitalist economies are the excessive expansion or contraction of credit in the interest-based banking system, glaring inequalities of income and wealth and, as well put by Heilbroner, "the anarchic and planless character of capitalist production."[118] It is again not possible to remove these sources of instability without the introduction of healthier fiscal and monetary policies and the restructuring of capitalist economies.

A third problem is the rising debt-servicing burden created by the financing of large budgetary deficits through extensive borrowing, both internal and external. This has been further aggravated by relatively high interest rates and excessive exchange rate instability. While these have made the financing of deficits expensive for all countries they have made it particularly burdensome for developing countries. The inability of these countries to service their debts has jeopardised the health and stability of the entire international monetary system. A number of programmes have been proposed for providing relief to the severely indebted countries. However, these programmes have not yet gained momentum because of lack of adequate funding. Some countries have already announced their resolve to service their debts only to a certain proportion of their export receipts. If some of the major debtor countries were also to announce their conversion to this strategy, the problem faced by banks would undoubtedly be severe.

A fourth problem, an automatic consequence of the undue rise in unnecessary spending by both the public and the private sectors, is the decline in savings. As savings and investment are highly correlated, investment has also declined. Aggregate saving and investment has gone down in 13 major OECD countries from 17.5 and 17.6 per cent respectively in 1960–71 to 10.7 and 10.8 per cent in 1980–87.[119] Since the demand on these declining savings is expected to rise due to the increased demand for investment funds from Soviet Russia, Eastern Europe and united Germany, the prospect of higher real interest rates is looming large on the world economic horizon. This may tend to have adverse implications for investment, growth, employment and stability of the stock, commodity and foreign exchange markets, particularly because savings in a high-saving country like Japan have also been declining.

A fifth problem, also the result of undue emphasis on want satisfaction and growth has led to an accelerated depletion of non-renewable resources and created a number of ecological hazards which have endangered life on earth. It is now being realised that "addressing the global environmental crisis requires nothing less than a radical change in the conduct of world policy and the world economy."[120] Although a number of useful proposals have been made, there seems to be little realisation that one of the indispensable needs is a move towards commitment to moral values and simpler life-styles, away from the "inertia of affluence".[121]

The Dilemmas

There are however only two options for ensuring price stability within the framework of capitalist analysis. Either push down costs or reduce aggregate demand.[122] The first prescription requires resorting to some form of wage-price controls while the second requires a return to the principle of the 'balanced budget'. The former can be adopted only as a stop-gap arrangement. Its prolonged use is not possible, particularly in an inflationary climate, because it is unjust to labour whose real wages decline, and leads to black markets, long-run supply shortages, and distortions in resource allocation. When the lid of regulations is taken off, both prices and wages tend to rise with a vengeance. The balanced budget prescription does help on the inflation front, but leads to lower growth rates, greater unemployment, and a substantial cut in welfare spending, given the determination of governments not to cut their other (particularly defence) spending, and the resistance of a value-free society to cut its 'unnecessary' and 'wasteful' spending. This has thrown capitalism into a crisis.

There is an irresoluble conflict between the avowed objectives of capitalism and a healthy, non-inflationary economy.

Thus, while the Keynesian strategy has generated dilemmas without solving the problems of unemployment and inflation, the goals of need fulfilment, eliminating poverty and reducing glaring inequalities of income and wealth still remain unfulfilled. These goals have, however, acquired intellectual prominence over the years under the irresistible influence of socialism, giving rise to the welfare state which has now taken firm root in the Western market economies.

The welfare state incorporates not only the Keynesian proposal of a balancing role for the government in the economy but also a welfare role through 'proper' regulation and greater welfare spending. Greater welfare spending, without any offsetting reduction elsewhere in the public and private sectors, has led to an excess of claims on resources and, hence, a backlash against the welfare state. The solution to the crisis, as seen by the social Darwinists, lies in a reduction in welfare spending. But is it possible to reduce welfare spending or abandon the goal of full employment and high rate of growth for a prolonged period in a democratic society where the humanitarian goals of society are still alive? Since this is not possible, the question is: What is wrong? As indicated earlier, there are basic flaws in the espistemology and method of the whole capitalist system.

Social Ills

The tragedy of the secularist philosophy of capitalism was not merely that the unhindered pursuit of self-interest by individuals did not, and could not, serve the interest of all, but that it also led to a number of other insoluble social evils. The undermining of Divine Authority and collective values that it stood for have created a permissive society in which the trammels of earlier ages have been cast off leading to a breakdown of moral values. The lust for conspicuous consumption and status symbols has intensified this further by the desire to acquire wealth by any means, right or wrong.

The individualism and self-centredness that were continually preached have substantially weakened the institution of family, which has historically served as the basis of healthy social development. It is not possible to keep husband and wife together in a mutually-loving relationship unless there is mutual trust and dependence. This was not possible within the framework of sexual permissiveness which reduces commitment to family and estranges husband and wife. Hence, fast on the heels of "God is dead" pronouncements, came the call of the commercial culture for "crush the family". The family became denounced as the "nest of oppression and pathology".[123] This was no doubt a natural outcome of the call of the Enlightenment movement to free the "human being, from the shackles of tradition" and "from all concrete collective bonds".

The sacrifices that the raising of children requires could also not be in harmony with the maximisation of pecuniary self-interest and sexual permissiveness. The love, care and upbringing, which children need from both parents and which are necessary to create a future generation that is better than the present one, could not hence be provided. Day-care centres could not take the place of mothers in the most crucial period of children's upbringing. Juvenile delinquency has hence been continually on the rise and has given birth to a generation which has no respect for social values and for either parents, brothers and sisters, or other human beings. Can a civilisation survive with such a decline in the quality of human beings?

The domination of the economy by large-scale enterprises and the sharp decline in the proportion of population managing their own businesses and farms has led to an exodus of population from rural areas and small towns to large urban centres.[124] This exodus, combined with the breakdown of the family, has led to the 'atomisation of society'[125] and deprived it of the mutual care of members for each other. This has put nearly the entire burden for the care of the poor, the sick, the old and the handicapped on the state which does not have the resources or the machinery to shoulder this huge responsibility.

The breakdown of the family and of community life has eroded the most effective channels of social control and contributed to a rise in crime. Index crimes (like robbery, burglary, rape and personal assault), committed mainly by the poor, and white collar crimes (like bribery, consumer fraud, misleading advertising, marketing of substandard products, unfair labour practices and under-reporting of taxable income), committed mainly by the rich, have risen steeply and continue to rise. The crimes which are officially reported reflect only the tip of the iceberg.

There is also a rise in all the symptoms of anomie. These indicate lack of inner happiness in the life of individuals. If the single-minded pursuit of wealth, want satisfaction, and sensual pleasures could have been the source of human happiness, these symptoms would not have become so dominant and widespread that they have become a threat to the survival of civilised society.

Most governments do not realise that more police does not demonstrably mean less crime. Something else is needed and that something is socio-economic justice along with moral transformation of society. Talking of the latter without serious efforts to actualise the former is meaningless and bound to fail. The actualisation of socio-economic justice however requires a socio-economic restructuring which only a Divinely-revealed moral system can help bring about, but which does not fit into the worldview and strategy of capitalism.

Because of the absence of socio-economic restructuring, even the advanced capitalist countries have failed to minimise poverty and unemployment, to satisfy the needs of a substantial proportion of their populations, and to reduce inequalities of income and wealth, in spite of their rapid development and vast resources. In the United States alone, there are 32.4 million people living below the poverty line, 13.6 per cent of the population.[126] Of these, about one-quarter are "caught in a vicious circle of poverty and despair". They live in the "decayed hearts of major cities", and are "prisoners of ghetto pathology". They are "the denizens of a self-perpetuating culture" marked by teenage pregnancy, fatherless households, chronic unemployment, crime and drug use.[127] This is despite the welfare state of the sixties and seventies, when the hold of *laissez-faire* philosophy had loosened substantially and poverty was considered a responsibility of society as a whole. What will happen now when the *zeitgeist* has shifted under the influence of Reagan and Thatcher and poverty is being blamed on the poor and the system of government support created to help them? If one adds to these the parameters of slow growth rates and other macroeconomic imbalances starkly facing the world, one cannot fail to see the dire need for a completely new model of economic organisation.

Notes and References (Chapter 1)

1 Tibor Scitovsky, *The Joyless Economy* (1976).

2 There is no doubt that few economists would now be willing to support this view. It is however a logical outcome of the assumed symmetry between public and private interests and was widely held by economists, like J. B. Clark, who felt that factor incomes in the real world closely approximated the marginal product and its value (See G. Stigler, *Production and Distribution Theories: The Formative Period* (1941). It therefore provided the rationale for the much-cherished government non-intervention principle.

3 George Dalton, *Economic System and Society* (1974), p. 68.

4 Samuel Brittan, *Two Cheers for Self-Interest: Some Moral Prerequisites for a Market Economy* (1985), p. 16.

5 Crane Brinton, "Enlightenment", in *Encyclopaedia of Philosophy* (1967), vol. 2, p. 521.

6 Will Durant, *The Story of Civilisation* (1953), vol. 5, p. 572.

7 E. A. Burtt, *The Metaphysical Foundations of Modern Science* (1955), p. 17.

8 Voltaire wrote in his *Treatise on Toleration*: He would have borne with the absurdities of dogma had the clergy lived up to their sermons and had tolerated differences, but "subtleties of which not a trace can be found in the gospels are the source of the bloody quarrels of Christian history." Selected Works, p. 62, cited by Will Durant, *The Story of Philosophy* (1970), p. 237.

9 Durant, *The Story of Civilisation* (1953), vol. 5, p. 571.

10 See John Passmore, "Logical Positivism", *Encyclopaedia of Philosophy* (1967), vol. 5, p. 53.

11 Quoted by Durant, *The Story of Philosophy* (1970), p. 241.

12 Littre and Robin defined the human soul as "anatomically, the functions of the neck and spinal column; physiologically, the sum of functions of the power of perception in the brain" in their Dictionnaire (1809 ed.) – cited by Owen Schadwich, *The Secularisation of the European Mind in the Nineteenth Century* (1975), p. 173. Julien La Mettrie, a physician, concluded that: "the soul is clearly an enlightened machine . . . Soul is therefore but an empty word of which no one has any idea, and which an enlightened man

should use only to signify the part in us that thinks''. La Mettrie, *Man a Machine*, p. 128 – cited by Durant, *The Story of Civilisation* (1953), vol. 9, p. 619.

13 Bertrand Russell, *A Free Man's Worship – Mysticism and Logic* (1918), p. 46 ff; see also Burtt (1955), p. 24.

14 Bertrand Russell, *The Impact of Science on Society* (1953), p. 6.

15 See, R. H. Tawney, *The Acquisitive Society* (1948), p. 12. For an excellent presentation of a cross-section of views on the meaning of life, see Paul Edwards, ''Life, Meaning and Value of'', *Encyclopaedia of Philosophy* (1967), vol. 3, pp. 467–77.

16 Bertrand Russell, *A Free Man's Worship* (1918) p. 46.

17 The position that human life cannot be meaningful without religious belief is ably defended in C. H. D. Clark, *Christianity and Bertrand Russell* (1958).

18 Jean-Paul Sartre, *Being and Nothingness*, tr. by Hazel Barnes (1957), p. 38. For a clear presentation of Sartre's views, see Anthony Manser, *Sartre: A Philosophic Study* (1966), and Leslie Stevenson, *Seven Theories of Human Nature* (1974), pp. 78–90.

19 Durant, *The Story of Civilisation* (1953) vol. 9, p. 618.

20 Among the important schools of modern thought, existentialism is probably the major one which is not determinist and considers man to be free in making his choices.

21 See, Jacques Barzun, *Darwin, Marx, Wagner* (1958), p. 3.

22 E. F. Schumacher, *Small is Beautiful* (1973), p. 81.

23 Crane Brinton, ''Enlightenment'', *Encyclopaedia of Philosophy* (1967) vol. 2, p. 523. See also Michael Prowse, ''Why the Church is losing its Market'', *Weekend Financial Times*, 31 March/1 April, 1990, p. I of Section II. According to Prowse: ''The erosion of the Church of England seems strongly to confirm the 'secularisation' thesis advanced by social scientists in the 1960s and 1970s.''

24 According to the *Economist*, ''more than half of all Americans say that religion is 'very important in their lives' (in the 1950s, three-quarters said so): two-thirds are members of a church and about 40 per cent go to church regularly'' (*Economist*, 16 May 1987, p. 25). But, it adds that ''the United States is an unusually religious country''. This statement may be true because in France and Britain only about 12 to 14 per cent attend church regularly while in Norway, Sweden and Denmark merely about 5 per cent do so (See ''Man and Religion in Secular Europe'', in *Focus on Christian Muslim Relations*, monthly newsletter issued by The Islamic Foundation, Leicester, U.K., 5/1988, pp. 9–10.

25 This is reflected in the teaching of ethics in schools. Most ''schools have scrubbed all the traditional religious references out of their curricula,

leaving only a musky indecision on matters of basic morals''. (''Values in Schools'' reproduced from *Washington Post* by *International Herald Tribune*, 17 March 1987, p. 4).

26 Sherry Buchanan, ''As Ethics Courses Multiply, Prospective Tycoons Shrug'', *International Herald Tribune*, 9 July 1987, p. 9; see also ''The Business Ethics Debate'', *Newsweek*, 25 May 1987, p. 44.

27 Arnold Toynbee, *A Study of History*, abridgement by D. C. Somervelle (1958), vol. 2, p. 380 and vol. 1, pp. 495–6.

28 Will and Ariel Durant, *The Lessons of History* (1968), p. 51.

29 George A. Miller, *Psychology: The Science of Mental Life* (1962), pp. 230–1, see also Bertrand Russell, *A History of Western Philosophy* (1945), pp. 773–82.

30 Quoted by George Lichtheim, *A Short History of Socialism* (1978), p. 20.

31 Bertrand Russell, *A History of Western Philosophy* (1945), p. 775.

32 Richard A. Posner, *The Economics of Justice* (1981), p. 33.

33 See John Rawls, *A Theory of Justice* (1973); see also Brittan (1985), pp. 25–6.

34 See the views of many rebels against the tyranny of normless sciences in Quentin Skinner, ed., *The Return of Grand Theory in the Human Sciences* (1986).

35 According to Rawls: ''During much of modern moral philosophy the predominant systematic theory has been some form of utilitarianism.'' (John Rawls, *A Theory of Justice* (1973), p. vii.) For the history of utilitarianism, see especially H. Sidgwick, *Outlines of the History of Ethics* (1946).

36 Russell, *A History of Western Philosophy* (1945), p. 779.

37 Alexander Solzhenitsyn, *A World Split Apart* (1978), p. 49.

38 W. Schneider, *Adam Smith's Moral and Political Philosophy* (1948), p. 52; see also Piero V. Mini, *Philosophy and Economics: The Origins and Development of Economic Theory* (1974), p. 76.

39 Frank Hahn and Martin Hollis (eds.), *Philosophy and Economic Theory* (1979), p. 13.

40 W. S. Jevons, *The Theory of Political Economy*, reprint of the 1871 edition (1965).

41 See, Milton Friedman, *Capitalism and Freedom* (1972), p. 133.

42 F. Y. Edgeworth, *Mathematical Psychics: An Essay on the Application of Mathematics to the Moral Science* (1881), p. 16.

43 Milton L. Myers, *The Soul of Modern Economic Man: Ideas of Self Interest, Thomas Hobbes to Adam Smith* (1983), p. 2.

44 Adam Smith, "Invisible Hand", in L. S. Stepelevich, ed., *The Capitalist Reader* (1977), p. 20. See also, Wilhelm Roepke, "Ordered Anarchy", *ibid.*, p. 32.

45 See Milton Friedman, "The Methodology of Positive Economics", in F. Hahn and M. Hollis, *Philosophy and Economic Theory* (1979), p. 19.

46 Harvey Leibenstein, "Notes on Welfare Economics and the Theory of Democracy", *Economic Journal*, June 1962, pp. 299–317, cited by Mini (1974), pp. 136–7. It is relevant to quote here the view of John Rawls that one must never act solely to increase general happiness if in doing so one makes any particular person unhappy (John Rawls, "Justice as Fairness", *Philosophical Review*, vol. 67/1958, pp. 164–94). Charles Schultz has called the 'Pareto optimum' as the "do no direct harm" principle – the precept that government actions must never harm anyone directly. He argues that this principle is a major reason why sensible economic reforms rarely prevail in the political arena. See Charles Schultz, *The Public Use of Private Purpose* (1957), Chapter 4.

47 Robert A. Solo, "Values and Judgements in the Discourse of the Sciences", in Robert Solo and Charles Anderson, eds., *Value Judgement and Income Distribution* (1981), p. 38. See also Amartya Sen, *On Ethics and Economics* (1987), p. 32.

48 Solo (1981), p. 32.

49 T. Malthus, *An Essay on the Principle of Population* (2nd ed., 1803), p. 531.

50 Lichtheim, (1978), pp. 17–18. According to Hofstadter, "the survival of the fittest" has acquired a permanent niche in the American mind (Richard Hofstadter, *Social Darwinism in American Thought* (revised edition, 1962), pp. 200–4).

51 See Harry K. Girvetz, "Welfare State", *International Encyclopaedia of the Social Sciences* (1968), vol. 16, pp. 513–14.

52 Karl Polanyi, *The Great Transformation* (1944), p. 57.

53 See, Elizabeth Jay and Richard Jay, *Critics of Capitalism: Victorian Reactions to Political Economy* (1986).

54 Henry George, *Progress and Poverty* (1955), p. 10.

55 Jay and Jay (1986), pp. 15–16.

56 Hyman Minsky, *Stabilising an Unstable Economy* (1986), pp. 5–6.

57 Vance Packard has expounded this phenomenon at the popular level in a series of books. Typical of these is *The Hidden Persuaders* (1957), an exposé of the wiles of Madison Avenue. Decisions hence become far less rational than they ought to be. See also Charles Lindholm, *Politics and Markets*, p. 79.

58 John K. Galbraith, *The New Industrial State* (1972), p. 153; see also, Edward S. Greenberg, "The Corporate State", in Edward S. Greenberg and Richard Young, *American Politics Reconsidered* (1973), p. 61.

59 A number of expressions are used by economists to describe this phenomenon. These include the 'bandwagon' effect, the 'snob' effect, and the 'Veblen' effect. For representative definitions of these, see Harvey Leibenstein, *Beyond Economic Man* (1976), pp. 51–2.

60 Daniel Bell, *The Cultural Contradictions of Capitalism* (1976), p. 21.

61 Tawney, *The Acquisitive Society* (1948), p. 12.

62 Arthur Okun, *Equality and Efficiency: The Big Trade-off* (1975), p. 11.

63 There is no doubt that there is 'surplus' milk production in the EEC countries. But this 'surplus' is due to the high prices paid to producers as a result of subsidies which have become a burden on the public exchequers. The benefit of these subsidies goes to the producers of milk and not to the consumers. If it went to the consumers through a lower equilibrium price the 'surplus' would be eliminated and the consumers would also benefit.

64 Brittan (1985), p. 17.

65 Paul A. Samuelson, *Economics* (1980), p. 591.

66 John K. Galbraith, *The Affluent Society* (1958); see also, Girvetz, "Welfare State", pp. 519–20.

67 Schumacher, *Small is Beautiful* (1973), p. 40.

68 Michael Harrington, *Twilight of Capitalism* (1977), p. 32.

69 See Paul A. Baran and Paul M. Sweezy, *Monopoly Capital: An Essay on the American Economic and Social Order* (1966), p. 6.

70 See Andrew Hacker, *et al.*, "Corporation, Business", the *New Encyclopaedia Britannica* (1973–74), vol. 5, p. 182.

71 Quoted by David Owen, "Go Broke, Young Man", *Financial Times,* 31 January 1987, p. I.

72 See Edward S. Mason, ed., *The Corporation in Modern Society* (1980), for a useful anthology on the subject.

73 Lindholm, *Politics and Markets,* p. 356.

74 Edward S. Greenberg, *Serving the Few: Corporate Capitalism and the Bias of Government Policy* (1974), p. 247.

75 Cited by Greenberg, *Serving the Few* (1974), p. 45, from Reagan, "What 17 Million Shareholders Share", p. 102.

76 Robert Sheehan, "Proprietors in the World of Big Business", *Fortune,* 15 June 1967, p. 179.

77 See Gabriel Kolko, *Wealth and Power in America: An Analysis of Social Class and Income Distribution* (1964), pp. 68 and 127.

78 Michael Reich, "The Evolution of the U.S. Labour Force", *The Capitalist System* (1972).

79 Edward S. Mason, "Corporation", *Encyclopaedia of Social Sciences,* vol. 3, p. 401.

80 David Reisman, *Galbraith and American Capitalism* (1980), pp. 58–68.

81 Hacker, *et al.* (1973/74), vol. 5, p. 185.

82 *Ibid.,* p. 187. See also Kolko, *Wealth and Power* (1964), p. 67.

83 C. Wright Mills, *The Power Elite* (1956), p. 116.

84 Hacker, *et al.* (1973/74), p. 185.

85 *Ibid.*

86 Greenberg, *Serving the Few* (1974), p. 40.

87 Hacker, *et al.* (1973/74), p. 185.

88 David Owen (1987), p. 1.

89 Hacker, *et al.* (1973/74), p. 185.

90 Adolf A. Berle, Jr., *The Twentieth Century Capitalist Revolution* (1954), p. 39.

91 Galbraith, *The New Industrial State* (1972), p. xiv.

92 Galbraith, *Economics and the Public Purpose* (1973), p. 209.

93 Greenberg, *Serving the Few* (1974), p. 99.

94 Galbraith, *Economics and the Public Purpose* (1975), p. ix.

95 Alice Rivlin, *American Economic Review,* May 1975, pp. 5–6, cited by R. Lekachman, *Economists at Bay* (1976), p. 92

96 Paul A. Samuelson, *Economics* (1980), p. 499.

97 Stanley Lebergott, "Income Distribution II (Size)", *International Encyclopaedia of the Social Sciences* (1968), vol. 7, p. 146.

98 George Soule, *Ideas of the Great Economists* (1952), p. 53.

99 Harrington, *Twilight of Capitalism* (1977), p. 320.

100 Soule, *Ideas of Great Economists* (1952), p. 53.

101 William G. Sumner, *The Challenge of Facts and Other Essays,* edited by Albert G. Keller (1914), p. 90.

102 Dalton, *Economic System and Society* (1974), p. 77.

103 Reported by Stanley Lebergott in "Income Distribution", (1968), p. 151.

104 Lester Thurow, "The Illusion of Economic Necessity", in Solo and Anderson (1981), p. 250.

105 Kolko, *Wealth and Power in America* (1964), p. 126.

106 Galbraith pointed out that "Left to themselves, economic forces do not work out for the best except perhaps for the most powerful" (Galbraith, *Economics and the Public Purpose* (1975), p. xi).

107 For a review of some of the literature on this, see Jacob Mincer, "The Distribution of Labour Incomes: A Survey with special reference to the Human Capital Approach", *Journal of Economic Literature,* March 1970, pp. 1–26.

108 Galbraith, *Economics and the Public Purpose* (1975), pp. 186–7.

109 *Ibid.*, p. 297. The term 'planning system' is used by Galbraith in sharp contrast with the classical model of a perfectly competitive market. It refers to a market dominated by a few large oligopolistic corporations, each dominating a significant part of the market and able to exercise control over its prices and products. The consumer plays a relatively passive role by responding to persuasive advertising (*ibid.*, pp. 11–50).

110 Richard J. Barnett and Ronald E. Muller, *Global Reach: The Power of the Multinational Corporations* (1974), p. 24.

111 John Maynard Keynes, *Economic Consequences of the Peace* (1920), p. 3, cited by Mini (1974), p. 233.

112 Lawrence R. Klein, *The Keynesian Revolution* (1954), p. 90.

113 J. M. Keynes, *Tract on Monetary Reform* (1924), p. 88.

114 See Klein, *The Keynesian Revolution* (1954), Chapter 7 (pp. 165–87); see also, Greenberg, *Serving the Few* (1974), pp. 230–1.

115 For prices since 1950, see International Monetary Fund, *International Financial Statistics,* various *Yearbook* issues; for earlier years, see William Rees-Mogg, *The Reigning Error: The Crisis of World Inflation* (1974), p. 69.

116 The rate of inflation, which had declined in the OECD countries to 3.9 per cent per annum in 1987 from the average of about 8 per cent from 1968–86, rose to 4.8 in 1988 and 5.9 per cent in 1989. It is expected to be around 7 per cent in 1990. (See "Latest Trends in Consumer Prices", OECD *Press Release,* 1990.)

117 Nicholas F. Brady, *et al.,* Report of the Presidential Task Force on Market Mechanisms (Washington, D.C.: U.S. Government Printing Office, January 1988).

118 R. Heilbroner, *The Limits of American Capitalism* (1966), p. 88.

119 Bank for International Settlements, *59th Annual Report* – April 1988–March 1989 (Basle: BIS, June 1989), Table on "Saving and Investment: A Longer-Term Comparison", p. 32.

120 Mostafa Tolba, Executive Director of the United Nations Environment Programme, reported in "The Flight to Save the Planet", *Time,* 18 December 1989, p. 51.

121 Bill McKibben, *The End of Nature* (1989).

122 Solo (1981), p. 37.

123 For bibliographical details, see, Khurram Murad, ''On the Family'', in *The Muslim World Book Review*, No. 1, 1984, pp. 44–9.

124 See ''Rural America'', *Economist*, 8 November 1986, pp. 21–5.

125 Soule (1952), p. 73.

126 Isabell V. Sawhill, ''Poverty in the U.S.: Why is it so Persistent'', *Journal of American Literature*, September, 1988, p. 1075.

127 Richard Stengel, ''The Underclass: Breaking the Cycle'', *Time*, 10 October 1988, p. 26.

CHAPTER 2

The Retreat of Socialism

The innate goodness of human nature could not readily accept the misery and suffering of the poor that were characteristics of *laissez-faire* capitalism. There was hence a reaction which took different forms, one of the most important of these being socialism. Socialism is, however, not a precise term, there being several different versions of it: utopian, Fabian, syndicalist, guild, Marxist, market, democratic and others.[1] It is neither possible nor desirable to go into the details and mutual differences of all these variants of socialism.

There are however certain characteristics that are common to most of them. They were nurtured in the then dominantly secularist environment and hence all of them (except a few like those of Paul Tillich, R. H. Tawney, and Kurt Schumacher) had the same secularist worldview as capitalism.[2] They contained a common critique of the capitalist mode of production and argued that the free and uncontrolled markets on which it rested are bound to bring about an allocation of resources that favours the rich and perpetuates injustices and enormous inequalities of income and wealth. They considered private property and the wage system to be the source of evil and insisted that justice cannot be rendered to the poor without socialising private property to varying degrees. They felt that even democracy was not workable effectively as long as there are inequalities and special interests. They conceived of a future in which the masses would either forcibly or democratically take control of the levers of government from the capitalists and create an egalitarian and democratic society, free from class conflict and based on comprehensive planning and public control of the means of production. In other words, they attacked capitalism and proposed a different system for allocation and distribution.

The difference between them was however not essentially in the worldview but rather in the strategy or mechanism.

Of the various strands of socialism, only three – Marxist, market and democratic – will be discussed below. The others are forerunners or variants of these three mainstreams of socialism and, since they did not attain the political dominance that these three have, their discussion would not add significantly to the clarification of central issues.

MARXISM

WORLDVIEW AND STRATEGY

Militant Atheism

Marxism is a synthesis of many ideological currents of the early and middle nineteenth century. These currents were the secularist thought of the Enlightenment, the dialectics of Hegel, the materialism of Feuerbach, the class-war theories of Michelet, the economic doctrines of Smith and Ricardo and the militant slogans of the French Revolution. Marx was brought up in the midst of these ideological currents, primarily secularist and anti-religious, even though he was one of seven children of Jewish parents. His father was not notably strict in his religious observances. This is clearly indicated by his conversion to Protestantism, not out of conviction but because his profession required it.[3] From his youth Marx was known to be a hard-core atheist whose creed was (and remained): "Criticism of religion is the foundation of all criticism."[4]

Like any social thinker Marx also tried to diagnose the condition of man in society and to arrive at a prescription for its cure. In this process he used a number of key concepts like alienation, exploitation, surplus value, private property, class struggle, wage slavery and economic determinism, which, because he was not a rigorous and lucid writer, remain elusive and obscure.[5]

The principal concept in Marx's analysis is 'alienation' or 'estrangement', which arises in a capitalist society from the exploitation of the proletariat by the bourgeoisie. The proletariat are the industrial workers who lack their own means of production and hence become subject to wage slavery, selling their labour to live. The bourgeoisie are the capitalists, the owners of means of production. While all economic value comes from the proletariat, they do not get more than a subsistence wage, a wage which is just enough to keep them alive and reproducing themselves. The balance (surplus value) is expropriated by the bourgeoisie, who thus become continually more and more powerful and subject the proletariat to a state of perpetual wage slavery. This 'degrades' and 'dehumanises' them and reduces them to 'fragments of human beings' (alienation). They become 'incapable of developing to the full their human potentialities'. Their exploitation leads to the division of society into antagonistic classes and sets in motion the class struggle which shapes human history and constitutes the core of the historical process. Human beings are not free; they are pawns on the chessboard of history. Their fate is determined by the inevitable conflict of economic interests within the various classes in human society (economic determinism).

According to this argument, the key to history lay not in men's ideas but in the economic conditions of their lives. Religion and the state in a bourgeois society were an integral part of this conflict and were used by the bourgeoisie to exploit the proletariat. They have thus played a crucial role in man's alienation. The alienation would disappear when a classless society has been established and the state has withered away after passing through the various stages of the historical process. The categorical imperative therefore is to overthrow "all those conditions in which man is an abased, enslaved, abandoned, contemptible being".[6] There is thus an irresolvable dualism in Marxist philosophy. On the one hand there is an undue emphasis on the overbearingly pessimistic aspects of economic determinism, exploitation and class conflict from which there is no escape. On the other hand there is the idealist strain that looks forward to the deliverance of humanity from economic determinism.

According to Marx, "there was no such thing as individual human nature", which refers to a set of relatively basic and general human characteristics and hence to something which by definition remains constant or unchanged.[7] Since human beings did not have a basic nature, their consciousness and much else in the social, political and intellectual processes of their lives was always changing and this change was determined by "the material conditions of life" and specifically "the mode of production or the material means of existence".[8]

Norman Geras rejects this widely-held view about Marx's concept of human nature.[9] However, his case is not convincing. Acceptance of it would repudiate the material concept of history on which the Marxist edifice substantially rests. If man does have an unchanging human nature then the material conditions of life could not succeed in determining everything in human history and he could not be reduced to the position of a pawn on the chessboard of history. The basic characteristics inherent in his nature would assert themselves against the historical process. This however never happened in the Marxist historical process. One may also emphasise that the difference of view is the outcome of an inherent contradiction in the different concepts that Marx propounded. While his historical materialism does not logically permit any concept of inherent human nature, his concept of alienation requires such a nature because otherwise there is no criterion against which alienation may be understood. The two concepts are mutually inconsistent, which is no doubt one of the main reasons for the general complaint about the obscurity and inconsistency in Marx's writings.

Misdirection of Strategy

The only way to end 'alienation' was to abolish private property, its main cause. This would bring to an end the social privileges of the bourgeoisie and also break their political and exploitative power. The most effective means to this end was a revolution by the proletariat to forcibly overthrow the capitalist system. Marx rejected the avenue of 'social utopias' (small humanitarian experiments in community proposed by the utopian socialists) as deadening the class struggle. He also rejected gradualism because he believed that all efforts to transform capitalism gradually would be defeated by the entrenched power of the 'capitalist ruling class'. Efforts by governments to modify patterns of distribution cannot lead to successful socialism. To create a genuinely communist society reflecting the ideal of "from each according to his ability to each according to his needs'', the capitalist system must undergo a revolutionary transformation.[10] After the masses have liquidated the bourgeoisie and collectivised the privately-owned means of production, there would succeed a progressive rational society with no wages, no money, no social classes and, eventually, no state – ''a free association of producers under their [own] conscious and purposive control''. The fall of the bourgeoisie and the victory of the proletariat were equally inevitable.

While the goals of removing alienation of the proletariat by giving them political and economic power, improving their living and working conditions, and eliminating the class conflict are no doubt admirable, the strategy proposed by Marx was defective. If the philosophical trappings of Marx's theory, embedded in his 'historical materialism' are set aside, what remains as strategy is the liquidation of the bourgeoisie, state ownership of all means of production, and central planning. He was unable to show convincingly how this strategy would be able to eliminate wage slavery and exploitation, and raise the socio-economic condition of the proletariat to ensure the disappearance of alienation and the creation of a classless society in the higher phase of Communism, when the state would also wither away.

If the state machinery and all other institutions in human society were instruments for exploitation under capitalism, there is every reason to believe that, in a system which is built on dialectics and 'liquidation' of some human beings by others as the foundation stones of its philosophy, things may become worse if the power of those individuals is intensified through state ownership and central planning. It is not possible to create a 'brotherhood' of human beings in a system which believes in dialectics, indiscriminate liquidation and expropriation. Brotherhood requires sacrifice and service by the powerful for those who are not so endowed and dialectics smacks of that same 'survival of the fittest' notion inherent in social Darwinism.

What is the assurance that the proletariat who have killed and expropriated in their self-interest will abstain from becoming exploiters after they have entrenched themselves in a position of absolute power through a totalitarian state in place of the bourgeois state, which is at least not all pervading? It must be realised that the totalitarian state is not governed by all members of the proletariat. This would not be practical. It has to be run by a few, and those few can be worse than the bourgeoisie. While private property creates a system of decentralised decision making and leaves at least some freedom for the workers, the totalitarian state, with all means of production under its control, concentrates power in a few hands and does not leave any freedom. Is there any guarantee that the 'dictatorship of the proletariat' will not betray the Marxist revolution in the same way as the French Revolution was betrayed by the very class which made it?

If alienation were caused only by private property then one might have conceded the Marxist view that the solution lay in abolishing private property. However, private property is only one of the sources of power in human society. There are other sources of power like physical prowess, mental ability, education, creativity, ambition and hard work, family relations, and positions of leadership in society and state. While it may be possible to reduce private holding of property and also to blunt its exploitative edge through various non-Marxist measures, it may not be possible to remove the other sources of power in the Marxist way without destroying the foundations of stability and progress in civilisations. It must also be borne in mind that alienation is not necessarily inflicted by only one class or group. Anyone who gets power can exploit it, irrespective of whether the power comes from property or position and whether the person exercising it is from the bourgeoisie or the proletariat. However, in the Marxist strategy, while the power exercised through private property is removed, absolute power is vested in the hands of the politburo members through a state-owned centrally planned production system – the power to allocate jobs and resources, the power to reward and punish, the power to send to labour camps. No wonder the Marxist strategy has failed to eliminate, or even reduce, alienation in any of the societies where it has succeeded.[11] A false prescription can only exacerbate the evil it wishes to cure.

What Marx's ideas essentially reflect is a distrust of human beings. You cannot reform them. You must take private property away from them because it is a source of power and leads to exploitation. But the officials in a totalitarian state also exercise immense power, far greater than the powers of property owners. If individual human beings cannot be trusted in a decentralised decision-making system to manage their private businesses within the overall constraint of social well-being, how can they be trusted to manage the whole nation's means of production in a totalitarian system? Will not the politburo officials come from the same people who cannot be trusted, or will they be angels, unlike the capitalists? If not, what is the guarantee that they will not exploit the tremendous power at their command through their control over all means of production to serve their self-interest? Marx was probably aware of the possibility of such exploitation and this may have been the prime reason for his dream of a stateless society. But Marx did not realise that a stateless society carries the potential for even greater exploitation and injustice through the unhindered collusion of individual vested interests against other members of society.

THE FLAWS AND THE EFFECTS

The Marxist strategy in its post-revolution phase – state ownership of means of production and central planning – hoped to bring about such 'efficiency' and 'equity' in the allocation of resources that its vision of "from each according to his ability to each according to his needs" would be realised. The rationale was that once the privileges that private property provides had been eliminated, the state machinery would be able to end the distortions, misallocations and inequities that the blind operation of market forces introduces. In practice this hope has proved to be misplaced because of serious flaws in the reasoning.

The False Assumptions

Like capitalism, socialism also made a number of false assumptions about background conditions. The absence of these has frustrated the realisation of both efficiency and equity. But a lay person does not realise this because the assumptions have not been spelt out clearly in the literature. It is not possible to specify all the various assumptions underlying the Marxist strategy. However, the discussion of a few of these assumptions would help.

Distrust and Trust

Firstly, while the Marxist analysis implied a total distrust in the ability of human beings to manage private property within the constraints of social well-being, it was tacitly assumed that, after the introduction of socialism, the same human beings in their capacity as consumers, workers, managers of enterprises, and government officials, would always be motivated to do their best for the social good without caring for their self-interest. This implied that: (a) workers would work efficiently, honestly and selflessly without the incentive of proportionate material rewards; (b) managers of enterprises would operate efficiently without being able to serve their self-interest, without being exposed to the pressures of competition, and without having the ability to take their own decisions and to purchase and sell their inputs and outputs wherever they consider best; and (c) government officials would not take undue advantage of their enormous decision-making and executive powers. It also implied that in return for all this they would, in their capacity as consumers, restrict their claims on resources to only what fulfilled their needs, to avoid excessive pressure on resources.

These assumptions were highly unrealistic. In a secularist system where there is no concept of accountability before the All-Knowing God and where the total life-perspective of an individual does not go beyond the limited span of this world, it is simply illusory to expect individuals to ignore their pecuniary self-interest. There is no rational reason to believe that in a socialist society, just as in a capitalist society, individuals will not give priority to serving their self-interest, which in the absence of a spiritual basis for life, consists primarily in maximising their incomes as well as the satisfaction of their material and sensual desires. It was not anticipated that their inability to serve their self-interest would adversely affect their motivation and productivity, and seriously jeopardise the realisation of social goals even if coercion were used.

Harmony of Interests

Secondly, it was assumed that the state machinery would be run by a group of persons whose interests were in harmony with those of the whole society and who themselves had no axe to grind. This assumption was also false. Even a totalitarian state cannot be free from plurality of interests and privileges arising from factors like position in the power structure, race and geographical area. In the absence of a moral orientation, there is no mechanism by which a harmony of interests may be created. Even in a centrally planned economy, allocation in accordance with social goals requires the resort to collective value judgements in addition to the expression of choice by consumers. The planners have to have a basis for determining the goals they need to serve and values they must abide by – goals and values which serve the interest of all individuals and not of any vested group. Who will provide these goals and values? Since socialism is as secularist as capitalism, if not more so, and since its conventional wisdom also has no place for Divine guidance, how will these goals and values be determined? If human beings cannot be trusted with private property for fear that they will exploit their position of strength to serve their vested interests, how can they be trusted with the responsibility of determining goals and values and the configuration of goods and services to be produced for the whole society? Will they not serve their own self-interest? How will the society guide and discipline them in such a way that a 'socially-desired' configuration of goods is produced?

Moreover, the question is, "who plans the planners?", as aptly posed by Karl Mannheim.[12] There seems to be no valid rationale for giving a few individuals the right to determine what the whole society should produce. If the planners are human beings, as they are bound to be, then their own preferences and vested interests will tend to take the upper hand in a system not steered by a clearly defined set of goals and values provided by Divine guidance. But even if the planners are to operate on the basis of Divine guidance, as some Muslims suggest in their simple-minded justification of socialism, vesting control over all means of production in the hands of a few individuals is too dangerous. Such enormous power cannot but give rise to a dictatorial and inflexible bureaucracy interested in preserving its own power and benefits and oblivious to the welfare of the masses. It is also bound to lead to ruthless struggles for power and to intrigues, purges and concentration camps.

Availability of Information

Thirdly, it was assumed that the central planning machinery would have at its disposal all the information about consumer preferences, production costs and prices necessary for taking numerous decisions. However, such information does not exist. It is not possible to have such information without the free interaction of supply and demand in the market place. Hence Hayek's argument that a socialist solution to the problem of resource allocation was impracticable simply because complete knowledge of all the relevant data would not be available to the authorities.[13]

But even if the information were available, the task of making decisions about the allocation of resources among thousands of consumer and capital goods and services is so formidable that a handful of persons in the central planning authority could not possibly cope. Even if they tried they would find it too cumbersome and time-consuming to collect and analyse the data. They would therefore be slow in decision-making and responding to changing circumstances. The task is moreover so crucial to the welfare of all members of the society that it should not even be assigned to a few individuals. Decentralised decision-making is in the best interest of society. Any system which does not allow those who are directly affected to participate in the decision-making cannot be serious about general well-being.

If however the consumers are to be allowed to participate in the decision-making process, then why not allow them to express their preferences through the price system within the framework of moral constraints? The price system, which decentralises the decision-making process and allows thousands of consumers and producers to interact with each other, can respond more easily and readily to the needs of individuals than any cumbersome centralised planning machinery with thousands of producing and consuming units operating under its authority. The decentralised market system is also more flexible and any errors in decision-making made by individual units can be not only less costly for the society but can also be corrected more promptly. Nevertheless, if the market mechanism is to be adopted by socialism for decisions on resource allocation then, without any effective role by Divine guidance and without goal-related socio-economic restructuring, even socialism cannot avoid the same problems and inequities that are characteristic of capitalism.

Benefit of Subsidies

Fourthly, it was assumed that the large general subsidies implied in the Soviet pricing system would benefit the poor. This has also proved to be wrong. General subsidies, as will be shown in the discussion on the welfare state, benefit the rich and the privileged persons far more than they benefit the poor whose purchases are limited.[14] Food subsidies have constituted about 10 per cent of gross national product in the Soviet Union – about 5 times their share in the EEC.[15] While these benefit the rich more, they penalise the farmers who get lower prices for their produce and whose incentive to work efficiently and to produce more is hence killed.

Large subsidies are natural and implicit in the Soviet planning system. The all-powerful State Committee for Prices has to fix prices for more than 20 million items ranging from nails to tractors.[16] This task is so difficult that it is almost impossible for a single government organisation to manage it, no matter how well-staffed it may be. It cannot possibly have all the information on consumer preferences, demand and costs needed for this purpose. Hence, it tends to adopt the easier course of not changing prices. Prices have thus remained unchanged for years, particularly retail prices, changes in which are also politically sensitive. Such a rigid price structure leads to hidden subsidies and to serious inefficiencies and inequities in the allocation of resources.

The existence of large subsidies has brought a criminal waste of scarce resources. The extent of the waste may be visualised from Mr. Mikhail Gorbachev's statement at one of his press conferences that: "One can see children using a loaf of bread as a ball in their games."[17] Hence, as rightly observed by Mr. Valentin Pavlov, chairman of the Soviet state committee for prices: "Prices play little role in creating balance between supply and demand, leading to continual shortages both for retail and wholesale goods."[18] The severity of shortages is not corrected because central planning has to be enforced in a totalitarian state by a controlled press and stifling of all democratic processes. Decisions in Soviet Russia are made at the top, and obeyed. In a one-party system which was reinforced in the past by a powerful KGB (the Soviet Union's Committee for State Security), with widespread powers to arrest and send to 'psychiatric hospitals' and 'labour camps', and with limited safeguards against abuses, there is bound to be an inherent inflexibility in decision making. Such a totalitarian system lacks an automatic mechanism for responding to consumer needs and for rewarding the right decisions or punishing the wrong ones.

Isn't rigidity of prices, one may ask, good for consumers? Not necessarily. When prices are kept stagnant by fiat and not allowed to move in conformity with demand and supply conditions, they become a source of inequity and inflict a great deal of harm on the economy through the adverse effect they have on the efficient use of resources, work incentives and long-term supplies. Consumers use the products wastefully, while workers and producers do not get adequate compensation. Quality of output therefore suffers and fails to meet consumer expectations. The quantity also does not expand in response to the secular expansion in demand with the rise in incomes and population, giving rise to shortages and queues. This leads to the existence of large secondary and black markets where the rich and high officials are able to buy what they want, but the poor, who cannot afford to pay the higher price, have to forego the goods or waste a lot of their valuable time in queues.[19] Since production is on the basis of command from above, shortages of some goods are accompanied by overproduction of others. These remain unsold; yet no one suffers any loss or penalty and production continues uncorrected.[20]

Efficiency of Large Farms and Enterprises

Fifthly, it was assumed that the large monopolistic farms and state-enterprises would operate efficiently in spite of diseconomies of scale, lack of competition, and absence of market signals. This has also been belied. The large farms usually cultivated many crops, kept many kinds of livestock and had a large labour force scattered over a number of villages and hamlets. This made the task of supervision very difficult. A peasant proprietor or crop-sharing farmer does this job properly and efficiently as he is directly interested in the outcome. But the many and varied tasks on a collective farm may or may not be performed well and this may remain unnoticed, the consequences unseen. Accordingly, while private plots constituted only 0.5 per cent of agricultural area in the USSR in 1989, they provided 27 per cent of all agricultural output, indicating a much higher productive efficiency than that of the state-owned and cooperative farms.[21] In addition to loss of output, there are losses resulting from inefficient maintenance of agricultural equipment and theft of inputs and output that may not be serious on privately-owned plots.

Permanent absence of competition removes any incentive to state enterprises to economise the use of inputs or to introduce innovations. This is a rational response to the system: why should managers do something that may not necessarily benefit or may hurt them? Since the price mechanism that gives signals, and the prospect of additional profits or losses (and bankruptcy), are not there, there is nothing to induce management to do its best. What the market does under the market system – create a link between the consumer and the independently responsive producer – is missing under socialism. Management thus becomes an encrusted mass of officials used to receiving and transmitting orders. State ownership, as Weber had predicted, intensified bureaucratisation of economic life and depersonalised all participants by imposing a deadening routine.[22] Efficiency has thus suffered. For example, the Soviet Union uses two-and-a-half times as much energy as the OECD for each unit of output produced.[23]

The Soviet manager does not, moreover, have any control over the sources, quality or costs of his inputs, and the market, quality or prices of his output; these are determined in Moscow by the central authorities under the five-year plan. Suppliers and clients are not free to choose each other. They have to make requests to the state supply committee (GOSNAB) which has neither the intimate knowledge of the circumstances faced by each individual enterprise nor the time and the will to analyse their individual cases separately and to take prompt decisions that would solve their problems. A change in the nature of the product or its quantity is also not possible in response to the enterprise's own evaluation of market preferences. In addition, any gains made by increased efficiency or improved product do not necessarily benefit the manager and his workers. It is in fact possible that an enterprising manager may be hurt by the inefficient industrial and political bureaucracy that pervades in the system. This leaves the enterprises little room for flexing their muscles or incentive to introduce better management, technology or products. In consequence, resources do not move quickly in the Soviet system from the least to the most efficient uses.

There is, moreover, no mechanism for deciding how much to invest and how to strike a balance between present and future needs and to induce people to make the needed sacrifices willingly. In a centrally-planned economy, investment decisions are clearly the responsibility of the planning organisation. Without market signals and socially-agreed values, it does not have any basis for determining efficiently the scale of capital accumulation and its allocation among different goods and services. Decisions are thus made on the basis of political considerations and the whims of the planners.

One may retort by arguing that even under capitalism conditions are not necessarily better. Instead of a few state-owned enterprises in each sector of production, capitalism has a few giant corporations which not only play a dominant role in the economy but also exercise tremendous social and political influence in the country. The absence of meaningful consumer sovereignty and divorce of ownership from control are now well-recognised. Consumers and shareholders do not play a significant role in decisions about what and how to produce. It is the management which plays a dominant role in policy-making and running the corporation's affairs. Since the management consists of a few hired professionals and directors coming mainly from the rich and upper strata of society, what is the difference between socialism and capitalism?

In spite of the inefficiencies and inequities prevalent under capitalism, the above argument is not valid. The product quality, quantity and prices of even the big corporations are not determined in the same way under capitalism as those of the individual enterprises under socialism. The market has an important role to play and, even though there may be only two, three or four dominant firms in a given industry, and there may be some clandestine understanding between them about prices and markets, there is still some degree of competition between them, even though substantially less than what the logic of capitalism assumes. The firms can take their own decisions in response to their perception of the market and will themselves incur losses from their errors. They can also correct their own mistakes without having to refer to a central authority. While they can benefit from their creativity and efficiency, they face the threat of competition from substitutes and imports and the possibility that they may be eliminated if they do not act efficiently. These characteristics are absent under state socialism.

The Sour Fruits

Inefficient Allocation

The above appraisal could easily have been brushed aside as misguided and prejudiced if socialism had performed better in practice. The inability of the system to motivate both labour and management to excel, combined with a centralised and cumbersome decision-making process, which hampered the transfer of resources from less efficient to more efficient uses, has had an almost paralysing effect on the Soviet economic machinery. It was unwieldy and unresponsive to changing social and economic needs. Production therefore suffered in both quantity and quality in all sectors of the Soviet economy, and conspicuously in agriculture.

The record of Soviet collectivised farming is dismal. Even though one in three of the working population lived on the land, there has been a chronic grain deficit which has had to be made up by imports. Consequently, Soviet Russia, which was at one time the world's largest grain exporter, has become the world's largest grain importer.[24] The country's enormous agricultural potential could not be fully utilised in spite of the maximum use of force. As Joseph Stalin personally informed Winston Churchill, "millions of men and women had been blotted out or displaced for ever simply because they resisted the process of collectivisation."[25] This underlines the reality that force cannot replace either self-interest or higher values which motivate human beings to work for themselves or others.

The Central Planning Authority (GOSPLAN) in the Soviet Union did not have, in a secularist environment without any market-determined prices to serve as signals for consumer needs, anything other than the interests and inclinations of its own members and party officials to go by. This led to a frightful perversion of priorities in Soviet planning. The Soviet Union concentrated on prestige-oriented heavy industries and defence build-up at the expense of need-fulfilling consumer goods. The result is that, even though the Soviet Union is rich in human and physical resources and has the potential to satisfy all the needs of all its people, the country has been suffering for a long time from shortages of many need-satisfying goods. Although the workers have the money, the goods they need are not available.[26] The shortages have now acquired crisis proportions such that even the Soviet leadership has been alarmed.

The inefficiency of the system has now become reflected in low growth rates. Initially the growth rates were high – 5.8 per cent per annum during the period 1928–1940, followed by low growth rates (2.2 per cent per annum) during the years 1940–50 due to the War. The economy, however, picked up after the War and returned to high growth rates of 5.7 per cent per annum during the period 1950–60. This generated an ebullience of confidence in the Soviet system, which began to be heralded as the wave of the future and the model for developing countries. There has been a continuing decline in Soviet growth rates since then – 5.2 per cent per annum during 1960–70, 3.7 per cent during 1970–75, 2.6 per cent during 1975–80, and 2.0 per cent during 1980–85.[27] The "corrected, but more accurate" estimates produced by Mr. Aganbegyan, one of the brains behind *perestroika* (restructuring), suggest that there was really no growth at all in the first half of the 1980s.[28] This has reduced the appeal of the system, particularly because the growth record of other countries like Japan, West Germany and South Korea, with vastly smaller resources, has been more impressive. Stalin's famous call in 1931 for making good the distance between the Soviet Union and the advanced countries in ten years has thus proved to be an illusion. Even Khrushchev's dream of closing the gap within the decade of the sixties has remained unfulfilled.[29] The decline in growth rates has reversed the trend of decline in the absolute gap between the United States' and the Soviet economies; the gap has been widening in recent years.[30]

Inequitable Distribution

The primary *raison d'être* of socialism was equity, but in practice socialism has reduced inequalities only to a minor extent. The propertyless labourer continues to be a propertyless labourer; instead of being an employee of the individual capitalist, he has become the employee of a more powerful employer, the monopolist state enterprise, with unhindered powers to punish or reward. The worker is completely divorced from the power centres, far more than in capitalist countries, where he exercises at least some influence through the labour unions, the news media, and the elections. His dream of control over the means of production and over what was produced is hence non-existent. His *de facto* position has in fact worsened.

The wage slavery which Marx sought to abolish thus continues with greater intensity. In the capitalist system the labourer is at least free to choose his employer, there being so many of them; in the Soviet system he is not free to do so. He is stuck with one firm and does not enjoy the same freedom to shift that he does under capitalism. Everything depends on the immediate boss. If the boss is benevolent, the worker may be well off; although even if he is more competent, works harder, and performs his duties more conscientiously, he may not necessarily get a higher reward. If, however, the boss is vindictive, the worker has to suffer in silence. He has nowhere to go. If he fights for his rights he may end up in the concentration camp. State socialism thus turned out to be more tyrannical than private capitalism.[31] Is not this alone sufficient to increase the wage earners' alienation? As Crosland, a social democrat, rightly indicated: "The underlying fact of the alienation of workers from the means of production" still remains. This is because "the control centre is separated from the workers; and the possibility of exploitation, and of all the other features of 'capitalism', is present."[32]

Social inequalities and class distinctions also continue unabated. As Murray Yanowitch remarked, "Soviet society may be characterised as a class system."[33] The higher and better paid jobs go, as under capitalism, to those who come from the higher stratum of society.[34] A number of sociological studies have demonstrated that the great majority of workers' children who have high ambitions are "destined to remain disappointed".[35] Hence the need to glorify "workers' dynasties" (families in which successive generations have been workers) and stressing opportunities for short-range mobility. The once popular equation that state ownership will create a classless society has thus been falsified. There is no logical reason to assume that when the state expropriates industry, no one class will control the state.[36] The class system is bound to continue in a more intensified form in a centralised system, the underlying philosophy of which is not based on any concept of human brotherhood and accountability before the Supreme Being, but rather on dialectics and the elimination or domination of one class by the other.

To reinforce all these alienating factors is, as already indicated, the absence of priority in Soviet Russia to need fulfilment. Hence housing, food and other essentials of life are in short supply. The labourer has to wait in long queues to get some of his essential requirements. The powerful and the influential by contrast enjoy privileged access to everything through "lavish perquisites: not only free cars and country houses, but also secret additional salaries and special shops with reduced prices and, in the case of top people, with goods completely free of charge."[37] This is a clear manifestation of the existence of social classes – an aristocracy that has access to all comforts and luxuries and an ordinary public deprived even of adequate need-fulfilment.[38] This has a serious effect on the workers' morale and discipline. In the famous Novosibiris

Report, leading economists however blamed merely economic overcentralisation for the creation of an indisciplined, corrupt and apathetic work force.[39] They did not see the impact of moral failure, social inequalities and class distinctions.

Even in terms of education and training, the workers' children do not have as great an opportunity to be accepted in institutions of higher learning as that enjoyed by children coming from families of higher social strata with their greater 'influence' and resourcefulness. The Soviet education system has a strong tendency to transmit economic and social inequalities across generations even when all levels of schooling are tuition free. The critical link is the position of the family unit in the hierarchy of classes and strata. Yanowitch observes that "the more 'promising' the future occupational status associated with completion of any given type of schooling, the lower is the share of manual workers' children and the higher the proportion of non-manual strata in the student body".[40]

The system is also highly unjust in other ways. The peasants and labourers not only lost their lands, they also received low prices for their products – prices determined by officials. In the Soviet Union and, for that matter, in the entire socialist world, incomes hardly conform to need.[41] Inequality in the USSR may be less than that in France and the United States but it is certainly not less than in Norway and the United Kingdom.[42] In fact Sweezy, himself a socialist, views Soviet society as containing large disparities in income and privileges.[43] Under these circumstances, even the use of force is unable to induce the peasants and the workers to put in their best. Thus, the system not only abolished private property, it also became a great source of injustice to the proletariat producers, by paying them less, as well as the proletariat consumers, by not fulfilling their needs. The 'dictatorship of the proletariat' had to suppress the proletariat to 'cure' their alienation. Hence Sweezy is constrained to remark that the Soviet Union does not come near to living up to the principles of a Marxist socialist society.[44]

THE FALSE DREAM

The Marxist dream of an egalitarian, fraternal society with no wages, no social classes and eventually no state thus remains grossly unfulfilled. The labourer remains a wage earner with little freedom to move. Social classes also persist without any significant change. The dictatorship of the proletariat was not established. The 'withering' of the state is nowhere to be seen. If anything, the state has become more powerful and more firmly entrenched.

The reason for the failure is evident. The goals are not in harmony with the underlying philosophy and strategy. The goals are humanitarian – a classless society where no one exploits anyone else, where everyone works for the social good, where needs are fulfilled, where there are no inequalities of income and wealth, and where there is hence no alienation. The underlying philosophy and the strategy are however in conflict with these goals. They promote dialectics – hatred, conflict and elimination – and transfer the management of all means of production into the hands of a few. With immensely increased power in the hands of a small proportion of the population, no motivating force to check self-interest and serve social interest, and no socially-agreed filter mechanism to guide decision-making, the system is bound to promote privileges and a power struggle to perpetuate these. Any effort to promote democratic institutions in such a system may be frustrated because it may not be in the interest of the powerful bureaucracy who wishes to prolong its perquisites and socio-political privileges. Only sycophants and those who are collaborators in intrigues and power play can hope to have access to similar privileges in such a totalitarian society.

The system was hence a non-starter from the very beginning. An earlier indictment of the system was that of Leon Trotsky who in the mid-1930s argued that 'true socialism' is not automatically attained merely by public ownership of the means of production but rather requires the spread of democracy, freedom and greater equality.[45] However, Trotsky's wish for the spread of democracy could not be realised in a system where a few people in the politburo exercised control over everyone's means of livelihood and who had a vested interest in keeping the workers divorced from the power centres. Why would the power-wielding politburo officials act differently from the property-holding bourgeoisie? The human tendency to serve self-interest, unless kept within bounds by some effective mechanism, would prevent the realisation of Marx's utopian vision of a society whose desired goal is "from each according to his ability, to each according to his needs". People do not give the maximum of their ability for nothing. They try to take as much as they can in return. There has to be some mechanism to motivate them to do their best and to restrict their claims on resources to the limits defined by social well-being. Marxism had no mechanism other than force to restrain human self-interest. Thus while Marx provided a powerful critique of the capitalist system, he failed to provide a constructive and feasible alternative.

To keep human self-interest within bounds and to create an ideal human society, it is important to rise above class conflict and to conceive of a mechanism that would motivate human beings to treat each other as brothers and to work for the common good within the framework of agreed values that everyone accepts as uncontestable. As will be discussed later, only religion can provide such a mechanism, but Marx called for the rejection of all religion and the values that it stands for. After the destruction of the rich heritage of human values, all that he produced was a totalitarian state with all means of production under its control, no agreed criteria to guide state policies, no mechanism to restrain human self-interest, and all the power to be cruel, unjust and ruthless. Marx wishfully believed that such a totalitarian state would ultimately wither away. How? He did not explain. If the bourgeoisie is not willing to yield power, would the proletariat have done so after getting into positions of power in the politburo?

The fact is that the state, far from withering away, became ever more powerful and an instrument of oppression in communist countries; 'the society in balance with nature' did not come into being. The proletariat continued to be wage slaves. So what did they gain by the Marxist revolution – a rise in their incomes? But so they have in the capitalist countries like the U.S., West Germany and Japan, substantially more than in Soviet Russia, Eastern Europe and China, although not as much as those of the bourgeoisie. Consequently, Marx's prophecy of the 'inevitable doom' of capitalism has also been falsified. Nearly all the lessons to be drawn from the Soviet experience – economic inefficiency, bureaucracy, hierarchy, despotism, and frustration of grass-roots initiative – are negative.[46] Thus, considered against the background of what Marx visualised, the results are not less than frustrating. The claimed blessings – a stateless society with no wages, no money and no social classes – has simply remained unrealised. The frustration is even greater when one considers the total absence of grass-roots democracy and ruthless suppression of criticism.

COMPLEXITIES OF REFORM

> Haphazard attempts to introduce aspects of market economies to the command economy were no more successful than a vine graft on a telephone pole.
>
> George Arbatov[47]

As a result of its unrealism, Marxism, which had a dominant intellectual influence over the socialists in the pre-war period, has come increasingly under attack.[48] Revisionism has gained ground and come close to a repudiation of the Marxist system. There has been an increasing realisation among the Soviet economists themselves that a drastic reform of the Soviet economic machine is overdue. The leadership has now started emphasising the vital need for political and economic reform, reflected in the policies of *glasnost* (openness) and *perestroika* (restructuring) initiated by Mikhail Gorbachev.[49]

The problem, however, is that nobody is yet clear about the extent of restructuring necessary to enable socialist countries to realise their goals. It is being argued that the remedy lies in decentralisation and reintroduction of private property and the market mechanism into the socialist economies. While this is no doubt necessary, a number of closely related issues have yet to be clarified by both *glasnost* and *perestroika*. These are: the extent of decentralisation, competition, price reforms, privatisation and property rights that a socialist economy is willing to tolerate without changing its identity totally. While half-baked reforms and piecemeal changes may be ineffective, bold moves in the direction of capitalism would, given the absence of background conditions, only aggravate the existing socio-economic inequities and lead to a permanent burial of the original *raison d'être* of socialism.

The glaring question remains whether the patching on to socialism of certain elements of capitalism, which has itself failed, can bring about the kind of revolutionary restructuring that is necessary to overcome the prevailing economic problems and social unrest and to realise the professed goals of socialism. Unfortunately, the entire debate about restructuring the socialist economies in both the capitalist and the socialist intellectual circles reflects a lack of awareness of the dire need for a change in the socialist worldview. While *glasnost* has reduced to some extent the repression of religion, there is decidedly no change in the socialist worldview. The role of the moral dimension in motivation and socio-economic restructuring has not been given even a stray mention, as if it were of absolutely no importance.

It is not realised that if centralised decision-making and lack of private property and market-determined prices were the only factors responsible for shortages of need-satisfying goods and services in the socialist countries, the capitalist countries would certainly have been able to realise their goals. But needs cannot be satisfied without an immensely larger allocation of resources for this purpose. The essential counterpart of increased allocation for need satisfaction is a substantially reduced allocation for some other purposes – defence, space programmes, heavy industries, prestige symbols, luxuries and privileges of the elite, and numerous other economic sectors and geographical areas which enjoyed a disproportionate allocation of resources in the past.

Such reallocation is not an easy task. It requires not only socially-agreed criteria but also a strong motivation on the part of the privileged individuals or geographical areas to sacrifice. Why should they do so in a secularist society with only a short, this-worldly frame of life? If, however, the 'unnecessary' spending which is in conflict with need satisfaction is not reduced, where are the resources to come from? Monetary expansion? This will lead to the same excessive claims on resources and the associated macroeconomic and external imbalances that capitalism and the welfare state are facing. The magnitude of the problem may be appreciated better if the need to reduce substantially the existing unhealthy fiscal deficits is also borne in mind. These have risen in the Soviet Union from under 3 per cent of GDP in 1980–85 to about 7 per cent in 1987 and 14 per cent in 1988.[50] How will these be reduced without hurting need-fulfilment, employment and growth? This crucial question remains unanswered. If heavy doses of borrowing are used to solve the problem, the Soviet Union may, after a few years, experience the same acute debt-servicing problems that the heavily-indebted developing countries are now facing.

Thus the Soviet Union has an impossible task before it – that of restructuring its economy to fulfil needs without a filter mechanism of socially-agreed values, that of serving social interest without any mechanism to restrain self-interest in the face of rising individualism, that of reducing budgetary deficits without generating unemployment and further reducing the rate of growth, and that of containing inflation in spite of introducing realistic prices in an economy plagued by suppressed inflation. The introduction of realistic prices and exchange rates and the reduction of subsidies to lower the high budgetary deficits will mean the dismantling of the existing paternalistic system where retail prices bear no relationship to production or import costs, where cheap food, clothing and housing are at least theoretically assured, and where employment is supposed to be guaranteed. Realistic prices are bound to have an inflationary impact.

If wages and pensions are not raised simultaneously, there will be a steep decline in the standard of living, particularly of the poor. This will create social unrest and political problems if *glasnost* is also to be maintained. If however, wages are raised with prices, then *perestroika* would not be effective. *Perestroika* would demand that wage increases not be guaranteed or uniform. They will have to be linked rather to labour productivity and enterprise revenues. If this is done, then some workers will be affected more adversely than others by price and wage changes. This will accentuate the differences in real incomes and contribute to greater income and wealth inequalities, thus leading to social unrest, as it did in China. In a market system where such changes occur in small doses every year, they may not be noticed as much as they will be in a system where the errors of decades are designed to be rectified in a few years. Hence moral regeneration and socio-economic restructuring are now more urgently needed by a privatising command economy than any other economy in the world.

Moreover, the demand for increased efficiency cannot be meaningful unless the enterprises are also free to select the quality, quantity and sources of their inputs and also to hire and fire employees on the basis of their performance. The privilege of a guaranteed market, which enterprises now enjoy, may also have to be withdrawn. This may increase the losses of many of them and lead to unemployment when they stop being paternalistic and fire employees in their quest for greater efficiency. Since the state enterprises are large, the problems resulting from the liquidation of loss-making enterprises, especially unemployment, will also be great. The Soviet system is not geared to handle the problems resulting from the move toward the market system. Hence a programme of partial restoration of the market is a contradiction in terms, as long as the paternalistic goals continue. However, if these goals are abandoned along with central planning and collective ownership to realise greater efficiency, then what is it that is left of socialism to identify it as a distinct system?

Even the question of privatisation is fraught with serious difficulties. Since all nationalised property now belongs essentially to the people, transfer of property rights through privatisation needs to be brought about in a just manner. There does not seem to be, so far, any clear-cut programme for this.

The idea apparently gaining some ground is the auctioning of shares in state-owned industries and farms. However, before any such auction can take place, a realistic appraisal of value is necessary, something that is a time-consuming and difficult job in the absence of market-related prices and returns. Without such appraisal, the risks would be too great for those not having insiders' knowledge. Moreover, the auction of shares has the disadvantage of giving an edge to those who had amassed wealth during the socialist period; they are the ones who will be able to buy the shares. Hence, those who were privileged without ownership rights will now add another feather to their caps – that of ownership. So where then will the proletariat be in whose name socialism was brought about and in whose name it is now being dismantled?

However, if the property rights are to be passed on equitably to the people, then the perplexing question is about how this should be done – who gets a share in what and to what extent? If the workers are to be given shares in farms and enterprises in which they work, how about those who are not working or those who are working in less fertile areas or in enterprises that are, or will soon become, bankrupt? If coupons are to be issued to everyone to purchase, then privatisation may have to wait until the appraisal of all saleable enterprises and farms has been completed. This will require time, which the system does not have. Moreover, those who had amassed wealth in the past will again have an edge if they can use this wealth along with the coupons to purchase.

The social-Darwinist weeding out process may also create problems. It has determined the make up of the socialist leadership over the last several decades and created a vested interest in the continuation of the existing situation. *Perestroika* may not be able to change this mood by itself in the absence of moral transformation. Officials of state enterprises may not be psychologically prepared to face the realities of market competition. The leadership will therefore need to be ruthless in weeding out inefficient managers. Since this may tend to create unrest and discontent, the leadership will find itself at the same time struggling to pacify the vested interests in order to keep itself in power. Avoiding overconcentration of power, over-centralisation of management, and diseconomies of scale, the major defects of socialism, will therefore be an uphill task. "Virtually everyone in the Soviet Union has an excellent reason to favour reform and an excellent reason to fear it."[51] The power struggle that is bound to result between those who wish to cling to the existing privileges of power and the revisionists who cannot succeed unless such privileges are ended, could not but reduce the speed of reform and also blunt its effectiveness through inevitable compromises.

MARKET SOCIALISM

While the Soviet Union has just started injecting a market dimension into the management of its economy, the Eastern European countries (Bulgaria, Czechoslovakia, East Germany, Hungary, Poland and Rumania), Yugoslavia and China had already pioneered a route to what has come to be referred to as 'market socialism'. China had even abandoned the emphasis on its unnatural and inhumane commune system which had been forcibly imposed by Mao Zedong.[52] The central Soviet model with state ownership of most means of production nevertheless continued to serve as the pivot for all these economies.

The primary theme of the reforms was to bring about a partial decentralisation of the decision-making machinery in the economy by allowing market signals and private initiative to play a greater role in the allocation and distribution of resources. State enterprises were to be granted greater autonomy in planning their operations, securing their inputs, and pricing their outputs. Most controls on these enterprises were to be relaxed in favour of self-management. Market-related prices, wages, and exchange rates were to be introduced and subsidies were to be cut to bring down budgetary deficits. The undue emphasis placed previously on heavy industry was to be reduced and greater weight was to be given to agriculture and consumer goods industries.

Failure and Overthrow

These reforms were not uniformly introduced in all countries.[53] They were more extensive in Yugoslavia, Hungary, Poland and China, and less so in Bulgaria, Czechoslovakia, East Germany and Rumania. None of these countries, however, went as far in decentralising the economy and trusting the markets as market socialists had in theory visualised. The basic superstructure of the highly centralised, highly bureaucratised system remained intact practically everywhere. Hence the problems that these countries sought to address – falling productivity and growth, rising shortages, and low-quality goods – continued unresolved. When these reached intolerable levels, communist regimes fell like dominoes in all the six East European countries in 1989. The Chinese regime would probably also have been overthrown had it not been for the use of brute force to suppress the freedom movement which found its expression at the Tiananmen Square in 1989. The question is, why did market socialism not fare any better than the Soviet model in realising its goals?

Political Democracy?

Economic reforms were not accompanied by political democracy. Political dictatorship and suppression continued. The absence of political freedom crippled economic reforms and did not allow them to take their full course. Reforms took the direction that suited the vested interests of the suppressive regimes. Partial and half-hearted fulfilment of reforms could not lead to the needed revitalisation of the economies. Goals hence remained unrealised. Corruption and inefficiencies also took a heavy toll of resources leading to serious shortages and difficulties.

However, even if political democracy had accompanied economic reforms, it would not have been sufficient. The replacement of bureaucratic red tape by decentralisation and market signals would no doubt have helped introduce greater efficiency in the allocation of resources, but not more than exists in nationalised industries in the market economy countries. The absence of private ownership of means of production and the initiative that this creates, would still have hurt.

Moreover, greater equity, which even market economies have failed to deliver, cannot be attained unless the reforms envisaged by market socialism were designed within the framework of an enabling worldview. Only this would have made possible the kind of filter mechanism, motivating system, and socio-economic and financial restructuring that goal realisation requires. An effective strategy could not hence be developed. These countries were thus not only unable to fulfil needs, they also got themselves enmeshed in a number of macroeconomic problems which had long been considered by the socialists to be characteristic of capitalism – budgetary deficits, inflation, unemployment, and high foreign debt. Inequalities also rose and gave rise to social turmoil.

Inflation, Unemployment and Debt

Yugoslavia, Poland, Hungary and China, which had gone the farthest in liberalising, are good examples. Yugoslavia and Poland are groaning under hyperinflation and a wave of labour unrest. The annual rate of inflation has continually accelerated in both countries. In Yugoslavia, the rate of inflation rose from 21.2 per cent in 1979 to 1,240 per cent in 1989. In Poland, it rose from 7.1 per cent in 1979 to 245 per cent in 1989. It has continued to accelerate in both these countries and stood at, respectively, 2,685 and 640 per cent per annum in December 1989.[54]

The rate of inflation in Hungary and China, though relatively smaller, has also been accelerating continually. In China, it accelerated nearly six times from 2.0 per cent in 1983 to 11.9 per cent in 1985.[55] This rise in prices came as a shock to the Chinese who had been accustomed to unchanging prices for more than 30 years. As a result there were protests and student unrest, and Hu Yaobang, Chief of the Chinese Communist Party and the man behind economic reforms, had to resign in disgrace. The government announced a freeze on price increases and, at least temporarily, suspended the plans to move towards a more market-oriented economy. There was hence a temporary respite in 1986 when the rate of inflation decelerated to 7.0 per cent. The lid could not, however, be held tightly and the rate of inflation rose to 8.8 per cent in 1987 and 20.7 per cent in 1988. Because of repressive measures, the rate declined to 16.3 per cent in 1989. However, it retains the potential of rising to a much higher level if suppressed inflation is allowed expression through real liberalisation of the economy.

Unemployment has also started to rise. It is bound to do so in socialist countries when they try to reduce the inefficiencies plaguing their productive machineries and do not restructure their economies and financial systems sufficiently to provide alternative income-earning opportunities to those unemployed. Initially there was an effort to deny the existence of unemployment. However, the problem became too big to hide in Yugoslavia, Hungary and China. In Yugoslavia, the jobless rate stands at 15 per cent, double the OECD average and is expected to rise further.[56]

The external debt of Eastern European countries and Yugoslavia has also risen steeply. During the four years from 1985–89, it rose from $71.7 billion to $101.2 billion. The outstanding gross debt of Hungary, Poland and Yugoslavia, the most indebted of these countries, was estimated to be $20.6

billion, $43.3 billion and $19.7 billion in 1989. During the four years from 1985–89 it rose from $66.8 billion to $83.6 billion. The external debt of China has been rising even faster. It shot up from $4.5 billion in 1980 to $44.9 billion in 1989 and is expected to rise even faster in the near future.[57]

Problems of Reform

The strategy for reform that is being recommended to these countries is tailored within the secularist framework of capitalism – reduce government spending and credit expansion to restore macroeconomic stability; let prices find market-clearing levels; remove bureaucratic controls; and privatise. Although all these are no doubt indispensable, they would require a burial of the socialist goal of equity unless there is a thorough degree of socio-economic and financial restructuring, which cannot be attained without a proper value and motivating system which the secularist worldview is not capable of providing.

Cutting government spending is necessary to remove the macroeconomic imbalances, but is difficult to attain when welfare is dependent primarily on the government's paternalistic spending programmes. Rolling these back significantly would accentuate political unrest, particularly when subsidies are removed, prices are allowed to find market-clearing levels, wage increases are restrained, and there is a deep erosion of real incomes. Moreover, reduced government spending along with the effort of privatised government enterprises to cut losses may lead to unemployment. This will further accentuate political unrest unless there is an effective social security net to support and retrain the unemployed. Privatisation will also raise equity-related issues, as already discussed under the complexities of reform in the Soviet Union.

This shows how difficult it is to initiate reforms without a properly designed transition strategy to serve the goals of both efficiency and equity. A privatisation strategy prepared within the framework of secularism will enable the rich and the powerful to exercise the same kind of influence against need fulfilment as they do under capitalism. The poor and the vulnerable will thus suffer tremendously. Crime may also be expected to rise, there being nothing other than state coercion in the tool-box of totalitarian systems to prevent these.

The 'reformed' socialist economies therefore face a double dilemma – how to get rid of the past inequities and imbalances that have led to current socio-political discontent, and how to realise both efficiency and equity without exacerbating crime and the prevailing imbalances? Adoption of the strategy of democratic socialism and the welfare state, which these countries now treat as a model, may not help because social democracies do not face the high rates of suppressed inflation and unemployment or the serious shortages that East European countries are now facing. Unless a different strategy is adopted, East European countries may encounter far more serious macroeconomic imbalances and other problems than faced by the social democracies. Unless a moral dimension is injected into their reforms and a thorough socio-economic and financial restructuring is undertaken, the East European countries will probably resort primarily to substantial doses of borrowing to accelerate their development and to overcome the shortages and imbalances they are facing. While this will help appease the people temporarily, it will create other problems which are equally perplexing, as most developing countries have now realised to their great chagrin.

DEMOCRATIC SOCIALISM

Democratic socialism does not have the Marxist ideological trappings and does not believe in the use of force and violence or the inevitable collapse of capitalism. It rather believes that socialism as an ideal is inseparable from democracy and should be brought about peacefully in a gradual manner through democratic processes (the free consent of the governed) without revolution. Complete state ownership of means of production and central planning were nevertheless considered necessary in the earlier discussions for realising socialist aims. Schumpeter defined socialism as an institutional pattern in which the control over means of production and over production itself is vested with a central authority.[58] His distinguished contemporary, Oscar Lange, viewing the scene some years later, agreed that socialism signified state control and central planning, although he spoke of "social ownership of the principal means of production".[59]

Divorce from the Soviet Model

However, as a consequence of the repressive measures used in the Soviet Union and the inefficiency of the Soviet economic machinery, the emphasis on both these was gradually abandoned. It came to be assumed that the market system was capable of bringing about an efficient allocation of resources and of solving all the problems of production and that, since the failures of capitalism lay mainly in the area of distribution, the main task of socialism lay in removing the distributive injustice and inequality inherent in the capitalist system. This, it was presumed, could be done through a mixed economy in which the public sector plays an important role and adopts a number of measures to "modify the nature of capitalism to a serious extent" and "lead to socialism" in the end.[60] Although there was a considerable difference of opinion on what these measures should be, democratic socialism in general became equated with the welfare state with its emphasis on political and economic democracy combined with regulation, nationalisation of 'key' industries, labour reforms and welfare services (unemployment benefits, free or subsidised education, health and transport services, and welfare payments). In contrast with this, communism became synonymous with revolution, central planning and state ownership of all means of production. This was in essence the success of the 'inevitability of gradualism' that the English Fabians and the German revisionists had preached around the turn of the nineteenth century.

Radical socialist theoreticians had however felt unhappy at this development. According to them the revisionists' tools of parliamentary party and labour unions were condemned to frustration while they operated within a capitalist environment. Parliament and labour unions could only reflect the interests dominant in society and, in a capitalist society, bourgeoisie interests predominate. The revisionists' tools could not therefore succeed in bringing about the downfall of capitalism. They could only serve to strengthen the institutions of capitalist society. Consequently, it was argued, the reformist programme would merely prolong the existence of capitalism.[61] The radicals did not therefore consider the welfare state as their ultimate goal. They continued to cling to the hope of eventually bringing about 'real' socialism which would go beyond the welfare state toward a society in which class distinctions have been erased and wealth has been equitably distributed by the abolition of wage relationships, and through the state ownership of all means of production. But this radical approach which, as indicated earlier, only accentuated wage slavery and undermined efficiency, no longer constitutes the political platform of the socialist parties who have become equated with the welfare state.[62] Moreover, with the abandonment of the radical approach by even the Soviets, there is little chance of its gaining converts in the foreseeable future.

The question that hence arises is: is it possible to realise the goal of an ideal society of brothers where poverty is abolished, everyone is assured of need fulfilment, and income and wealth are equitably distributed, by making a few cosmetic changes in the distributive machinery of capitalism through a greater role of the state in the economy? The answer would have been 'yes' only if the market system had been successful in allocating resources 'efficiently' and its failure lay mainly in distribution. Since, as has been shown, the market system has also failed to allocate resources 'efficiently', there is no question of democratic socialism succeeding with its minor adjustments in the operation of the market system's distributive machinery. The long experience with democratic socialism has clearly established this.

Socialist parties have come to power at different times in almost all of the Western European countries. Their principal objectives were: abolition of poverty, provision of social services by the state, greater equalisation of wealth, full employment and economic stability.[63] Although these parties have succeeded in introducing a number of most welcome reforms in their economies and in improving the condition of labour, it must be admitted that they have largely failed in realising their principal objectives. In spite of the great wealth of their economies: poverty still persists, needs remain unfulfilled, inequalities of income and wealth have in fact risen, unemployment has taken a higher toll, and imbalances and instability have risen, with unhealthy consequences for economic growth, efficiency and equity.

Principles Compromised

While the ideals of democratic socialism remain remote from achievement, its strategy has already come under attack because of the unhealthy budgetary deficits and the heavy tax burden it has brought, as will be discussed in the following chapter. The socialist movement has thus lost much of its earlier élan. In many countries, where socialism had gained strength, "there is resurgence of the 'New Right'; anti-socialism has become a vote-getter".[64] The result is that in 1983 and again in 1987, the British Labour Party "failed to unseat a Conservative government that had presided over an economic contraction sharper than that of 1929."[65] Labour's inability to translate three million unemployed into a winning issue induced the *Economist* to declare that: "Socialism, that bountiful and revolutionary doctrine in the heyday of growing public spending, now seems old and stale. . . . Socialism no longer inspires what may soon be a post-Socialist Europe."[66]

Some of the front-line socialist thinkers are even questioning the wisdom of the socialist attack on some fundamentals of capitalism, particularly private ownership of property and profit. Crosland concludes in his *Future of Socialism* that "the definition of capitalism in terms of ownership, whether or not it was helpful 100 years ago, has wholly lost its significance and interest now that ownership is no longer the clue to the total picture of social relationships: and that it would be more significant to define societies in terms of equality, or class relationships, or their political systems."[67] Nationalisation is no longer considered to be important and accordingly the British and many European socialist parties are only 'mildly' collectivist.[68] The importance of profits in the efficiency and development of society has also come to be increasingly recognised. Thus, Crosland states that "it is a mistake to think that profit, in the sense of a surplus over cost, has any special or unique connection with capitalism. On the contrary, it must be the rationale of business activity in any society, whether capitalist or socialist, which is growing and dynamic."[69] Hence one would tend to agree with Novak when he concludes that "socialists seem to be in retreat both from theory and from programme."[70] Even Mr. Kjell-Olof Feldt, Finance Minister of Sweden, declared that "we must not let ourselves become the anti-capitalist party. Capitalism has many large problems but we have not got a wall-to-wall alternative."[71]

However, if private ownership of property and profit are both to be embraced by socialism, then what is it that would distinguish socialism from capitalism, particularly when inequalities have risen even under democratic socialism and social classes also continue to dominate? Since even the rightists now support the collective provision of essential services, strong support for the trade unions remains the main characteristic of democratic socialism. But with the prevalent high rate of unemployment, the trade union movement has also considerably weakened and is "unable to effect a radical transformation of power relationships".[72] Hence William Pfaff has been led to remark: "The liberal left – and illiberal left, for that matter – simply has no large and convincing programme for society."[73] Irving Howe comes out even more forcefully by saying that "socialism is now identified neither with the abolition of poverty nor with the nationalisation of industry."[74]

A major problem with democratic socialism is that, in its effort to achieve power by peaceful and legal means in advanced industrial countries, it has had to compromise so much with the dictates of election politics that it has lost the vigour of conviction and the capacity to bring about fundamental change – change that would lead to a real 'modification' of capitalism.[75] Democratic socialism is only conceivable on condition that a majority of the population desire it. The results of elections in many countries have shown that the electorate has vacillated in its commitment, in spite of recession and unemployment. The movement has been unable to gain firm roots. It continues to be at the mercy of public fads and the strength of conservative or socialist leadership. People are not willing to stand firmly for it and to fight and die for it as they would for a religious ideal. Can such vacillation of the public mood provide assurance for the ultimate success of democratic socialism? A revolution is no solution either. The communist revolutions in Russia and China killed millions, leaving behind unsavoury memories that could not be entertained by anyone serious about democracy and human rights. Even in some developing countries, where socialism has been brought to power by revolutionary means or military *coups,* it has largely destroyed what humane aspects there were in the original traditions.[76]

Loss of Élan

Judging it against performance, one can say of democratic socialism that it has not succeeded in realising its goals and, even if it returns to power in future elections, there is little likelihood that it will make much headway. This is because the lack of harmony between its goals and its worldview disables it from developing an effective strategy. Like capitalism, democratic socialism is also an extension of the post-Enlightenment secularist philosophy. All it has done is to introduce some 'realistic' changes in the distributive machinery of capitalism. The effort to get a mango tree out of a lemon seed by some changes in the fertilisers and the soil has not and cannot succeed. Without a radical change in the worldview, transformation of human beings, the most important element in the scene, and substantive change in the strategy, all efforts to realise the humanitarian goals of socialism, are bound to be frustrated.

However, instead of doing radical rethinking to arrive at a real solution, 'Americanisation' of the Left has taken place. There is an effort to identify democratic socialism with issues like environmentalism and peace. Even though these are important, embracing them does not in any way ensure the realisation of need fulfilment, greater equality, and erosion of class differences. Such prescriptions could come with an equal ardour from bourgeois parties. Mr. Roy Hattersley's recent book, *Economic Priorities for the Labour Government,* shows how narrow the base for democratic socialism has become.[77] In his speech at the Labour Party Conference, Mr. Neil Kinnock "set out an agenda of social-market policies as impeccably capitalist as any put forward by the two centre parties in the previous fortnight." Labour's aim, according to its leader, "should be to manage the market economy better than the Conservatives."[78] Mr. Kinnock's election as Labour Party chief has effectively committed the party to 'better-managed' capitalism. Hence it seems that without ever realising its ultimate goals, democratic socialism has lost its élan.

Notes and References (Chapter 2)

1 The term 'socialism' became well established in England in the 1830s, although its first use can be traced back to at least 1826. Less than a century later a British social scientist compiled over 260 definitions of socialism. See D. F. Griffith, *What is Socialism? A Symposium* (London: Richards, 1924), cited by J. Wilczynski, *The Economics of Socialism* (1978), p. 21.

2 Lichtheim's verdict is that "socialism is generally associated with secularism." This is because the socialist movement inherited the basic worldview of humanism in the French Revolution. In fact socialism in France, Belgium, Ireland, Italy, Spain and the Luso-Hispanic cultures of Latin America has historically been associated with militant aetheism (George Lichtheim, *A Short History of Socialism* (1978), pp. 308–9).

Marxism

3 See Lewis S. Feuer, "Marx", *The New Encyclopaedia Britannica*, 15th ed. (1973–4), vol. 11, p. 549.

4 Neil McInnes, "Karl Marx", *The Encyclopaedia of Philosophy* (1967), vol. 5, p. 172.

5 See John Plamenatz, *Karl Marx's Philosophy of Man* (1975), pp. 11–13.

6 Cited by Plamenatz (1975), p. 233, from Karl Marx, *Early Writings*, p. 521.

7 See Plamenatz (1975), pp. 37–8; and Leslie Stevenson, *Seven Theories of Human Nature* (1974), p. 54.

8 "The mode of production in material life determines the general character of the social, political, and intellectual processes of life. It is not the consciousness of men that determines their being, but, on the contrary, their social being determines their consciousness." Karl Marx, *Selected Writings in Sociology and Social Philosophy*, tr. T. B. Bottomore, eds., T. B. Bottomore and M. Rubel (1963), p. 67.

9 See Norman Geras, *Marx and Human Nature: Refutation of a Legend* (1983).

10 See Karl Marx and Friedrich Engels, *Basic Writings on Politics and Philosophy*, ed. Lewis Feuer (1959), "The Communist Manifesto", p. 9; see also Bottomore (1963), p. 263.

11 Cf. C. A. R. Crosland, *The Future of Socialism* (1963, ed. reprinted in 1985), p. 37.

12 Ben B. Seligman, *Main Currents in Modern Economics* (1971), vol. 1 (*The Revolt Against Formalism*), p. 107.

13 F. A. von Hayek, *Individualism and Economic Order* (1948), pp. 77ff.

14 See Gyorgy Szakolczai, "Limits to Redistribution: The Hungarian Experience", in D. Collard, R. Lecomber and M. Slater (eds.), *Income Distribution: The Limits to Redistribution* (1980), pp. 206–35; see also, Maksymiban Pohorille, "Collective Consumption in Socialist Countries: A Theoretical Approach", in R. C. O. Mathews and G. P. Stafford, *The Grants Economy and Collective Consumption* (1982), p. 77. For example, in Poland official car prices are about 40 per cent of the market price, so gains from privileged access are huge ("Stranded Red Elephants", *The Economist,* 30 May 1987, p. 72).

15 Commission of the European Communities, Directorate General for Economic and Financial Affairs, *European Economy,* No. 45, December 1990, p. 52.

16 N. D. Nordhaus, "Soviet Economic Reform: The Longest Road" (1990), vol. 1, pp. 287–307. See *European Economy,* No. 45, December, 1990, p. 52; L. Sirc, *Economic Devolution in Eastern Europe* (1969); and Russell Lewis, *The Survival of the Capitalist System: Challenge to the Pluralist Societies of the West* (1977), p. 9. Retail prices of bakery products, sugar and vegetable oil were last changed in 1955. Prices of milk and milk products were last raised in 1962 and have been static ever since. The nominal prices of some basic foodstuffs have been the same for some 20 years. (Patrick Cockburn, reporting from Moscow, "Now for the Prices", *Financial Times,* 17 September 1986, p. 16.) Soviet rents have not changed since 1928, utility rates for electricity and gas since 1946 (Patrick Cockburn, "Doubts over Prices: Soviet Prices Chief Calls for Overhaul", *Financial Times,* 14 July 1987, p. 2, quoted from a pamphlet issued by Mr. Valentin Pavlov, Chairman of the Soviet state committee for prices.

17 *Financial Times,* 8 October 1987, p. 2.

18 Cockburn, 14 July 1987 (see note 16 above).

19 See Quentin Peel (in Moscow), "Soviet Black Market 'Beyond Control' ", *Financial Times,* 5 April 1988. In this note Peel reports the admission by the Head of the Soviet campaign to stamp out the country's rampant black market that, "the problem is beyond the capacity of the police to control."

20 For example, in 1984, the Soviet Union, with a population of 275 million produced 740 Million shoes – more than those in the U.S., Britain, France and West Germany combined (Cockburn, 17 September 1986, see note 16 above).

21 *European Economy,* No. 45, December 1990, p. 37. See also, Nove (1983), p. 87.

22 See Ben Seligman, *Main Currents in Modern Economics* (1971), vol. 1, p. 26.

23 *European Economy*, No. 45, December 1990, p. 40; see also Jan Winiecki, *Economic Prospects, East and West* (1987), and Winiecki, *The Distorted World of Soviet-Type Economies* (1988).

24 Marshal I. Goldman, *U.S.S.R. in Crisis: The Failure of an Economic System* (1983), p. 2; see also, Russell Lewis (1977), p. 8. There are a number of works published in E. Europe on the subject of chronic and recurrent shortages. One of the more important of these available in English is, J. Kornai, *Economics of Shortage* (1980); see also Alec Nove, *The Economics of Feasible Socialism* (1983), p. 71.

25 Winston Churchill, *The Hinge of Fate* (1950), pp. 498–9. See also Roy Medvedev, *Let History Judge*, tr., George Shriver (1989).

26 See Jan Winiecki, *The Distorted World of Soviet-Type Economies* (1988). See also, "Why Planned Economies Fail?" *The Economist*, 25 June 1988, p. 69.

27 For growth rates, see Gur Offer, "Soviet Economic Growth: 1928–1985", *Journal of Economic Literature*, December 1987, Table 1, p. 1778.

28 See Abel Aganbegyan, *The Challenge: Economics of Perestroika* (1988); see also, N. Shmelev and V. Popov, *The Turning Point: Revitalising the Soviet Economy* (London: Tauris, 1990), pp. 298–9; *European Economy*, No. 45, December 1990, p. 21; and "The Soviet Economy: Survey", *The Economist*, 9 April 1988, p. 3.

29 See Offer (1987), p. 1798; and Gregory Grossman, "Communism in a Hurry: 'The Time Factor' ", in Abraham Brunberg (ed.), *Russia Under Khruschev* (1962), pp. 205–18.

30 Offer (1987), p. 1781.

31 Norman Furniss and Timothy Tilton, *The Case of the Welfare State: From Social Security to Social Equality* (1977), p. 42.

32 Crosland (1963), p. 37.

33 Murray Yanowitch, *Social and Economic Inequality in the Soviet Union* (1977), p. 108.

34 *Ibid.*, Table 4.2, p. 109.

35 *Ibid.*, p. 131.

36 Crosland (1963), p. 38.

37 Cited by Russell Lewis (1977), p. 27, from Tibor Szamuely's postscript to Sir Tufton Beamish's Half Marx (London: Tom Stacey, 1970).

38 Brezhnev prided himself on a motley collection of foreign luxury cars – Rolls-Royce, Lincoln, Mercedes, Cadillac. See, Raveendra N. Batra, *The*

Downfall of Capitalism and Communism: A New Study of History (1978), p. 227. According to Pravda, the perks of high officials included the following grocery list for their dachas in the Ryazan region, south-east of Moscow, for the first six months of 1988: 394 kilos of caviar, 6,000 tins of crab, liver paté and sundry other delicacies, 565 kilos of cured sturgeon, and much more. "And this in a country where meat is still rationed in eight of the 15 republics, if it can be found at all." ("Perestroika Throws a Party", *The Economist*, 1 October 1988.

39 See, "Privatisation, Soviet-Style", *Financial Times*, 20 November 1986, p. 16.

40 Yanowitch (1977), p. 69.

41 Abram Bergson, "Income Inequality Under Soviet Socialism", *Journal of Economic Literature*, September 1984, p. 1052.

42 Bergson (1984), p. 1092.

43 Paul M. Sweezy, "Lessons of Soviet Experience", *Monthly Review*, November 1967, pp. 9–21.

44 *Ibid.*

45 Leon Trotsky, *The Revolution Betrayed* (1937/72).

46 See also Nove (1983), p. 68 and back cover.

47 George Arbatov, "Soviet Economic Reform: Challenge by the Radicals", *Financial Times*, 2 May 1990, p. 17.

48 See Crosland (1963), p. 2.

49 See Mikhail Gorbachev, *New Thinking for Our Country and the World* (1987); See also Abel Aganbegyan (1988, 1989); Anders Aslund, *Gorbachev's Struggle for Economic Reform* (1989); and A. Hewett (ed.), *Reforming the Soviet Economy* (1988).

50 See "Alas, Poor Perestroika", *The Economist*, 24 September 1988, p. 30; and "Budget Perestroika", *The Economist*, 8 October 1988, p.75.

51 Jerry Hough, *Russia and the West: Gorbachev and the Politics of Reform* (1988).

52 For the heavy loss of lives (20–30 million) and the disasters that had befallen China, see John K. Fairbank, *The Great Chinese Revolution 1800–1985* (1986). See also, Warren Lerner, *A History of Socialism and Communism in Modern Times: Theorists, Activists and Humanists* (1982), pp. 212 and 241.

For some 50 years Mao was referred to in Western literature as Mao Tse-tung. However, in 1979 the *pinyin* version of Chinese names was adopted for English-language usage. Hence the revised spelling is used here (see Warren Lerner (1982), p. 153).

Market Socialism

53 See Michael Karen, "The New Economic System in the GDP: An Obituary", *Social Studies,* April 1973, pp. 554–87; Janos Kornai, "The Hungarian Reform Process: Visions, Hopes and Reality", *Journal of Economic Literature,* December 1986, pp. 1687–737; U.S. Congress, Joint Economic Committee, *East European Economies: Slow Growth in the 1980s* (1986), vol. 3; Dwight H. Perkins, "Reforming China's Economic System", *Journal of Economic Literature,* June 1988, pp. 601–45; and William F. Robinson, *The Pattern of Reform in Hungary* (1973).

54 For data on inflation, see IMF, *International Financial Statistics,* Table on Consumer Prices.

55 These and the following data on Chinese inflation are also from *ibid.*

56 "Marx Turned Upside Down", *The Economist,* 24 September 1988, p. 17.

57 Data are from World Bank, *World Debt Tables, 1990–91,* vol. 1, p. 105, and vol. 2, pp. 66 (China), 162 (Hungary), 298 (Poland) and 414 (Yugoslavia); and Bank for International Settlements, *60th Annual Report,* 1989/90 (Basle: BIS, June 1990), p. 48.

Democratic Socialism

58 Joseph Schumpeter, *Capitalism, Socialism and Development* (1950), p. 167.

59 Oscar Lange, *Political Economy* (1963), vol. 1 (General Problems), p. 81.

60 Crosland (1963), p. 26

61 See Rosa Luxemburg, *Reform or Revolution* (1963), p. 41. See also George Lichtheim, *Marxism* (1961), p. 329; Furniss and Tilton, (1977), pp. 69–70.

62 See Lewis A. Coser, "Socialism", *Encyclopaedia Britannica,* 15th ed. (1973–74), vol. 16, p. 973.

63 See Crosland (1963), p. 1.

64 See Nove (1983), p. xii. See also "Europe's Socialists: Has Anybody Seen Our Philosophy?" *The Economist,* 30 September, 1989, pp. 21–4.

65 George F. Will, "A Turning Point in History: British Socialism's Demise", *International Herald Tribune,* 18 June, 1987, p. 5.

66 "Labour's Wilderness", *The Economist,* 10 January 1987, p. 16.

67 Crosland (1963), p. 42.

68 Cf. John Lloyd, "Why it will not be Easy to Kill Off Socialism?" *Financial Times,* 23 March 1987, p. 14.

69 Crosland (1963), p. 16.

70 Michael Novak, *The Spirit of Democratic Capitalism* (1962), p. 197. The Socialist International, which groups more than 80 left-wing and social-democratic parties from around the world, embraced the market economy at its 100th anniversary meeting in Stockholm on 22 June 1989 and rejected the idea of nationalisation as a "remedy for social ills". This is without doubt a major revision of its basic principles. (Robert Taylor, "Socialists Revise Objections to Market Economy", *Financial Times*, 23 June, 1989, p. 3.)

71 Kjell-Olof Feldt, "The Acceptable Face of Socialism", *Financial Times*, 16 June 1988, Section IV, p. iv.

72 John Lloyd (1987), p. 14.

73 William Pfaff, "When the Left has Nothing to Offer, the Right Wins", *International Herald Tribune*, 9 July 1987, p. 4.

74 See Irving Howe, "Introduction" in Irving Howe (ed.), *Twenty-Five Years of 'Dissent': An American Tradition* (1979), pp. xiv and xix.

75 See also Barrington Moore, *Reflections on the Causes of Human Misery and upon Certain Prospects to Eliminate Them* (1972), p. 193.

76 Moore (1972), p. 193.

77 Roy Hattersley, *Economic Priorities for the Labour Government* (1987).

78 "A Battle Won, A Battle Joined", *The Economist*, 8 October 1988, p. 41.

CHAPTER 3

The Crisis of the Welfare State

> Those who care deeply about social justice have often felt themselves to be conducting a dialogue with the deaf.
>
> Michael Prowse[1]

The welfare state was no doubt a welcome development in capitalist countries. It gained momentum, first after the Great Depression and then after the Second World War, as a response to the challenge posed by socialism and the difficulties created by the Depression and the War.[2] Its immediate objective was to mitigate some of the most conspicuous excesses of capitalism and thus reduce the appeal of socialism. Hence it attracted all sections of the population, workers as well as capitalists. According to some of its critiques, it represents "a movement of social management from above aimed to ensure social order without the transfer of essential power from the ruling stratum to the plebeian majority."[3]

Its underlying philosophy indicates a movement away from the social-Darwinist principles of *laissez-faire* capitalism and towards the belief that the welfare of the individual is too important a goal to be left merely to the operations of market forces. The philosophy implies a formal recognition by mainstream economics that poverty and inability to provide for one's own needs are not necessarily evidences of personal failure. Workers may be underpaid, unemployed or impoverished through no fault of their own. Hence it was necessary to assure every member of society protection against social risks including industrial accidents, disability and unemployment, and to provide social services like education, housing, medical care and public transportation, which are essential for the effective functioning of individuals in modern society but which may not be accessible to people having limited means. The philosophy also recognises full employment and equitable distribution of income and wealth among the important goals of state policy. This calls for the playing of a far more active role by the state in the economy than would be permissible under *laissez-faire* capitalist, or even the Keynesian, versions of the welfare state.

This should not lead to an impression that there exists a consensus over the nature and functions of a welfare state. On the contrary, political analysts have been unable to reach a generally accepted agreement on its precise definition in spite of their discussions for decades – so much so that Titmuss calls it an "indefinable abstraction".[4] Accordingly, there are several different practical examples of the welfare state ranging from the tepid version of the United States to the fuller version of Sweden.

However, the welfare state was not able to break away from the secularist trappings of the Enlightenment philosophy or the belief in sanctity of the market system. The Enlightenment attitude against value judgements continued unperturbed. Means tests came to be regarded as an anathema to the welfare state.[5] It was assumed, in step with democratic socialism, that the allocation of resources could be handled efficiently by the market system with the help of some government intervention aimed at reducing the imperfections, which create inefficiencies in the operation of the market, and offsetting market failure, which prevents the market from reaching certain desirable results in resource use. The public sector's main role lay in the area of distribution, particularly through transfer payments and provision of public goods and services. The entitlement to these was not, however, to depend on being rich or poor, but rather on the badge of citizenship to which all members of society have an equal right.[6] Accordingly, "the principle of benefits paid as a social right rather than according to individual need is the basis of most social insurance schemes."[7] The rationale behind this is that the distribution of benefit on the basis of a means test would not only require value judgements but also violate the criterion of Pareto optimality.

THE STRATEGY

The welfare state did not therefore recognise the need for introducing any radical changes in the market system to realise its objectives. A greater role by the state was considered sufficient to improve the functioning of the market and to redress the inequities created by *laissez-faire* capitalism. This could be accomplished through the tools of the welfare state, six of which have acquired great prominence: regulation, nationalisation of certain key industries, a strong labour movement, fiscal policy, high rate of economic growth, and full employment. It is therefore necessary to examine the effectiveness of these welfare state tools in the realisation of its goals.

(a) Regulation

There can be no doubt that regulation of private enterprise is important to ensure competition, maintain order and standards, and safeguard the rights of others. However, regulation requires agreed criteria or collective values in the light of which to regulate. If such criteria and values are not available or not universally recognised then, in pluralist societies where everyone pursues his self-interest, the state becomes a neutral springboard for all groups and vested interests, and its activities simply become the bargained outcomes of the political struggle.[8] Assuming that all vested interests will try vigorously to protect their interests, regulation in the absence of socially-agreed values is bound to favour one or the other group and to reflect a tendency to overregulate or underregulate depending on which pressure group has the upper hand in terms of voting, control over news media, financing election campaigns, and lobbying. Since economic and organisational power and resources at the disposal of various interest groups are not equally distributed, they are not mutually counterbalancing, as has been claimed by Strachey, Galbraith and others. The ultimate outcome of the efforts to regulate may, in this case, tend to favour the rich and the powerful because they will use their resources to control news media, and to finance election campaigns and aggressive lobbying, to have regulation tilted in their favour.

Moreover, even if the right legal framework is prepared for regulation, government coercive power may itself be inadequate to enforce regulations effectively. It has to be backed by a powerful motivating mechanism which only proper upbringing and moral transformation of society can provide. Unless there is an inner urge on the part of individuals to comply conscientiously with regulations, if necessary at the cost of their own self-interest, every effort will be made to evade regulations and to take advantage of loopholes, which are bound to exist in all regulations, irrespective of how carefully they are drafted. Hence it is just wishful thinking to expect that balanced regulations designed to further socio-economic justice can be drafted and effectively enforced by government coercive machinery without the backing of socially-agreed goals and values and a motivation among all social classes to sacrifice their self-interest for the realisation of these goals. Both of these forces are denied any role by secularism which constitutes, like capitalism, the main pillar on which the edifice of the welfare state rests.

When welfare state ideas were gaining momentum under the onslaught of socialism, even the rich and powerful in capitalist societies supported increased regulation, considering this to be a better alternative to socialism. Now, however, when the welfare state is facing fiscal problems and questions are being raised about its long-term feasibility, business interests have joined hands with conservative governments to push for deregulation, which is gaining momentum in many industrial countries. It is argued that regulations do not allow the economy to flex its muscles and add to public as well as private costs in enforcing or complying with regulations. What this clearly indicates is that, in the absence of unshakable social conviction in socio-economic justice combined with socially-agreed values and a mechanism to motivate the various groups to give others their due and to hold their own claims on resources within the constraints of social welfare, it is difficult to have balanced regulations and to enforce them in order to realise justice in pluralist societies; whatever regulations are enacted under the pressure of political winds may tend to be diluted or removed with a change in political expediency.

(b) Nationalisation

The movement for nationalisation of major industries has also lost its momentum. This is not only because of the general disenchantment with the performance of nationalised industries, but also because of the large doses of subsidies which these industries have normally required for their survival, sometimes due to the political constraints that prevent them from charging market-related prices. The budgetary problems generally encountered everywhere are making it difficult for public exchequers to finance these subsidies. Hence, more as a matter of financial necessity and less as a matter of political choice, privatisation has become a worldwide trend and is gaining momentum under governments of both right and left-wing persuasion.

Privatisation programmes of one kind or another are planned or under way in Western Europe and enthusiasm has even spread to countries and regions as far-flung as Japan, India, Latin America, Canada, Africa and even China, Eastern Europe, and the Soviet Union.[9] In Spain, moves toward privatisation have been started under the first fully socialist government the country has ever had.[10] In Britain, the privatisation movement started by the Conservatives in 1979 had provided more than $17 billion to the Treasury by 1988, and it was expected that this figure would rise to $33 billion in the following three years. The contribution of nationalised industries accordingly declined from 10 per cent of GDP in 1979 to about 6 per cent in 1988.[11] Since the political climate has now changed, even the Labour Party does not express its allegiance to nationalisation any more, and the privatisation movement is likely to gain further momentum with the persistence of slower growth rates and budgetary constraints faced by governments.

(c) Labour Movement

The trade union movement which was considered to be a panacea for raising the incomes of labour, improving their working conditions, and providing them with a sense of economic security, has now lost its momentum as a result of inflation and high unemployment. Continually rising wages are being unjustly, or perhaps justly, blamed for cost-push inflation, and wage rigidity is generally being considered a major cause for unemployment. Consequently, non-unionism has risen in many industrial countries and labour unions are suffering both an absolute decline in membership and a decline in their share of the work-force. A clear majority of workers in Britain, where the movement has been strongest, no longer belongs to a trade union. In manufacturing, the traditional base of the British trade union movement, union membership had slumped by 24 per cent when employment had fallen by 13 per cent. The proportion of workers in the Trade Union Congress unions in Britain is now below 40 per cent. Of those who are members, most are not actively involved. Rank and file commitment to the unions has slackened and "people simply do not want to be in unions".[12] This indicates the weakening of the trade union movement even in its stronghold. It is more so in West Germany, Japan and France, where the union density figures are lower, and the U.S., where only 19 per cent of workers are in unions.[13]

It does not appear likely that labour unions will be able to achieve a major breakthrough in the foreseeable future in the face of unemployment, which looks set to continue at around current levels. However, it is not just unemployment which is to be blamed. Some of the excesses of the unions themselves, spurred only by the 'unhindered' pursuit of self-interest by aggressive and vocal members and their lack of concern for any adverse impact of their policies on social well-being, have also been an important factor in eroding the support they enjoyed from the industrialists and the wider public.

The industrialists had acquiesced to the trade union movement, not necessarily because of their conviction in socio-economic justice, but rather because of their realisation that the unions constituted a positive benefit to the industrial system through the contribution they could make to harmonious management-labour relations. They negotiated contracts that were binding on all members; they standardised wage contracts between competing industrial firms; and they sanctioned strikes only at the expiration of a contract, thus ending wildcat strikes. Thus they added to stability and predictability of the economic environment which are indispensable to capital accumulation and growth of production.[14] However, the corruption of union leadership and the large number of strikes led to a breakdown of the tacit social contract between the industrialists and the labour unions and removed the rationale behind the industrialists' support for labour unions. During the 'winter of discontent' in 1978/79, there were so many strikes in Britain that they accentuated public misery and turned even public sentiment against them. This seems to have been one of the major reasons why Mrs. Thatcher was swept to power.[15]

There are doubts whether the unions have been able to contribute significantly to the rise in real wages. In the United States, while the average real hourly wages rose by 58 per cent over the two decades from 1947–1967, they did not rise at all during the two following decades. In 1987, they were close to where they were in 1968.[16] Given the strong winds of conservatism and the erosion of political support for minimum wage legislation, the unions have been unable to bring about an adequate rise in the United States in the federal nominal minimum wage, which has remained unchanged at $3.35 an hour since 1981. The recent decision to raise it to $4.25 an hour in April 1991 will be significantly short of the minimum wage of $4.86 necessary even to offset adequately the erosion of around 45 per cent which will have taken place over the decade in its real value as a result of inflation.[17] If this process of erosion in the real value of the minimum wage continues, inflation rather than legislation will have effectively repealed it.

(d) Fiscal Policy

Public Spending

Fiscal policy has been the major tool of the welfare state. It includes the use of public expenditure, progressive taxation and borrowing to realise the desired goals. Public spending has to be not only for the traditional functions recognised by even the *laissez-faire* state (defence, public administration and economic services), but also for the welfare state functions of promoting growth, economic stability, and greater income equality. With the continued expansion in the responsibilities of the state in pursuance of these functions, there has been an exponential growth in public spending and taxation over the last fifty years, particularly because of a steep rise in defence spending and transfer payments. The latter incorporate a vast array of benefits, including social security entitlements (like unemployment compensation), social assistance grants (like old age benefits and child care), subsidies (on food and public utilities), and public services (like education, health care, housing, and public transport), which are not restricted merely to the poor and which every interest group therefore lobbies for.

Between 1960 and 1982 the average size of government expenditure as a percentage of GDP at current prices rose by 15 percentage points to 41.3 per cent in the OECD countries. Thereafter it has tended to come down gradually to 40 per cent in 1988. Among individual countries, it rose to as high as 66 and 62 per cent in Sweden and the Netherlands in 1982 and declined thereafter to around 59 and 58 per cent respectively in 1988. The lowest ratio of spending has been in Switzerland (30 per cent).[18] The ratio also rose continually in the United States, which was not as committed to the welfare state as Sweden, from around 10 per cent of GDP in 1940 to 37 per cent in 1986, coming down thereafter marginally to 36.3 per cent in 1988.[19] Spending rose not only during periods of recession and unemployment but also during periods of prosperity and full employment, a position which could not be theoretically justified under the Keynesian analysis. Government spending had to continue rising because *laissez-faire* capitalism was inherently unstable and inequitable and the revolution in rising expectations in terms of physical goods and services, which the materialist culture had brought about, could not be satisfied without a high rate of economic growth.

The rise in expenditures has however been accompanied by two major changes in the structure of government spending in the OECD countries. One of these is a steep rise in defence spending and transfer payments and a fall in government investment outlay, and the other is the downward inflexibility in total spending. Since growth rates in most countries are below the level required for reducing the high rate of unemployment, a reduction in spending has serious social repercussions and is politically sensitive. Government expenditures have hence become out of control.[20] The governments are therefore under pressure to cut spending. However, instead of first setting priorities in the light of agreed socio-economic goals, the governments have followed "the strategy of small cuts hither and thither", which are "soon reversed".[21]

The general tendency seems to be to "trim the meat rather than the fat".[22] The primary candidates for cuts are normally government investment outlay and welfare spending for the rich and the poor alike. Since such cuts cannot be sustained for long without hurting the country's future growth prospects and social stability or eroding political support for the ruling party, the chances of reversal remain strong. This is one of the main reasons why governments have not been able to fulfil their promises to the electorate for sustained long-term cuts in spending.

The decline in East-West tensions has made it possible to reap a large 'peace dividend' in the form of lower deficits and higher appropriations for a number of sectors that could play a crucial role in raising economic efficiency and equity. Nevertheless, the general feeling seems to be what the *New York Times* aptly stated in a recent editorial, "political leaders will be reluctant to cut Pentagon spending, even where they believe cuts to be wise, until they are confident that their communities will not face economic ruin."[23] This indicates that it is not so much the economic management role of the large Pentagon budget that may prevent deep cuts in it, but rather pressure-group politics. It is always possible to handle the economic management part of the budget by additional allocations for improving health, education, research, infrastructure, environment and employment. But a small number of giant corporations who command great political clout would prefer economic management through greater military spending.

A cut in agricultural subsidy, which benefits primarily the big farmers through the price support programme and which hurts the poor through higher prices, could also be beneficial. The subsidy has nevertheless continued to rise. It has risen as a percentage of farm income for all OECD countries. Between 1979 and 1986, it rose from 14.7 per cent to 35.4 per cent in the U.S., from 44.3 per cent to 49.3 per cent in the European Community and 64.3 per cent to 75 per cent in Japan.[24] The direct cost to the taxpayer is also a great burden: around $40 billion a year in the U.S.; about the same in Japan; and around

$30 billion in the EEC in spite of the recent farm reforms. The indirect costs of higher food prices and inefficient production are even higher. A recent OECD estimate of the total cost to taxpayers and consumers in its member countries is $245 billion a year.[25] A *Financial Times* editorial laments that rarely "has so much been lavished by so many upon so few".[26] Since politicians in rich industrial countries are the prisoners of their farm lobbies, the concern that these data rouse is unlikely to have a perceptible effect.

High Tax Levels and Deficits

The obvious way to finance increased spending is raising taxes or resorting to increased public borrowing. Taxes have, however, already risen substantially in the OECD countries from 27.7 per cent of GDP at current prices in 1960 to 38.4 per cent in 1988 – the highest ratios being in Sweden (55.3 per cent) and Denmark (52.1 per cent), and the lowest in the United States (29.8 per cent), and Turkey (22.9 per cent).[27] Accordingly there is a reaction that has come to be termed as the 'welfare state backlash', a resistance to the taxation on which welfare programmes have been based.

Since this backlash has made it difficult to raise taxes in step with expenditures, the obvious choice has been greater reliance on public borrowing to finance the rising deficits. While in 1960 there was an overall budgetary surplus of 1.3 per cent of GDP in the OECD countries, in 1984 there was a deficit equal to 4.4 per cent of GDP; the deficit has come down since then, but is still expected to be around 2 per cent in 1990 for the major industrial countries in spite of a long period of economic expansion – an expansion which could have been used profitably to minimise the deficit.[28] The large deficit has a number of implications. It is inflationary, raises interest rates, and crowds out private sector investment. It has also contributed to a rise in government interest payments from an average of 5 per cent of total government spending in 1975 to almost 10 per cent by 1982. Since the public debt has continued to rise, the only factor that has had a redeeming effect has been the decline in interest rates since then. Interest rates have, however, been rising since 1988.[29]

The high level of both taxes and borrowing to finance expenditure thus represents a problematic and unhealthy dimension in the overall structure of public finances in all welfare states. For the United States the persistent deficits have been even more problematic. They have not only absorbed the country's entire private sector saving but have also led to external borrowing to finance the excess. This has not only tended to crowd out private sector investment but has also turned the United States, one of the richest countries in the world, into one of its biggest debtors. If the deficits continue, the need for attracting foreign capital will force the country to maintain higher interest rates, with adverse effects on economic growth, employment and current account, not only in the United States but also other countries, particularly the developing countries whose debt-servicing burden will rise as a result and further squeeze their ability to finance development from internal resources.

The Inequitable Subsidies

While public spending, tax burden, and deficit have all risen exponentially, the inequalities of income and wealth, which the welfare state aimed at reducing, have not gone down. Indeed government spending could not have succeeded in reducing the inequalities created by the undisturbed continuation of all capitalist institutions. The productive system, operating in accordance with capitalist norms, has also operated against the use of scarce resources for the need fulfilment of all. The lack of an agreed filter mechanism of humane values created an anathema to value judgements, and has not only deprived the welfare state of well-established, long-term priorities in expenditure planning, but also led to the 'equal' treatment of rich as well as poor in the access to benefits from public spending on education, health care, and a wide variety of subsidised goods and services. This has, on the one hand, reduced the redistributive effect of government spending and, on the other hand, subjected public sector finances to unnecessary pressures which they are unable to bear. It was not appreciated that if the means test was applied and cost recovery pricing techniques were used for the rich, the poor could have derived greater benefit from the same or even a lower level of government spending. Consequently, even some of the stop-gap and makeshift expedients adopted within the framework of capitalism have failed to produce the desired result of reducing inequalities.

Julian Le Grand has examined the effect of public expenditure on education, health care, housing and public transport on the overall pattern of inequality. His well-argued conclusion is that in each of the four cases public expenditure as a whole favours the better off rather than the poor. As a result, the desired equality in the provision of benefits to the rich and the poor has not been achieved. The relevant inequalities have not even been diminished significantly. He concludes that the strategy has failed and there seems to be not much "prospect of retrieving the situation through any piecemeal reform".[30]

Richard Titmuss, the doyen of universalist benefits, admits that fifteen years of experience with the universal, free-on-demand, provisions of Britain's National Health Service have shown that "the higher income groups know how to make better use of the Service; they tend to receive more specialist attention; occupy more beds in better equipped and staffed hospitals; receive more elective surgery; have better maternity care, and are more likely to get psychiatric help and psychotherapy than low income groups."[31] The poor are often relegated to inferior services or wind up at the end of the line.[32] Even in the United States, the Medicaid and Medicare programmes have neither broken nor even seriously damaged the relationship between social class and health care. They have not only failed to improve substantially the situation of the disadvantaged but have actually improved the situation of certain groups among the advantaged.[33] In fact, according to Greenberg, "Government spending in the U.S. is a prime contributor to the maintenance of class inequality."[34]

A number of other studies have also indicated that general subsidies tend to benefit the rich more than the poor, the proportion of subsidised goods and services being consumed by the rich being large. Witt and Newbould investigated the distribution of subsidies on bread, butter, milk, cheese, flour and tea introduced in Britain by the Labour Government immediately after their election victory in 1974. Their conclusion is that these food subsidies benefited the better off to a greater extent than the less well off.[35] Food subsidies are widespread in socialist countries and Gyorgy Szakolczai has shown that the same pattern appears there. His investigation of the Hungarian system of redistribution through lower commodity prices indicates that even though the extent of food subsidies was substantial, the net impact of the whole system was to discriminate against the poor.[36]

Price subsidies offered through nationalised industries yield the same perverted results. Since the rich spend more on electricity, gas, coal, postal services and telephones, Le Grand has shown that the subsidies introduced on these services as a part of anti-inflation policies in Britain in the early 1970s (by holding down the prices of these commodities and paying compensation to the relevant industries to meet their resultant deficits) benefited the rich more than the poor.[37] Thus the expansion of free or subsidised public services in the welfare state has benefited the rich far more than the poor. Inequalities have accordingly risen.

Progressive Taxation

The other element of welfare state fiscal policy, progressive taxation, has not fared any better. Initially the faith in the ability of progressive taxation to reduce inequalities was so great that Henry Simons made a categorical statement:

> Thus I would suggest . . . not merely that progressive taxation is a sound and promising method for mitigating inequality, but that it is the only sound and promising method which has seriously been proposed and that other currently popular schemes are unsound and incompatible with the kind of total arrangements which we wish to preserve against the recently prevailing world trend.[38]

Progressive taxation appealed to everyone because it did not create any fundamental disturbance in the capitalist system.

In reality, however, progressive taxation has failed to reduce income inequalities. A number of studies related to the United States have shown that, while the rate structure maintained the facade of progressivity, the numerous exclusions, exemptions, deductions and credits reduced it effectively. ''Every item removed from the tax reduces revenue and probably makes the income tax less fair.''[39] Strayer accordingly observes that ''as now applied, the individual income tax is not as effective an instrument of income redistribution as generally believed.''[40] Other studies have come up with similar conclusions.[41] Pechman has gone even farther by observing that in the last 20 years the tax system has become more regressive due to increased reliance on payroll taxes and the declining importance of corporate taxation, a trend that he notes in other developed countries as well.[42] A recent study by the British Institute of Fiscal Studies also found the tax system to have increased in severity for the great majority of Britain's population since 1979.[43] Even in the case of Sweden, apparently an ideal welfare state, the position is that: ''Income tax may be steeply progressive on paper, but the rich have learned to use a complex system of deductions to lighten their tax burdens. Once income from capital is taken into account, the progressivity of the tax system looks a lot less draconian . . . People can stay rich by exploiting asymmetries in the tax system.''[44] Thus, there seems to be a widespread recognition now that progressive taxation has not only not played a significant redistributive role anywhere, but has rather also possibly operated in the reverse direction in some countries.

However, even though the tax systems did have great potential for accomplishing a significant redistribution, if properly designed and administered, the welfare state backlash and the supply side onslaught have led to calls for reductions in individual and corporate tax rates instead of a reform of the tax systems in the direction of greater equity. Redistributive taxation, it is claimed, hampers growth. Accordingly, tax rates are being lowered in many countries. In the United States, the 1986 tax reform ''lowered the income tax rates to levels not seen since the 1920s.''[45] The result is that, while previously the tax system at least gave the semblance of having income redistribution as its objective, it will fail to convey this impression after the proposed reductions in tax rates have been carried out.

Persistent Inequalities

The bitter fact is that in spite of the rise in government spending and the apparent progressive taxation, inequalities of income and wealth have risen – the poor have become poorer and the rich richer, particularly in the U.S.[46] According to the U.S. Bureau of the Census, the poverty rate (per cent below poverty level) rose in the United States from 11.4 per cent in 1978 to 13.6 per cent in 1986.[47] The income gap between the rich and the poor has also increased. In 1980, one-fifth of all families at the bottom of the income ladder received 5.3 per cent of aggregate income while the upper fifth received 38.2 per cent. In 1986, only six years later, the share of the bottom fifth had dropped to 4.6 per cent while that of the top fifth had risen to 43.7 per cent.[48] Accordingly, the Democrats on the U.S. Congress's Joint Economic Committee concluded in a recent report that "the concentration of wealth has greatly increased in the past two decades." While 0.5 per cent of the population controlled 25.4 per cent of the net wealth in 1962, they controlled 35.1 per cent in 1983. The share of the assets held by the poorest 90 per cent of American households dropped during those 21 years from 34.9 per cent to 28 per cent.[49] Commenting on the Report, the Chairman of the Joint Economic Committee, Representative David R. Obey, said, the figures are "proof that the rich get richer". He added: "If wealth is power, then most Americans have less power today than in the early 1960s." The position is not significantly different in other industrial countries. In the supposedly ideal welfare state of Sweden, the share of the highest 10 per cent of families rose from 21.3 per cent of aggregate income in 1972 to 28.1 per cent in 1981.[50] Although the share of the lowest fifth also rose marginally from 6.6 per cent to 7.4 per cent, the rise was not sufficient to enable them to fulfil all their essential needs in an inflationary environment.

(e) High Growth

While the previously discussed tools of the welfare state have failed to make any significant contribution towards reducing the inequalities of income and wealth, the strategy of high growth rate has not fared any better. High growth was the only tool in the tool-kit of the welfare state which was fully in conformity with the self-imposed constraint of not making value judgements or interpersonal comparisons, and which hence received unanimous support. Since the concept of the welfare state gained momentum after the Second World War against a background of sustained economic growth, great faith was placed in its ability to lead to a classless society. Social policy became "an *ad hoc* appendage to economic growth."[51] In fact some writers considered redistribution without growth to be dubious. Even a leading socialist like Anthony Crosland felt growth to be the only feasible method of redistribution because "any substantial transfer involves not merely a relative but an absolute decline in the real incomes of the better-off half of the population . . . and this they will frustrate."[52] Some prominent policy advisers even consider faster growth to be the solution to all the problems of developed as well as developing countries.[53]

However, two decades of unexpectedly high growth rates and continually rising wealth have failed to remove poverty, fulfill needs and reduce inequalities. Even in the world's richest countries, irrespective of whether we look at the less welfare-oriented countries like the U.S. and Japan or the high welfare-oriented countries like West Germany, the U.K., and Sweden, some of the essential needs of the poor – particularly education, medical facilities and housing – remain unfulfilled. Moreover, the phenomenal rise in the volume of goods and services that economic growth has brought about has not by itself contributed to a rise in human happiness. There is an increased manifestation of the symptoms of anomie. "Tension", says Mishan, "is everywhere more evident than harmony, disproportion more evident than proportion."[54]

While the undeterred pursuit of economic growth did not help realise the distributive goals, it did contribute to high rates of inflation and interest rates because of the accelerating rates of rise it required in public and private sector spending. It also led to a high degree of pollution and rapid depletion of non-renewable natural resources. Hence, the very idea of high growth rates has come under attack. The concept of 'sustainable development' has been popularised since 1987 by the World Commission on Environment and Development (the 'Brundtland Commission'). This emphasises the realisation of growth without adversely affecting both intergenerational and intragenerational equity. If some of the phenomena that adversely affect such equity – rising levels of inflation, interest rates, debt-servicing, pollution and depletion of non-renewable resources – are taken into account, the prognosis cannot but be a lower rate of sustainable development.

Moreover, return to the high growth rates of the 1950s and the 1960s is unlikely in the industrial countries in the near future. According to IMF projections, the real rate of growth in the first half of the 1990s is expected to be only around 3 per cent.[55] Given these projections, the strategy of depending primarily on economic growth to solve the distributional, macroeconomic and external imbalances of many industrial and developing countries does not inspire general confidence. What is called for is a new but more effective strategy.

(f) Full Employment

The objective of a high rate of employment which was an important way of improving the condition of the poor has also soured with unemployment becoming one of the most intractable problems of all Western industrial nations. Unemployment stood at 8.1 per cent in OECD Europe in 1990, three times its level of 2.7 per cent in 1970, in spite of some decline from the high of 9.9 per cent in 1986.[56] It is not expected to fall significantly below this level in the near future.[57] The 'nonaccelerating inflation rate of unemployment' (NAIRU) has also increased sharply in all the major industrial countries since the late 1960s.[58] Even more worrying is the higher than average rate of youth unemployment because it hurts their pride, dampens their faith in the future, increases their hostility towards society, and damages their personal capacities and potential contribution.[59]

Nevertheless, the only major tool available in the welfare state strategy for increased employment is a high rate of growth. In Europe, a real growth of 3.5 per cent is required to prevent unemployment from rising. European growth had been below this benchmark for more than a decade since 1976. The performance improved during 1978–79, but expectations for the medium-term are not very encouraging. Even in the U.S., a growth rate of 2.5 to 3 per cent is required according to the BIS to prevent a rise in U.S. unemployment. The U.S. growth is estimated to be 1.7 per cent in 1990 and is expected to be even lower in 1991. Expectations are that, if the U.S. becomes seriously determined to reduce its budgetary deficit, the growth rate may continue to be low for some time with an upward creep in its unemployment rate.[60] Given the budgetary constraints, the ever-looming threat of inflation, and the prospect of low growth rates continuing in the foreseeable future, the possibility of attaining full employment in the Western world is not very bright.[61] This pessimism is clearly reflected in the statement of Louis Emmerij that: "If we put both sides of the equation together, the lower rate of growth and the growing labour force, we get the inescapable result that full employment as we understand it today is an almost unattainable goal."[62]

THE SOURING OF THE STRATEGY

The welfare state was no doubt a great improvement over the social-Darwinist philosophy of capitalism. The inequities generated by capitalism could not be tolerated by the innate revulsion in human beings against injustice and misery, which even three centuries of secularism has been unable to destroy. However, while its goals were humanitarian, it could not develop an effective strategy to realise its goals. It did not introduce any fundamental change in the worldview or strategy of capitalism. Hence, it lacked an effective mechanism and motivating system that would help prevent the use of scarce resources for purposes that obstruct the realisation of its egalitarian goals. The same capitalist life-style, the productive machinery, and all the capitalist institutions which play a dominant role in widening the gap between the rich and the poor, have continued undisturbed. The idea that the secularist market system would by itself be able to bring about an 'efficient' allocation of resources and that the inequities created by the market could be undone by an active government role, without the help of collective value judgements and without any significant restructuring of the economy, has proved to be just wishful thinking.

Even though the welfare state has ameliorated somewhat the condition of the poor in industrial countries, the problems of poverty and disadvantage remain profound. Poverty is stubbornly persistent and even the essential needs of the poor remain unfulfilled. The distance between the prosperous and the poor is widening, not only in real incomes but also in access to health care, housing and higher education. The perplexing dilemma is that, in spite of spending a substantial proportion of the GDP on health care (over 9 per cent in Sweden), the poor and the old are unable to secure prompt and adequate treatment. They have to wait for an intolerably long period of time for some badly needed operations, ranging from heart surgery to cataract removal. Pharmaceutical prices are high and lobbying by the pharmaceutical industry has dissuaded governments from pressing for the use of cheaper, but therapeutically equivalent, generics in place of trade-marked medicines.[63]

In the United States, where most health care is privately financed, 31.3 million Americans (13.3 per cent of the population) have no health insurance. Of these, 8.6 million are children – nearly one out of every six children in the country.[64] Housing markets have tightened for nearly everyone, but particularly for the poor. "Almost no houses are within reach of the really poor."[65] Hence most poor families rent, and rents have risen faster than incomes in the past decade. The cost of college education has accelerated even faster, making a mockery of the principle of equal opportunity. A more perplexing paradox is that the prevailing socio-economic conditions not only keep the poor poor, they also perpetuate poverty in families, a black hole from which few people are able to escape. Millions of human beings in the richest and economically strongest nations of the world are trapped in festering inner city ghettos which have gone from bad to worse in spite of the welfare state. They have become a perplexing nightmare of fatherless children, crime, gangs, drugs and despair.

Thus the dream of an egalitarian society remains far from realisation in spite of the great wealth of the welfare states.[66] Given the existing state of affairs, one may say without fear of challenge that the welfare state has failed to bring about an efficient and equitable allocation of resources. It is, nevertheless, argued that untrammelled market relations would have produced still greater social inequality without the welfare state. While this is no doubt true, it does not exonerate the welfare state of its now widely recognised failures. Thus, even though the dream of a 'good-society' that the welfare state had visualised remains unfulfilled, its strategy has been exhausted. All the tools in its tool-kit have now been tried and dented, including regulation, nationalisation, labour movement, fiscal policy, economic growth, and full employment. Hence "there is widespread loss of confidence in the capacity of the welfare state to deliver either full employment or welfare services."[67] Albert Hirschman is bold enough to admit "that the welfare state is in trouble can be hardly contested."[68]

The rapid growth of government spending on social services in the 1950s and the 1960s in the OECD countries was made possible by the high rates of economic growth attained by them. The lower growth performance since the early 1970s and the high level of budgetary deficits have disrupted the growth of programmes and benefits. The result is that funding for constructing new hospitals, community health centres, and teaching institutions has been too low. Existing facilities have hence become overcrowded and less efficient, and unable to cope with the increasing demand. Within the philosophical constraint of the welfare state, more money is clearly a major answer. Even according to the British Labour Party, more public spending and borrowing are essential to create more investment and jobs.[69] But how this can be done without raising taxes or accelerating inflation, they have not been able to show.

The large budgetary deficits and their inflationary implications make it difficult to provide the increasing funding made available during the fifties and the sixties. In fact the goal of avoiding the double-digit inflation of the seventies requires lower government deficits and smaller credit expansion. However, in view of the backlash against taxes, the decline in deficits is not possible except through a cut in spending. Powerful lobbies, in the 'justified' pursuit of their self-interest, do not allow a deep cut in defence and other such public sector spending which have been given maximum priority in the 'national' interest. Hence a range of social policies including unemployment compensation, minimum wages, medical aid, and other welfare benefits are being re-examined. The resulting clash between economic and social policies has put the welfare state in crisis. "The ruling thought nowadays is more probably that the continued growth of the welfare state is neither likely nor even desirable."[70] In fact, Harold Wilensky reports on the basis of a study of 64 countries that in the 1970s there was already evidence of growing resistance to further expansion of state services in many rich countries.[71]

This trend of thought has led to a conservative tide which has swept almost all welfare states.[72] Such a reaction is, however, unwarranted. It is not possible for any large human society to realise its humanitarian goals without the state playing an important role in the economy. Even the success of Western managed-market economies has been built largely on the dream of a 'good society' that the welfare state has provided. The frontiers of the welfare state cannot therefore be rolled back for long. If the elected representatives of society have to face the electorate periodically, they cannot afford not to fulfil the promises they have made, promises which cannot be fulfilled without an effective welfare role for the state. The welfare state is thus in a double bind. Has something gone wrong?

THE LOGICAL FLAWS

The problem arises because the welfare state faces the same scarcity of resources that any other state faces. If it increases the claims on resources through welfare services, it must reduce other claims on resources or else the bind in which the welfare state now finds itself cannot be removed. However, by resorting merely to the price system, the reduction in claims cannot be attained in such a way that social goals are actualised. It is necessary to establish priorities on the basis of a socially-agreed filter mechanism and to motivate people to reorient their preferences and claims on resources in conformity with these priorities. But, since the welfare state operates within the secularist framework of capitalism, it does not have at its disposal a mechanism with which to arrive at a consensus on priorities, or to motivate individuals and the pluralist groups to hold their claims consistent with the demands of macroeconomic and external balance and the distributive goals of society. On the contrary, the self-imposed constraints of abstaining from making value judgements and of formulating policies within the framework of Pareto optimality, leads to an avalanche of claims on scarce resources generated by both the private and the public sectors. The race for status symbols fuelled by value-free advertising and continued credit expansion leads to an acceleration of private demand even in the welfare state's secularist society, where the satisfaction of a maximum number of wants is the ultimate objective of life. The public sector accentuates this further through its large fiscal deficits resulting from its provision of welfare services within the self-imposed constraint of Pareto optimality.

The welfare state has thus become overloaded with demands which its value system has directly sanctioned. Although, initially, this contributed to a higher rate of economic growth, it has since led to a rapid widening of the gulf between resources and the claims on them. This gulf has become reflected in macroeconomic and external imbalances in a number of countries.

In countries like the U.S. and the U.K. where the imbalances had become unduly large and were considered undesirable, it was necessary to reduce budgetary deficits. Within the framework of the Reagan and Thatcher philosophies, this could be accomplished primarily by placing a greater trust in the market-place. While this strategy did help the British Government improve its financial balance, it was at the cost of social welfare priorities. This proved to be very expensive for Mrs. Thatcher at the popularity polls. The U.S. did not pursue the policy seriously and the government financial balance has not improved significantly as a per cent of the GNP in spite of promises made to the electorate.

In countries like Sweden, which have had a better record for providing welfare services, there are problems resulting from the high level of taxation and government spending. It is widely recognised that the excessively high tax rates are discouraging work, saving, and personal initiative. The rate of inflation in Sweden is currently more than double that in the industrial countries. This is eroding its competitiveness, reducing its market share, and enlarging its current account deficit, in spite of a relatively large devaluation of the Swedish kroner. The heavy tax burden has adversely affected private savings; the net private saving ratio was only 0.8 per cent of national disposable income in Sweden during 1980–87 compared with 9.3 per cent in major industrial countries.[73] This is bound to raise interest rates and further reduce investment and economic growth, thus accentuating economic problems in the future. There is hence public pressure for reducing tax rates. But it is not possible to reduce taxes without at the same time reducing spending, or else the budget deficit, inflation and external imbalances will escalate. The easiest target for saving will be across-the-board cuts in welfare spending as has been the case in other countries. Hence, within the secularist frame of reference, the call for reducing tax rates is essentially a signal for reducing the welfare role of the state.

In countries like West Germany and Japan, which do not face macroeconomic imbalances but which have also failed to realise the welfare state goals in varying degrees, there is difficulty of another kind – pressure from large deficit countries to heat their economies in the interest of symmetrical adjustment and international policy coordination. Such pressure makes it difficult for surplus countries to continue following their healthy monetary and fiscal policies over a long stretch of time unless all countries do the same simultaneously. Both West Germany and Japan had to yield to the pressure by lowering their central bank discount rates from 4.5 per cent and 5.0 per cent in 1984 and 1985 respectively to the historical low of 2.5 per cent in 1987. Both consequently suffered from undesired monetary expansion, price increases and speculative excesses. They had therefore to raise the discount rate in short successive steps to 6.0 per cent by October 1989 (West Germany) and August 1990 (Japan). During the low interest rate period Japanese stock and real estate markets rose to dizzy heights, which could not be sustained for long. It is not realised that while the heating of surplus countries may reduce the health of their economies, it may not necessarily help the deficit countries unless they simultaneously adopt healthy monetary and fiscal policies and undertake a restructuring of their economies. Since this is not done, healthy economies also become destabilised. Short-term speculative capital movements are thus accentuated.

This tends to poison the international economic and financial climate and to create volatility in the foreign exchange, commodity and stock markets.

Thus, while capitalism generated an overload of demands through its value neutrality, the welfare state has aggravated the problem further without genuinely redeeming the condition of the poor. To remedy the unacceptable outcome of capitalism, the welfare state has created other equally insoluble problems.[74] The reason for this is that the welfare state policies were essentially patchwork remedies to the secularist and social-Darwinist philosophy of capitalism – a random outcome of the conflict between pluralist groups each of which is trying to serve its maximum self-interest and to make the minimum sacrifice. The humanitarian goals which the welfare state tacitly recognises and the hedonism and social Darwinism on which its strategy is unconsciously based cannot coexist for long without creating tantalising and baffling socio-economic problems. The numerous minor adjustments and modifications undertaken so far have failed to do the job. Such adjustments solve some problems but create others. There is need for a fundamental restructuring of the society and the economy in such a way that the humanitarian goals of the welfare state may be actualised without exceeding the limits set by resource availability.

This fact is now well recognised by many scholars. Maurice Bruce, observes: "No one . . . ever planned the Welfare State, nor has it been the direct outcome of any political or social philosophy. It has been, in fact, no more than the accumulation over many years of remedies to specific problems."[75] Piet Thoenes, expressing a similar dissatisfaction with the philosophy of the welfare state, observes: "A remarkable feature of the welfare state is that nobody has the courage to propagate it properly and completely. To the socialist it is nothing but semi-socialism, to the liberals only semi-liberalism."[76] Hence Sidney Hook asserts that "the social philosophy behind the welfare state is vague and inchoate."[77] According to Barrington Moore, proponents of the welfare state can muster no more than negative and incomplete answers on even the most basic questions: What are its ends? How does it conceive of welfare? He observes that the "welfare state was brought into being after a world crisis and a world war, in a period of scarcity in which it was patently obvious to everybody what it was they did *not* want, and that was: danger, hunger, thirst or cold, unemployment, dictatorships or squandering of either food or talents." Hence, these "negative aims are the most compelling for the welfare state."[78] Accordingly, Myrdal observed that the governmental interventions which the welfare state policies stand for were caused by events not by ideology.[79] This is probably the reason why the welfare state has not been able to go far enough for socio-economic reform. It does not have a single coherent and compelling philosophy to develop an effective strategy, all the different elements of which may be self-consistent, designed to realise its humanitarian goals.

The forces which create and perpetuate poverty and inequalities, are too strong to be overcome merely through *ad hoc* measures by the welfare state social services. The 'backdoor' methods of redistribution are not powerful enough to overcome the social and economic forces that create poverty and perpetuate inequalities. It is necessary to tackle these forces directly and to attend to the source of the problem rather than just the symptoms. What is needed is a thorough reform of the socio-economic structure and the values of life on which capitalism or its reformed version, the welfare state, are based. This will also help solve a number of other social problems, including unemployment, economic instability, social unrest and crime, which have acquired alarming proportions in spite of socialism and the welfare state.

To be frank, the welfare state could not have developed a coherent philosophy, free from self-contradictions, even if the scholars writing on the subject had so desired. Is it possible to develop a social welfare philosophy on the foundations of utilitarianism and social contract theory of justice? Can the concepts of rational self-interest and social contract take us beyond the Pareto optimum? These philosophies cannot inspire human beings to live and die for the supremacy of agreed values, infuse them with the spirit of brotherhood, and motivate them to cooperate and sacrifice for the welfare of others. The inculcation of these qualities requires human beings to rise above self-interest and to cut their claims on resources even though this may hurt their own immediate self-interest.

All values conceived on the basis of utilitarianism and

self-interest can be disputed whereas human society needs to be based on values for 'good' or 'evil', and 'right' or 'wrong' which are not disputed even if they benefit the have-nots at the expense of the haves. A secularist society is uncommitted to any one vision of a social order. "In a genuinely pluralistic society", writes Michael Novak, "there is no sacred canopy. *By intention* there is not. At its spiritual core, there is an empty shrine. That shrine is left empty in the knowledge that no one word, image, or symbol is worthy of what all seek there."[80] Only Divine guidance can provide such a sacred canopy and the motivation to stay under it even in the face of serious odds. Without the feeling of a moral obligation to make a sacrifice, what is it that can motivate a rich man to forego his luxuries and to economise resource use for the need satisfaction of all?

THE SILVER LINING

Every cloud, however, has a silver lining – and the silver lining in the clouds of the Western sky is the ongoing critique of the epistemology of both capitalism and the welfare state. It is being increasingly recognised that selfishness does not necessarily constitute the main motivating force behind human action. The importance of need fulfilment and of value judgements in human society is also being emphasised. Different schools of thought have accordingly developed – schools which do not fall strictly within the bounds of mainstream classical economics. All these schools are however closely related, the difference between them being primarily in the degree of emphasis. Three of these schools deserve special mention.

One of these is Grants Economics which asserts that "it is no longer necessary to regard unselfishness as an aberration from rationality" to explain individual behaviour.[81] In fact some economists doubt whether the rationality assumption is realistic enough. According to Hahn, "Economics probably made a mistake when it adopted the nomenclature of 'rational' when all it meant is correct calculations and an orderly personality."[82] It is also being argued whether unrealistic assumptions can yield a correct theory. Notwithstanding Friedman's positive answer, some economists feel otherwise.[83] It may be proper to state that, if the function of economic theory is to yield valid and meaningful predictions about phenomena not yet observed, then the assumption of rational behaviour within the framework of altruism, and not self-interest, may probably yield more meaningful predictions. Hence the 'Boulding optimum' has been proposed as an alternative to the Pareto optimum, "bringing within the scope of economic analysis a human flair assumed away in the name of value-free science."[84]

A second school of thought is the need-based Humanistic Economics designed to "promote human welfare by recognising and integrating the full range of basic human values."[85] Instead of the conventional emphasis on wants and wealth, Humanistic Economics emphasises need satisfaction and human development to move towards what Abraham Maslow calls 'self-realisation' or 'self-actualisation'.[86]

A third school of thought is Social Economics which involves a "reformulation of economic theory in the mould of ethical considerations."[87] Commitment to the imperative of scientific neutrality, the sacred ideal of the Enlightenment scientists bequeathed by economists, is now being considered as both untenable and undesirable – untenable because scientific inquiry is based on assumptions which tacitly involve value judgements; undesirable because scientific inquiry has to address itself to questions of public goals and priorities. Any discipline committed to value neutrality cannot succeed in evaluating policies and recommendations for public choice. Such an evaluation necessarily involves ethical judgements. Hence, according to Prof. Sen, "the distancing of economics from ethics has impoverished welfare economics and also weakened the basis of a good deal of descriptive and predictive economics." His conclusion is that economics "can be made more productive by paying greater and more explicit attention to ethical considerations that shaped human behaviour and judgement."[88] The problem however is that values cannot be derived scientifically. In Arnold Brechts' words, "Anyone who claims scientific authority for a system of values is scientifically in error."[89] If values cannot be established 'scientifically' and if 'judgement' has to be exercised, then the question is: whose judgement? Can a consensus be brought about – a consensus forceful enough to become a social sanction such that anyone who acts against the established norms stands censured?

The decline in the sanctity of 'self-interest' and 'economic man' and the emphasis on need fulfilment and value judgements are welcome developments. They show that man is not necessarily condemned to living with inequities. He is capable of rising to the occasion, of analysing his problems, and of knowing what is wrong. However, what is not so easy is the remedy. It does not lie in patchwork or cosmetic changes. The remedy lies in reorganising the whole society and economic system in such a way that, on the one hand, there is a transformation of the individual from the economic man to a morally-conscious human being who is willing to live up to the demands of brotherhood and socio-economic justice and, on the other hand, there is a restructuring of the entire economy in such a way that needs are fulfilled without generating imbalances, and inequalities of income and wealth are not only not generated but also substantially reduced.

Even though the revival of emphasis on values is laudable, their introduction into Western economics is bound to be an uphill task. First of all there is, as Galbraith has pointed out, "the vested intellectual commitment to established belief", which views economics as a science and sets "the standard of intellectual precision" by the hard sciences.[90] Moreover, the commitment to value neutrality has gone too far in the West over the last two centuries to allow any early retracing of steps, particularly without the consensus that only religion provides. As Schadwich has aptly observed, "social morality depends on agreed standards, upon a consensus which is received as so axiomatic that it hardly ought to be discussed", and that, "except in the case of a small number of exceptional groups of people morality never had been separated from religion in the entire history of the human race."[91] Utilitarianism and social contract theories do not carry the potential of providing values which everyone accepts as being given and which no one challenges. No wonder that Minsky should have remarked about the Western world: "there is no consensus on what we ought to do."[92] Without agreed values, it is difficult to arrive at such a consensus.

Notes and References (Chapter 3)

1 Michael Prowse, "The Isolation of the Individual", *Financial Times*, 4 May 1989, p. III of Supplement on "Audit of Revolution".

2 For one of the best historical examinations of the welfare state, see: Asa Briggs, "The Welfare State in Historical Perspective", *Archives Européenes de Sociologie* (1961); see also Richard Titmuss, *Essays on the "Welfare State"* (1963); Maurice Bruce, *The Coming of the Welfare State* (1966); and David Marsh, *The Future of the Welfare State* (1964).

3 A. H. Halsey, "Some Lessons from the Debates", in OECD, *The Welfare State in Crisis* (1981), p. 15.

4 Richard M. Titmuss, *Commitment to Welfare* (1976), p. 124; see also, D. Arnold Hancock and Gideon Sjoberg, *Politics in the Post Welfare State* (1972), p. 3; and Norman Furniss and Timothy Tilton, *The Case for the Welfare State: from Social Security to Social Equality* (1977), pp. 14–21.

5 Harry K. Girvetz, "Welfare State", *International Encyclopaedia of the Social Sciences* (1968), vol. 16, p. 515.

6 Neil Gilbert, *Capitalism and the Welfare State: Dilemmas of Social Benevolence* (1983), p. 47.

7 Peter Saunders and Friedrich Klau, *The Role of the Public Sector: Causes and Consequences of the Growth of Government* (1985), p. 25. The Beveridge Report of 1947, which set the framework for Britain's welfare state, also endorsed the view that health and welfare services should be made available to all citizens as a basic right.

8 See Ralph Millhand, *The State in Capitalist Society* (1969), and Edward S. Greenberg, *Serving the Few* (1974), p. 20.

9 According to estimates published in June 1987 by Salomon Brothers, a leading Wall Street investment bank, at least 55 state-owned entities have been shifted into the private sector worldwide since 1980, raising proceeds totalling about $48 billion, and another 2000 were earmarked for sale by 1990. (See Guy de Jonquieres, "Privatisation: Trusting the Market", *Financial Times*, 16 September 1987, Section III, p. 1.)

10 *Ibid.*, p. 8.

11 Simon Holberton, "A Turning Point in Privatisation", *Financial Times*, 6 November 1988, p. 3. See also Richard Hemming and Ali M. Mansoor, *Privatisation and Public Enterprise* (1988), p. 7.

12 Philip Bassett, "Britain's Trade Unions: At War with a Wasting Disease", *Financial Times*, 28 August 1986.

13 See *ibid.*, and also "Unions: Declining Force, Increasing Power", *The Economist*, 14 February 1987, p. 35. Only 27 per cent of the Japanese workforce is currently unionised, about half the proportion of 1948 ("Japan: All Together Now", *The Economist*, 30 September, 1989, p. 67).

14 See James O'Connor, *The Fiscal Crisis of the State* (1973), p. 138; Greenberg, p. 199; and John K. Galbraith, *The New Industrial State* (1972), p. 288.

15 Philip Bassett, "The Spectre Refuses to Rise Again", *Financial Times*, 2 June 1987.

16 IMF, *International Financial Statistics*, lines 64 and 65 of the page on U.S.; and "Flat Wages in America", *International Herald Tribune*, 8 September 1987; see also, Albert E. Rees, *Wage Inflation* (1957), pp. 27–8.

17 Calculated on the basis of consumer price index given for the U.S. in the IMF, *International Financial Statistics* (Yearbook for 1989 and July 1990) and projection for the period thereafter.

18 1960 data are from Saunders and Klau, *The Role of the Public Sector* (1985), Table 1, p. 29; data for later years are from the *OECD Economic Outlook, 47*, June 1990, Table R15, p. 195.

19 Data for 1940 are from the U.S. Department of Commerce, Bureau of the Census, *Statistical Abstract of the United States, 1986*, pp. 305 and 410; data for later years are from *OECD Economic Outlook, 47*, June 1990.

20 Saunders and Klau (1985), pp. 11–26.

21 John Burton, *Why No Cuts: An Inquiry into the Fiscal Anarchy of Uncontrolled Government Expenditure* (1985), p. 86.

22 *Ibid.*, p. 88.

23 "Retooling without Ruin", a *New York Times* editorial reproduced in the *International Herald Tribune*, 23 March 1990, p. 4.

24 OECD, *National Policies and Agricultural Trade* (1988) cited by the *Financial Times* in an editorial, "High Cost of Farming", 20 May 1988, p. 18.

25 See Peter Montagnon, *et al.*, "Governments Held to Ransom", *Financial Times*, 14/15 July 1990.

26 "High Cost of Farming", *Financial Times*, 20 May 1988, p. 18.

27 Saunders and Klau (1985), Table 1, p. 29; and OECD, *Revenue Statistics of OECD Member Countries, 1965–89* (1990), Table 1.

28 Saunders and Klau (1985), p. 29; and *OECD Economic Outlook, 47*, June 1990, pp. 15 and 194.

29 For general government interest payments, see Saunders and Klau (1985), p. 72; and IMF, *Government Financial Statistics Yearbook*, 1989, pp. 74–5. For OECD public sector debt, see *OECD Economic Outlook, 47*, June 1990, p. 119. For interest rates, see the IMF, *International Financial Statistics*, the pages on international and national interest rates.

30 Julian Le Grand, *The Strategy of Equality: Redistribution and the Social Services* (1982), pp. 3, 17 and 137.

31 Richard M. Titmuss, *Commitment to Welfare* (1976), p. 196.

32 Gilbert (1983), p. 71.

33 Greenberg (1974), p. 203. Medicaid provides federal and state funds for the medical needs of the poor. Medicare provides certain medical services to Americans over 65.

34 Greenberg (1974), p. 181.

35 Witt, S. F. and Newbould G. D., "The Impact of Food Subsidies", *National Westminster Bank Quarterly Review*, August 1976, pp. 29–36.

36 Gyorgy Szakolczai, "Limits to Redistribution: The Hungarian Experience", in D. Collard, R. Lecomber and M. Slater (eds.), *Income Distribution: The Limits to Redistribution* (1980), pp. 206–35. See also, Maksymilian Pohorille, "Collective Consumption in Socialist Countries: A Theoretical Approach", in R. C. O. Mathews and G. B. Stafford, *The Grants Economy and Collective Consumption* (1982), p. 77.

37 Julian Le Grand, "Who Benefits from Public Expenditure?" *New Society*, vol. 45, No. 833, 1978, pp. 614–16.

38 Henry C. Simons, *Personal Income Taxation* (1938), pp. vi and 29.

39 Joseph A. Pechman, *The Rich, the Poor and the Taxes they Pay* (1986), p. 59.

40 Paul J. Strayer, "The Individual Income Tax and Income Distribution", *American Economic Review*, vol. 45, No. 2, pp. 430–1.

41 See, for example, B. I. Page, "Why Doesn't the Government Promote Equality", in Robert A. Solo and Charles W. Anderson, *Value Judgement and Income Distribution* (1981), p. 83; Joseph A. Pechman and Benjamin A. Okner, *Who Bears the Tax Burden?* (1974), pp. 49 and 56; and Joseph A. Pechman, "The Rich, the Poor and the Taxes They Pay", *The Public Interest*, Fall 1969.

42 Pechman (1986).

43 See John Plender, "World Tax Reform: Another Wave of Change Ahead", *Financial Times*, 13 March 1987.

44 "Sweden's Economy", *The Economist*, 7 March 1987, pp. 23–4.

45 Joseph A. Pechman, *World Tax Reform: The Progress Report* (1988), p. 1. For some relevant details about the tax reform in other industrial countries see the various chapters of this book.

46 See S. Danziger, P. Gottschalk and E. Smolensky, "American Income Inequality: How the Rich have Fared", *American Economic Review*, May 1989, pp. 310–14; and Isabell V. Sawhill, "Poverty in the U.S.: Why is it So Persistent?" *Journal of Economic Literature*, September 1988, pp. 1085 and 1113.

47 *Statistical Abstract of the United States, 1988*, Table 713, p. 433.

48 Data for 1980 are from IBRD, *World Development Report, 1989*, Table 30, p. 223, while those for 1986 are from *Statistical Abstract of the United States, 1988*, Table 70, p. 428. For comparison with 1973, 1979, 1982, and 1987, see Danziger, *et al.* (1989), p. 311.

49 Reported by Michael Wines, "Rich in U.S. Get Richer: Study Finds", *International Herald Tribune*, 28 July 1986, p. 3. For a comparison with other countries, see Alan Harrison, *The Distribution of Income in Ten Countries* (1979).

50 See IBRD *World Development Report, 1980* and *1989*, Tables 24 (p. 157) and 30 (p. 223) respectively.

51 Richard M. Titmuss, *Commitment to Welfare* (1976), p. 164.

52 C. A. R. Crosland, *Socialism Now* (1974).

53 At the annual meeting of the Bretton Woods Committee on 21 January 1987, a number of speakers including Paul Volcker, Helmut Schlesinger, Rimmer de Vries and Senator Paul Sarbeans echoed the view that the prevailing low rates of growth in industrial countries were not conducive to growth and adjustment in developing countries. Higher growth was the only long-term solution to the problems of not only the developing countries but also of the United States and other major industrial countries (See *IMF Survey*, 26 January 1987, p. 21).

54 E. J. Mishan, *The Costs of Economic Growth* (1973), p. 204.

55 IMF, *World Economic Outlook*, May 1990, Table 5, p. 31 and Table A51, p. 197.

56 *OECD Economic Outlook, 47*, June 1990, Table R19, p. 199; and OECD *Press Release on Standardized Unemployment Rates*, 21 March 1991.

57 *OECD Economic Outlook, 47*, June 1990, Table 9, p. 23.

58 Charles Adams, Paul Fenton and Flemming Larson, "Differences in Employment Behaviour among Industrial Countries", IMF, *Staff Studies for the World Economic Outlook*, July 1986, p. 6.

59 For the high rate of youth unemployment, see OECD Employment Outlook (1987), Table 2.3; Commission of the European Communities, *European Economy*, Supplement A on Highlights on Employment and Unemployment, December 1989, Table 5, p. 4.

60 See, *OECD Economic Outlook, 44* (June 1990), *op. cit.*, pp. 1 and 181; and IMF, *World Economic Outlook*, May 1990, p. 31. See also Samuel Brittan, "Time to Tackle the Euro Malaise", *Financial Times*, 22 June 1987, p. 19. According to the BIS, the rate of growth that "older industrialised countries can hope to achieve without courting inflationary dangers" is somewhere around 2.5 per cent (BIS, *59th Annual Report*, June 1989, p. 3. See also IMF, *World Economic Outlook*, 1 May 1990, Table 1.

61 See Morgan Guarantee Trust Co. of New York, *World Financial Markets*, June/July 1986, p. 5.

62 Louis Emmerij, ''The Social Economy of Today's Employment Problem in Industrial Countries'', in *Unemployment in Western Countries* (1980), p. 58.

63 See ''Sick Health Services: Europeans Seek the Right Treatment'', *The Economist,* 16 July 1988, pp. 17–20.

64 *Statistical Abstract of the United States,* 1988, p. 92.

65 ''The Stretching of the Middle Class'', *The Economist,* 17 September 1988, p. 54.

66 Lindemann frankly admits that ''although the quantity of wealth in Western societies has increased immeasurably, its distribution has not fundamentally changed. Power continues to be exercised by narrow elites, whatever the formalities of democratic participation and control.'' (Albert S. Lindemann, *A History of European Socialism,* (1983), pp. 351–2.

67 Halsey, in OECD, *The Welfare State in Crisis* (1981), p. 17.

68 Albert O. Hirschman, ''The Welfare State in Trouble: Systematic Crisis or Growing Pains'', *American Economic Review,* May 1980, p. 113.

69 Philip Stephens (1987).

70 Bernard Cazes, ''Welfare State: A Double Bind'', in OECD, *The Welfare State in Crisis* (1981), p. 151.

71 Harold Wilensky, *The Welfare State and Equality* (1975), p. 47.

72 Ruud Lubbers, the Dutch Prime Minister, ''Beyond the Welfare State'', an interview by Laura Rann, *Financial Times,* 15 December 1986, p. 6.

73 Bank for International Settlements, *59th Annual Report,* June 1989, p. 32.

74 See Claus Offe, *Contradictions of the Welfare State,* ed., John Keane (1984), pp. 35–7.

75 Maurice Bruce, *The Coming of the Welfare State* (1968), p. 13.

76 Piet Thoenes, *The Elite in the Welfare State* (1966), p. 133.

77 Sidney Hook, ''Welfare State – A Debate that Isn't'', in C. I. Schottland (ed.), *The Welfare State* (1967), p. 165.

78 Piet Thoenes (1966), p. 133; Barrington Moore, *Reflections on the Causes of Human Misery* (1972).

79 Gunnar Myrdal, *Beyond the Welfare State* (1960).

80 Michael Novak, *The Spirit of Democratic Capitalism* (1982), p. 53.

81 Janos Horvath, ''Foreword'', in Robert A. Solo and Charles W. Anderson (eds.), *Value Judgement and Income Distribution* (1981), pp. ix–x.

82 Frank Hahn and Martin Hollis (eds.), *Philosophy and Economic Theory* (1979), p. 12.

83 Friedman states that: "Truly important and significant hypotheses will be found to have 'assumptions' that are widely inaccurate representations of reality, and in general, the more significant the theory, the more unrealistic the assumptions (in this sense)." (Milton Friedman, "Methodology of Positive Economics", in Hahn and Hollis (1979), p. 26.) See also Hahn's view in *ibid.*, p. 12.

84 Solo and Anderson (1981), p. x.

85 M. A. Lutz and K. Lux, *The Challenge of Humanistic Economics* (1979), p. ix.

86 Abraham Maslow, *Motivation and Personality* (1970).

87 Masudul Alam Choudhury, "The Micro-Economic Foundations of Islamic Economics: A Study of Social Economics", *The American Journal of Social Sciences* (1986), p. 237.

88 Amartya Sen, *On Ethics and Economics* (1987), pp. 78 and 9.

89 Cited by Solo in the "Introduction" to Solo and Anderson (1981), p. 1.

90 John K. Galbraith, *Economics in Perspective* (1987), p. 284.

91 Owen Schadwick, *The Secularization of the European Mind in the Nineteenth Century* (1975), pp. 229 and 234.

92 Hyman P. Minsky, *Stabilising an Unstable Economy* (1986), p. 290.

CHAPTER 4

The Inconsistency of Development Economics

Development economics does not have a separate identity of its own. It is an offshoot of either one of the three major strands of mainstream economics (neoclassical, Keynesian or socialist). All these have their roots in the Western worldview. The strategies proposed by development economics have also therefore been based on the Western worldview. The specific strategy pursued at any given time has, however, depended on which particular strand of mainstream economics has been in fashion at that time. Development economics has therefore witnessed a shift in allegiance back and forth from the Keynesian and socialist strategies to the neoclassical strategy.

THE WAVERING ALLEGIANCE

Development economics was born after the Second World War when a number of developing countries became independent and an analysis of problems related to their development began to attract attention.[1] The first issue of the first journal on development economics, *Economic Development and Cultural Change,* came out in 1952. At that time there existed only a handful of scholarly works specifically devoted to the subject.[2] Since Keynesian economics and socialism were gaining momentum in the West at that time as a result of the Great Depression and the problems of post-War reconstruction, development economics also moved away from its neoclassical base and preached a lesser reliance on the market and a greater role for the government in the economy. However, when the hold of Keynesian and socialist strategies began to weaken in the early 1970s and neoclassical economics started making a comeback, development economics started "going through a crisis". The current literature on the subject reflects an "atmosphere of questioning and self-doubt".[3]

While a majority of development economists still continue to believe in its usefulness, there are some who doubt even the very legitimacy of the discipline.[4] The debate has become polarised between those who do not advocate sole dependence on markets and prices and those who believe that liberalisation of markets with reduced role of the government in the economy is all that is necessary for solving the problems of developing countries. The dominant view at present seems to be anti-*dirigiste* and pro-free market, reflecting the resurgence of liberalism and neoclassical economics in the West. In consequence, many of the problems now experienced by developing countries are being blamed on the *dirigiste* policies pursued over the last three decades, whether it be the inefficient use of scarce resources, the unduly large macroeconomic and external imbalances, the rising inequalities of income and wealth, or the social tensions.

This wavering allegiance of development economics, from the market to the state and back again has deprived it of firm direction. This has led to conflicting analyses and policy prescriptions, and generated inconsistencies and uncertainties in the development programmes of developing countries, causing immense harm to the health and development of their economies. The task that these countries now face is doubly difficult. They not only have to develop their economies in a way that would lead to greater efficiency and equity in the use of their extremely scarce resources but also have to remove the imbalances that false prescriptions have generated. The question that arises is whether the new policies being prescribed in the light of neoclassical economics will help realise equity along with efficiency and stabilisation. It would therefore be appropriate to see the impact that the Western worldview has had on development economics and the problems that it has generated for the developing countries.

Since neoclassical, Keynesian and socialist economics all have their origin in the Enlightenment worldview, they are secularist in their approach to the realisation of human well-being and analysis of human problems. They place too much emphasis on consumption and material possessions as a source of human happiness. They disregard the role of moral values in individual and social reform and hence in development, and overemphasise the role of the market or the state. They are not inwardly committed to brotherhood and socio-economic justice and do not have a socially-agreed filter mechanism of moral values. Their strictly this-worldly perspective does not provide a rationale for anything other than materialism and social-Darwinism. Within this framework there is no motivation to serve social interest except where it is automatically served as an indirect result of serving self-interest.

The Pessimist Outlook

The social-Darwinist approach of economists along with their ethnocentricity led them to introduce a grain of pessimism in the development literature by ascribing poverty, underdevelopment and political subjugation of poor countries, which happened to be primarily non-European and non-white, to the cultural, racial and even mental inferiority of their people.[5] It was argued that these countries did not fulfil the preconditions that development required. Their social and value patterns were *a priori* considered to be inimical to the creation of these preconditions. Even a United Nations study prepared by a committee of five experts reflected this ethnocentric attitude and envisaged that the advancement of poor countries was not possible unless their social, economic, legal and political institutions were reformed to resemble those of the Western capitalist countries.[6] A similar point of view prevailed among experts of the World Bank who believed that the only way for the poor countries to achieve capital formation, productivity and consumption, comparable to those in developed countries, was to duplicate the social, economic and political institutions of the latter. This was the impression of both Kindleberger and Spengler after studying, respectively, three and ten World Bank reports prepared in the early 1950s.[7] The most brazen expression of these views was by Eugene Staley who said that the development of poor countries could be successful only if carried out in the image of the United States. They will have to adopt the social institutions and values of the West.[8] Even Myrdal, a less ethnocentric Western economist, believed that the "modernisation ideals", which were necessary for development, were "alien" to these countries because they "stem from foreign influences".[9] Thus the dominant view was that Western culture and its materialist values were the *beau idéal* for development and developing countries would not be able to advance unless they 'modernised'. Modernisation did not consist in merely adopting modern technology, and management and marketing techniques; it consisted rather in adopting Western materialist values and life-styles.

The continued, heavy emphasis on the lack of prerequisites for growth conceived within the perspective of Western culture led to widespread acceptance of the "vicious circle of poverty" in development literature. Nurkse defined this as "a circular constellation of forces tending to act and react upon one another in such a way as to keep a poor country in a state of poverty . . . a country is poor because it is poor."[10] The idea of a vicious circle became so ubiquitous in the literature that nearly every development economist became infected by it.[11] It would not be possible for the poor countries to overcome the vicious circle of overpopulation, lower incomes, lower savings, lower investment, lower exports and lower growth that the lack of 'modernisation ideals' created. They would hence be condemned to what Nurkse described as, a "low-level equilibrium that perpetuates itself". Even the savings that they did realise by squeezing consumption could not be translated into capital goods because of their inability to raise their exports and foreign exchange earnings. These countries would not find it possible to overcome the two gaps – saving-investment and import-export – that they faced, and would not therefore be able to extricate themselves from the poverty trap.

Even the theories of 'stages of growth' inherently implied the idea of a 'vicious circle'.[12] The strategic factors for development on which interest was focused in these theories implied a circular causation. The prevalence of certain social and institutional factors would prevent the poor countries from moving from one stage to the other. This would tend to have a more serious cumulative effect on their development than even the vicious circle.

Most of the development literature was thus imbued with a sense of deep pessimism about the prospects for growth in developing countries.[13] Since patterns of living and values of life other than those of the enlightened West were *a priori* considered inimical to growth, little thought was given to the formulation of a development strategy that would be consistent with the resource endowment and values of the poorer countries. Williamson rightly admitted this in the early 1950s by saying that "Economists generally have been too much concerned with static models and too culturally bound by a Western European framework of institutions to make the contribution to the subject of the economics of growth that might reasonably be expected from the profession."[14]

Experience has, however, clearly demonstrated that this pessimism concerning the prospects for development was seriously in error and that substantial growth has taken place in spite of widely varying initial endowments and circumstances. What continues to be a problem however is that, because of policies framed and pursued within the perspective of value neutrality, poverty has persisted and "the fruit of growth is concentrated in a few hands" in spite of growth.[15] In addition, the developing countries have become engulfed in macroeconomic imbalances and external debt of immense proportions. Why this is so will become clear in the following discussion.

The Socialist Strategy

The air of pessimism in the early years of development economics gave rise to the idea of a 'critical minimum effort'. If these countries wished to break the vicious circle, they must "find and marshal stimulants to development that are of sufficient magnitude."[16] In the absence of a critical minimum effort, attempts to develop will fail.[17] But how could this critical minimum effort be mustered when the people were culturally backward and the savings and private initiative needed for this purpose were not available? The discussion took two specific tacks. One of these favoured adoption of the socialist strategy of a dominant role for the government in the economy through comprehensive planning, controls, and public enterprises, in sharp contrast with the extreme neoclassical view of relying primarily on the private sector and the market.[18] The other was a playing down of the goal of socio-economic justice for developing countries.

The volte-face in favour of the socialist strategy in development literature was brought about by the initial success of totalitarian regimes in the USSR and China and of Keynesian economics in the West. It began to be argued that the neoclassical economic model with its emphasis on the markets and marginal economic adjustments in response to price changes was highly unrealistic for developing countries that were suffering from various cultural and structural rigidities.[19] The governments of developing countries should 'push' for development as hard as they could by playing a leading role in the economy. Only such a 'big push' could help them attain 'self-generating' or 'self-sustained' growth and the 'great leap forward'.[20]

The 'big push' was essentially a euphemistic expression for the Stalinist 'road of socialist industrialisation', which called for high-speed growth in the USSR by giving top priority to the development of heavy industry. This would serve as a driving force for the ultimate development of agriculture and other sectors of the Soviet economy, thus reducing dependence on imports from non-socialist countries.[21] The 'big push' in developing countries was also to be attained, as in the Stalinist model, through unbalanced growth with heavy emphasis on industrialisation, import-substitution and urban development. It was necessary to have "a wave of capital investments in a number of industries".[22] This was, according to Rosenstein-Rodan, "a necessary (though not sufficient) condition of success."[23] The theory of the big push had a built-in bias toward large-scale projects and capital-intensive techniques.[24] Concentration on industry, particularly heavy industry, was "propounded as the only course by which an underdeveloped country can be set firmly on the road to development."[25] Since the minimum economic size of a number of industrial projects was considered to be so large that private entrepreneurs were neither willing nor able to make such investments, "they have to be in the public sector".[26]

The outcome of the 'big push' theory was an undue emphasis on the role of the public sector in economic growth. Neoclassical economics thus went into disrepute. It was replaced by the new economics which placed greater emphasis on planning and government intervention, industrialisation, import-substitution, urban development and a host of other policies that led to a continually widening role for the government in the economy. Development economics generally acquired "a strong *dirigiste*, anti-free market, anticapitalist bias".[27]

Comprehensive planning became increasingly important in country after country. Most of these plans called for the government to make virtually all major investments and to operate all capital goods industries. Many of these plans also called for a wide range of direct controls. Planning was thus intended not just to provide guidance and a framework for development to maximise efficiency and equity, but was rather directed to the actual carrying out of investment projects by the government through public enterprises and the levying of direct controls.

The Neglect of Equity

The other impact of the air of pessimism was the belief that the goals of economic growth and socio-economic justice were incompatible and that, if the goal of accelerated growth was to be attained, the goal of equitable distribution must be compromised.[28] This could not however be stated baldly in development plans because of the adverse political implications it would have. Hence, the plans continued to pay lip service to the goal of socio-economic justice by mentioning it among the objectives of planning. The first plan in a developing country – that of India in 1952 – included "the attainment of economic equality and social justice" among the objectives of the Plan along with "maximum production" and "full employment".[29] The directive principles of state policy in the 1956 constitution of Pakistan contained an injunction in favour of "preventing the undue concentration of wealth and means of production and distribution, in the hands of a few, to the detriment of the interests of the common man."[30] The terms of reference given to the National Planning Board and the statement of objectives in the First Five Year Plan were also stated in egalitarian terms. Pakistan's Second Five Year Plan reiterated the egalitarian objectives of the First Plan.[31] Effective measures were however not taken in India, Pakistan and most other developing countries to make the goal of socio-economic justice a reality.

The anti-equity tone in development literature was in a way set in 1955 for almost a decade and a half by Sir Arthur Lewis, who wrote: "First it should be noted that our subject matter is growth and not distribution."[32] Bauer and Yamey argued in 1957 that "redistribution of income in favour of the poor is not likely to promote economic growth in the sense of greater output per head."[33] Even the United Nations ruled out distribution as a goal of policy by stating that "the most general objective of economic development is to maximise the national income or the rate of economic growth."[34] Prof. Harry Johnson, writing in 1962, emphasised that it would be "unwise for a country anxious to enjoy rapid growth to insist too strongly on policies aimed at ensuring economic equality and a just income distribution."[35] Poverty, inequality and income distribution were virtually absent from consideration in the first edition of the widely-used book of readings by Gerald Meier, *Leading Issues in Economic Development,* published in 1964. Even a conference of leaders in the field of economic development held in the mid-1960s made hardly any mention of the goals of reducing poverty and inequality, as is evident from the proceedings published in 1966.[36]

Some advocates of accelerated growth went to the extent of arguing in favour of "greater inequality of incomes on the grounds that the beneficiaries are likely to save a larger part of the income transferred to them and so add to capital formation."[37] Misleading empirical support for such views was sought in the inverted-U curve which has become associated with the name of Kuznets, even though it received little empirical support from Kuznets' own writings or from subsequent data. The Kuznets curve was taken to imply that inequality is bound to increase in the early stages of development and will decrease only in the later stages. No consideration was given to the possibility that the Kuznets curve may be the result of the economic system and the policies pursued, and need not necessarily reflect an iron law of nature.[38]

One of the most favoured explanations advanced for the rise in saving rate across industrial revolutions has been rising inequality. Ever since Adam Smith, economic historians have stressed the growth-inequality trade-off, which is central to the classical labour-surplus model considered to be *a priori* true for all Third World countries. The evidence, however, has not been kind to the trade-off thesis. Rising inequality has accounted for little of America's or of Britain's saving experience. It appears to have made little contribution to contemporary savings.[39]

Even a policy of inflation was espoused because it lightens the repayment burden of the public exchequer and also 'forces' the public to save. It was argued that inflation has the ability to "bring about a redistribution in favour of individuals and classes who are likely to save a larger part of the income transferred."[40] Professor Lewis also argued eloquently that price rises resulting from 'mild' inflation serve to increase the profits of the industrial and mercantile classes, and by so doing, increase their savings, which are invested.[41] This reasoning was based on the false assumption that every penny paid in wages is spent on consumption and that every penny not paid to labour is necessarily saved and invested productively.

This trend of thought had its influence on leaders and policy-makers in developing countries. Even Jawaharlal Nehru, apparently a staunch believer in socio-economic justice, justified the trend toward increasing economic inequality in India by saying: "To some extent that is inevitable in a growing economy."[42] Some Muslim economists also joined the bandwagon, in spite of the clear and unequivocal emphasis of Islam on socio-economic justice, and projected the secularist, social-Darwinist view that indulgence in the goal of socio-economic justice was a luxury that only developed countries could afford. Dr. Mahboobul Haq, who later became the Minister of Finance and Planning in Pakistan, wrote: "The underdeveloped countries must consciously accept a philosophy of growth, and shelve for the distant future all ideas of equitable distribution and welfare state. It should be recognised that these are luxuries which only developed countries can afford."[43] It was probably not realised that within the Islamic value frame it is a cardinal sin for a Muslim to commit, propagate or even condone injustice.

The socialist tendency in development economics therefore did not reflect the concern for equity that it did in Western and socialist countries. It reflected only the desire to accelerate growth through the use of planning and the coercive power of the state, with an even greater commitment to social-Darwinism than was true for neoclassical economics. Socialism in the developing countries was "thus of a third type, different from that of the Communist countries as well as that of the Western world."[44] All that socialism really connoted in the Third World was a "commitment to nationalisation, and more generally, to state ownership and management of a large sector of the economy."[45] Socialism thus became "merely equated with planning."[46] Even though there were a number of economists who continued to be concerned about equity even during this period, they were in the minority.[47] The prevailing view was that the 'trickle-down' mechanism would ultimately solve the poverty and income distribution problems if only growth were fast enough.[48] The trickle-down mechanism, however, proved to be highly ineffective. This was bound to be the case. Poverty and income inequality are so sticky and pervasive that it was highly unrealistic to expect that they could be removed without making major structural changes in the economy and the financial system, and without creating values and a motivating system that would be conducive to their removal.

THE STERILE CONTROVERSIES

The lack of commitment on the part of development economics to a filter mechanism of socially-agreed values and particularly to socio-economic justice, made it difficult to resolve the several hair-splitting controversies which have plagued it over the last three decades. The twin pillars of materialism and inequality on which development economics was founded could not provide a filter mechanism that could help resolve these controversies on different issues of social importance. The whims and personal preferences of the discussants, without any agreed criteria to guide them, led the discussion along an endless circular path. This was clearly the case irrespective of which controversy we look at: agriculture versus industrialisation, rural versus urban development, balanced versus unbalanced growth, import-substitution versus export promotion, and market forces versus planning. Looked at from the point of view of realising the twin goals of efficiency and equity the controversy appears to be sterile and unproductive. It reflects the absence of socio-economic justice as a goal of development. It also indicates a lack of awareness of the different phases in which developing countries are, the diversity of their socio-economic circumstances, the complexities of human society, and the factors which motivate human beings to work for their self-interest without crossing the bounds of social interest. The harm that the controversy has done is reflected in the bottlenecks, imbalances, slow growth rates, higher inflation, burdensome debt and social unrest that most developing countries are now facing. If a filter mechanism of agreed values were available and socio-economic justice had been a clear target of policies, the strategy for development would not have been involved in as much controversy as the development literature has witnessed.

Agriculture Versus Industry

Since a majority of the population in developing countries lives in rural areas, their well-being could not have been ensured without rural and agricultural development. Rural development was therefore not an option. It was indispensable. Rural development could not, however, have taken place without support from industrial development. To enable the farmers to undertake investments in fertilisers, better seeds and improved technology, it was necessary to raise their incomes. This was not possible without providing employment to the unemployed and underemployed members of rural families. It would not be possible to do so without simultaneously developing small-scale and micro industries in rural areas. Thus, for a great majority of developing countries, industrialisation, like agricultural development, was also not an option. It had to be a fundamental part of the policy objectives. It was necessary to attain balanced development if the objective was to expand employment opportunities, satisfy the basic needs of the entire population, and reduce inequalities. Neither agriculture nor industrialisation could by itself help developing countries realise such development. Diversification and modernisation of all sectors of their economies was necessary.

Agricultural and industrial development were therefore not alternatives to choose from. They were rather complementary and mutually supporting with respect to both inputs and outputs. The issue was not industrial or agricultural development but rather the human being and how his well-being can be improved. If the well-being of all were the goal, the interrelationship between industry and agriculture and the contribution that each can make to the other and to the realisation of agreed socio-economic goals would have been appreciated. Within this context any development programme that propounds unbalanced growth and overemphasises industrialisation relative to agriculture or agriculture relative to industry could not but lead to injustice and misery and also create bottlenecks, which it would be difficult to remove without a reversal of policies to restore a balance. Such reversals are normally difficult and traumatic.

Import-Substitution Versus Export Promotion

If industry and agriculture are both to be developed, then the strategic importance of both import-substitution and export promotion in the socio-economic advancement of developing countries needs to be clearly visualised. There is no reason to emphasise one to the exclusion of the other. Both are necessary, even though their importance may vary over a longer time horizon in step with the different phases in a country's development.

This does not mean that import-substitution should be undertaken at any cost.[49] Since the ultimate goal is efficient and equitable use of scarce resources to realise general well-being, all tariff and non-tariff barriers must be weighted against the realisation of socio-economic justice and the promotion of economic development. The rational principles of resource allocation cannot therefore be lost sight of; the cost of economic inefficiency will be reflected in the non-realisation of goals and will ultimately have to be borne by the people; this cannot be justified. Nevertheless, import-substitution at all cost became an anchor of policy in many developing countries because it satisfied the vested interest of the rich and the powerful. The slogan of reducing external dependence was used to appeal to the national sentiment of the masses.

It was therefore not the policy of import-substitution *per se* which was wrong; it was rather the way in which this policy was implemented. If equity had been one of the primary goals of development, the policy of import-substitution would have been used initially to support primarily agriculture and small and micro enterprises (SMEs) in developing countries. This would have helped fulfil needs and expand employment opportunities in rural areas and small towns. Workers would have found jobs either in their own villages and towns or near them. They would have thus not been uprooted from their families and social surroundings. What was done instead was the promotion of large-scale industries in urban centres through full government support in the form of subsidised inputs, overvalued exchange rates, and unduly high tariffs on competing imports. International support was also available mainly for such industries. Large projects were "eye-catchers and even international agencies tend to prefer large-scale projects."[50]

Agriculture and SMEs suffered from lack of any subsidy or protection and from overvalued official exchange rates. Techniques remained antiquated, productivity low, and income, savings and investment could not rise significantly. Unemployment and underemployment rose. Import-substituting large-scale industries prospered because of the low cost of their capital and inputs and the protection they received through high tariff walls and overvalued exchange rates. Moreover, since equity and need-fulfilment were not the primary goals of policy, even the selection of import-substituting industries did not take this into consideration. If this had been done, there would have been a positive advance in the direction of need-fulfilment, although the employment goal would still have suffered. Many of the import-substituting large-scale industries were not related to needs; they were rather related to consumer durables and heavy capital goods – industries in which a need-oriented development programme would not have taken a serious interest in the initial phase of development. Such industries also became constrained by the size of the domestic market. Being inefficient, they could not compete in the export market. They nevertheless led to an increase in the volume of imports, particularly in the case of industries which had to import not only capital goods but also raw materials. The imports they needed could not be cut back. Hence what many of them accomplished in reality was to substitute one kind of imports for another.

The growth of large-scale import-substituting industries, many of which depended on imported capital goods and raw materials, did not increase significantly the demand for the output of agriculture and SMEs. The 'linkage' effect did not therefore take place. The benefit mostly leaked abroad through increased induced imports. Moreover, the technologies adopted in these industries were predominantly capital-intensive, being designed for countries having abundance of capital and scarcity of labour.[51] Employment directly generated by expansion of these industries was therefore relatively small. Even a substantial part of the meagre domestic savings came to be diverted into these industries at lower or subsidised rates of interest compared with what prevails in the rural areas. The proportion of savings going into agriculture and SMEs was thus small – not necessarily because of lack of savings in these sectors but rather because of the misallocation of savings. The unduly large support given to large-scale industries therefore ruined handicraft industries, particularly handlooms. The bulk of the rural population had no choice but to remain underemployed in rural areas or to migrate to the overcrowded urban centres.[52] This is not an argument against large-scale capital-intensive industries *per se,* which do have a place in development. However, since expanding self-employment and employment opportunities enjoy a priority, large-scale capital-intensive industries should get the green light when they are indispensable and the job that they can do cannot be done effectively by labour-intensive SMEs.

The particular trend that import-substitution took was natural, given the propagation of Western life-styles, the lack of an indigenous development philosophy, and the absence of a motivating system to induce people successfully to abstain from unnecessary and conspicuous consumption. This was exacerbated by the vested interest of Western manufacturers of capital goods and raw materials in the production of goods for conspicuous consumption. They did effective salesmanship and also arranged financing through suppliers' credits and loans from banks and official lending institutions. Imports therefore rose without a corresponding rise in exports. The foreign exchange bottleneck became more acute.

However, if the policy of industrialisation and import substitution had been pursued to promote equity, an entirely different approach would have been adopted. The objective would have been to fulfil needs, enlarge employment opportunities and reduce inequalities rather than to serve the vested interest of foreign exporters and rich domestic investors. Everything would have been done to encourage and help rural and urban entrepreneurs to produce the needed consumer and capital goods for the domestic market and for export. The help would have included not only tariff protection but also creation of an efficient physical, social and financial infrastructure in rural areas in addition to import or domestic development of simple but efficient technology for the SMEs. This would have enabled them to increase production and also, ultimately, compete effectively with foreign goods. Employment and income would have risen in rural areas, with less congestion in urban centres. The rising incomes of the rural population would also have helped agriculture by enabling the farmers to use better agricultural inputs.

Import-substitution policy implemented within this framework would have enabled the SMEs initially to meet the domestic demand and ultimately to export. Exports do not necessarily have to be goods which are not also in demand in the domestic market. Production can be for both the domestic and the foreign markets. In the first stage, however, production can be for the domestic market; later on, when capacity has increased and the external economies have been realised, the fruits of the export market can also be reaped. Such a policy would have helped developing countries utilise their advantage in the production and export of simple, need-fulfilling goods and services and the capital goods related to these. This course of initial industrialisation does not imply that at a later stage of development, when needs have been largely fulfilled and the unemployment problem has been solved, import-substitution and export promotion in the field of consumer durables and heavy capital goods cannot become a target of national policy.

While import-substitution did not take the right course,

export promotion did not take place either. Many of the capital-intensive industries that were established did not have a comparative advantage in the initial phase of development and, in spite of overt and covert subsidies, they could not compete in the export market. Agriculture and labour-intensive small-scale industries which could have been made to have a comparative advantage did not get the needed official support and credit to expand their output. The overvalued exchange rate also hurt them and they could not compete effectively in the export market. Exports therefore did not rise as much as they could have.

The recent reversal of emphasis on export promotion needs to be considered with caution.[53] If import-substitution at all costs is bad, export promotion at all costs is also not desirable. The ultimate impact of any policy on socio-economic justice must never be lost sight of, given the fact that a number of inefficient large-scale industries have been established. A heavy dose of devaluation of the local currency along with freezing of nominal wages (two of the crutches on which the export strategy stands) may enable the inefficient urban industries established by the rich and the influential to export and thus survive, but would hurt the poor by substantially lowering their real wages. It would thus be at variance with the objective of socio-economic justice. Thus, before jumping on to the bandwagon of export promotion, all necessary measures should be taken to ensure that the benefit goes to the poor rather than the rich.

Those who overemphasise the strategy of export promotion to the neglect of import-substitution, may also wish to bear in mind that the exports of developing countries have always faced and continue to face all kinds of tariff and non-tariff barriers in industrial countries and that their imports have been influenced by dumping and predatory pricing by industrial countries. According to *The Economist,* "Poor countries are the main victims of some of the most pernicious barriers to trade, such as Europe's common agricultural policy and the rich countries' Multi-Fibre Agreement."[54] Government aid to agriculture and industry has grown substantially in the industrial countries over the last three decades and barriers against imports have proliferated. According to Boonekamp, such "restraints mainly affect developing countries.''[55] As a result of such support programmes and protectionist measures, the imports of agricultural products from developing countries are severely affected. For example, virtually no rice imports are permitted in Japan and the domestically produced rice is sold at about nine times the world price, despite recent reductions in support prices.[56] While tariffs have been steadily reduced, protection via non-tariff barriers has been assuming increased importance. Such non-tariff barriers involve major trade, employment and welfare costs for developing countries.[57] Moreover, any developing country that tries hard and manages to become a big exporter soon faces solid walls of quota ceilings imposed by industrial countries, thus finding it difficult to expand its exports further. UNCTAD has estimated the total economic cost of protectionist barriers against Third World countries to be as high as $700 billion annually in terms of export earnings – more than 50 per cent of the total current external debt of these countries.[58]

THE UNANTICIPATED PROBLEMS

While the pundits of development economics emphasised a substantially large government role to overcome the ruling pessimism about the prospects for growth, they did not give any serious thought to the development of a strategy for making an offsetting reduction in claims on resources elsewhere. Wholesale adoption of Western consumer culture was in fact propagated, and even developing countries in their initial stages of development were pushed into the high living and gadgetry of Rostow's fifth stage. This raised the import of luxury goods and unwarrantably widened the import-export gap. It also lowered the propensity to save and the internally generated savings were thus inadequate to satisfy the rising need for investment. Hence, the savings-investment gap also widened. Squeezing wasteful and inessential absorption would have required value judgements, which the value-free development economics could not entertain. Within its tool-kit, taxes and inflation were the main tools available for squeezing consumption.

However, tax revenues could not be raised in step with

spending because of the narrow tax base and the inefficient and corrupt tax administration in developing countries. Budgetary and current account deficits thus rose steeply. To finance these deficits, Keynesian economics encouraged monetary expansion and the 'two-gap' approach pointed towards foreign aid.[59] Those who encouraged monetary expansion probably did not realise that developing countries, with their structural bottlenecks and supply constraints, were prone to a higher rate of inflation and greater import-export gap than the developed industrial countries. Those who emphasised aid probably did not realise that only a very small portion of aid takes the form of grants; most of it is usually in the form of loans, which must be repaid with interest. Monetary expansion and heavy borrowing (both internal and external) thus became the crutches on which governments heavily relied. Once the governments become dependent on these, it is difficult to reverse the steps; a deep cut in spending or a steep rise in taxes, which the reversal demands, have always been politically unpopular.

Inflation

Inflation became rampant, but this was also initially justified.[60] The Phillips curve offered policy-makers the needed rationale in the form of a trade-off between inflation on the one hand, and higher growth and employment on the other. Most Keynesian economists felt little concern about inflation and continued to urge expansionary policies throughout the post-World War II period.[61] Prof. Henry Bruton said, in a series of lectures delivered at the University of Bombay in 1961, that "a case could be made for making inflation an instrument of policy, rather than the control of inflation an objective of policy."[62] Warnings were, no doubt, usually added against monetary mismanagement by saying that "a naive note printing extravaganza does nothing but harm."[63] But such warnings were usually not taken seriously by planners and finance ministers in most developing countries. Inflation offered a way of 'covert taxation without consent'. It did not immediately raise the political uproar that higher taxes would raise and was thus an easy way of financing the burgeoning deficits. If there were any unpleasant consequences, it would be their successors, and not they themselves, who would have to face them. Such behaviour should have been expected as the most natural in a system where socio-economic justice is not a fundamental goal, and the pursuit of self-interest is the primary objective of life. There was no reason to expect that bureaucrats and political leaders would act differently in a value-free environment.

Inflation tended to redistribute income upward, thus tilting the balance against the goal of socio-economic justice. This alone would probably not have given development economists pause for thought. There were, however, other adverse effects which have hurt development adversely and will continue to do so for quite some time in the future.

Inflation led to price controls and subsidies on foodgrains and other essential items of consumption. While price controls hurt the growth in long-term supply of these goods, subsidies loaded the government budget with a heavy burden which the governments now find it difficult to bear. Inflation also led to overvalued exchange rates which were adopted by governments to hold down inflationary pressures. This encouraged imports and hurt exports by making them uncompetitive in the international market. Agriculture and SMEs were particularly hard hit because they did not get the support that large-scale industries received. The dependence on imports increased and the foreign exchange deficit rose further. This raised the need for borrowing and exacerbated the debt-servicing burden. Even though the governments would now like, under the IMF and World Bank pressure, to remove price controls and subsidies, and to adopt realistic exchange rates, they find it politically difficult to do so because of the adverse impact on cost of living. Sir Arthur Lewis was thus led to exclaim: "The principal lesson we have all learned, less-developed countries and more-developed countries alike, is that inflation is a scourge."[64]

Debt Burden

As a result of heavy doses of borrowing, both internal and external debts of developing countries have risen steeply.[65] This was at first justified serenely. But now, the internal and external imbalances faced by developing countries have become so serious that they have created a nightmare for all those concerned with development policies and the health of the domestic as well as international financial systems. The use of shallow domestic financial markets for large government borrowings not only crowded out the private sector but also made financial institutions weak; loaded down with low-yield government debt, they were unable to provide for adequate reserves against losses through bad debts. The heavy resort to multinational banks for external borrowing, initially justified on the basis of the supposed insolvency of sovereign debtors, has raised the debt burden to such an unbearable level that the inability of debtor countries to service the debt is threatening the very survival of these banks. Even the developmental process has now become jeopardised. Real rates of growth have slowed down. Efforts to reduce inflation and the external imbalance may slow it down even further.

Planning Difficulties

While the problems of excessive government spending were not anticipated, even the difficulties of comprehensive planning were underestimated and the expected results overestimated. The ability to formulate development plans was severely limited by the lack of requisite data and the imperfect character of such statistics as are available. Errors tended to be large because the data were inadequate to calculate such strategic variables as total saving, capital coefficients, the extent of underemployment, or the value of an investment project.

Moreover, there was a tendency to expect too much from a planning model. It was not realised that a planning model could not remove or simplify the hard choices that policy-makers had to make. Conflicts among multiple objectives that were frequently encountered in development programmes could not be resolved without establishing priorities. An econometric model could not take the place of a development philosophy which provides guidelines in terms of agreed goals and values, such as cannot be established within the framework of Pareto optimality. A development philosophy and motivation on the part of policy-makers and the public was needed to take and accept decisions ungrudgingly in the larger interest of general well-being. The absence of such a philosophy and motivating system explains why almost all development plans placed equity among the goals of planning but none of them laid down an effective programme to realise it.

Problems of implementing the comprehensive plans were also not given adequate attention. Many development plans met on paper the tests of efficiency and consistency (though not equity), but failed in practice due in large measure to deficiencies in political and administrative requirements. The implementation of plans tended to be extremely difficult because their formulation had been based on the most advanced econometric models. The plans were too refined for practical implementation. Most developing countries could have benefited "more from sound application of fundamental elementary principles of economics than from attempts to use the highest style theory."[66]

The macroeconomic models had a built-in preference in favour of the quantifiable to the relative neglect of components that are not quantifiable but are of crucial importance for realising the plan's objectives, particularly socio-economic justice. The more rigorous an econometric model, the less likely it was to incorporate noneconomic components. As Professor Galbraith observed: "On even the most preliminary view of the problem, effective government, education, and social justice emerge as critically important. In many countries, in diagnosing the barriers to advancement, it is lack of these that is of critical importance. And it follows that until these barriers are removed little will come from capital investment and technical assistance. While plans will be big on paper they will be small in result."[67]

THE RESURGENCE OF NEOCLASSICAL ECONOMICS

The difficulties now faced by developing countries have led to a resurgence of neoclassical economics. The blame is being laid squarely on the socialist strategy of big government and comprehensive planning followed over a period of about three decades. It is being argued that heavy reliance on public sector investments and controls for promoting growth has led to not only distortions in resource allocation but also macroeconomic and external imbalances. It has hindered full realisation of the initiative and investment potential of the private sector. The enthusiasm for large-scale capital-intensive heavy industries has led to inefficient industrialisation at the cost of rural and agricultural development. As Mr. Michael Camdessus, Managing Director of the IMF, has clearly emphasised: "Economies that suffer from rampant inflation, large budget deficits, pervasive trade restrictions, misaligned exchange rates, unrealistic interest rates, heavy external debt and repeated bouts of capital flight cannot and do not grow rapidly for any sustained period of time."[68] Even more disconcerting than the lagging growth and imbalances has been the failure of poor countries to alleviate the numbers in absolute poverty, the increasing numbers in unemployment and underemployment, and the persistence of inequality. The problems faced by the poor have increased rather than decreased. The expectations that independence and promises made by national governments had raised have remained unfulfilled.

The resurgence of neoclassical economics in the wake of failure of the socialist strategy has thus brought the developing countries back to where they started – the problem of realising both efficiency and equity in the use of scarce resources. Development economics, it must be admitted, has a different face this time around, at least so it appears. It is not concerned merely with growth, it is also concerned with equity. This has been so since the beginning of the 1970s when it began to be recognised that development must mean not only growth in average per capita income but also a reduction in poverty.[69] It began to be realised that for poor, heavily populated nations like India, Bangladesh, Pakistan and Indonesia, only long-term sustained, equitably distributed growth of per capita income offers the majority of people any hope of economic advancement. It simply may not be possible to "grow first and redistribute later."[70] Development economics is thus no longer worshipping merely at the altar of GNP, praying only for its growth, it also claims to be a devotee of redistribution. The call is for "growth with redistribution", "reduction of absolute poverty", and "meeting basic human needs". Neoclassical economics does not now purport to be just the "guardian of rationality", it also wishes to be the "trustee of the poor".[71]

Addressing the World Bank's Annual Meeting in Nairobi in 1973, Mr. McNamara, the then President of the Bank, called upon the world to focus on those in "absolute poverty" – those "who suffer a condition of life so degraded by disease, illiteracy, malnutrition, and squalor as to deny its victims basic human necessities."[72] Theodore Schultz, while accepting the Nobel Prize in 1979, stated: "Most of the people in the world are poor, so if we knew the economics of being poor we would know much of the economics that really matters."[73] Gerald Meier, from the first edition of whose *Leading Issues in Economic Development* published in 1964, poverty, inequality and income distribution were virtually absent, led off the fourth edition (1984) with a substantial emphasis on income distribution in developing countries and went even to the extent of saying that "emerging from poverty" is the "economics that really matters" in another book of his also published in 1984.[74] This concern for distribution is eloquently epitomised by Dudley Seers when he says: "The questions to ask about a country's development are therefore: what has been happening to poverty? What has been happening to unemployment? What has been happening to inequality? If all three of these have declined from high levels, then beyond doubt this has been a period of development for the country concerned. If one or two of these central problems have been growing worse, especially if all three have, it would be strange to call the result development even if per capita income doubled."[75]

The Crucial Question

Thus we see that socio-economic justice, which had been declared to be an outcast in the interest of rapid capital formation and growth, has been readmitted. This is without doubt a welcome change. Development economics now gives at least the same outward appearance that neoclassical, Keynesian and socialist economics have always given – aspiring to realise both equity and efficiency. However, the crucial question is whether the value-neutral neoclassical economics is capable of providing an effective strategy for realising both these goals in developing countries. The strategy being currently emphasised by neoclassical economists in every paper and at every international or regional conference, is 'adjustment'. No one can challenge the need for adjustment. Given the severe imbalances faced by developing countries, adjustment is no longer an option, it has become a must. What is more important however is the components of an adjustment programme, and it is doubtful whether the components that neoclassical economics stands for can help realise both equity and efficiency.

Everyone will probably agree that the 'right' adjustment is that which addresses itself to both the demand and the supply sides of the problem in such a way that there is a 'minimum sacrifice of growth'. On the demand side, it is necessary to reduce domestic absorption, which refers to the aggregate of private and public consumption and investment outlays (C+I+G). However, if future growth is to be ensured, then the reduction in absorption should be primarily in the consumption component of absorption and not in investment. Moreover, if socio-economic justice is also to be realised, then the decline in consumption needs to be brought about in such a way that the adverse effect falls on those who are better off and strong enough to bear the required austerity, and that the condition of the poor is at least not made worse off, if it cannot, for some strong reason, be made better off, which is the most desirable alternative. On the supply side also, socio-economic justice demands that the rise in output be brought about in such a way that needs are fulfilled, employment rises and inequalities are reduced.

In contrast, the adjustment programme proposed by neoclassical economics, of which the World Bank and the IMF are the bastions, "will result", as Mr. Barber Conable, President of the World Bank, has frankly admitted, "in some temporary unemployment, and in real difficult short-term reductions in living standards – which sometimes affect the poorest segment of the population most harshly."[76] An economic system strongly committed to socio-economic justice cannot however permit the poorest segment of the population to be affected "most harshly". The palliative that the harsh effect may be "temporary" and "short-term" does not reduce the shock because the likelihood is that this effect may not only be permanent but probably also cumulative. Mr. Conable is not however wrong in his prediction about the impact of adjustment on the poor. His prediction is made within the framework of neoclassical economics. It is therefore important to see why the poor, who had been hit harshly by the secularist development economics during the expansion phase, will be hit harshly once again by neoclassical economics during the adjustment phase.

Contents of Liberalisation

The adjustment programme offered by neoclassical economics hangs mainly by the thread of liberalisation. This call for liberalisation is couched essentially in the value-neutral terms of Enlightenment theory. In spite of a great deal of talk about economists being "trustees of the poor", there is no commitment to a filter mechanism of socially-agreed values or to a motivating system that could induce the rich and powerful to absorb the harsh effect of adjustment, thus helping ensure socio-economic justice. The harsh effect on the poor is expected to be offset only indirectly – mainly by establishing an environment for higher growth through the restoration of internal and external balance.

The most important components of neoclassical liberalisation, as articulated by the IMF in its adjustment programmes, are: (a) reduce the role of government in the economy; (b) allow the market to play its role; and (c) liberalise foreign trade. Stabilisation and efficiency, which are the main targets, are to be attained by achieving "a sustainable external balance" and by "restraining aggregate domestic demand, promoting supply, and, most important, improving economic efficiency." It has been honestly admitted that "distributional issues are primarily an internal political concern."[77] Hence, "mitigation of the adverse distributional implications of exogenous shocks or of the economic adjustments necessitated by past, inappropriate policies has not been an explicit objective of Fund-supported programmes", even though these adjustment programmes have "important distributional implications".[78] Consequently, none of the IMF annual consultation reports on member countries ever discusses a member country's progress in removing poverty, fulfilling needs, and reducing inequalities. A country gets full laurels from the IMF if it succeeds in reducing the imbalances irrespective of whether this has been attained with or without adversely affecting equity.

It is argued that a reduced role for the government in the economy will help reduce domestic absorption by introducing fiscal restraint and cutting the budgetary deficit. The private sector will thus be able to play a greater and more active role in the economy and, being better motivated in its own self-interest, will contribute to greater efficiency. Restraints on credit expansion will help reduce private sector absorption. Greater reliance on the market will help in 'getting the prices right' (including interest rates and exchange rates) and in giving the 'right' signals to economic agents. This will remove distortions and lead to a more efficient allocation of resources. While such a policy would lead to a rise in the prices of most goods and services in developing countries, the neoclassical prescription calls for a restraint on real wages. Although this will "impose hardship on organised labour",[79] it will ultimately be offset by higher employment and growth. Outward orientation will help the adjusting country take advantage of international trade to promote growth and to offset the recessionary effect of reduction in domestic absorption. All import restrictions should be removed and imports and exports should both be encouraged. Realistic exchange rates will themselves go a long way in expanding exports and reducing imports and in thus reducing the current account deficit. If tariffs have to be used, they should preferably be low and uniform. Any discrimination will require value judgements which are not desirable; it will only lead to distortions which will adversely affect efficiency. Import-substitution, it is argued, has only a limited potential because its target is basically the domestic market, which is limited, while exports do not face such a quantitative limitation.

While liberalisation calls for a cut in overall government spending, it does not address itself to a change in the composition of government spending to improve the equity performance of the budget. There is no discussion of the ways of 'saving' resources needed for raising the quality and quantity of educational, health, housing, transport and sanitation facilities for the poor to uplift the quality of the human factor in development. Even a discussion of the supply side of Fund programmes is concerned primarily with providing better incentives to promote savings, investments and exports through realistic prices, interest rates, exchange rates and taxes. There is no discussion of economic restructuring to increase the supply of need-satisfying goods and services. 'Getting the prices right' through reliance on the market to give the 'right' signals to economic agents is thus the linchpin of the neoclassical prescription for solving the allocation and distribution problems of developing countries.

It has already been shown in Chapter 1 that without the prevalence of background conditions, the reliance on merely the price mechanism and the interest-based banking system to allocate resources cannot but operate against need fulfilment and equitable distribution of income and wealth. This aspect of liberalisation is not expressly spelt out by neoclassical economists. It is however at the back of their minds when they make the stark prediction about the effect on the poor. They assume, and their assumption is realistic within their value-free framework, that nothing can be done to avoid the "most harsh" effect on the poor. Any effort to avoid the result of market forces will create distortions that will lead to inefficiency and lower growth. Accordingly, the only preferable alternative is to allow higher growth attained through liberalisation to improve the position of the poor. However, the question is: will higher growth automatically lead to equity? If it could, the rich industrial countries would have long succeeded in eliminating poverty and reducing inequalities. This clearly shows that social-Darwinism is unmistakenly present at the core of neoclassical economics even though outwardly it presents a smiling face to the poor – a wolf in sheep's clothing.

The Wrong Examples: Not Just Liberalisation

In support of the neoclassical prescription are being cited the examples of Far Eastern countries like Japan, Taiwan, the Republic of Korea (South Korea), Hong Kong and Singapore, which resorted to policies of liberalisation and export-orientation to promote efficiency and growth. It is argued that liberalisation helped accelerate their development by motivating their private sectors to greater initiative and efficiency. The outward-orientation enlarged their export surplus and increased not only employment opportunities in these countries but also enabled them to meet the foreign exchange needs of their expanding economies with smaller reliance on foreign aid.

While there is no doubt that liberalisation and export-orientation have played a significant role in the accelerated growth of these countries, it is not correct to give the entire credit for their economic success to these two factors. There are several other factors which were equally, if not more, responsible. Some of these are: substantial government intervention, socio-economic justice and social harmony brought about by extensive land reform and social values, high propensity to save and invest, and active support of import-substitution as well as export-promotion for industrialisation. Not all of these factors fit into the neoclassical model; in fact some of them are clearly in conflict with it.

Government Role

Governments in these countries have played, and continue to play, an important role. Only in the case of Hong Kong has anything close to *laissez-faire* been practised. In other countries there is extensive intervention in the form of state enterprise, subsidies, regulations and other measures affecting the capital market, domestic savings, trade, and almost every aspect of the economy. The governments have also directed private business into targeted channels through their control over industrial licences, foreign loans and technology agreements, and use of selective incentives and threats.[80] It is not possible to call Japan, South Korea, Taiwan and Singapore liberal in the neoclassical sense.[81] With respect to Japan, Yasuo Masai says that: "Although the extent of direct state participation in economic activities is limited, the government's control and influence over business is stronger and more pervasive than in most other countries. This control is not exercised through legislation or administrative action but through constant – and to an outsider almost obsessive – consultation with business and through the authorities' deep indirect involvement in banking. . . . In addition, there are several agencies and government departments that concern themselves with such aspects of the economy as exports, imports, investment, and prices, as well as overall economic growth. . . . The need for large-scale government participation in economic activities is thereby obviated and unlike many governments in the free-enterprise world, the state appears to be reluctant to extend its direct role.''[82] It is doubtful if these countries could have achieved as much as they did without an active and strong role by their governments.

It must however be admitted that the government role in these countries has not necessarily been restrictive in the form of controls that inhibit the initiative and drive of the private sector. It has rather been positive, to facilitate and encourage the private sector. Of course, the pragmatic, growth-oriented and dedicated leadership of these countries has enabled the taking of right decisions in the interest of the country, and the stability of government has removed uncertainties about policies and inspired the confidence of investors.

Land Reforms and Wealth Distribution

Thoroughgoing land reforms were introduced in Japan, South Korea and Taiwan after the Second World War by the occupation authorities with the objective of destroying psychologically and materially the feudal lords who constituted the driving force behind these countries' war effort. These reforms had the far-reaching side effects of equalising rural income distribution and keeping rural/urban differentials much narrower than in other countries. In all three cases, land reforms were extensive. They destroyed the power base of feudal lords and virtually eliminated farm tenancy, which was widespread before the reforms. The land reforms reduced the average family holding in Japan to about 2.5 acres and in South Korea to about 2.25 acres of arable land.[83] The scale of landholdings has remained unchanged over the last 30 years. Even in 1985, the average farm size amounted to 1.2 hectares (2.9 acres) in Japan, with only 4 per cent of all farms operating on land of more than 3 hectares (7.41 acres).[84] According to Sachs, land reforms in these countries ''were probably more extensive than in any other case in modern history and could be accomplished because of the extraordinary national circumstances in each country'' – Japan and South Korea were under U.S. occupation while Taiwan was under the Nationalists. The landlords in these countries could not therefore effectively mobilise political opposition.[85] The land reforms in essence also brought about a substantial expropriation of landlords because compensation was either not paid or was inadequate.

The redistributive effect of these land reforms was further reinforced by the destruction of wealth by war in all three countries and the erosion in the real value of compensation received as well as of financial assets (bonds and cash holdings) by the high rate of inflation. Annual inflation rates reached 334 per cent in Japan in 1947, 500 per cent in the Republic of Korea and 3400 per cent in Taiwan in 1950.[86] All these factors had the effect of substantially narrowing income and wealth distribution and of creating the background conditions (discussed in Chapter 1), without which liberalisation would have probably led to greater inequity.

The creation of a large body of small independent proprietary farmers in place of a tiny class of rich, unpopular landlords shifted the balance of political power in favour of the peasantry. The peasants could now assert their newly-gained political clout to tilt decisions in their favour by governments who needed their support and who thus became obliged to give protection to agriculture and to develop rural infrastructure. The infrastructure, along with the transfer of land ownership, enabled the peasants to serve their self-interest and thus provided the necessary motivation to make improvements and long-term investments in agriculture. Given the small size of land holdings, the farmers successfully used simple, labour-intensive techniques (superior seeds, better methods of crop cultivation, and increased input of manures and fertilisers) to generate a substantial rise in output and incomes. This not only supplied the food needed by the rapidly growing population but also the savings and the market needed for industrial expansion.

What liberalisation did was to enable the *nouveaux riches* to become a dynamic element within the economy by making it possible for them to invest their savings in Western technology and machinery. This led to a rapid expansion in industrial output through the establishment of a large number of mutually competing manufacturing units. There was thus a simultaneous and balanced growth of both agriculture and industry. In the absence of liberalisation, the *nouveaux riches* may have been led into the unproductive fields of conspicuous consumption and capital flight, as has been the case in many developing countries.

Social Equality

The broad sharing of the benefits of growth that land reforms brought about ushered in greater social equality. As Myrdal has rightly observed: social inequality "in all its forms is detrimental to productivity."[87] Social equality also reduced conspicuous consumption and the related investments that income inequality promotes among the rich. This released resources for the need fulfilment of the poor, thus improving their health and educational level. A well-fed, healthy and better-educated labour force established a firm foundation for faster and sustained growth. Reduction in the suffering of the poor removed antisocial feelings among them, improved their motivation for work and efficiency, and reduced the waste resulting from strikes and conflict. According to Sachs, economic success in Latin America is impeded by social conflict over vast income inequalities, the distribution of income in Latin America being more unequal than in most other parts of the world. In Brazil the richest fifth have 33 times as much as the poorest fifth, whereas in Taiwan they have only a little over four times as much. On average the richest 20 per cent are 21 times as rich in Latin America, but nine times as rich in East Asia.[88]

Labour-Intensive Techniques

Equity was further reinforced by the choice of labour-intensive policies which have helped the cause of employment in these countries. However, unlike Japan and South Korea, Taiwan also opted for an effective role by small enterprises in both agriculture and manufacturing, and did not allow the establishment of large conglomerates in domestic business.[89] This policy not only provided further support to the labour-intensive techniques in reducing unemployment and underemployment – a constant problem in other industrial and developing countries – but also gave small farmers good opportunities for rural earnings. This gave a boost to rural incomes; by 1980, almost three-quarters of the income of rural families came from nonagricultural income.[90] Thus Taiwan was transformed over time from an economy having an abundance of labour in the 1950s to one having a scarcity in the 1970s. The achievement of full employment in rural as well as urban areas led to a rise in the incomes of all families and further improved the income equality already attained as a result of land reforms.[91] As a consequence, the Gini coefficient has continually declined in Taiwan from 0.56 in the 1950s to 0.31 in the early 1980s.[92] Taiwan has thus achieved a greater degree of income equality than any of the developing economies. The ratio of income of the richest 20 per cent of the population to income of the poorest 20 per cent declined from 20.5 in 1953 to 4.2 in 1980 and is probably the lowest ratio in any developing country.[93]

Cultural Values

The cultural values of these countries and the homogeneity of population in most of them also helped promote a closely-knit society with social peace and stability. Their value system is centred on personal obligation – obligation to one's parents, employer and employees, friends and neighbours, and the community. These obligations need to be fulfilled in order for one to be accepted as a member of society. If one were to refuse or neglect them, the inevitable consequence was social ostracism. In a society where obligation occupies such an important position, group discipline is strong, employer treats employee humanely and pays due attention to his well-being, employee works hard and conscienciously, and employer/employee relations are congenial. This aspect of social values which keeps self-interest under check and serves social interest even when the two may not coincide is certainly not in harmony with the value-free liberalisation of neoclassical economics.[94]

The perplexing question, however, is, why these same cultural values remained dormant before the War? The answer is that such values require an enabling environment for their observance. One of the factors which created such an environment was socio-economic equality which postwar political and economic restructuring brought about. In such an environment everybody is obliged to conform and unable to get away without being castigated, as is possible in an environment of extreme social, economic and political inequalities, and of common, uninhibited violation of social mores. Another factor was the difficulties faced by people in a war-ravaged economy. Everyone knew clearly what national reconstruction required – economy in the use of resources. This realisation provided a binding authority to the cultural values of simple living and abstinence from conspicuous consumption,[95] thus leading to their unchallenged observance by all without exception. Individual families tended to be extremely frugal.

This helped moderate consumption and generate a high rate of saving in these countries. Gross domestic saving as a percentage of gross domestic product was 33.4, 30.7, 39.9, 37.6 and 37.0 per cent in Japan, Hong Kong, Singapore, South Korea, and Taiwan in 1987 as compared with the average of 19.8 per cent for Latin America and the Caribbean, 13.0 per cent for Sub-Saharan Africa, 17.0 per cent for the Middle East and North Africa, and 19.3 per cent for South Asia.[96] The high rate of saving provided the domestic resources needed for capital formation, and expansion of output and exports. The contribution that this high rate of saving has made to the economic success of these countries should not be underestimated. It kept interest rates in these countries relatively lower than elsewhere and thus encouraged investment. It enabled the government as well as the private sector to finance their investments without resort, as in other developing countries, to unduly large monetary and credit expansion and external borrowing. This kept inflation under control and enhanced their competitiveness in the export market. It also enabled them to enlarge their productive capacity and laid the foundation for the success of their outward-looking policy without loading their economies with a high debt-servicing burden, as has happened in other developing countries.

Import Control and Export Promotion

While the social values have helped promote savings in these countries, they have also helped substantially in restraining inessential imports. In other developing countries this legitimate national need has been fulfilled by high import tariffs and stiff exchange controls (which lead to smuggling, under-invoicing and corruption). In the non-legal consensus societies of these countries, the need was satisfied by social norms which it is not possible to violate without being socially castigated. Therefore, while it might seem that these economies were outward-oriented they were so primarily in terms of exports and not imports, even though the absence of strict import controls may make them appear to be so.[97] Moreover, as Lester Thurow has observed with respect to Japan: "How does a foreign firm break in as a new supplier of industrial components, for example, when Japanese firms place a premium on maintaining long-term intimate supply relationships with nearby suppliers in the just-in-time inventory system?"[98]

Moreover, the role of outward-orientation in these countries is being unduly overemphasised. Export-led growth is new to Japan. In the 1950s and 1960s Japan had a chronic trade deficit. Companies became successful by winning at home and then, by exploiting economies of scale, to venture overseas: domestic demand fuelled the export drive, not the other way round. Korea, Taiwan and a number of countries which have succeeded in promoting their exports have "all initially followed the import-substitution path."[99] All these countries resorted to a substantial degree of protection initially, and only later on was there a shift from import-substitution to export promotion, but without any significant change in the development philosophy. They were almost forced to do so because their limited foreign exchange earnings had to be diverted to the purchase of foreign technology and machinery which they could not initially produce themselves. The whole economy was organised to minimise imports of non-essential goods. While protection is not sufficient for successful industrialisation, the argument that it is not necessary seems largely an *a priori* assumption. Most historical examples from Germany and the U.S. to Japan have involved protection. Even now, all these countries resort to a substantial degree of protection with respect to both industry and agriculture. Asking developing countries to do what even the developed countries have themselves not done, and are not doing, is unrealistic advice.

Low Defence Spending

A distinguishing feature of Japanese public finance has been the low level of spending on defence. Military spending has been held down to less than one per cent of GNP compared with an average of around four per cent in industrial countries and about three per cent in developing countries.[100] This has released resources for building an efficient infrastructure in spite of the relatively low level of total government spending. It has also helped keep taxes at a lower level compared with other countries. In Japan, taxes constituted 21 per cent of GDP in 1975 and 31.3 per cent in 1988 compared with 33 per cent and 40.8 per cent respectively in the EEC.[101] While South Korea and Taiwan have maintained a higher profile in defence spending as compared with Japan, their fiscal burden has been substantially reduced by foreign aid, primarily from the United States.

A Peep into the Future

One may thus see clearly the decisive role that a number of factors have played in the rapid growth of these countries, particularly in reducing the conflict between the objectives of growth and equity. It would therefore be improper to attribute the credit for all these factors to liberalisation alone, even though liberalisation has also played an important role. A crucial question that one may, however, wish to raise here is whether it would be possible for these countries to sustain the equity that they were able to realise due to exceptional circumstances? Some of the factors that have been eroding equity in these countries lead one to a negative answer.

South Korea, unlike Taiwan, opted for large family-run conglomerates (chaebol) in the industrial sector. The chaebol have continually grown bigger with the help of Government and financing from banks. By 1984, the 10 largest chaebol accounted for 64 per cent of GNP and 70 per cent of exports.[102] Even though the preference for labour-intensive techniques generated a substantial expansion in employment opportunities, these became available mainly in urban centres and not in rural areas. Consequently, unlike Taiwan, there was a large shift of population from rural areas to urban centres.[103] Almost half of the country's population is now crammed in four major urban centres (Seoul, Pusan, Taegu and Inchon). This has led to a pressure on housing and other facilities in these urban centres, making the life of rural migrants miserable. The chaebol, helped in their expansion by the urban bias and the banking system, have tended to widen income disparities in South Korea. In 1965, the bottom 40 per cent's share of income was 19.3 per cent, but by 1987 it had declined to 16.9 per cent – that of the top 20 per cent had risen to 45.3 per cent from 41.8 per cent.[104]

Thus even though income distribution is more equitable in South Korea than in comparable developing countries, the choice of chaebol as the preferred form of business organisation has sown the seeds of income disparity, conspicuous consumption and industrial strife. From 1981 to 1985, there were only 100 strikes a year. In 1986, there were 276. But in 1987 the number of strikes mushroomed to 3008.[105] This indicates that the growing inequalities and hardships faced by migrant labour in urban areas is eroding the harmonious industrial relations fostered by the socio-economic equality created by land reform and cultural values. "For three decades Korea sought economic development regardless of the social consequences. Attitudes are now changing."[106] Parvez Hasan has thus rightly remarked that "the past experience of lagging rural income and excessive migration to urban areas has underscored the need for a comprehensive strategy to deal with the economic imbalance of rural and urban areas."[107]

In Japan also, the prognosis for the future is a gradual increase in inequalities. The post-war dissolution of zaibatsu (family controlled groups of monopolistic companies like Mitsui, Mitsubishi, Sumitomo and Yasuda) along with land reform spread economic power more evenly over the population, making it difficult for a small group of people to dominate the national economy and politics. This led to a proliferation of small and medium-scale enterprises and created intense competition in all industries. Efficiency increased, making it possible for Japan to be competitive internationally. However, the law which led to their abolition (The Elimination of Excessive Concentration of Economic Power Law) became a dead letter from the late 1940s and was finally repealed in the mid-1950s. This rendered ineffective the dissolution of zaibatsu, as is evident from the rise of the Mitsubishi, Mitsui and

Sumitomo companies virtually to their previous positions.[108] Even though these companies are now structured quite differently from their zaibatsu days, they still exercise considerable economic and political clout. The zaibatsu banks, which have been gradually becoming more powerful, have become the hand-maidens of these companies, and it is most likely that their hold on the economy will increase, gradually but continually.[109]

While it is true that small businesses proliferate in Japan, they now account for a much smaller share of sales.[110] Most of these firms are, besides, company-affiliated stores not having the freedom to set their own prices. Thus, the system, aided by the banking setup, is gradually leading to concentration of wealth which, even though it may not be of the same nature and intensity as that of the zaibatsu days, it is moving closer to it.[111] No wonder Japan already has six of the world's ten richest men even though only four decades have passed since the near elimination of inequalities after the War.[112] Such excessively rich people are able to exercise, as in other countries, an increasing influence on the economy and the polity.[113] The process of ongoing liberalisation may intensify concentration, particularly if the Agricultural Land Act, which has prevented the revival of the landlord system, and the Large-Scale Retail Store Law, which has impeded the entry of large stores into the retail sector, are repealed or diluted significantly.

A substantial part of the savings in these countries are now going into stock market and land speculation and boosting share and land values, thus providing momentum to the trend towards concentration. The Nikkei index rose from an average of 102 in 1950 to 1,117 in 1960, 2,193 in 1970, 6,870 in 1980, and 26,646 just before the October 1987 crash. Prices, however, recovered faster in Japan than in any other major stock market and the index rose to the high of 38,916 in December 1989.[114] The Japanese stock market has thus seen share prices double on average every four years. The average price/earnings ratio for Japanese equities has accordingly risen from 10.7 in 1970 to 19.1 in 1980 and the high of 61.4 in April 1988. Thereafter it declined to 50.4 in July 1989 due primarily to a rise in interest rates. Comparative price/earnings ratios for other major countries in July 1989 were: United States, 13.3; United

Kingdom, 11.7; West Germany, 15.7; and France, 12.5.[115] The dizzy height of the Japanese price-earnings ratio carries the seeds of a serious crisis, which could unfold at any time and have an extremely destabilising effect not only on the Japanese economy but also the world financial markets.

Land values have also risen steeply. The average price of land for commercial, residential and industrial use in six major cities has doubled on an average every four years taking the index of average land prices from 100 in March 1955 to 12,848 in 1989.[116] Commercial, residential and industrial properties have hence become so expensive in Japan that they are now beyond the reach of most middle-class families. This shatters their dream of one day owning their own business and home. The high cost of office and residential property also adds a high premium to all goods and services purchased by the Japanese, thus reducing their real income. Japan has now become one of the most expensive countries in the world. The internal purchasing power of the yen has thus been outstripped by its exchange rate.

Speculation in both shares and property, nevertheless, continues to be fanned by credit extended for this purpose by banks to those who have the collateral. Since the value of the collateral (shares and property) was escalating, credit was also expanding simultaneously. The speculative boom was thus accentuating wealth inequalities and deeply eroding the socio-economic equity that had been realised after the War. This time around the shares and property-owning *nouveaux riches* have different attitudes. They are spending on conspicuous consumption, thus increasing social inequalities and loosening the social glue that strengthened social solidarity.[117] The same speculative boom with its adverse effect on socio-economic equality is also taking place in both South Korea and Taiwan.[118]

Thus, even though these countries started after the War with relative equality and met the background conditions for growth with equity, they have found it difficult to sustain socio-economic equity within the framework of the capitalist economic and financial systems that prevail in these countries. This shows that even if inequalities are minimised initially by unusual circumstances, they would re-emerge and lead to concentration of wealth unless the total economy is restructured and the financial system is reorganised in a way that would help to sustain as well as promote equity. Important elements of such a restructuring, particularly of the financial system, which has a strong tendency to promote concentration of wealth, will be addressed in Chapters 8 to 10.

THE MISSING LINK

Thus, while the Far Eastern countries have been able to attain higher growth with equity, it would be a mistake to overemphasise the role of liberalisation in this achievement. Even neoclassical economists accept that "the emphasis on the market did not mean that the government must accept the practice and results of *laissez-faire,* but rather that the government should improve and strengthen the market price system."[119] The answer to the question whether neoclassical liberalisation, along with the 'improvement' and 'strengthening' of the market system by the government, can sustain equity is negative, as discussed above.

The primary reason for greater equity in Far Eastern countries is not liberalisation but rather exceptional circumstances which prevailed in these countries after the War, government policies and cultural values. Such a combination of equity-creating circumstances cannot be duplicated in other developing countries under normal peace-time conditions. Without the background conditions that these factors created, neoclassical liberalisation will only worsen the equity picture unless it is accompanied by an effective strategy for advancing the cause of equity. Even though such cultural values are also present in other countries, their effectiveness has been blunted by the prevailing high level of socio-economic inequality, the continued moral degeneration, and the onslaught of Western consumer culture. Hence the challenge that faces us is how to realise and sustain equity in countries where it has not been created by force of circumstances.

Development economics, in spite of reintroducing equity as a goal, has even now been unable to propose an effective strategy for realising it in countries which do not have the background conditions created by exceptional circumstances. As Morawetz has pertinently indicated after a study of 25 years of development: "There exists a vast and easily accessible literature on the subject of how to grow: on what policies have been tried, where and with what results. But on the question of how to redistribute, the contributions though many are more disparate."[120] Even though this statement was made more than a decade ago, it is still factually true. Reliance continues to be primarily on growth for improving distribution. But as Fields has rightly concluded: "Although rapid economic growth generally reduces poverty, growth is neither necessary nor sufficient for poverty alleviation. . . . Whether inequality increases or decreases with economic growth depends on the type of growth rather than on the level of GNP or the rate of GNP growth *per se*."[121]

The continued poverty of development economics in suggesting an effective programme for reducing inequalities gives the impression that even the concern for equity that is now being expressed may be temporary and "just one more fashion in a fashion-prone discipline."[122] This feeling is further reinforced by the widening circle of neoclassical economists who would prefer equity to remain an indirect goal of policy rather than become a direct, express and fundamental goal. For them, the 'poverty' of development economics lies not in its indirect and inadequate discussion of equity, but rather in its getting involved in such a discussion.[123]

An effective strategy for realising equity requires socially-agreed values, a motivating system and economic restructuring. These are not attainable within the value-free framework of neoclassical economics. If appropriate policies can be suggested, why should or would others accept them? As Meier has rightly indicated, the most underdeveloped part of development economics is the question of "how to gain the acceptance of more appropriate policies?"[124] Why, one may ask, is it relatively easy to suggest policies but extremely difficult to gain their acceptance and implementation? The reason is, as Meier has again indicated, there is "a rare public policy from which everyone gains. Some in the country will gain and some will lose from the policy action."[125] It is hence necessary to have a mechanism by which to motivate even those who will be worse off to accept the policies suggested.

Neoclassical economics fails here. It can be effective only as long as the question is that of serving everyone's self-interest, which is necessary to induce greater initiative and efficiency. But equitable distribution cannot be attained by everyone serving just his self-interest; such behaviour in fact tends to worsen income distribution. Equitable distribution requires a motivation to serve social interest even if this involves sacrifice of self-interest. Social interest will be served under the neoclassical model only as long as it coincides with self-interest. The secularist value-free approach of liberalism does not have any mechanism to motivate people to sacrifice self-interest for social interest when the two do not coincide. According to a World Bank Report, if income were distributed differently at the global level, present output of grain alone could supply every man, woman and child with more than 3,000 calories and 65 grams of protein per day – far more than the highest estimates of requirements.[126] Compared with this, the daily calorie supply per capita was lower in 1985 than in 1965 in most developing countries.[127]

Needs remain unsatisfied, not necessarily because of lack of sufficient production of all need-satisfying goods, but because of inequitable distribution. The neoclassical model is not capable of bringing about an equitable distribution of wealth. If it was capable, it would have succeeded in the rich industrial countries with their far greater resources and growth, and the Development Committee would not have been led to admit that "it has proved extremely difficult to address poverty problems successfully."[128] It was the failure of the neoclassical model to promote equity, for reasons already discussed in Chapter 1, which gave birth to socialism. But socialism also failed to promote equity in most countries; it had the added disadvantage that in almost all countries it also failed to promote efficiency. Since equity is the most urgent socio-political imperative of developing countries, revival of neoclassical economics cannot now be expected to promote what it has failed to do in the past.

Inequities may hence be expected to persist in developing countries if they revert to the neoclassical model. This carries the potential of further exacerbating discontent, which has already heightened in recent years. The political upheaval that this may initiate may tend to tilt the balance once again in favour of anti-liberalism, this time with a vengeance. But will such a revival of anti-liberalism succeed in promoting equity in developing countries when it has failed to do so in the past in both the developing and most socialist countries? Probably not. Hence, instead of being swung like a football by the two systems from one extreme to the other, the developing countries need to develop their own strategy in the light of their own socio-economic imperatives.

Notes and References (Chapter 4)

1 E. E. Hagen, *On the Theory of Social Change* (1962), p. 36; see also H. W. Arndt, ''Development Economics before 1945'', in Jagdish Bhagwati and Richard Eckaus, *Development and Planning: Essays in Honour of Paul Rosenstein Rodan* (1972), pp. 13–29.

2 See, for example, K. Mandelbaum, *The Industrialisation of Backward Areas* (1945); United Nations, *Measures for the Economic Development of Underdeveloped Countries* (1951); Paul Baran, ''On the Political Economy of Backwardness'', *The Manchester School of Economic and Social Studies*, January 1952, pp. 66–84; Bert F. Hoselitz, *The Progress of Underdeveloped Areas* (1952); Moses Abramovitz, ''Economics of Growth'', in B. F. Haley, *A Survey of Contemporary Economics* (1952), vol. 2, pp. 132–82; and Jacob Viner, *International Trade and Economic Development* (1952). See also David Morawetz, *Twenty-five Years of Economic Development: 1950 to 1975* (1977).

3 D. Colman and F. Nixson, *Economics of Change in Less Developed Countries* (1986), p. vi.

4 For a spectrum of views on the subject, see, Deepak Lal, *The Poverty of Development Economics* (1984); Ian M. D. Little, *Economic Development: Theory, Policy and International Relations* (1982); Albert O. Hirschman, ''The Rise and Decline of Development Economics'', in Gersovitz, Diaz-Alejandro, Ranis and Rosenweig, (eds.), *The Theory and Experience of Economic Development* (1982); Henry Bruton, ''The Search for a Development Economics'', *World Development Oct/Nov (13)*; and Paul Streeten, *Development Perspectives* (1981).

5 See H. W. Arndt, *Economic Development: The History of an Idea* (1987).

6 United Nations, *Measures for the Economic Development of Underdeveloped Countries* (1951), pp. 13–16.

7 See C. P. Kindleberger, ''Review of The Economy of Turkey; The Economic Development of Guatemala; Report on Cuba'', *Review of Economics and Statistics*, November 1952, pp. 391–2; and Joseph P. Spengler,

"IBRD Mission, Growth Theory", *American Economic Review,* May 1954, pp. 586–7.

8 Eugene Staley, *The Future of Underdeveloped Countries* (1954), pp. 4, 21 and 24; see also Bert F. Hoselitz, *Sociological Aspects of Economic Growth* (1960), p. 56. Staley has been described by Arndt as "the man who more than any other brought the theme of economic development into the American discussion." Arndt, in Bhagwati and Eckaus (1972), p. 26.

9 Gunnar Myrdal, *Asian Drama* (1968), vol. 2, p. 73. According to Streeten, Myrdal's *Asian Drama* is on the whole pessimistic about the development prospects of developing countries (Paul Streeten, *Development Perspective,* 1981, p. 425). Myrdal's "modernisation ideals" are: rationality, social and economic equalisation, efficiency, diligence, orderliness, punctuality, frugality, scrupulous honesty, rationality in decisions on action, preparedness for change, alertness to opportunities, energetic enterprise, integrity and self-reliance, cooperativeness and willingness to take the long view. (Myrdal, *ibid.,* vol. 1, pp. 57–69). It is surprising how Myrdal could believe that all these ideals are "indigenous" to the West and "alien" to all developing (including Muslim) countries.

10 Ragnar Nurkse, *Problems of Capital Formation in Underdeveloped Countries* (1953), p. 4.

11 See H. W. Singer, "Economic Progress in Developed Countries", *Social Research,* March 1949. See also Gunnar Myrdal, *Rich Lands and Poor* (1957), pp. 11–38, and *Asian Drama* (1968), vol. 3, pp. 1844–5.

12 There was considerable literature on the theories of stages of growth. For a review, see, Bert F. Hoselitz, "Theories of Stages of Economic Growth", in B. F. Hoselitz, *et al., Theories of Economic Growth,* (1960), pp. 193–238.

13 For examples of relatively pessimistic predictions for particular countries, see IBRD, *The Basis of a Programme for Columbia* (1950); Willard Thorp, "Some Basic Policy Issues in Economic Development", *American Economic Review,* May 1951, pp. 407–17; G. E. Britnell, "Factors in the Economic Development of Ceylon", *American Economic Review,* May 1953, pp. 115–25. See also W. A. Lewis, "A Review of Economic Development", *Manchester School,* May 1965, pp. 1–16.

14 H. F. Williamson in his comments on the Abramovitz paper in Haley (1952), vol. 2, p. 182.

15 W. Arthur Lewis, "Reflections on Development", in Gustav Ranis and T. Paul Schultz, *The State of Development Economics: Progress and Perspectives* (1988), pp. 3–14 and 16–19.

16 Harvey Leibenstein, *Economic Backwardness and Economic Growth* (1957) pp. 96, 98.

17 *Ibid.,* p. 96.

18 Some of the economists whose writings were influential in providing various elements of the socialist strategy were: Nurkse, Myrdal, Hirschman, Balogh, Rosenstein Rodan, Chenery, Prebisch, Singer and Streeten. Those who continued to emphasise the superiority of the market were: Haberler, Viner, Bauer and Yamey, and Schultz. For detailed references see Deepak Lal, *The Poverty of Development Economics* (1983), p. 5.

19 See for example, Albert Hirschman, "The Rise and Decline of Development Economics", in *Essays in Trespassing* (1981); and Gunnar Myrdal, *Economic Theory and Underdeveloped Regions* (1957).

20 See W. W. Rostow, "Take-off into Self-sustained Economic Growth", *Economic Journal,* March 1986.

21 For a brief description of the Stalinist model from Russian sources, see Dong Fureng, "Development Theory and Problems of Socialist Development Economics", in Ranis and Schultz (1988), pp. 235–7.

22 Nurkse, *Problems of Capital Formation in Underdeveloped Countries* (1953), p. 13.

23 P. N. Rosenstein-Rodan, "Notes, on the Theory of the 'Big Push' ", in Howard S. Ellis, ed., *Economic Development for Latin America* (1961), p. 1.

24 Myrdal, *Asian Drama* (1968), vol. 3, p. 1899.

25 *Ibid.*, p. 1900.

26 M. L. Qureshi, *Strategy of Industrial Planning and Development in Pakistan* (1965), p. 6.

27 Gottfried Haberler "Liberal and Illiberal Development Policy", in Gerald M. Meier, (ed.), *Pioneers in Development* (1987) p. 66.

28 The literature on economic development is full of assertions that an improvement in income distribution is in direct conflict with economic growth. For a summary of these views, see William R. Cline, *Potential Effects of Income Redistribution on Economic Growth* (1973), Chapter 2.

29 Government of India, Planning Commission, *The First Five Year Plan: A Summary* (1952), p. 8.

30 Government of Pakistan, *The Constitution of the Republic of Pakistan,* (1962), p. 13.

31 Government of Pakistan, National Planning Board, *The First Five Year Plan 1955–60,* (1957), pp. 1 ff; and *The Second Five Year Plan 1960–65* (1960), pp. xv, 1.

32 Arthur W. Lewis, *The Theory of Economic Growth* (1955), p. 9.

33 Peter T. Bauer and Basil S. Yamey, *The Economics of Underdeveloped Countries* (1957), p. 168.

34 United Nations, ECAFE, "Criteria for Allocating Investment Resources among Various Fields of Development in Underdeveloped Countries", June 1961, p. 30.

35 Harry G. Johnson, *Money, Trade and Economic Growth* (1962), p. 159.

36 G. Fields, "Income Distribution and Economic Growth", in Ranis and Schultz (1988), p. 460; Irma Adelman and Erik Thorbecke (eds.), *Theory and Design of Economic Development* (1966).

37 Bauer and Yamey (1957), p. 168. See also W. Galenson and H. Leibenstein, "Investment Criteria, Productivity and Economic Development", *Quarterly Journal of Economics*, August 1955, pp. 343–70.

38 Simon Kuznets, "Economic Growth and Income Inequality", *American Economic Review*, March 1955; "Quantitative Aspects of the Economic Growth of Nations: VIII, Distribution of Income by Size", *Economic Development and Cultural Change*, January 1963; and *Modern Economic Growth* (1966).

39 See J. G. Williamson and P. H. Lindert, *American Inequality: A Macro-Economic History* (1980); J. G. Williamson, *Did British Capitalism Breed Inequality?* (1985); and J. G. Williamson, "The Historical Content of the Classical Labour Surplus Model", *Population and Development Review*, June 1985, pp. 171–91. See also Williamson's comments on Lewis' paper in Ranis and Schultz (1987), p. 29.

40 Bauer and Yamey (1957), p. 206, see also p. 168.

41 W. Arthur Lewis, *The Theory of Economic Growth* (1955).

42 "Strategy of the Third Plan", *Problems in the Third Plan – A Critical Miscellany*, p. 50.

43 Mahboobul Haq, *The Strategy of Economic Planning: A Case Study of Pakistan* (1963) p. 30.

44 Myrdal, *Asian Drama* (1968), vol. 2, p. 740.

45 *Ibid.*, p. 808.

46 *Ibid.*, p. 807.

47 One such economist was Gunnar Myrdal. Stress on economic and social equality runs through all his writings and particularly so in the *Asian Drama* (1968).

48 Morawetz (1977), p. 9.

49 This may be clearly seen from the identity, Y=C+I+G+X-M, where Y = gross domestic product; C = consumption; I = gross domestic investment; G = government spending; X = exports; and M = imports. If C+I+G = A, where A represents gross domestic absorption, then Y = (A-M) + X. For developing countries, which are encountering both internal and external imbalances, a successful strategy to raise Y and lower the imbalances would require a rise not only in X but also in (A-M), which is the domestic absorption of domestically-produced goods and services. Since A needs to be reduced to remove the internal imbalance, the only way (A-M) may be raised is by

lowering M more than in proportion to the decline in A. Although import-substitution would be an important way to realise this goal, it would not be sufficient. It would also be necessary to squeeze substantially the import of luxury and inessential consumer goods so that the import of essential consumer and capital goods proceeds as desired.

50 Douglas Dosser, "General Investment Criteria for Less Developed Countries", *Scottish Journal of Political Economy,* June 1962, pp. 93–8.

51 Hla Myint, "Neoclassical Development Analysis: Its Strengths and Limitations", in Meier (1987), p. 118.

52 See ILO, *Employment Objectives in Economic Development: Report of a Meeting of Experts* (1961), pp. 28–32.

53 UNCTADs 1989 *Trade and Development Report* pours some cold water on the idea that trade policy reforms necessarily promote the economic growth of developing countries. A study of 32 developing countries which followed varying trade policies during the 1980s, revealed that favourable export performance was not always synonymous with good overall economic performance. See also, "Export Reforms No Guarantee of Economic Growth", *Financial Times,* 6 September 1989, p. 6.

54 *The Economist,* 22 July 1989, p. 65.

55 Clemens Boonekamp, "Industrial Policies of Industrial Countries", *Finance and Development,* March 1989, p. 17.

56 Peter Winglee, "Agricultural Trade Policies of Industrial Countries", *Finance and Development,* March 1989, p. 10.

57 See Sam Laird and Alexander Yeats, "Non-tariff Barriers of Developed Countries, 1966–68", *Finance and Development,* March 1989, pp. 12–13.

58 United Nations Conference on Trade and Development (CTAD), *Trade and Development Report, 1985,* pp. 123–4. For the external debt of developing countries, see note 65.

59 See Hollis Chenery with A. Strout, "Foreign Assistance and Economic Development", *American Economic Review,* September 1966; and Henry Bruton, "The Two-gap Approach to Aid and Development", *American Economic Review,* September 1966.

60 The average rate of inflation has continually risen in developing countries from 10 per cent per annum in 1965–73 to 26 per cent in 1974–82 and 51 per cent in 1983–87. IBRD, *World Development Report,* 1989, p. 62.

61 Haberler, in Meier (1987), p 70.

62 Henry Bruton, *Inflation in a Growing Economy* (1961), p. 57.

63 *Ibid.,* p. 58.

64 Lewis, in Ranis and Schultz (1988), p. 22.

65 The total external debt of all developing countries rose from $639 billion in 1980 to a projected $1,341 billion in 1990. (IBRD, *World Debt Tables: External Debt of Developing Countries 1990–91*, vol. 1, p. 12.)

66 Gerald Meier, *Leading Issues in Development Economics: Selected Materials and Commentary* (1964), p. 563.

67 J. K. Galbraith, *Economic Development in Perspective* (1962), pp. 9–10.

68 Michael Camdessus, ''Opening Remarks'', Vittoria Corbo, *et al.*, *Growth-Oriented Adjustment Programmes* (1987), p. 7.

69 Morawetz (1977), p. 10.

70 *Ibid.*, p. 71.

71 Gerald Meier, *Emerging from Poverty: The Economics that Really Matters* (1984), pp. 5 and 184.

72 Cited by *Ibid.*, p. 29.

73 Cited by *Ibid.*, p. 2.

74 *Ibid.*

75 Dudley Seers ''The Meaning of Development'', *International Development Review*, December 1969.

76 Barber Conable, ''Opening Remarks'', Corbo, *et al.* (1987), p. 6.

77 IMF, *Fund-Supported Programmes, Fiscal Policy, and Income Distribution*, IMF Occasional Paper No. 46 (September 1986), p. 1.

78 IMF, *The Implications of Fund-Supported Adjustment Programmes for Poverty: Experience of Selected Countries*, Occasional Paper No. 58 (1988), pp. 1 and 32. See also Occasional Paper No. 55, *Theoretical Aspects of the Design of Fund-Supported Adjustment Programmes*, September 1987.

79 IMF, Occasional Paper No. 58 (1988), p. 17.

80 See Ronald Findlay, ''Trade, Development and the State'', in Ranis and Schultz (1988), pp. 92–3; see also Myint in Meier, *Pioneers in Development* (1987), p. 117.

81 See Ronald Findlay's comments on Haberler in Meier, (1987), p. 96; see also Bhagwati and Kruger, ''Exchange Control, Liberalisation and Development'', *American Economic Review*, 2/1973, pp. 419–27.

82 Yasuo Masai, ''Japan'', *The New Encyclopaedia Britannica*, 15th ed., vol. 10, p. 49.

83 Marius B. Jansen, ''Japan, History of'', *The New Encyclopaedia Britannica*, 15th ed., vol. 10, p. 88; South Korea, Agriculture in Korea (1970), pp. 5–17; and Oh Young-Kyun, ''Agrarian Reform and Economic Development: A Case Study of Korean Agriculture'', *Koreana Quarterly*, 1969, p. 99.

84 Australian Bureau of Agricultural and Research Economics, *Japanese Agricultural Policies,* Policy Monograph No. 3, Canberra, 1988.

85 Jeffrey D. Sachs, "Trade and Exchange Rate Policies in Growth-Oriented Adjustment", in Corbo, *et al.* (1987), p. 301.

86 *Ibid.*, p. 303.

87 Myrdal, *Asian Drama* (1968), vol. 2, p. 747.

88 Jeffrey Sachs, *Social Conflict and Populist Policies in Latin America* (Cambridge, Mass.: National Bureau of Economic Research, Paper No. 2897).

89 Pranab Bardhan's comments on Ranis and Fei, in Ranis and Schultz (1988), p. 138.

90 Meier, *Emerging from Poverty* (1984), p. 61.

91 See Hla Myint, "Comparative Analysis of Taiwan's Economic Development with Other Countries", *Academic Economic Papers,* March 1982; see also Myint, in Meier, *Pioneers in Development* (1988), p. 133.

92 Ranis and Fei, in Ranis and Schultz (1988), p. 121.

93 See Meier, *Emerging from Poverty* (1984), p. 63; Tibor Scitovsky, "Economic Development in Taiwan and South Korea", Food Research Institute Studies, No. 4, 1985, pp. 215–64; and "Unequalled Economic Failures", *The Economist,* 17 June 1989, p. 83. According to Meier, Taiwan "is probably the most egalitarian of all capitalist countries" (Meier, *Emerging from Poverty* (1988), p. 63). This statement is probably inaccurate because a number of other countries have a lower Gini coefficient and better welfare services than those of Taiwan.

94 With respect to Japan, see R. Benedict, *The Chrysanthemum and the Sword* (1946); see also Yoshihara Kunio, *Japanese Economic Development: A Short Introduction* (1979), pp. 80–2.

95 For Japan, see T. Nakamura, tr. J. Kaminski, *The Postwar Japanese Economy: Its Development and Structure* (1981), p. 96.

96 World Bank, *World Tables, 1988-89,* vol. 1, pp. 66–9; and Directorate General of Budget, Accounting and Statistics, Republic of Taiwan, *Statistical Yearbook of the Republic of China, 1988,* p. 90.

97 In 1983, Japan's average tariff rate was 4.5 per cent for dutiable imports and 2.5 per cent for all imports, lower than in America or Europe. Even in textiles the tariff of 13.8 per cent was lower than America's 22.7 per cent and about the same as in Europe. "An Open and Shut Case", in "Japan: A Survey", *The Economist,* 7 October 1985, p. 20.

98 Lester Thurow, "A Time to Dismantle the World Economy", *The Economist,* 9 November 1985, p. 23.

99 Findlay, in Ranis and Schultz (1988), p. 90.

100 See IMF, *Government Financial Statistics Yearbook*, 1989, pp. 92–3, for data on worldwide defence spending except Japan, for which data have been obtained from other sources.

101 OECD, *Revenue Statistics of OECD Member Countries, 1965–89* (1990).

102 "Republic of Korea (South Korea)", *The Europa Yearbook, 1987*, pp. 1661–2.

103 See Parvez Hasan, *Korea: Problems and Issues in a Rapidly Growing Economy* (1976), p. 23.

104 Data for 1965 from Michael Prowse, "Unequal Society Rethinking its Priorities", *The Financial Times*, 15 June 1989, p. XII; and those for 1987 from the IBRD, *World Development Report, 1989*, p. 223.

105 Liz McGregor, "Labour Unrest, the Price of Success", *The International Herald Tribune*, 5 July 1989, p. 7.

106 Prowse (1989).

107 Hasan (1976), p. 23.

108 Kunio (1979), p. 111.

109 The ten largest Japanese banks, many of them associated with the names of zaibatsu families, are Dai-Ichi Kangyo, Mitsui Taiyo Kobe, Sumitomo, Fuji, Mitsubishi, Sanwa, Tokai, Daiwa, Bank of Tokyo, and Kyowa. Some of these banks are among the largest in the world. (See "Wedding Bells for Japan's Big Banks", *The Economist*, 2 September 1989, p. 79; and "Ranking the World's Largest Banks", *Institutional Investor*, June 1989, p. 119 ff.)

110 Forty-eight per cent of all wholesale stores and 83 per cent of all retail stores were classified as small-scale in 1985 (i.e., they had less than 5 employees). These, however, accounted for only 5 per cent of the value of all wholesale sales and 31 per cent of retail sales in that year. (Japan: Ministry of International Trade and Industry, *Commercial Statistics and White Paper on International Trade (1988)*.)

111 This is clearly reflected in the Gini coefficient for Japan, which rose from 0.380 in 1965 to 0.420 in 1971 (see Scitovsky, *op. cit.*).

112 *Forbes Magazine*, cited by *Arab News*, 10 July 1989, p. 14.

113 See Karel van Wolferen, *The Enigma of Japanese Power* (1989).

114 Yamaichi Research Institute of Securities and Economics, *Monthly Digest of Statistics*, January and September 1989 and July 1990, p. 1.

115 *Ibid.*, pp. 6 and 126.

116 Nikko Research Centre, *Analysis of Japanese Industries for Investors, 1990* (January 1990), p. 202.

117 According to Bill Emmott, "By leading a fancier and more visibly opulent life, the new rich are setting an example to the millions who have only moderate wealth. The effect of their riches is trickling down, affecting what people spend, why they buy and what they aspire to. The old, austere homogeneity of Japanese life is breaking down." (Bill Emmott, *The Sun also Sets: Why Japan will not be Number One* (1989).

118 See, "South Korea: Land to the Dweller", *The Economist,* 16 September 1989, p. 80; and "A Dangerous Game in Taipei: Taiwan's Stock Market was once a Sleepy Casino, Now it's Hyperactive", *ibid.,* 9 September 1989, p. 113. See also the special surveys on Taiwan and South Korea, *Financial Times,* 10 October 1989 and 16 May 1990.

119 Meier, "On Getting Policies Right", in Meier, *Pioneers in Development* (1987), p. 70.

120 Morawetz (1977), p. 71.

121 Gary Fields, "Income Distribution and Economic Growth", in Ranis and Schultz (1988), pp. 468–9.

122 Morawetz (1977), p. 7

123 See Deepak Lal (1984).

124 Meier, *Emerging from Poverty* (1984), p. 233

125 *Ibid.,* p. 228.

126 *Ibid.,* p. 90.

127 Development Committee, *Strengthening Efforts to Reduce Poverty* (1989), p. 3.

128 *Ibid.,* p. 5.

PART II

THE ISLAMIC RESPONSE

يَٰٓأَيُّهَا ٱلَّذِينَ ءَامَنُوا۟ ٱسْتَجِيبُوا۟ لِلَّهِ
وَلِلرَّسُولِ إِذَا دَعَاكُمْ لِمَا يُحْيِيكُمْ

O Believers! Respond to God and to His Prophet when he calls you towards that which will give you life (Qur'an, 8: 24)

إِنَّ ٱللَّهَ لَا يُغَيِّرُ مَا بِقَوْمٍ
حَتَّىٰ يُغَيِّرُوا۟ مَا بِأَنفُسِهِمْ

God does not change the condition of a people until they change their own inner selves (Qur'an, 13: 11)

CHAPTER 5

The Islamic Worldview and Strategy

The first four chapters have discussed the reasons for the inability of the rich capitalist and socialist countries as well as the developing economies to realise simultaneously the goals of both efficiency and equity by means of strategies based on the secularist Enlightenment worldview. The Muslim countries have therefore no reason to accept these strategies as models if they wish to realise the *maqāṣid al-Sharī'ah,* which are far more comprehensive in their coverage of elements necessary for overall human well-being than any secularist system is ever likely to envisage. Nor do the Muslim countries have much time in which to act. There is already considerable unrest and dissatisfaction and, unless they give utmost priority to the realisation of the *maqāṣid,* socio-political discontent will intensify, leading to near disintegration of their societies.

The Muslim countries therefore need a different economic system – a system able to provide all the elements necessary for human well-being in accordance with the demands of brotherhood and socio-economic justice. The system should be able not only to remove the imbalances but also to bring about a reallocation of resources in such a way that the goals of both efficiency and equity are simultaneously realised. It should be able to motivate the participants to abide by its principles and to give of their best not only in their own interest but also in the interest of society. The system cannot succeed unless it is able to create a positive environment through comprehensive socio-economic restructuring. Such restructuring may be difficult to realise unless all centres of power in the society are so adapted through political, economic and social reform such that no individual or group is able to derive an undue advantage by violating the basic principles of the system.

To create an equilibrium between scarce resources and the claims on them in a way that realises both efficiency and equity, it is necessary to focus on human beings themselves rather than on the market or the state. Human beings constitute the living and indispensable element of an economic system. They are the ends as well as the means, and unless they are reformed and motivated to pursue their self-interest within the constraints of social well-being, nothing can succeed, neither the 'invisible hand' of the market nor the 'visible hand' of central planning, in actualising socio-economic goals. Individuals in turn receive important impulses from the economic system and its institutions, and no reform of individuals can be effective unless it also penetrates the economic system and brings about such a restructuring of life-styles and the economic-financial machinery that unnecessary claims on resources are minimised and all sources of injustice, exploitation, and instability are substantially reduced, if not eliminated. There is thus a two-way relationship between human beings and the economic system. Both need to be addressed. Any system that gives primary emphasis in its strategy to only the market or the state, albeit in the pious hope of solving human problems, will ultimately end up degrading human beings and increasing their misery.

Human beings cannot become the end and the means of an economic system unless the system is based on a worldview that restores to them their enviable place of importance at centre stage, around whom everything else is made to revolve. The worldviews of both capitalism and socialism do not give such importance to human beings and, being based on social Darwinism or dialectics, do not incorporate an inherent belief in human brotherhood, socio-economic justice and the trust nature of resources. There is an overly exaggerated emphasis on 'survival of the fittest' or 'class struggle' and 'maximum want satisfaction' or 'material conditions of life'. They do not have a motivating system to induce human beings to work in the interest of society, which is not always served by the pursuit of self-interest by individuals, but also requires sacrifice of personal comfort and gain for the sake of others. These worldviews intensify claims and strife and lead not only to inefficiency and inequity in the allocation of resources but also to disillusion, crime, family and social breakdown, and, ultimately, to degradation of human beings.

The money and banking system exercises such a tremendous influence in modern-day economies that no economic system can sustain its health and vigour or contribute positively to the achievement of its socio-economic goals without its positive support. The money and banking system should therefore be reformed to eschew the excesses and imbalances which promote inequalities, conspicuous consumption, unemployment and unhealthy monetary expansion to the ultimate detriment of all. It should, in general, support need satisfaction, high rate of employment, and broad-based ownership of means of production.

Is it possible to design such a just and sane economic system? The primary aim of this chapter is to indicate briefly that it is, provided the system is rooted in the Islamic worldview and strategy. The translation of this worldview and strategy into specific policies will be addressed in Chapters 6 to 11.

Islam has a worldview and a strategy which are in harmony with the *maqāṣid* and which can enable it to provide the blueprint for a just and workable solution to the problems faced by Muslim countries, provided that there is the necessary political will to adopt its teachings and to implement its reforms. Since the economies of a number of Muslim countries are still in the earlier stages of development, it may not be too difficult for them to adopt a new design and direction for their economies and their financial systems. However, with the passage of time it may become more and more difficult to do so.

THE WORLDVIEW

Islam is a universal faith which is simple and easy to understand and rationalise. It is based on three fundamental principles which are: *tawḥīd* (unity), *khilāfah* (vicegerency), and *'adālah* (justice). These principles not only frame the Islamic worldview, they also constitute the fountain-head of the *maqāṣid* and the strategy. Thus there is no question of a patchwork or an after-thought in response to the conflicting demands of pluralist groups or social classes. The Islamic worldview, *maqāṣid* and strategy are blended together into a consistent whole and there is complete harmony between them. For the benefit of those who are not familiar with these concepts and to indicate how the Islamic worldview, *maqāṣid* and strategy are dovetailed into a consistent whole to enable the Islamic economic system to realise its goals, it is desirable to state briefly the meaning and significance of these three fundamental principles.

TAWḤĪD (Divine Unity)

The foundation stone of the Islamic faith is *tawḥīd* (Oneness and Unity of God). On this concept rests its whole worldview and strategy. Everything else logically emanates from it. It means that the universe has been consciously designed and created by the Supreme Being, Who is One and Unique, and did not come into existence by chance or accident. (Qur'ān, 3: 191, 38: 27 and 23: 15.) Everything created by Him has a purpose. It is this purpose which gives meaning and significance to the existence of the Universe, of which man is a part. After creating the Universe, the Supreme Being did not retire. He is actively involved in its affairs (Qur'ān, 10: 3 and 32: 5) and is aware of and deeply concerned with even the minutest details (Qur'ān, 31: 16 and 67: 14).[1]

KHILĀFAH (Vicegerency)

The human being is His *khalīfah* or vicegerent on earth (Qur'ān, 2: 30, 6: 165, 35: 39, 38: 28 and 57: 7) and has been endowed with all the spiritual and mental characteristics, as well as material resources, to enable him to live up to his mission effectively.[2] Within the terms of reference of his *khilāfah* he is free, and also able to think and reason, to choose between right and wrong, fair and unfair, and to change the conditions of his life, his society and the course of history, if he so wishes. He is by nature good and noble (Qur'ān, 15: 29, 30: 30 and 95: 4) and is capable of preserving his goodness and nobility and rising to the challenges before him if he receives proper education and guidance and is properly motivated. Since he is good by nature, he feels psychologically happy and satisfied only as long as he stays in, or moves closer to, his inner nature, and feels unhappy and miserable when he deviates from it.[3]

The resources with which God has endowed this world are not unlimited. They are however sufficient to cater for the well-being of *all,* if used 'efficiently' and 'equitably'. The human being is free to choose between the alternative uses of these resources. However, since he is not the only one who is a *khalīfah* and there are millions of other human beings who are *khalīfahs* like him and who are his brothers and equals, one of his real tests lies in utilising the God-given resources in such an 'efficient' and 'equitable' manner that the well-being *(falāḥ)* of all is ensured. This is possible only if the resources are used with a sense of responsibility and a constraint determined by Divine Guidance and the *maqāṣid.*

The concepts of *tawḥīd* and *khilāfah* are inherently in conflict with the concepts of 'born sinner', or 'pawn on the chessboard of history', or 'tabula rasa', or 'condemned to be free'.

Why would the Great, Merciful God create a 'born sinner' and condemn him eternally for no fault of his? As Kant rightly pointed out, "the most awkward way to understand the spreading of moral evil and its continuation within human history is to imagine that it comes to us from the first parents through 'inheritance'."[4] The idea of original sin implies that sinfulness is genetically transferable and that each human being comes into this world already influenced by the failures and sins of others. Moreover, if a 'saviour' had to come to 'atone' for the 'original sin' which he did not commit, why did he come so late in history and not with the appearance of the first human beings on earth? If man is a 'born sinner' how can he be held responsible for his deeds? The concept of 'original sin' is thus in sharp conflict with individual responsibility for all deeds that the Qur'ān unequivocally emphasises (e.g., 6: 164, 17: 15, 35: 18, 39: 7 and 53: 38). Such a concept can, as rightly pointed out by Lewis, "do great harm" by "undermining the sense of responsibility, for collective guilt is not the guilt of anyone in particular".[5] The concept of original sin is also in conflict with God's attributes of *al-Raḥmān* and *al-Raḥīm* (the Most Merciful and the Most Compassionate), which a Muslim repeats most often during his lifetime. It is beyond human capacity to understand why such a Merciful God would act so unjustly as to load all human beings with the sin of their first parents. It would be impossible for Him to do so, given that He is a Loving and Forgiving God and has all conceivable good attributes (Qur'ān, 7: 180). No wonder even the Rationalists and the Romantics of the nineteenth century rejected the notion of an inherent flaw in human nature (original sin), as do almost all modern philosophers.[6]

Similarly the concepts of 'pawn' and 'tabula rasa' which are built into most Western theories of human nature dwarf human beings into insignificance by denying the existence of an immortal soul having an identity of its own and capable of steering its own destiny by influencing the forces around it. All these theories imply that the human mind is like a blank slate upon which external factors record whatever impressions they choose to. Human beings are, in this view, passive and helpless; they have no mission to live for. Their lives are determined by material forces of history (Marx), or conditioned by psychological (Freud), instinctive (Lorenz) and environmental (Parolv, Watson, Skinner and others) influences. This leads to the verdict, in step with Skinner, that "individual freedom is a myth".[7] Determinism and human responsibility cannot be reconciled with each other.[8] Determinism not only lowers human dignity but also negates human responsibility for the prevailing conditions, and for the inefficient and inequitable distribution of resources.

Determinism implies that the human condition cannot change until the psychic forces, social structures and the material conditions of life change. But who will change these if human beings are passive and their life is determined and conditioned? Moreover, if life is determined, then 'alienation' is also an integral part of it and neither the bourgeoisie nor the proletariat can be held responsible for it. Why then blame the bourgeoisie for the 'alienation' of the working class or ask the workers to rise? The determined nature of man's existence should by definition be unchangeable by human effort. The Marxist prescription of eliminating the bourgeoisie and private property, and establishing in its place state despotism, could not but introduce another kind of determinism in human life, that imposed by the politburo.

At the other extreme to the determinists is Sartre's existentialism.[9] There being no God, man is "condemned to be free". There is no limit to his freedom except that he is not free to cease being free.[10] Every aspect of man's mental life is intentional, chosen and his responsibility. This is no doubt an improvement on determinism. But for Sartre, this freedom is absolute – everything is permitted. There is no ultimate meaning or purpose inherent in human life. There are no transcendent or objective values set for human beings, neither laws of God, nor Platonic Forms nor anything else. Human beings are 'forlorn' and 'abandoned' in the world to look after themselves completely. The only foundation for values is human freedom, and there can be no external or objective justification for the values anyone chooses to adopt.[11] Such a concept of absolute freedom can only lead to the capitalist notions of *laissez-faire* and value neutrality. There can be no question of having agreed values, and of imposing restrictions on individual freedom to create harmony between individual and social interest, or of leading to an efficient and equitable allocation and distribution of resources, not brought about automatically by market forces.

In sharp contrast with these ideas, the concept of *khilāfah* raises human beings to an honourable and dignified status in the universe (Qur'ān, 17: 70) and provides the life of both man and woman with a meaning and a mission. The meaning is provided by the conviction that they have not been created in vain (Qur'ān, 3: 192 and 23: 115), but rather to fulfil a mission. Their mission is to act in accordance with Divine tenets in spite of being free. This is what is implied by *'ibādah* or worship (Qur'ān, 51: 56) in the Islamic sense, an inviolable imperative of which is fulfilling one's obligations towards other human beings *(ḥuqūq al-'ibād),* to promote their well-being and to actualise the *maqāṣid.* No wonder that Islam, like some other great religions, places a greater emphasis on duties than on rights.[12] The fundamental wisdom behind this is that if duties are fulfilled by everyone, self-interest is automatically held within bounds and the rights of all are undoubtedly safeguarded.

Success in this Mission requires spiritual uplift through total commitment to the Creator, Who is the Wise, the Just, the

Benevolent and the Loving God, and to the Guidance provided by Him. Human beings must submit to none but Him, to no other values but His, and to live for no other mission but His. They are responsible to Him for all their deeds in this world. They are, however, accountable only for their own actions (Qur'ān, 6: 164, 17: 15 and 35: 18) and not for the actions of others, past or present, except to the extent to which they are themselves the ultimate cause. Even though they are destined to die (Qur'ān, 3: 185, 4: 78 and 29: 57), their life is not confined to this world alone, which is a place of trial and test, and hence temporary. Their real abode is the Hereafter, where they will be rewarded or punished in accordance with how they have discharged their responsibilities in this world. They can never succeed in escaping their accountability before God. Their life is thus not "destined to extinction in the vast death of the solar system", and the whole temple of man's achievement will not be "buried beneath the debris of a universe in ruins", as Bertrand Russell pessimistically expected.[13]

The concept of *khilāfah* has a number of implications, or corollaries. These are:

(1) *Universal Brotherhood*

Khilāfah implies the fundamental unity and brotherhood of mankind. Everyone is a *khalīfah* and not any single privileged person, or members of a particular race or group or country. This makes the social equality and dignity of all human beings, white or black, high or low, a cardinal element of the Islamic faith. The criteria for determining a man's worth are not his race, family or wealth but rather his character (which is a reflection of his faith and practice) and service to humanity.[14] The Prophet, may the peace and blessings of God be on him, said categorically: "All human beings are dependents of God and the most beloved of them before Him are those who are best to His dependents."[15]

Within the framework of this concept of brotherhood, the right attitude towards other human beings is not 'might is right', struggle to serve only one's own 'self-interest', or 'survival of the fittest', but rather mutual sacrifice and cooperation to fulfil the basic needs of all, to develop the entire human potential, and to enrich human life.[16] Competition is hence to be encouraged to the extent to which it is healthy, raises efficiency, and helps promote human well-being, the overall objective of Islam. As soon as it crosses the limits and contributes to snobbery and jealousy and promotes ruthlessness or mutual destruction, it must be corrected.[17]

(2) *Resources are a Trust*

Since all resources at the disposal of human beings have been provided by God, man as *khalīfah* is not their primary owner. He is just a trustee *(amīn)*.[18] While this trusteeship *(amānah)* does not mean "a negation of private property", it does carry a number of very important implications which create a revolutionary difference in the concept of private ownership of resources in Islam and other economic systems.[19]

Firstly, the resources are for the benefit of all and not just a few (Qur'ān, 2: 29). They must be utilised equitably for the well-being of all.

Secondly, everyone must acquire resources rightfully, in a manner indicated by the Qur'ān and the *Sunnah*. Acting otherwise constitutes a violation of the terms of *khilāfah*.[20]

Thirdly, even the resources so acquired, should not be disposed of except in accordance with the terms of the trust, which are the well-being not only of one's own self and family but also that of others.[21] It is not becoming for man as a trustee to be selfish, acquisitive and unscrupulous, and to work merely for his own well-being.

Fourthly, no one is authorised to destroy or waste the God-given resources. Doing so has been equated by the Qur'ān with the spreading of *fasād* (mischief, viciousness and corruption), which God abhors (Qur'ān, 2: 205). Accordingly, when Abū Bakr, the first Caliph, sent Yazīd ibn Abī Sufyān on a war assignment, he exhorted him not to kill indiscriminately or to destroy vegetation or animal life even in enemy territory.[22] If this is not allowed even in war and enemy territory, there is no question of its being allowed in peacetime and home territory. Hence there can be absolutely no room for destroying output, by say, burning or dumping into the ocean, to force up or to maintain prices at a higher level.

(3) *Humble Life-Style*

The only life-style that suits the *khalīfah* of God is one that is humble. It should not reflect arrogance, pomp and grandeur, or moral laxity. Such life-styles lead to extravagance and waste and result in unnecessary pressure on resources, reducing a society's ability to satisfy the needs of all. They also promote unscrupulous ways of earning and generate inequalities of income beyond the normal distribution that is warranted by differences in skill, initiative, effort and risk. They also erode the feeling of equality and weaken the bonds of brotherhood that are an essential characteristic of a Muslim society.[23]

(4) *Human Freedom*

Since human beings are the *khalīfahs* of God, they are subservient to none but Him. Serfdom of any kind, irrespective of whether it is social, political or economic, is, therefore, alien to the teachings of Islam. The Qur'ān states that one of the primary objectives of the Prophet Muḥammad, may the peace and blessings of God be on him, is to release mankind from the burdens and chains that have been imposed upon them (Qur'ān, 7: 157). Accordingly, no one, not even the state, has the right to abrogate this freedom and to subject human life to any kind of bondage or regimentation. It is this teaching which prompted 'Umar, the second Caliph, to ask: "Since when have you enslaved people although they were given birth as free individuals by their mothers?"[24]

This does not imply that human beings are free to do anything they want. They are subject to the *Sharī'ah,* which aims at the well-being of all by subjecting everyone to a discipline. They are thus free only within the bounds of social responsibility as specified by the *Sharī'ah.* Any system, which either subjects human beings to serfdom or gives them undue freedom to overstep the constraints imposed by the Creator Himself through the *Sharī'ah,* is in conflict with the dignity and accountability embodied in the concept of *khilāfah* and cannot contribute to the well-being of all human beings.

'ADĀLAH (Justice)

Brotherhood, which is an integral part of the concepts of *tawḥīd* and *khilāfah* would remain a hollow concept having no substance if it were not accompanied by socio-economic justice.[25] Justice has been held by the jurists to be an absolutely indispensable ingredient of the *maqāṣid al-Sharī'ah,* so far so that it is impossible to conceive of an ideal Muslim society where justice has not been established. Islam is absolutely unambiguous in its objective of eradicating from human society all traces of *ẓulm,* which is a comprehensive Islamic term referring to all forms of inequity, injustice, exploitation, oppression and wrongdoing, whereby a person deprives others of their rights or does not fulfil his obligations towards them.[26]

Establishment of justice and eradication of all forms of injustice have been stressed by the Qur'ān as the primary mission of all God's Messengers (Qur'ān, 57: 25). There are no less than a hundred different expressions in the Qur'ān embodying the notion of justice, either directly in such words as *'adl, qisṭ, mīzān,* or in a variety of indirect expressions. Besides, there are over two hundred admonitions in the Qur'ān against injustice expressed in such words as *ẓulm, ithm, ḍalāl* and others.[27] In fact the Qur'ān places justice 'nearest to piety' (Qur'ān, 5: 8) in terms of its importance in the Islamic faith. Piety is naturally the most important because it serves as a springboard for all rightful action, including justice. The Prophet, peace and blessings of God be on him, was even more emphatic. He equated the absence of justice with "absolute darkness" and warned: "Beware of injustice for injustice will lead to absolute darkness on the Day of Judgement".[28] No wonder, Ibn Taymiyyah felt encouraged to assert that: "God upholds the just state even if it is unbelieving, but does not uphold the unjust state even if it is believing", and that "the world can survive with justice and unbelief, but not with injustice and Islam."[29] Injustice and Islam are at variance with each other and cannot coexist without either of the two being uprooted or weakened.

The intense commitment of Islam to brotherhood and justice demands that all resources at the disposal of human beings, a sacred trust from God, be utilised to actualise the *maqāṣid al-Sharī'ah,* four of which are particularly important within the framework of discussion here. These are: (1) need fulfilment; (2) respectable source of earning; (3) equitable distribution of income and wealth; and (4) growth and stability.

(1) *Need Fulfilment*

The logical implication of brotherhood and of the trust nature of resources is that these resources must be utilised to satisfy the basic needs of all individuals and to assure everyone a standard of living that is humane and respectable, and in harmony with the dignity of man inherent in his being the *khalīfah* of God.[30] The Prophet, may the peace and blessings of God be on him, went to the extent of saying: "He is not a man of faith who eats his fill when his neighbour is hungry."[31] Since resources are relatively limited, this goal cannot be actualised unless claims on the available resources are made only "within the limits of humanity"[32] and general well-being. Need fulfilment must be within the framework of simple-living and, while it should include comforts, it cannot take the dimension of waste and snobbery, which have been prohibited by Islam but which have nevertheless become rampant in Muslim countries.

This stress on need fulfilment in Islam should not be construed as an after-thought arising out of the recent Western discussion of the subject.[33] It has received an important place in the *fiqh* and other Islamic literature throughout Muslim history. The jurists have unanimously held the view that it is the collective duty *(farḍ kifāyah)* of Muslim society to take care of the basic needs of the poor.[34] In fact, according to Shatibi, this is the *raison d'être* of society itself.[35] All modern scholars, including Mawlana Mawdudi, Imam Hasan al-Banna, Sayyid Qutb, Mustafa al-Sibā'ī, Abu Zahrah, Baqir al-Sadr, Muhammad al-Mubarak and Yusuf al-Qaradawi, are also unanimous on this point.[36]

(2) *Respectable Source of Earning*

The dignity attached to the status of *khalīfah* implies that need fulfilment must be through the individual's own effort. Accordingly, the jurists have emphasised the personal obligation of every Muslim *(farḍ 'ayn)* to earn a living to support himself and his family.[37] They have further stressed that without fulfilling this obligation, a Muslim cannot maintain his body and mind in a state of health and efficiency adequate to carry out even his devotional obligations.[38] Since a Muslim may not be able to fulfil the duty of earning an honest living unless opportunities are available for self-employment or employment, it may be inferred that it is the collective obligation of a Muslim society to ensure for everyone an equal opportunity to earn an honest living in keeping with his ability and effort.

Nevertheless, there are bound to be those who are unable to earn enough through their own effort because of some handicap or inability. It is the collective obligation of the Muslim *ummah (farḍ kifāyah)* to help such people fulfil their needs, without stigma or recrimination. In a closely-knit, brotherhood-oriented Muslim community, this collective obligation of the *ummah* is to be discharged first by the family, friends, neighbours and *awqāf* (trusts) or altruistic organisations. Only when these are unable to fulfil their collective obligation, should the state enter into the picture. This will impose a smaller economic burden on the Islamic state. The ultimate objective of all help should be to enable those so helped to stand on their own feet through an increase in their ability to earn more. But until this becomes a reality, the help must also include income supplements. Islam has a built-in institutional arrangement to get the necessary wherewithal for this purpose through the obligatory payments of *zakāt* (including *'ushr*) and voluntary contributions in the form of *ṣadaqāt* and *awqāf*. The government should also make the maximum possible budgetary appropriations.

(3) *Equitable Distribution of Income and Wealth*

In spite of need fulfilment, there could be extreme inequalities of income and wealth. Inequalities can be admitted in a Muslim society primarily insofar as they are more or less in proportion to skill, initiative, effort and risk. These are bound to be normally distributed in a society where Islamic teachings are sincerely followed. Extreme or highly skewed inequalities are incompatible with Islamic teachings, which emphasise that resources are not only gifts of God to all human beings (Qur'ān,

2: 29) but also a trust (Qur'ān, 57: 7). There is accordingly no reason why they should remain concentrated in a few hands. Lack of an effective programme to reduce inequalities is bound to destroy, rather than foster, the feelings of brotherhood that Islam wishes to create. Hence Islam not only requires the fulfilment of everyone's needs, primarily through a respectable source of earning, but also emphasises an equitable distribution of income and wealth so that, in the words of the Qur'ān "wealth does not circulate only among your rich" (Qur'ān, 59: 7).

The Islamic stress on equitable distribution has been so intense that there have been some Muslims who have held the opinion that equality of wealth is essential in a Muslim society. Abū Dharr, a companion of the Prophet, may the peace and blessings of God be on him, was of the opinion that it is not proper for a Muslim to possess wealth beyond the essential needs of his family. However, most of the Prophet's companions did not agree with him in this extreme view. Abū Dharr was, however, not a proponent of equality of flows (incomes). He was in favour of equality of stocks (wealth accumulations). This, he asserted, could be attained if the entire surplus over 'genuine' expenses *(al-'afw)* was spent by the rich to improve the lot of their less fortunate brothers.[39] It is the general opinion of Muslim scholars that if the social behaviour pattern and the economy are restructured in accordance with Islamic teachings, there cannot be extreme inequalities of income and wealth in a Muslim society.

(4) *Growth and Stability*

It may not be possible for the Muslim *ummah* to realise the objectives of need fulfilment and a high level of self-employment and employment without using the available resources with maximum attainable efficiency, and generating a reasonably high rate of economic growth. Even the goal of equitable distribution of income and wealth would be realised faster and with smaller sacrifice on the part of the well-to-do if a higher rate of growth is attained and the poor are enabled to reap a proportionately larger share of the fruits of that growth. A better performance in terms of economic stability would also help reduce the suffering and inequities that recession, inflation and erratic movements in prices and exchange rates necessarily bring about. Accordingly, even in a Muslim society, which does not depend on Pareto optimality in the formulation of policies and does not emphasise economic growth for its own sake, the realisation of an optimum rate of economic growth and minimisation of economic instability would be necessary to fulfil the implications of *khilāfah* and *'adālah.*

THE STRATEGY

It is evident that, unlike both capitalism and socialism, the goals of Islam are absolute and a logical outcome of its underlying philosophy. They do not constitute a hotchpotch of incongruous elements resulting from the struggle for survival and domination between pluralist groups or social classes. They are so integral to the Islamic system that their realisation constitutes the criterion for measuring the level of Islamisation of a Muslim society. Of course, the harmony of goals with the worldview is not sufficient. It is also necessary to have a strategy that is also the logical outcome of the underlying philosophy, and, if put to work seriously, can enable the Muslim society to actualise its goals. Islam does have such a strategy. It consists of reorganising the entire economic system with a set of four indispensable and mutually-reinforcing elements:

(a) a socially-agreed filter mechanism;
(b) a strong motivating system to induce the individual to render his best in his own interest as well as in the interest of society;
(c) restructuring of the whole economy, with the objective of realising the *maqāṣid* in spite of scarce resources; and
(d) a positive and strong goal-oriented role for the government.

It is now important to see how the Islamic worldview, along with these specific elements of its strategy, can help the Islamic economic system to influence the allocation and distribution of resources in the direction of goal actualisation.

(a) THE FILTER MECHANISM

The relative scarcity of resources compared with the unlimited claims on them necessitates a filtering device. All claims on resources must be passed through this filter to serve the dual purpose of making them equal to the resources available and to realise the desired socio-economic goals. Whether or not the filter mechanism performs this dual function effectively will determine the success of the system.

Capitalism, as discussed in Chapter 1, gives license to the consumers to consume what they want in accordance with their individual preferences to maximise their utilities. It also gives license to the producers to produce what they want in response to consumer preferences with whatever combination of factors of production they deem fit to minimise their costs and to maximise their profits. Market-determined prices serve as the filtering device. Such prices bring about an equilibrium between demand and supply by determining not only what, but also how much, the utility-maximising consumers will consume and the profit-maximising producers will supply.

Since the background conditions are not fulfilled, the use of merely the price system as a filter mechanism, frustrates the realisation of socio-economic goals. Unhindered individual preferences, combined with value-free advertising and easy access to credit, creates unlimited wants, while the highly skewed income distribution enables the rich to transfer scarce resources for the satisfaction of their unnecessary wants. This not only squeezes the resources available for need satisfaction but also widens the savings-investment and export-import gaps and worsens the macroeconomic and external imbalances. Reliance on merely the price mechanism as a filtering device does help restore an equilibrium between demand and supply but at the expense of the poor, who are unable to fulfil their needs at the resulting higher prices from the limited means they have at their disposal. Their well-being thus suffers.

Replacement of the decentralised filter mechanism of the market system by planning and state control makes the position worse. It makes the system despotic without introducing any improvement in goal realisation. Centralising control over the allocation of resources into the hands of a bureaucracy, which does not have an effective way of getting information promptly about consumer preferences and producer costs, makes the decision-making process cumbersome, slow and inefficient. The bureaucracy does not even have the socially-agreed values or the motivating system to ensure the well-being of all. The only criterion it has at its disposal for allocation of resources is its own personal judgement which, without the help of socially-agreed values and market signals, cannot ensure an allocation of resources that takes into account the relative scarcity of resources or the relative urgency of need satisfaction. Moreover, the powerful position of its members gives them all the leverage they need to serve their own vested interest. The resultant allocation and distribution of resources is hence bound to be neither efficient nor equitable.

The best strategy for injecting equity into the allocation of resources is hence not the removal of the decentralised decision-making process of the market system. The decentralised system democratises the decision-making by enabling all individuals (consumers as well as producers) to participate. It also introduces greater efficiency by enabling prompt decision-making in response to changing circumstances. It would be better rather to complement the price mechanism by some other device that would eliminate or at least minimise unnecessary claims on resources – claims that lead to imbalances and serve as an obstacle in the way of need fulfilment.

Islam does this by introducing the moral filter. Allocation of resources is to be brought about by a double layer of filters. The first filter attacks the problem of unlimited wants at the very source, the inner consciousness of individuals, by changing the individual's preference scale in keeping with the demands of both *khilāfah* and *'adālah*. Islam makes it incumbent upon all Muslims to pass their potential claims on resources through the filter of Islamic values so that many are eliminated before they can be expressed in the market place. In this way claims on resources that do not contribute positively to or which divert from the realisation of human well-being are eliminated at source before exposure to the second filter of market prices.

The moral filter makes the claims on resources a function of human well-being and does not allow their use for other purposes. It does not, for example, permit the use of resources for morally prohibited activities – activities that would kill or harm human beings, animals or plants wantonly, either now or in the future and thereby reduce their well-being. It requires a humble life-style and does not allow extravagance or the use of resources for ostentation or vain competition – uses that do make a real difference in well-being. It also does not permit the destruction or wasteful use of resources (e.g., burning food to raise prices). If the banking system is also reorganised in such a way that it plays a complementary role in the filtering, claims on resources could be made to stay within the proper limits. The moral factor thus moderates and humanises the influence that wealth and power and financial intermediation are able to exercise in the allocation and distribution of resources.[40] As Barrington Moore has rightly indicated: "No human society can afford to permit all kinds of human behaviour. If it did permit them, it would soon cease to be a society."[41]

However, one of the basic issues of every society is who is capable of providing such a moral filter? Must a moral code have a Divine Origin and must it be backed by belief in accountability before God? The view of Islam, as that of some other religions, is that Divine sanction and belief in life-after-death are both necessary.

Firstly, the Divine sanction makes the rules of behaviour absolute and beyond dispute. Without the Divine sanction, they become the subject of personal judgement and dispute as happened in the West after its secularisation, until "their value came to be questioned altogether".[42] After their extensive but deep study of various civilisations, the Durants have drawn a very important lesson from history that: "There is no significant example in history before our time, of a society successfully maintaining moral life without the aid of religion."[43]

Secondly, who among human beings could be absolutely impartial and totally committed to the well-being of all? If human beings were to try to develop these norms themselves, there would be a natural tendency on their part to frame norms that are skewed in favour of the powerful and the vested interests, and not capable of serving the well-being of all. Even the slightest doubt about impartiality would negate the chances of a consensus.

Thirdly, human beings do not have the knowledge to assess

the effects of their own actions on others, especially those more remotely affected by them. Therefore, they need a well-meaning and knowledgeable outsider capable of visualising such effects to provide them with rules of behaviour that can save others from the adverse effect of their actions.[44]

Fourthly, the Supreme Being who has created human beings is alone capable of understanding their nature, their needs, their strengths and their weaknesses, and of serving as the Sole Guide and the Only Source of all values. In His Infinite Kindness He has not left human beings to grope in darkness; He has provided the needed Guidance through a chain of prophets starting from Adam himself – Guidance that can ensure the well-being of all.

Within the context of this logical framework, value neutrality is inconceivable. Value neutrality can be in harmony with only that system which glorifies individualism and self-interest or dialectics. It is without doubt in conflict with Islam which attaches primary importance to social responsibility and well-being of all. Values define the terms of reference of all *khalīfahs*. They all have to act in conformity with these values to actualise the *maqāṣid*. Collective value judgements are accordingly indispensable and any attempt to refrain from making such value judgements is bound to create confusion and chaos and frustrate the realisation of the well-being of all. After the claims on resources have been passed through the filter of socially-agreed values and unnecessary claims thus eliminated or minimised, the filter mechanism of market prices would be the more effective in bringing about an allocation of resources that is both efficient and equitable.

(b) THE RIGHT MOTIVATION

Efficiency and equity cannot be realised by merely having a proper filter mechanism. It is also necessary to motivate individuals to act accordingly. Capitalism assumes that self-interest will induce an individual to maximise efficiency while competition will serve as a constraint on his self-interest and help safeguard social interest. It was thus assumed by Adam Smith that the market system would be able to harmonise self-interest and social interest. Socialism did not trust the individual and assumed that his pursuit of self-interest would necessarily hurt the social interest. Therefore, it proposed the abolition of private property and profit and established strict state control over the allocation and distribution of resources to safeguard social interest.

But the pursuit of self-interest by individuals is not necessarily bad. Indeed, it is necessary for human development and an economic system cannot succeed in realising efficiency unless it allows it. The pursuit of self-interest becomes socially destructive only if it crosses certain limits and individuals are not willing to do things that need to be done to create a society which has brotherhood and socio-economic justice as its central objectives. However, while a rational individual would in any society normally be willing to render his best in his self-interest if he is able to get an adequate reward for his contribution, the question is: what would motivate him to work in the interest of society? Why should a consumer hold his claims on resources "within the limits of humanity" and make sacrifices for others, and why should a businessman not try to stifle competition or use questionable means to enrich himself? It is here that belief in accountability before God and the Hereafter become indispensable.

A self-interest whose vision is restricted to this finite world is bound to cultivate the evils of greed, unscrupulousness, and disregard for the interest of others. "Whenever they get a chance", observes *The Economist,* "rational economic agents try to benefit themselves at the expense of everybody else. So for many kinds of spillover a market solution is frustrated by the very force that usually makes markets work."[45] In a secularist, this-worldly society, self-interest cannot motivate individuals to fulfil their social obligations conscientiously except where doing so contributes to their this-worldly benefit. Pareto optimality is hence the only logical behaviour norm for such a society, irrespective of whether it is capitalist or socialist. Pareto was not wrong within the this-worldly framework in which his mind worked, like that of all other secularists.

Capitalism does not have an effective mechanism to motivate an individual to work in the interest of society unless that interest is served automatically by the pursuit of self-interest. Since the two interests are not necessarily harmonious and since the background conditions are not satisfied, reliance on the price system alone enables the rich to divert scarce resources to the satisfaction of their inessential wants at the expense of even the need-satisfying goods for the poor. Capitalism thus becomes inequitable. Socialism is worse because, by preventing the individual from pursuing his self-interest, it has deprived itself of a mechanism to motivate the individual to work efficiently. Moreover, its this-worldly perspective does not provide the individual with a motivation to work in the social interest either. Thus socialism fails to realise efficiency as well as equity.

If, however, the dimensions of accountability before an All-Powerful Being, from whom nothing can be hidden (Qur'ān, 5: 3), and a life-after-death are introduced, a higher rationality is created. These beliefs supply a powerful motivating force for socially-oriented action by giving self-interest an infinitely longer perspective. They imply that an individual's self-interest is not served only by improving his condition in this world but also in the Hereafter. Hence, if he is rational and seeks what is truly in his best interest, he will not act merely for his short-term this-worldly well-being but will also try to ensure his long-term well-being by working for the well-being of others through a reduction in his wasteful and unnecessary consumption in spite of the financial ability to be profligate. The resources which are thus saved can be diverted to the increased production and distribution of need-fulfilling goods, thus serving the interest of the poor. Similarly, the belief that this world is infinitesimally small compared to the Hereafter can prevent a businessman from enriching himself through questionable means, and so help others by not shrinking their frontiers of opportunity and depriving them of their independent livelihoods. These beliefs thus have the potential to work as a voluntary mechanism to motivate an individual to respond to the questions of what, how, and for whom to produce, in a way that would lead to an allocation and distribution in conformity with the dictates of general well-being.

While Islam provides a longer-term perspective for human action, it does not require individuals to deny their self-interest in this world. This would not have been practical. Any value system that does so cannot work. Islam in fact requires an individual to satisfy all his essential needs to remain physically and mentally healthy and efficient to be able to fulfil his responsibilities towards himself and his society and, in doing so, to develop his total potential. There is no point in shunning the good things that God has provided (Qur'ān, 7: 32). However, since resources are limited, it does not befit him as vicegerent of God to go to the extreme of becoming an economic man and ignoring the well-being of others. As Alec Nove has rightly remarked: "Societies concerned only with profit will fall to pieces. Corruption in the literal and the figurative sense can flourish where the making of money becomes the primary aspiration, the dominant criterion of success."[46] Similarly, Joseph Schumpeter also observed that "'no social system can work . . . in which everyone is supposed to be guided by nothing except his own short-run utilitarian interest."[47] A balance (*mīzān,* in the terminology of the Qur'ān, 55: 7–9) is absolutely necessary to ensure social well-being and continued development of human potential.

What Islam has done to create such a balance is to provide a spiritual and long-term dimension to self-interest. The individual must look after his interest in this world, which is infinitesimally short, as well as the Hereafter, which is eternal. While the interest in this world may be, though not necessarily, served by being selfish and unscrupulous, the interest in the Hereafter cannot be served except by fulfilling one's obligations towards others, though without resorting necessarily to self-denial. The belief in accountability before an All-Powerful and All-Knowing Being can thus play a powerful role in containing self-interest and encouraging social welfare-oriented behaviour. State coercion cannot perform this function because the chances of being detected by the state are not fool-proof and there are possibilities of escaping the adverse consequences of official prosecution through bribery or exploitation of one's political and economic leverage.

Thus, Islam recognises, what Marxism seeks to deny, the contribution of individual self-interest through profit and private property to individual initiative, drive, efficiency and enterprise. Islam, however, overcomes the evils of greed, unscrupulousness and disregard for the rights and needs of others, which the secularist and short-term, this-worldly perspective of both capitalism and socialism inevitably promote. This it does through the internal, self-regulating mechanism instilled in the inner consciousness of the individual himself, with its constant emphasis on belief in accountability before God, human brotherhood and socio-economic justice. This structure of beliefs can provide a strong motivating force to prevent self-interest exceeding the limits of social health and well-being.

Competition and market forces are no doubt indispensable for their contribution to efficiency of the allocative machinery. But these must operate within the constraints of the filter mechanism of moral values if the realisation of social goals is to be ensured. Only within these constraints will competition be 'healthy' and market forces 'humane'. Neither competition and market forces nor central planning and regimentation have the potential to instil in human beings the powerful motivating force for equitable use of scarce resources that the belief in accountability before God has. While in both the capitalist and the socialist systems, the powerful, vested interests have no inner mechanism to prevent them from manipulating policies and resources to their selfish advantage, or to encourage them to spend in accordance with the dictates of social well-being, in the Islamic system, as in any other effective religious system, they would be strongly motivated to do so. If they don't they will be acting against their long-term self-interest.

(c) SOCIO-ECONOMIC AND FINANCIAL RESTRUCTURING

The filter mechanism and the motivating system may both become blunted if they are not complemented by a socio-economic and political environment that is conducive to goal realisation. The social environment should be conducive to the observance of the rules of trust by not allowing material possessions and conspicuous consumption to become a source of prestige. The economic and financial environment should also be such that the economic man does not get born, and, if born, does not survive. If the society's value system hurts the prestige of the economic man, and if this is further strengthened by economic and financial restructuring such that the allocative and distributive machineries of the economy do not support the use of scarce resources for purposes that frustrate goal realisation, greater quality and meaning may be introduced into the consumption, earning and investment behaviour of individuals. The social and economic dimensions of restructuring may be further reinforced by political reform such that there is a dilution in the power centres of society, making it difficult for anyone to derive an undue advantage by exploiting his social, economic or political position. The absence of such restructuring would not only perpetuate inefficiency and inequity in the use of resources but also exacerbate the imbalances in the long-term.

Such a restructuring cannot be achieved through random, *ad hoc* measures. It must be systematic and coherent, and pursued steadfastly with a well-conceived, goal-oriented and long-term reform programme. The restructuring must address itself to:

(a) Invigorating the human factor by motivating and enabling the individual to perform his tasks with the aim of realising both efficiency and equity.

(b) Reducing the existing concentration of wealth and of economic and political power.

(c) Reforming all social, economic and political institutions, including public finances and financial intermediation, in the light of Islamic teachings, to help minimise wasteful and unnecessary consumption and to promote investment for need fulfilment, exports, and increased employment and self-employment.

In other words, what is needed is a reform of the human being, and a total restructuring of patterns of consumption, investment, ownership of means of production and of social, economic and political institutions. The greater the scarcity of resources or imbalances and the wider the gulf between the *maqāṣid* and the reality, the greater may be the restructuring required.

Certain key elements of the restructuring make up an integral part of a Muslim's beliefs – since his fate in the Hereafter depends on faithful compliance with them, his motivation to do so would be strong. Hence the restructuring in an Islamic environment is likely to be more successful than its counterpart in a secularist environment. Once such restructuring has been effectively enforced, the resultant system should be radically different from capitalism, socialism, or the welfare state. It is, however, neither possible nor necessary to review in this book all of the Islamic values and institutions involved in socio-economic restructuring. The Qur'ān, the *Sunnah,* and the *fiqh* literature are available for this purpose. Nevertheless, four key restructuring ingredients, which have been given especial importance by Islam, but which have been either ignored or misunderstood, are: (a) conscientious use of the trust resources, (b) social self-help through the payment of *zakāt* and other *ṣadaqāt* payments, (c) inheritance, and (d) reorganisation of the financial system. The implications of these for formulating a package of policies to realise the *maqāṣid* will become clear in the following chapters.

(d) ROLE OF THE STATE

Such a comprehensive restructuring may not be possible unless the state plays an active role in the economy. It must try to give practical expression to the goals and values of Islam.[48] This is because even in a morally-charged environment, it is possible for individuals to be simply unaware of the urgent, unsatisfied needs of others, or of the problems of scarcity and social priorities in resource use. Moreover, there are a number of functions which need to be performed in the interest of general well-being, but which individuals may not be willing or able to perform individually or collectively because of market failure or inability to mobilise adequate resources. Under such conditions, moral uplift and the price system, no matter how indispensable, cannot be sufficient to realise the kind of restructuring needed for equity as well as efficiency in the allocation and distribution of resources. Hence the role of the state in the economy has always occupied an important place in Muslim political thought from the earliest times to the present day, discussed under a number of subjects, including *al-aḥkām al-sulṭāniyyah* (government regulations), *maqāṣid al-Sharīʻah, al-Siyāsah al-Sharʻiyyah* (policy of the *Sharīʻah*), and *al-ḥisbah* (public reckoning).[49]

The role of the state in an Islamic economy is not, however, in the nature of an 'intervention', which smacks of an underlying commitment to *laissez-faire* capitalism. It is also not in the nature of collectivisation and regimentation which suppress freedom and sap individual initiative and enterprise. It is also not in the nature of the secularist welfare state which, because of its aversion to value judgements, accentuates claims on resources and leads to macroeconomic imbalances. It is, rather, a positive role – a moral obligation to help realise the well-being of all by ensuring a balance between private and social interest, maintaining the economic train on the agreed track, and preventing its diversion by powerful vested interests. The greater the motivation people have for implementing Islamic values, and the more effective socio-economic institutions are in creating a just equilibrium between resources and claims and in realising the *maqāṣid,* the smaller will be the role the state will have to play in the economy. But whatever the role of the state, it should not be played arbitrarily; it should be within the constraints of the *Sharī'ah* and through the democratic channels of 'consultation' *(shūrā).*

Thus, while Islam recognises individual freedom and the role of the price mechanism in promoting efficiency, it does not regard market forces as sacred. The blind operation of market forces does not automatically reward socially-productive effort, curb exploitation, or help the weak and the needy. It is therefore the responsibility of the state to ensure the realisation of the *maqāṣid.* This does not mean that the Islamic state must function as a police state. It need not resort to the use of force to realise its goals, or depend on owning and operating a substantial part of the economy. The requirement to use wisdom, conviction and tact in the enforcement of the *Sharī'ah* (Qur'ān, 2: 256 and 16: 125), and the abolition of interest would not permit these. It would rather try to motivate and help the private sector play its role effectively within the constraints of social well-being. For this purpose it would have to rely on raising the moral consciousness of people, accelerating social, economic and political reform, and providing incentives and facilities. It would be responsible for creating the right framework for the proper interaction of human beings, values and institutions to realise its goals. The role will become clearer in the following chapters which discuss the policy implications of Islamic values.[50]

A COMPREHENSIVE APPROACH

Thus, it may be seen that Islam does not propose any 'magic' formula, or mechanism or strategy for making the allocation and distribution of resources efficient and equitable. Claims about the 'magic' properties of any mechanism indicate a lack of realisation of the complexities of human society, and the difficulties involved in harmonising individual and social interests and realising social goals. They also reflect an effort to divert attention from the weaknesses of the system and to create a 'scientific' rationale for the enrichment of vested interests.

Islam is more realistic. It appreciates the difficulties involved in solving problems arising from scarcity and emphasises the need for a strategy consisting of a package of tools, all in harmony with its worldview and *maqāṣid.* In the absence of such a comprehensive approach there cannot be an effective strategy; there will rather be just a hotchpotch of incongruent policies conceived by way of compromises with the conflicting demands of pluralist groups and social classes.

Some writers have nevertheless tried to convey the false impression that the Islamic programme is based only on three measures: the behaviour norms, the *zakāt* and the prohibition of interest.[51] Even though these three measures have an important role to play in economic restructuring, they do not constitute the whole of the Islamic economic system. The effectiveness of even these measures lies in being supported and strengthened by an appropriate filter mechanism, a strong motivating system, effective restructuring, and a positive role for the government. Alone, the three measures cannot carry the burden and responsibility of realising the *maqāṣid.* It is just like looking at the skull, chest and legs of a skeleton and saying that this is the human being. Although these are important parts of the human body, they have significance only as long as the soul is there and muscles, tendons, heart, mind and all other systems of the body are healthy and functioning properly. Separately none of these is able to play the role of a human being. This shows the difference between individual ingredients and the whole recipe. Separately the ingredients do not provide the food with its taste, flavour, colour and wholesomeness, no matter how important the ingredients may be in the whole recipe.

It is not wise, as already discussed, to belittle the potential of beliefs and behaviour norms in transforming human beings and motivating them to act in a socially-responsible manner. In fact, without such beliefs and norms, no system, irrespective of whether the visible or the invisible hand guides it, can survive. Such beliefs and norms continue to exist even under capitalism and socialism. Secularism has not been able to obliterate them; it has only been able to weaken them substantially. In spite of being de-emphasised, they serve the function of reconciling, though to a limited extent, individual and social interests, and of maintaining a minimal degree of equity in the allocation and distribution of resources. Without this the relevant societies would either tear themselves to pieces or become engulfed in revolution. In their highly diluted state, however, they are not powerful enough to motivate most individuals to keep their self-interest within the bounds of social well-being to the extent to which it is necessary to bring about the quality of restructuring needed for actualising socio-economic justice. As Samuel Brittan has rightly pointed out: "The biggest mistake of the hard-boiled cynic is to underrate the role of moral legitimacy in human action. Without some kind of rules constraining the pursuit of self-interest no human organisation could function."[52]

The institutions of *zakāt,* inheritance, and the abolition of interest are not just values that every Muslim has to comply with faithfully for his personal well-being in this world and the Hereafter, they also have an important role to play in economic restructuring and realising the *maqāṣid.* It is incorrect to underrate their significance, given the effective revival of the other ingredients of Islamic strategy, including the role of government. However, all these are parts of a total socio-economic reorganisation and their full potential cannot be realised if applied in an isolated manner. The Islamic programme has to be accepted and enforced as a whole, and not just in parts, for total effectiveness. Partial acceptance and enforcement cannot ensure the actualisation of goals. Hence the Qur'ān stresses:

> Is it only a part of the Book that you believe in, and do you reject the rest? But what is the punishment for those among

you who do this except disgrace in this world and severe punishment on the Day of Judgement? (2: 85).

O Muslims! Enter into Islam in its totality, and follow not the footsteps of the Devil, for he is your obvious enemy (2: 208).

God does not change the condition of a people until they change their own inner selves (13: 11).

Notes and References (Chapter 5)

1 For a more detailed discussion of *tawḥīd,* see M. Nejatullah Siddiqi, "*Tawḥīd,* the Concept and the Process", in K. Ahmad and Z. I. Ansari, *Islamic Perspectives: Studies in Honour of Sayyid Abul A'lā Mawdūdī* (1979), pp. 17–33.

2 For a brief but comprehensive introduction to the concept of *khilāfah* in Islam, see 'Abd al-Qādir 'Awdah, *Al-Māl wa al-Ḥukm fī al-Islām* (1389 A.H.), pp. 12–25. This is the generally held view and supported by most early and modern-day Qur'ān commentators and scholars. It has its roots in both the Qur'ān and the *Sunnah.* See, for example, Sayyid Muḥammad Rashīd Riḍā, *Tafsīr al-Manār* (1954), pp. 257–61; Sayyid Quṭb, *Fī Ẓilāl al-Qur'ān* (1986), vol. 1, pp. 50–1; Sayyid Abul A'la Mawdudi, *Tafhīm al-Qur'ān* (1967–73), vol. 3, pp. 417–20 and 592, vol. 4, pp. 238 and 483; and Imam Hasan al-Banna, "Al-Insān fī al-Qur'ān", in *Ḥadīth al-Thulāthā' li'l Imām Ḥasan al-Bannā',* ed. Aḥmad 'Isā 'Āshūr (1985), pp. 19–25. However, there have been, and are, some scholars who do not accept the idea of man being the vicegerent of God. For this viewpoint, see Abdul Rahman Hasan al-Maydānī, *Baṣā'ir li'l Muslim al-Mu'āṣir* (1988), pp. 152–66; and Jaafar Sheikh Idris, "Is Man the Vicegerent of God?" *Journal of Islamic Studies,* 1/1990, pp. 99–110.

3 See, Jaafar Sheikh Idris, "Al-Taṣawwur al-Islāmī li'l Insān: Asās li Falsafat al-Islām al-Tarbawiyyah"; and Shaykh Abdul Rahman Hasan al-Maydānī, "Mafāhīm Qur'āniyyah Ḥawla al-Nafs al-Insāniyyah wa mā Tashtamilu 'alyahi". Both the above papers were presented to the First Islamic Educational Conference, Makkah, 31 March–8 April, 1977.

It is only this concept of the inner goodness of human nature which can answer the question of why a natural disaster like an earthquake brings out the best in people and makes them respond heroically to the call for help from their fellow human beings. (See, "A Disaster Brings out the Best in People. Why? Science Has Theories But No Complete Answer", *Newsweek,* 6 November, 1989, p. 9.) Evolutionary theory, depending for its answer on the survival instinct, does not explain why people sometimes sacrifice even their own life for the sake of strangers from whom they cannot possibly anticipate reciprocity, and why some people are more inclined to sacrifice than others. Even explanations provided by social psychologists are inadequate and raise more questions than they answer. The Islamic answer in terms of innate human goodness and Divine reward enjoys a clear advantage. Human beings need the right motivation to act selflessly in spite of their innate goodness. The innate human goodness and the right motivation can together explain the heroic deeds performed by individuals for the sake of others at a great this-worldly cost to themselves.

4 Cited from Immanuel Kant's *Religion within the Limits of Reason Alone* by Maurice Boutin, "The Fall: Its Factual Acceptance and Practical Meaning in Contemporary Society", in Durwood Foster and Paul Mojzes (eds.), *Society and Original Sin: Ecumenical Essays on the Impact of the Fall* (1985), p. 14.

5 H. D. Lewis, "Guilt", *The Encyclopaedia of Philosophy* (1967), vol. 3, p. 397. For the sake of comparison, see Sulayman S. Nyang, "The Islamic Concept of Sin", in Foster and Mojzes (1985), pp. 52–61.

6 See Claude Welch, *Protestant Thought in the Nineteenth Century* (1972), vol. 1 (1799–1870), p. 34; see also Paul Tillich, *A Complete History of Christian Thought* (1968), pp. v, 34 and 47.

7 B. F. Skinner, *Science and Human Behaviour* (1953); see also Leslie Stevenson, *Seven Theories of Human Nature* (1974), p. 104.

8 Problems of determinism and responsibility are discussed by several authors in Sidney Hook (ed.), *Determinism and Freedom in the Age of Modern Science* (1958), which is a selection of papers by contemporary philosophers, and Sidney Morgenbesser and James Walsh, (eds.), *Free Will* (1962), which brings together carefully selected discussions from classical and modern writers and is intended mainly for students. See also A. J. Alden, *Free Action* (1961), which offers elaborate and penetrating analysis of a wide range of concepts that have always been central to the free will controversy. Although the author does not try to prove directly that men have free will, he attacks the bases of certain widely held determinist theories.

9 Jean-Paul Sartre, *Being and Nothingness*, tr. by Hazel Barnes (1957). See also Stevenson (1974), pp. 78–90; and Anthony Manser, *Sartre: A Philosophic Study* (1966).

10 Sartre (1957), pp. 439 and 615.

11 *Ibid.*, p. 38.

12 For a comprehensive treatment of the duties of a Muslim towards himself and others, see M. Fazlur Rahman Ansari, *The Qur'ānic Foundations and Structure of Muslim Society* (1973), vol. 2.

13 Bertrand Russell, *A Free Man's Worship: Mysticism and Logic* (1918), p. 46.

14 This has been very clearly brought out in the Qur'ān and the *Ḥadīth*.

The Qur'ān says: "O mankind! We have created you from a male and a female and made you into nations and tribes so that you may know each other. Verily, the most honoured of you before God is the most righteous of you; surely, God is most Knowing, Aware" (49: 13).

The Prophet, may the peace and blessings of God be on him, said: ''Your God is One, your father is one, and your faith is one; your father is Adam, and Adam was created from dust; an Arab has no superiority over a non-Arab nor a white over a black except by righteousness'' (The Prophet Muhammad, may the peace and blessings of God be on him, in *Majma' al-Zawā'id*, 1352, v. 8, p. 84, from Abū Sa'īd, on the authority of al-Ṭabarānī; the quotation is a combination of two *ḥadīths*).

''God looks not at your faces or your wealth; He looks at your heart and your deeds'' (*Ṣaḥīḥ Muslim*, 1955, vol. 4, p. 1987:34, from Abū Hurayrah).

''The noblest of you are the best in character'' (*Ṣaḥīḥ al-Bukhārī*, vol. 8, p. 15, from 'Abdullāh ibn 'Umar).

Accordingly, the Qur'ān addresses itself to all human beings and not merely to Muslims or Arabs: O mankind! Surely I am the messenger of God to you all (7: 158).

15 *Mishkāt al-Maṣābīḥ* (1966), vol. 2, p. 613:4999, from Abū Hurayrah, on the authority of Bayhaqī's *Shu'ab al-Īmān*.

16 For the role of sacrifice in the life of a Muslim, see Khurram Murad, *Sacrifice: The Making of a Muslim* (1985).

17 The Qur'ān exhorts: ''Seek to excel each other in all that is good'' (2: 148), and ''Cooperate with one another in kindness and piety but not in sin and transgression'' (5: 2). The Prophet, may the peace and blessings of God be on him, stressed: ''Do not despise each other, do not turn your back toward each other, and do not vie with each other [in worldly things], but be like brothers, creatures of the One God'' (*Ṣaḥīḥ Muslim*, 1955, vol. 4, p. 1986:31, from Abū Hurayrah).

18 ''And believe in God and His Prophet, and spend of that in which He has made you a trustee'' (Qur'ān, 57: 7). For a brief introduction to the trust nature of resources and its implications, see 'Awdah, *Al-Māl wa al-Ḥukm fī al-Islām*, 1389 A.H., pp. 26–50.

19 Munawar Iqbal (ed.), *Distributive Justice and Need Fulfilment in an Islamic Economy* (1988), ''Introduction'', p. 15; see also Zubair Hasan, ''Distributional Equity in Islam'', *ibid.*, pp. 41–5, for a discussion of the concept of *amānah* in Islam; see also the comments and discussion on the paper, pp. 63–90, particularly that by Dr. Erfan Shafey and Dr. Said Martan.

20 ''Do not acquire wealth from each other wrongfully, nor knowingly offer it to officials with the objective of unjustly acquiring the wealth of others'' (Qur'ān, 2: 188).

21 ''And seek, with the wealth that God has given you, the abode of the Hereafter, but do not forget your share in this world. And do good (to others) as God has done good to you, and spread not mischief, for God does not like those who do mischief'' (Qur'ān, 28: 77). ''And they prefer others over themselves even though they are themselves destitute'' (Qur'ān, 59: 9). ''And in their wealth is a known right for the needy who asks and the deprived'' (Qur'ān, 70: 24).

22 Abū al-Ḥasan 'Alī ibn Muḥammad al-Māwardī, *al-Aḥkām al-Sulṭāniyyah* (1969), p. 34.

23 See the Qur'ān, 7: 31, 17: 26–7 and 25: 67 for verses against waste and extravagance. The Prophet, the peace and blessings of God be on him, also spoke against extravagance and in favour of simplicity and humility in life-style. He emphasised that waste of resources was forbidden not only in times of scarcity but also in times of abundance (*Mishkāt,* 1966, vol. 1, p. 133: 427); see also Othman Llewellyn, "Islamic Jurisprudence and Environmental Planning", *Journal of Research in Islamic Economics,* vol. 1, No. 2, Winter 1984, p. 34). The Prophet said: "God has revealed to me to teach you to be humble so that no one wrongs others or shows arrogance" (*Sunan Abū Dāwūd,* 1952, vol. 2, p. 572, from 'Iyāḍ ibn Ḥimār); and that: "God does not look at those who wear clothes reflecting arrogance" (*Ṣaḥīḥ al-Bukhārī,* vol. 7, p. 182 and *Ṣaḥīḥ Muslim,* 1955, vol. 3, p. 1651:42). He also said: "Whoever abstains from wearing an expensive dress out of humility, in spite of being capable of doing so, will be summoned by God in the presence of all humanity on the Day of Judgement and given the option to wear any of the distinguished attires of faith that he wishes" (*Jāmi' al-Tirmidhī* with commentary, *Tuḥfat al-Aḥwadhī,* vol. 3, pp. 312–13 from Mu'ādh ibn Anas al-Juhanī); and: "Eat and drink, give in charity, and dress up without extravagance or conceit" (Suyūṭī, *al-Jami' al-Ṣaghīr,* vol. 2, p. 96, from Ibn 'Umar, on the authority of *Musnad Aḥmad,* Nasā'ī, Ibn Mājah and *Mustadrak Ḥākim*). Accordingly, the weight of the Qur'ān and the *Sunnah* is on the side of a simple life-style for its followers and the jurists have concluded that vainglory and vying with each other for worldly symbols of prestige is *ḥarām* (prohibited). (See "Kitāb al-Kasb" of al-Shaybānī in al-Sarakhsī, *Kitāb al-Mabsūṭ,* vol. 30, pp. 266–8.)

24 'Alī al-Ṭanṭāwī and Nājī al-Ṭanṭāwī, *Akhbāru 'Umar* (1959), p. 268.

25 For a comprehensive treatment of the various aspects of socio-economic justice in Islam, see Sayyid Quṭb, *Al-'Adālah al-Ijtimā'iyyah fī al-Islām* (1964).

26 See M. U. Chapra, *Towards a Just Monetary System* (1985), pp. 27–8.

27 See Majid Khadduri, *The Islamic Conception of Justice* (1984), p. 10.

28 *Ṣaḥīḥ Muslim* (1955), vol. 4, p. 1996:56, Kitāb al-Birr wa al-Ṣilah wa al-Ādāb, Bāb Taḥrīm al-Ẓulm, from Jābir ibn 'Abdullāh. The Prophet, peace and blessings of God be on him, has used the word *ẓulumāt* in this *ḥadīth*. *Ẓulumāt* is the plural of *ẓulmah* or darkness, and signifies several layers of darkness, leading ultimately to 'pitch' or 'absolute' darkness, as is also evident in the Qur'ānic verse 24: 40.

29 Imām Ibn Taymiyyah, *Al-Ḥisbah fī al-Islām* (1967), p. 94. For translation see Muhtar Holland, *Public Duties in Islam: The Institution of the Hisba* (1982), p. 95.

30 The Prophet, may the peace and blessings of God be on him, said: "Any Muslim who plants a tree or cultivates a field that a bird, or a human being, or an animal eats from it, this act will be counted as an act of charity" (*Ṣaḥīḥ al-Bukhārī*, from Anas ibn Mālik, vol. 3, p. 128; and *Ṣaḥīḥ Muslim* (1955), vol. 3, p. 1189:12). This *ḥadīth* clearly indicates the importance of need-fulfilment not only of all human beings, but also of birds and animals.

31 Al-Bukhārī, from Ibn 'Abbās, *al-Adab al-Mufrad* (1379 A.H.), p. 52: 112.

32 Abdul Hamid Abu Sulayman, "The Theory of the Economics of Islam", in *Contemporary Aspects of Economic Thinking in Islam* (American Trust Publications, 1976), p. 20.

33 See Paul Streeten, "A Basic Needs Approach to Economic Development", in Kenneth P. Jameson and Charles K. Wilker (eds.), *Directions in Economic Development* (1973); Paul Streeten, *et al., First Things First: Meeting Basic Needs in Developing Countries* (1981); and Frances Stewart, *Basic Needs in Developing Countries* (1985).

34 See, for example, Abū Muḥammad 'Alī ibn Ḥazm, *Al-Muḥallā*, vol. 6, p. 156:725.

35 Abū Isḥāq al-Shāṭibī, *al-Muwāfaqāt fi uṣūl al-Sharī'ah*, vol. 2, p. 177.

36 For a brief introduction, see M. N. Siddiqi, "Guarantee of a Minimum Level of Living in an Islamic State", in M. Iqbal (1988), pp. 251–303; 'Abd al-Salām al-'Abbādī, *Al-Milkiyyah fī al-Sharī'ah al-Islāmiyyah* (1974–1975), vol. 3, pp. 81–95; Ibrahim Ahmad Ibrahim, *Niẓām al-Nafaqāt fī al-Sharī'ah al-Islāmiyyah* (1349 A.H.) and M. Anas Zarqa, "Islamic Distributive Schemes," in M. Iqbal (1988), pp. 163–219. According to Zarabozo, "A basic need approach is the Islamic approach to development", (Jamal al-Din Zarabozo, "The Need for an Islamic Approach to Economic Development", *Al-Ittihad*, October–December 1980, p. 24).

37 The Qur'ān instructs Muslims to go out into the world and seek of God's bounties after having attended to their prayers (62: 10). The Prophet, peace and blessings of God be on him, said that: "Earning a lawful livelihood is obligatory upon every Muslim" (Suyūṭī, *Al-Jāmi' al-Ṣaghīr*, from Anas ibn Mālik, p. 54), and elaborated this point further by saying: "A man has not earned better income than that which is from his own effort" (*Sunan Ibn Mājah* (1952), vol. 2, p. 723:2138, from Miqdām ibn Ma'dīkarib. According to the Prophet, the peace and blessings of God be on him, trust in God does not imply that a Muslim should refrain from making an effort. He should in fact do his utmost, but trust in God for the best results. This is the implication of his displeasure at a man who left his camel untied thinking that the camel would not stray because God would take care of him. The Prophet admonished him to tie the camel first and then trust in God (see "Kitāb al-Kasb" of Muḥammad ibn al-Ḥasan al-Shaybānī in al-Sarakhsī, *Kitāb al-Mabsūṭ*, vol. 30, p. 249). Caliph 'Umar emphasised the Islamic injunctions to earn one's own livelihood

by saying, "No one of you should refrain from seeking a livelihood and say, 'O God! Give me sustenance', for the sky will certainly not rain gold and silver" (Ṭanṭāwī and Ṭanṭāwī (1959), p. 268), and that: "Seek of the bounty of God and be not a burden on others" (Yūsuf ibn 'Abd al-Barr al-Qurṭubī, *Jāmi' Bayān al-'Ilm wa Faḍluhū*, vol. 2, p. 15).

38 A complete list of juristic references would be too long; the reader may however wish to see "Kitāb al-Kasb" of al-Shaybānī in al-Sarakhsī, *Kitāb al-Mabsūṭ*, vol. 30, pp. 344–87, particularly, pp. 245, 250 and 256; Abū Ḥāmid Muḥammad al-Ghazālī, *Iḥyā' 'Ulūm al-Dīn*, vol. 2, pp. 60–4; al-Shāṭibī, *al-Muwāfaqāt*, vol. 2, pp. 176–7 and al-'Abbādī (1974–75), vol. 2, pp. 22–5.

The Prophet, the peace and blessings of God be on him, disapproved of begging in his saying: "Do not beg anything from people" (Abū Dāwūd, 1952, vol. 1, p. 382, from 'Awf ibn Mālik), and that "The hand that is above is better than the hand that is below" (al-Bukhārī, vol. 2, p. 133, from 'Abdullāh ibn 'Umar and Ḥakīm ibn Ḥizām). The Prophet also declared unlawful the giving of charity to those who have no real need and who are healthy and able-bodied. (Abū Dāwūd, 1952, vol. 1, p. 379; Nasā'ī, 1964, vol. 5, p. 74 and Ibn Mājah, 1952, vol. 1, p. 589:1839).

He assigned a place of high esteem to earning one's own living by saying: "He who seeks the world lawfully to refrain from begging, to cater for his family, and to be kind to his neighbour, will meet God with his face shining like the full moon" (*Mishkāt*, 1381 A.H., vol. 2, p. 658:5207, from Abū Hurayrah, on the authority of Bayhaqī's *Shu'ab al-Īmān*).

39 For Abū Dharr's views, see the comments on verse 34 of *sūrah* 9 of the Qur'ān in the commentaries of Ibn Kathīr (*Tafsīr al-Qur'ān al-'Aẓīm*, vol. 2, p. 352), and al-Jaṣṣāṣ (*Aḥkām al-Qur'ān*, 1347 A.H., vol. 3, p. 130).

40 For a brief introduction to the role of morals in imbalances, see Mālik bin Nabī, *Al-Muslim fī 'Ālam al-Iqtiṣād* (1978), pp. 103–8.

41 Barrington Moore, Jr., *Reflections on the Causes of Human Misery and Upon Certain Proposals to Eliminate Them* (1972), p. 81.

42 J. G. de Beus, *Shall We Make the Year 2000?: The Decisive Challenge to Western Civilisation* (1985), p. 71.

43 Will and Ariel Durant, *The Lessons of History* (1968), p. 51.

44 For a very convincing discussion of why human beings need Divine Guidance to order their lives properly, see Muhammad Baqir al-Sadr, *Al-Insān al-Mu'āṣir wa al-Mushkilah al-Ijtimā'iyyah* (1388 A.H.), pp. 6–30.

45 "Schools Brief", *The Economist*, 13 December 1986, p. 83.

46 Alec Nove, *The Economics of Feasible Socialism* (1983), p. 7.

47 Joseph Schumpeter, quoted by W. Brus, *Journal of Comparative Economics*, vol. 4, 1980, p. 53.

48 See Imam Hasan al-Banna, *Majmū'ah Rasā'il al-Imām al-Shahīd Ḥasan al-Bannā'* (1989), p. 262; Sayyid Abul A'la Mawdudi, *Islām awr Jadīd*

Ma'āshī Naẓariyyāt (1959), pp. 161–2, and *Khilāfat-o-Mulūkiyyat* (1966), pp. 15–102; Muhammad Baqir al-Sadr, *Iqtiṣādunā* (1981), pp. 721–2; Muhammad al-Mubarak, *Niẓām al-Islām: al-Iqtiṣād, Mabādi' wa Qawā'id al-'Āmmah* (1972), pp. 106–27; and Hasan Turabi, "Principles of Governance, Freedom, and Responsibility in Islam", *The American Journal of Islamic Social Sciences*, 1/1987, pp. 1–11.

49 Of particular significance are the writings of: Al-Juwaynī, *Ghiyāth al-Umam fī al-Tiyāh al-Ẓulam*; Al-Māwardī, *Al-Aḥkām al-Sulṭāniyyah;* Abū Ya'lā, *Al-Aḥkām al-Sulṭāniyyah*; Ibn Khaldūn, *Muqaddimah*; Ibn Taymiyyah, *Al-Siyāsah al-Shar'iyyah fī Iṣlāḥ al-Rā'ī wa al-Ra'iyyah,* and *Al-Ḥisbah fī al-Islām.* For a summary of these views, see Rafiq al-Misri, *'Uṣūl al-Iqtiṣād al-Islāmī* (1989), pp. 66–84. In modern times, there have been several writings on the role of the state in the economy. Of particular significance are the views of Imam Hasan al-Banna, Sayyid Abul A'la Mawdudi, and Baqir al-Sadr.

50 See also the author's *The Islamic Welfare State and its Role in the Economy* (1979) for a more detailed discussion of the obligations, strategy and functions of the state in Islam.

51 See Timur Kuran, "The Economic System in Contemporary Islamic Thought: Interpretation and Assessment", *International Journal of Middle Eastern Studies,* 2, 1986, p. 135.

52 Samuel Brittan, "There Must be a Better Way", *Financial Times,* 20 November 1987, p. 17.

CHAPTER 6

The Malaise

Given the Islamic worldview and strategy, one may wonder why the Muslim countries are also suffering from the same inequities and imbalances as most other countries. The reason is obvious. Nowhere in the Muslim world is the Islamic strategy fully in operation. Islam is in fact conspicuous by its absence, particularly in the political and the economic fields. It is not possible to present here a comprehensive analysis of all the historical, political and sociological factors which have led to the deviation of Muslim countries from their professed ideals and which are responsible for their current malaise.[1] However, a brief review should help appreciate the magnitude of the task involved and the nature of policies necessary to face the challenge successfully.

POLITICAL AND MORAL DEGENERATION

After reaching the zenith of its glory, the Muslim society lost its momentum due to political and moral degeneration. The first thing to give in was the institution of *khilāfah* (caliphate), which reflected the Islamic political system in its ideal form. Its place was taken, in general, by autocratic and hereditary rule, which took little inspiration from the Islamic democratic imperative of *shūrā* (consultation), and which accumulated over time all the vices associated with such rule.[2] The emotional attachment to the faith nevertheless continued, but there was increasing laxity in the observance of Islamic teachings. The character of Muslims began to erode and move away gradually from the Islamic ideal. The three important characteristics of a Muslim society: strength of character, strong bonds of brotherhood, and incorruptible justice, became more and more tarnished. This weakened the Muslim person further, reduced his vigour and vitality, and led to a "loss of command over his physical environment", borrowing the words used by Toynbee in his general analysis of the decline of civilisations.[3]

The loss of command over the environment also set the stage for foreign domination which sapped the vitality even further. Muslim countries became deprived of effective nationhood and independent, Islamically-oriented governments that would feel an urge to take constructive measures to realise the *maqāṣid* by promoting balanced growth of their economies. Unlike the allied occupation authority, which implemented radical land reforms in Japan, South Korea and Taiwan, the colonial rulers in Muslim countries allied themselves with the privileged classes, particularly the landowners who, as Myrdal has indicated, were "primarily interested in preserving the social and economic status quo under which they were privileged".[4] This led to a further strengthening of the forces which were perpetuating exploitation and repression *(ẓulm)* of the masses and working toward degeneration and disintegration of the Muslim society. Public pressure for a return to Islam was also not allowed to gather momentum and policies that could lead to a realisation of the *maqāṣid* were not even formulated, let alone implemented.

ECONOMIC DECLINE

With the weakening of brotherhood and social equality, the Muslim society became more and more status-oriented and structured. Socio-economic justice, the prominent hallmark of a true Muslim society, became a major casualty and opportunities to rise vertically declined substantially. The possibility of receiving a just reward for hard, conscientious work and of getting due recognition for ability diminished, diminishing with it, in most able and competent people, the urge to be creative and to work hard for their advancement. There was an ever greater resort to corruption and improper means to achieve the wherewithal to make ends meet or to satisfy the demands of unhealthy customs and expensive life-styles which spread to all sectors of society. Corruption thus became pervasive.

This not only weakened further the solidarity and moral fibre of society, but also undermined the ability of the rich and middle classes to save. The exploitation of the poor gave them incomes which were inadequate to satisfy even their basic needs. Thus there was insufficient increase in capital formation by either the rich or the poor. Combined with the continued erosion of socio-economic justice, there was a substantial decline in enterprise, creativity and innovation.

In agriculture, the main occupation of most Muslim countries, tenant farmers and landless peasants, who had the potential of becoming dynamic entrepreneurs, became virtual slaves of the landlords, many of whom had obtained, and not earned, large chunks of land through machinations and loyalty to their colonial and local masters. Since the absentee landlords took away most of what the land produced, the farmers' incentive and drive suffered. They had no incentive to develop the land and use better techniques to raise output. They did not even have the means to enable them to undertake the necessary investments. In addition, they were under the excruciating burden of debt taken from money lenders and landlords. This killed their ambition even further. The absentee landlord himself made no investments in technology, training, improved seeds, fertilisers or insecticides. He also opposed all measures that would lead to the educational, social or economic uplift of tenant farmers and landless peasants. The agricultural sector therefore remained backward. Since historically an agricultural revolution has always preceded or accompanied industrial revolution, the sad state of agriculture in many Muslim countries has pre-empted the possibility of sustained, rapid development. The verdict of the World Bank is that: "In virtually all countries where agricultural development has been strong, economic growth has advanced at a rapid rate", and that: "While the role of agriculture in development has been debated for hundreds of years, the evidence, both historical and contemporary, is remarkably consistent. In Europe, Japan, and the United States, for example, a dynamic agriculture accompanied – and in some instances led – the process of industrialisation and growth."[5]

In industry, the craftsmen who prospered during the period of Muslim glory, were impoverished by the policies of the colonial rulers to increase their exports to the colonies. The colonial powers, as Myrdal has rightly observed, "used the dependent country as a market for the products of its own manufacturing industry . . . and took special measures to hamper the growth of indigenous industry."[6] The crafts therefore died. The pressure on land increased further and the farmers became poorer, being deprived of an opportunity to supplement their incomes from farming. They were forced to leave their kith and kin and migrate to urban centres where also they were exploited and faced, in addition, miserable living conditions.

Farmers, craftsmen and labourers are as rational in Muslim countries as elsewhere and can respond to economic incentives. Their lack of drive, creativity, conscientiousness, efficiency and high productivity are not innate characteristics. These have been forced upon them by their adverse political, social and economic environment and their inability to obtain a respectable standard of living through hard work. There cannot be two factors having a greater corrosive effect on the morale, vigour and creativity of a society than poverty and injustice. No amount of sermonising will be effective. Give them justice, training and proper tools to work with and their performance will improve manifold. If justice is not done, their response cannot be positive.

THE MISSED OPPORTUNITY

Independence from foreign domination brought a ray of hope. It was expected that national governments would work with dedication for the well-being of the people within the framework of Islamic values and development philosophy. This hope has, however, remained unfulfilled. Independence has only removed direct foreign domination. Its place has been taken in most countries by military dictators and unpopular rulers who have been insensitive to the aspirations of the people. Some of them have almost ruined their economies in the name of socialism or national defence. In spite of independence, the spirit of the colonial past has become incarnated in a secularist, inefficient, conceited and corrupt bureaucracy which has aligned itself with the vested interest of landlords, big business and the military.

The task of preparing policies for development fell upon this bureaucracy after independence. It was not trained or motivated for the task. It had been brought up in the secular Western tradition and had little understanding of Islam or its revolutionary concept of socio-economic justice. Thinking through the Islamic development philosophy, and preparing policies in the light of it, was a difficult task. It was much easier to adopt blindly the policy prescriptions coming from the pundits of development economics. Since development economics had itself developed in the West within a secularist background and lacked a serious commitment to socio-economic justice and moral values, it could not develop an agreed filter mechanism to sift the conflicting policy prescriptions and to lay down a firm policy framework for growth with equity and stability. Hence policies pursued in Muslim countries oscillated, as in other developing countries, on the waves of socialism and free enterprise, liberalism and anti-liberalism. This generated inconsistencies and uncertainties and caused immense harm to the health and development of their economies. Continued increase in spending was encouraged to promote development. Value judgements required to keep unnecessary spending under control were shirked. This led to a continually expanding resources gap. Monetary expansion and internal and external borrowing were promoted as a virtue to fill this gap. Those who opposed such borrowing were dubbed fundamentalists, opposed to modernisation and advancement. If the proof of the pudding is in the eating, the pudding provided by secular development economics has been bitter and expensive, involving large macroeconomic and external imbalances, a high debt-servicing burden, and social tensions.

The twilight which the common man saw on the horizon at the time of independence has not yet turned into the full light of day. His problems still remain unsolved. His basic needs are not fulfilled. Inequalities have risen and socio-economic justice has not been actualised. Excessive budgetary deficits have led to rapid monetary expansion and high rates of inflation in most Muslim countries. Large external imbalances have increased dependence on foreign aid. This has trapped them in the clutches of foreign lenders and aid-givers, who consider Islam an anathema and apply all the pressure they can to prevent the adoption of Islamic policies. They fail to realise the potential of

Islam for promoting growth, justice and political stability in Muslim countries.

The dream of establishing an Islamic society remains unfulfilled. Even the direction and destiny of most Muslim countries remain undetermined. The lip-service paid to Islam has not and cannot fulfil the aspirations of the masses. They are frustrated and craving for a change. The time is therefore ripe for Muslim leadership to read and understand the signs of the time, to work for the revival of Islam, and to eradicate *ẓulm.* Only those who respond to the challenges facing them can survive the wrath of the frustrated masses and also earn for themselves a place of eternal recognition in history. Unfortunately even those of the Muslim leaders who talk positively of Islam do not go beyond the level of implementing Islamic punishments, falsely equating the Islamic strategy with these punishments. This is unfair to Islam. They have done hardly anything worthwhile to establish justice. Trying to implement the punishments before laying down even a framework for restoring to justice its place of primary importance in a Muslim society is like putting the cart before the horse.

THE NEED FOR CHANGE

Political Legitimacy

There is need for change in the Muslim world. The deep emotional attachment of the Muslim masses to Islam has an immense potential for socio-economic reform and development. What is needed, however, is a mechanism to mobilise this potential by rekindling the flame of faith in the hearts of the people and to inculcate in them the characteristics of a true Muslim. Governments can perform this task more effectively by providing the moral leadership *(qudwah ḥasanah)* that the Muslim world needs for healthy social change, and by using the educational and material resources they have at their disposal. As Imam Hasan al-Banna has rightly stressed, governments are the heart of socio-economic reform; if they become corrupt, they may corrupt everything and if they are reformed, they may be able to reform everything.[7] Governments do not normally play their role effectively until they are legitimate. Unfortunately, governments have not been legitimate in the Muslim world over a substantial part of its history and unless their legitimacy is restored, the Islamic programme for realising the *maqāṣid* may continue to occupy only an ornamental place in the political life of Muslim countries.

Criteria for Legitimacy

Islam has its own rigorous criteria for a legitimate government. The first of these is that the government is accountable to God, Who is the Sovereign Lawgiver and the primary source of the *Sharī'ah*. This implies that the government's authority is limited and not absolute. The government must itself abide by the *Sharī'ah* and do all it can to ensure its fulfilment. The Qur'ān leaves no doubt about this by stressing: "Follow that which has been sent to you by your Lord, and follow not authorities other than Him" (7: 3), and that "those who do not rule in accordance with what God has sent are the transgressors" (5: 45).

Since one of the primary objectives of the *Sharī'ah* is the well-being of all people, and not of any specific group or family or region, it is the moral and legal obligation of the government to ensure the realisation of such well-being through the adoption of all necessary measures, including the efficient and equitable use of resources. The Prophet, may the peace and blessings of God be on him, said:

> Everyone of you is a shepherd and accountable for his or her flock.[8]
>
> Anyone who has been given the charge of a people but does not live up to it with sincerity, will not taste even the fragrance of paradise.[9]
>
> The most beloved of mankind and the nearest to God in rank on the Day of Judgement will be a just ruler, and the most despised of them and farthest from Him in rank will be an unjust ruler.[10]

The second criterion of legitimacy is the government's accountability before the people. This is because the government is a trust – trust from God as well as from the people given to those who manage the affairs of the government. The Prophet, peace and blessings of God be on him, emphasised this clearly to Abū Dharr, who wished to acquire a senior government position, by saying: "O Abū Dharr! You are weak and this position is a trust. It will be a source of disgrace and regret on the Day of Judgement except for him who acquires it deservedly and fulfils its obligations upon him."[11] Therefore, while the government is accountable to God for its success or failure in living up to the trust, it is also accountable to the people for realising their aspirations in conformity with the terms of the trust.

The government cannot fulfil its role of realising the people's aspirations effectively unless it is open to their suggestions and criticism. Hence, the Prophet, peace and blessings of God be on him, emphasised that one of the demands of faith on Muslims is that they render sincere advice to their rulers – advice that would help the rulers perform their duties effectively.[12] But how can the people fulfil this obligation if there is no freedom of expression and they are not allowed to criticise the policies being pursued by the government? Unless the rulers consider themselves accountable to the people and are willing to get feedback from them, there can be no reform. Accordingly, when Abū Bakr became the first caliph, he categorically emphasised this Islamic imperative in his inaugural address by saying: "If I act rightly, help me, but if I act wrongly, correct me and set me right."[13] This establishes a two-way flow of rights and obligations. It is the right of people to participate in the formulation of policies and the obligation of rulers to enable them to do so. It is simultaneously the right of the rulers to get help and cooperation from the people if they are following the right policies, and the obligation of people to correct them if they are not doing so.

This statement of Abū Bakr is not a rare incident. 'Umar, the second Caliph, also followed the same practice. When someone tried to prevent a person from criticising him, 'Umar insisted on allowing the person to continue, saying: "They are not good if they do not speak out and we are not good if we do not accept what they say."[14] There are so many reports of the ordinary people criticising the caliphs, and the caliphs accepting such criticism gracefully, that there is no escape from the conclusion that people's right to freedom of expression and the leadership's obligation to be open to criticism had been an indispensable part of early Muslim political tradition, and remained so for some time even after the elimination of the caliphate and its replacement by hereditary succession.

The third criterion for legitimacy is the prevalence of a general atmosphere of *shūrā* (consultation) as required by the Qur'ān (42: 38). This is not an option, it is rather an obligation, as Imam Ibn Taymiyyah and Shaykh Muḥammad 'Abduh have both clearly emphasised.[15] What this essentially implies is that there is no argument in the *Sharī'ah* in favour of despotism, military dictatorship, and autocracy. This is because – as Shaykh Rashid Riḍa has approvingly reported the explanation of Shaykh Muhammad 'Abduh – "A group is generally farther from error than an individual, and the danger is much greater and far more serious for the *ummah* in entrusting its affairs to a single individual."[16] The *shūrā* that is required is not of the cosmetic kind, to rubber stamp decisions made by the rulers. What is required is an autonomous institution for a free, unhindered and fearless discussion of all issues related to public well-being within the framework of the *Sharī'ah,* and the serious and sincere implementation by the executive of all policies thus crystallised. The institution of *shūrā* demands the widest possible participation of the people in the affairs of the state, either directly or through representatives.[17] What specific form the fulfilment of this imperative may take is for the *ummah* to decide on the basis of its own circumstances.

A fourth criterion for legitimacy is the equality of all people before the law, and incorruptible justice, as required by the Qur'ān: "And when you judge between people, judge with justice" (4: 58). The rulings of the *Sharī'ah* should be applied equally to everyone, irrespective of status, wealth, or position of the person concerned in the social or government hierarchy.[18] Anything other than this is *ẓulm,* and *ẓulm,* as Shaykh Muhammad 'Abduh rightly emphasised, is the most hideous evil *(aqbaḥ al-munkar).*[19] It is important to note here what Caliph Abū Bakr declared in his inaugural address: "The weak person among you is strong before me until I have obtained for him his right, and the strong person among you is weak before me until I have taken the right from him."[20] The message this conveys is that the *raison d'être* for the coercive power of the government is to establish justice and to help the weak and the poor to obtain their rights.

Satisfying the Criteria

These four criteria for legitimacy may not be satisfied unless those who wield political power derive their authority from the people and are answerable to the people for the quality of their performance. This demands a system of free and fair elections. Without such elections people cannot fulfil the Qur'ānic imperative of giving "the trust to those who deserve it" (4: 58). The people must themselves give the trust willingly to those whom they consider to be deserving. It cannot be acquired by forceful imposition or heredity.

Hence, the leaders of two of the most prominent Islamic movements in the present-day Muslim world, Imam Hasan al-Banna and Mawlana Abul A'la Mawdudi, have both strongly endorsed democracy. Imam al-Banna finds the representative form of government to be closest in spirit to Islamic political teachings.[21] Similarly, Mawlana Mawdudi emphasises that: "The government should be constituted and run in consultation with the people. Its structure must be such that the people are able to express their viewpoint. It is their will which should prevail. And this can take place only in a state that is democratic in structure and in its working."[22] Even Shaykh 'Allāl al-Fa'sī, President of Ḥizb al-Istiqlāl, the Islamic movement of Tunis, expressed similar views.[23] It is only the accountability before people in a democratic system that can ultimately ensure that the rulers abide by the *Sharī'ah* with respect to the well-being of all and the enforcement of incorruptible justice. This does not necessarily mean that the democratic form of government in its prevalent form has no drawbacks. These drawbacks do not, however, justify military dictatorship or autocracy. To the extent to which Muslims can reform the democratic process and remove, or even reduce, the influence of money, power and manipulation in the choice of political leadership, they will bring it closer to the Islamic ideal of *shūrā*, and take another step in the right direction. This may however be difficult to accomplish in one stroke. It will take place over time through a process of evolution.

The Role of the *'Ulamā'*

While the political leadership has failed to provide the *qudwah ḥasanah,* even the highly-placed and influential *'ulamā'* (religious scholars) and professionals, who carry considerable clout in the political set-up, have failed to do so. Instead of being the standard-bearers of socio-political reform and of putting their weight behind the moral and material uplift of the masses, most of them have become sycophants, trying to secure for themselves as large a chunk of the social product as possible. They have failed to realise that Islamic values place a heavy responsibility on all those who occupy influential positions and require them to use their leverage fully in favour of socio-economic and political reform.[24] There is absolutely no justification by the *Sharī'ah* for such people to serve their this-worldly self-interest by becoming an instrument of, or even condoning, the prevailing forces of corruption and injustice. Such behaviour has been equated by the Prophet, may the peace and blessings of God be on him, with disbelief.[25] Within the existing unhealthy environment, even those who are selfless and conscientious, are unable to make significant headway, particularly when repressive governments feel threatened by reform and do their utmost to frustrate and persecute the reformers. Hence, the Prophet, may the peace and blessings of God be on him, had rightly predicted that:

> I am apprehensive of three things about my *ummah*: the lapse of the *'ulamā'*, the rule of despots, and the pursuit of worldly pleasures.[26]

This state of affairs may not however continue for long. The masses have become restless and are craving for a change. The ongoing awakening in the Muslim world is making the Muslim masses realise more and more that their salvation lies in the revival of Islam. This will ultimately force the ruling élite to adopt the Islamic strategy whether they like it or not.

RESTRUCTURING POLICIES

It is now time to translate the Islamic worldview and strategy into an integrated package of policies so that any government which is serious about actualising the *maqāṣid* may be able to consider it for adoption after making the necessary adjustments in it in the light of its own circumstances. Muslim countries are not starting from scratch with economies that may be put into the mould of Islam relatively easily. Many of them are suffering from serious inequities and imbalances, which makes the task of their Islamisation relatively more difficult and complex. Nevertheless, as the discussion so far will have indicated, they cannot avoid taking inspiration from Islam. The very logic of the human condition (scarcity of resources accompanied by unlimited claims on these) dictates that the *Sharī'ah* be taken seriously and that the value-neutrality inherent in Pareto optimality be abandoned. Any strategy that talks of increasing resources to realise socio-economic goals without effectively reducing their availability for other purposes is bound to be a non-starter.

If resources were unlimited, human beings would have been able to satisfy all their wants without facing any imbalances. In this case, even absolutely unrestricted freedom would have harmed no one, and socio-economic justice would be realised without rules. But since resources are limited, it is necessary to use them efficiently as well as equitably if the desired socio-economic goals are to be realised. Absolute freedom to use resources in accordance with individual preferences, the goal of secularist societies, is a sure way of perpetuating both imbalances and injustice. It is necessary to subject human beings to some constraints to realise both efficiency and equity. No economic system can operate without such constraints. Capitalism and socialism, even though they have refused to accept the constraint of Divine values, have had to accept constraints whether imposed by the market or the state. Nevertheless, these systems, as discussed in earlier chapters, have failed to realise simultaneously both efficiency and equity and to avoid imbalances.

In formulating policies for Muslim countries within the framework of the *Sharī'ah,* it is neither possible nor necessary to find a precedent for all of them in early Islamic history. Although the *Sharī'ah* has prescribed all the essential elements of a basic strategy, it has allowed flexibility over space and time by not spelling out detailed policy measures. The detailed measures have to be developed. It may be possible to emulate the experience of other countries with respect to specific policies. But, while doing so, it is necessary to ensure that the policy measures being considered for adoption fulfil two criteria – that they make a positive contribution to the realisation of the *maqāṣid* without creating a conflict with the *Sharī'ah*, and that they do not lead to an excessive increase in the claims on resources. The testing of all policy measures against these criteria will also strengthen the hand of governments in getting the policies publicly accepted, particularly policies which do not satisfy the criterion of Pareto optimality.

Only a well-conceived and effectively implemented adjustment programme can help restore social and economic health to Muslim countries. Such an adjustment programme may seem bitter. Its bitterness should not be attributed to the Islamic value system. Islam is not an ascetic religion and does not normally require the kind of austerity that is now called for. Under normal circumstances adherence to Islamic values would help avoid imbalances and realise both efficiency and equity without resort to such austerity. The contribution that Islam can undoubtedly make is to provide the filter mechanism and motivating system that would help redistribute the burden of adjustment from the poor to the rich, in sharp contrast to what a secularist adjustment programme conceived within the neoclassical or socialist framework, would normally propose.

FIVE POLICY DIMENSIONS

The policy measures suggested for solving the problems of Muslim countries are classified and discussed under five different dimensions, each in a separate chapter. The first dimension (Chapter 7) relates to the question of invigorating the human factor by motivating and enabling the individual to perform the tasks needed in the interest of improving his own economic condition as well as that of his society. The second dimension (Chapter 8) relates to the question of reducing the existing concentration of wealth in Muslim societies. The third and fourth dimensions (Chapters 9 and 10) relate to the kind of restructuring that would be needed in the life-styles, public finances, and economic and financial systems of Muslim countries if the realisation of Islamic goals is to be ensured. All these measures cannot be effectively undertaken without proper planning. The final dimension (Chapter 11) therefore relates to the kind of strategic policy planning that would be necessary.

A number of the policy measures suggested in these chapters may be familiar to those well-versed in development literature. What is important to bear in mind, however, is the integration of moral and material dimensions of life that, in keeping with the Islamic worldview and strategy, the whole package of policies reflects. In the absence of such an integration, it may not be possible to realise the *maqāṣid* without putting excessive pressure on the limited resources available.

Notes and References (Chapter 6)

1 Discussion of the causes of Muslim decline is very scanty in the available literature. The reader could however benefit from the following:

Abul-Hasan Ali al-Nadwi, *Mā dhā Khasira al-'Ālam bi Inḥiṭāṭ al-Muslimīn* (1974); Zakariyya Bashir Imam, *Ṭarīq al-Taṭawwur al-Ijtimā'ī al-Islāmī* (1397 A.H.), pp. 47–83; Z̲aghlul Raghib al-Najjar, *Qaḍiyyah al-Takhalluf al-'Ilmī wa al-Taqnī fī al-'Ālam al-Islāmī* (1409 A.H.); Amir Shakib Arsalan, *Our Decline and its Causes*, tr., M. A. Shakoor (1962); John J. Saunders, (ed.), *The Muslim World on the Eve of Europe's Expansion* (1966); Halil Inalcik, "The Heyday and Decline of the Ottoman Empire", and Ann Lambton, "Persia: The Breakdown of Society", in P. M. Holt, *et al.* (eds.), *The Cambridge History of Islam* (1970), pp. 324–31 and 430–67; Philip Hitti, *History of the Arabs* (1958), see in particular Chapters 33, 39 and 40.

2 For the best available analysis of the factors which led to this shift from the system of *shūrā* to hereditary and autocratic rule, see Sayyid Abul A'la Mawdudi, *Khilāfat-o-Mulūkiyyat* (1966), pp. 103–53. See also Sayyid Muḥammad Rashid Riḍa, *Tafsīr al-Manār* (1954), vol. 4, p. 204, and vol. 5, p. 198.

3 Arnold J. Toynbee, *A Study of History*, abridgement by D. C. Somervell (1946).

4 Gunnar Myrdal, *Rich Lands and Poor* (1957), p. 59.

5 IBRD, *World Development Report, 1982*, pp. iii and 39.

6 Myrdal (1957), p. 57.

7 Imam Hasan al-Banna, *Majmū'ah Rasā'il al-Imām al-Shahīd Ḥasan al-Bannā'* (1989), p. 255.

8 From Ibn 'Umar, in al-Mundhirī, *Al-Targhīb wa al-Tarhīb* (1986), vol. 3, p. 155:1, on the authority of al-Bukhārī and Muslim.

9 Al-Bukhārī, from Ma'qil ibn Yasār, vol. 9, p. 80, Kitāb al-Aḥkām.

10 From Abū Sa'īd al-Khudrī, in al-Mundhirī (1986), vol. 3, p. 167:7, on the authority of al-Tirmidhī and al-Ṭabarānī.

11 Muslim (1955), from Abū Dharr, vol. 3, p. 1457:1825, Kitāb al-Amārah.

12 The Prophet, may the peace and blessings of God be on him, said: ''Faith *(al-Dīn)* is sincere advice.'' The companions inquired: ''For whom, O Prophet of God?'' The Prophet replied: ''For God, His Book, His Prophet, the rulers and the common people'' (Muslim, 1955, from Tamīm al-Dārī, vol. 1, p. 74:95, Kitāb al-Īmān).

13 Ibn Hishām, *Sīrat al-Nabawiyyah* (1955), vol. 2, p. 661.

14 Abū Yūsuf, *Kitāb al-Kharāj* (1952), p. 12.

15 Ibn Taymiyyah, *Al-Siyāsah al-Shar'iyyah fī Islāḥ al-Rā'ī wa al-Ra'iyyah* (1966), p. 135; and *Tafsīr al-Manār* (1954), vol. 4, p. 45. See also Muhammad Salim al-'Awwā, *Fī al-Niẓām al-Siyāsī li al-Dawlah al-Islāmiyyah,* (1975), pp. 105–17.

16 *Tafsīr al-Manār* (1954), vol. 4, pp. 199–200.

17 See Abul A'la Mawdudi, *Human Rights in Islam* (1976), p. 37.

18 In this connection, the following *ḥadīth* reported by 'Ā'ishah should be very enlightening. She reports that the Quraysh were faced with the problem of a Makhzūmī lady who had stolen. They inquired about someone who could intervene on her behalf with the Prophet, may the peace and blessings of God be on him. They learned that Usāmah ibn Zayd, whom the Prophet liked very much, may be the only one who could have the courage to do so. Hence Usāmah talked to the Prophet, may the peace and blessings of God be on him. The Prophet thereupon said: Are you intervening to prevent the enforcement of Divine Law? Then the Prophet got up and addressed the people, saying: ''People before you were punished by God because if a highly-placed person stole they acquitted him, but if a lowly person stole they enforced the Law of God on him. By God! Even if Fāṭimah, the daughter of Muḥammad, steals, I will certainly cut her hand.'' (Reported from 'Ā'ishah by al-Bukhārī and Muslim – *Mishkāt,* 1381 A.H., vol. 2, p. 302:3610).

19 *Tafsīr al-Manār* (1954), vol. 4, p. 45.

20 Ibn Hishām (1955), vol. 2, p. 661.

21 See Imam Hasan al-Banna, *Majmū'ah Rasā'il* (1989), pp. 192–3 and 239–41.

22 Sayyid Abul A'la Mawdudi, *The Islamic Law and Constitution* (1967), p. 197.

23 'Allāl al-Fa'sī, ''Al-Islām wa Mutaṭallibāt al-Tanmiyyah fī al-Mujtama' al-Yawm'', a paper presented at the conference, ''Multaqā al-Fikr al-Islāmī'', held in Wahran, July 1971. He argues in favour of the people

themselves determining how they wish to be governed. He finds this to be possible only if there is a government through the people's representatives, elected to assemblies by means of free and fair elections, in which the wealthy and the powerful are not able to exercise any pressure or influence (pp. 42–3).

24 Said the Prophet, may the peace and blessings of God be on him: "Whoever sees something wrong should use his strength to set it right; if he cannot, he should speak against it; and if he cannot, he should at least consider it wrong in his heart; and this is the weakest of faith". (Muslim, from Abū Sa'īd al-Khudrī, vol. 1, p. 69:78, *Kitāb al-Īmān*). If this is required of every Muslim, then the obligation of those in positions of influence is much greater.

25 "Whoever goes along with an oppressor and strengthens his hands, knowing that he is an oppressor, has taken himself out of the fold of Islam" (from 'Aws ibn Sharaḥbīl, by al-Bayhaqī in his *Shu'ab al-Īmān*; cited by *Mishkāt* (1381 A.H.), vol. 2, p. 641:5136).

26 From 'Awf ibn Mālik, in al-Mundhirī (1986), vol. 3, p. 175:33, on the authority of al-Bazzār and al-Ṭabarānī.

CHAPTER 7

Invigorating the Human Factor

The most challenging task for realising the *maqāṣid* even in a conducive political environment is to motivate the human factor to do all that is necessary in the interest of efficient allocation and equitable distribution of resources. Individuals must be willing to render their best by working hard and efficiently with integrity, conscientiousness and discipline, and to make the sacrifices necessary to overcome obstacles in the path of development. They must also be willing to change their consumption, saving and investment behaviour in conformity with what is required to increase employment, raise the rate of growth, reduce macroeconomic imbalances, and realise the *maqāṣid*.

Motivation alone is, however, not sufficient to get the best out of human beings. They must also have the appropriate ability, which comes from proper training and access to finance. Unless an adequate arrangement is made for both, motivation alone may not be able to take the economic system far in realising the optimum potential of the human factor.

MOTIVATION

Unless individuals are properly motivated, no system can realise either efficiency in resource use or equity in distribution. To motivate individuals to render their best and to utilise the scarce resources with maximum efficiency, it is necessary that their self-interest be served by doing so. Socialism was naive and unrealistic when it expected individuals to work efficiently even though it deprived them of the opportunity to serve their self-interest. It therefore failed. Capitalism was also unrealistic when it assumed that self-interest and social interest would always be in harmony. Its secularism and this-worldly perspective did not provide any mechanism to motivate individuals to serve the social interest when this was in conflict with their self-interest.

It is not possible to motivate individuals to be both efficient and equitable unless a moral dimension is injected into their pursuit of self-interest so that social interest is not jeopardised even when it is in conflict with self-interest. However, depending primarily on sermons to motivate all human beings to conform to moral values would again be unrealistic. It is necessary to reinforce moral values by socio-economic restructuring such that the individual does not find it possible to serve his self-interest except within the constraints of socio-economic justice.

Socio-Economic Justice

In most Muslim countries material rewards have become so inequitable that most people are unable to get due reward for their hard work, creativity, and contribution to output. They have consequently become apathetic and their initiative, drive and efficiency have all suffered considerably. There are two factors responsible for this: firstly, biases and lack of realism in official policies, and secondly, concentration of wealth and power in a few hands in both rural and urban areas.

The biases and lack of realism in official policies have led to distortion of key prices which unconsciously result in lowering the incomes of tenant farmers, small and micro enterprises (SMEs), and workers, reducing their demand for needs and creating a misallocation of resources against need-fulfilment. The concentration of wealth and power, also due partly to official policies and partly to the exploitative economic system that has prevailed for centuries, has restricted competition, generated widespread collusion, and created a climate conducive to the misery of the masses.

Rural Uplift

The bias against agriculture and SMEs in government policies has retarded the development of human, physical and financial infrastructure in rural areas. This has not only reduced the rewards for the effort of tenant farmers and workers in rural areas but also lowered their ability to invest in better seeds, fertilisers and equipment and in SMEs to supplement their incomes from agriculture. It has also led to an influx of labour to urban areas, thereby depressing wages and living conditions there.

The bias of government policies in favour of urban development and large-scale businesses and industries, has unduly raised their comparative advantage. Along with heavy tariff protection, concessionary financing and subsidised inputs, this bias has boosted the rates of profit in such urban businesses and industries, reduced the competitiveness of rural and urban SMEs, and enhanced the concentration of wealth and power. While high tax evasion prevents the governments from reaping the benefit of their urban bias, urban congestion results in low wages and salaries and prevents urban employees from getting appropriately rewarded for their contribution to urban prosperity.

It is therefore necessary to remove the bias of official policies against agriculture and SMEs. This is, however, not enough. It is also necessary to introduce a number of socio-economic reforms that would help raise the real incomes of all workers, savers, investors and exporters, and particularly so if they are poor.

Labour Reforms

Islamic values require employers to consider employees as members of their own family. This demands that employees be treated with respect and compassion and that their well-being be ensured. Real wages in a Muslim society should ideally be at least at a level that would enable employees to fulfil all their and their families' essential needs in a humane manner.[1] They must also be provided with training, job security and, preferably, also a share in profits within the framework of a long-term, harmonious relationship.

In sharp contrast with this, real wages in most Muslim countries are so low that, in spite of nearly 10–14 hours of hard work, a labourer is unable to fulfil his own and his family's basic needs. In addition, employees do not enjoy any job security. The reasons for this are not merely low productivity, excess supply of labour, and lack of adequate opportunities for employment, as the neoclassical economists would have us believe. A substantial role is played by exploitation, which is made possible by a configuration of unjust forces, including inappropriate official policies, concentration of wealth and power, and lack of training and financing facilities for workers. Unless the forces of exploitation are substantially weakened, it may not be possible to do justice to workers and to induce them to work conscientiously and efficiently.

The prescription of minimum wages may not, nevertheless, be the immediate solution. It would be difficult to enforce and, if enforced, it could have two adverse effects. Firstly, it could lead to a difference in wages reported to the authorities and those actually paid. This would imply a reduction in the tax liability of the employer without any real benefit to the labourer. Secondly, it could exacerbate the prevailing high level of unemployment.

It would hence be better to resort to an entirely different package of policies – policies that would blunt the edge of exploitation by firstly, raising the productivity of workers, and secondly, expanding the opportunities available for self-employment in both rural and urban areas. Such policies should include: (a) provision of better vocational training to raise productivity; (b) extension of financing facilities to promote SMEs; and (c) restructuring of the entire economy in favour of need fulfilment and a more equitable distribution of income and wealth. These policies should be further reinforced by making profit-sharing and employee stock ownership plan (ESOP) as widespread as possible.

Every firm should be required to establish a profit-sharing scheme for employees. A certain agreed proportion of the firm's net profit should be required to be partly allocated for distribution among the employees as profit-sharing bonus and partly utilised to provide training facilities, improve their working conditions, and grant medical benefits, educational allowances for children, housing facilities, and food subsidies. Linking the increase in income and benefits of employees beyond a certain minimum needed for comfortable living to their firm's profitability should have a number of benefits. These would include: (a) reduction in the existing apathy through a boost in the employees' morale, thus leading to greater conscientiousness, less wastage and higher productivity; (b) improvement in labour-management relations through worker participation in management, thus helping revive an important characteristic of an ideal Muslim society; (c) keeping the employees' earnings flexible and responsive to the health of the national economy and the performance of their firms – the employees sharing amply in their firm's prosperity when profits are good but not being laid off when profits are low or the firm is suffering losses; (d) reduction in tax evasion (provided that the tax system is reformed), because the employees, in their own self-interest, would keep an eye on the firm's actual profits with respect to which they are currently indifferent; and (e) increase in the competitiveness of the economy and the firms, thus improving the general climate for investment and the macroeconomic performance of the economy. While implementing the profit-sharing scheme, it is necessary to ensure that this policy does not lead to exploitation. This could happen if the basic wage, which is not subject to risk, is not adequate to meet the basic needs of the employee.

The introduction of ESOP could also go a long way toward reducing concentration of wealth and power. It would enable workers to become equity owners, thus increasing their stake in the firm's success. A share in management and active participation in policy may not only improve worker-management relations but also reduce industrial strife, and make the workers more conscientious and efficient. It would raise savings, discourage the unproductive alternative of gold hoarding and also help raise their social status in the company and society. When ESOP has been adopted in even some capitalist countries like France, the U.K. and the U.S.A., there is no reason why it should not receive enthusiastic support in Muslim countries.[2]

Fair Return to Small Depositors and Shareholders

The low rates of return on deposits and shares in many Muslim countries because of administrative fiats and corporate corruption hurt mainly the small savers and investors. Big businesses use different devices to get their due return. They are, besides, alleged to keep most of their savings abroad to evade taxes, to protect themselves from the depreciation of the national currency, and to get a higher international market-related return. They do, however, borrow from local banks and government financial institutions at lower prime or concessionary rates for domestic investment. This accentuates inequalities. This is not a plea in favour of higher interest rates, which hurt investment, but rather a strong case in favour of equity financing and reform of banks and non-bank corporations in conformity with the *Sharī'ah.* This would not only enable savers and investors to get a just reward but would also help bring about greater allocative 'efficiency', economic stability and growth.[3]

Justice to Producers, Exporters and Consumers

Similarly, unrealistic exchange rates and unnecessary price controls hurt producers and exporters, while high protective tariffs hurt consumers. The plea that these measures serve the interest of the common man and promote the country's development is usually a facade. They do not. They serve rather the vested interest of the rich and powerful who have grown continually richer at the expense of the masses who have become more and more impoverished. They also prevent the authorities from adopting healthy policies that would curb inflation, expand the supply of need-satisfying goods and services, and expand employment and incomes.

All measures that enrich a minority of the population at the expense of the majority cannot be defended in the light of the *Sharī'ah.* It is necessary, however, to take adequate measures to safeguard the interest of the poor before exchange rates are realigned and price controls are removed. Such measures may take different forms, including income supplements or relief payments out of *zakāt* and other funds earmarked for this purpose, accompanied by incentives and facilities to expand the supply of need-fulfilling goods and services and income-earning opportunities.

The Moral Dimension

Although a *quid pro quo* relationship between work and reward is indispensable for eliciting hard and efficient work, it is not necessarily sufficient for inducing integrity and conscientiousness. It is also not adequate to motivate people to change their consumption, saving and investment behaviour in conformity with the *maqāṣid*. Secularism, which has tacitly been the dominant philosophy in most Muslim countries, regardless of whether their leaning is towards socialism or capitalism, has neither the filter mechanism necessary to serve social goals, nor the charisma to inspire people and motivate them to make the sacrifices required. Islam, however, has a great potential for creating the desired qualities in people and for making them identify the social interest with their personal interest. It not only demands these characteristics in its followers, it also commands the necessary charisma to inspire and change them.[4] However, since the Muslim masses have lost touch with the inner core of their faith due to many generations of decay and foreign domination, the implementation of a reform programme based on Islamic values is indispensable. It would help accelerate development substantially in Muslim countries by improving the quality and preferences of the human factor.

Fears may be expressed here about the cost and the time span involved in moral transformation. Fears about the cost may be exaggerated. The implementing machinery already exists in the form of mosques, which exist even in the remotest villages of Muslim countries, educational institutions, news media and social reform organisations. If all these are properly mobilised and effectively utilised for improving the quality of the human resource, the cost may not be very high. The governments need to get the *imāms* (prayer leaders), school teachers and social workers involved in the whole process of social change through the proper training and the preparation of necessary literature. The preparation of this literature may also not require a stupendous effort because, in addition to what is contained in the Qur'ān and the *Sunnah,* a great deal has been written over the centuries on the character of a true Muslim and his responsibility before God and fellow human beings. Hence an important task that the governments need to perform is to have this material put across in a simple, effective manner through the network of existing institutions, to mobilise the energies of the people for socio-economic reform and development.

Fears about the time span are, on the other hand, realistic. But, if moral reform is necessary for socio-economic development, then an effort has to be made in that direction. The lack of willingness to initiate the process of social change through moral reform will not reduce the time span. Changing the social mood may help reduce the time span substantially. Reform movements have been trying to accomplish this in Muslim countries but have not been able to make much headway because of the virtual apathy of, in fact antagonism from, governments. If the governments shed their secular tendency and throw their full weight behind the reform movements, the social mood may change faster and provide the needed momentum to social change, ultimately leading to the desired quality of people. If this is not done, the erosion in morals will continue and contribute to a further degeneration in the quality of people accompanied by its adverse impact on development and socio-political stability.

The effective use of educational institutions and news media may help the governments accelerate the pace of social change and eliminate or reduce more rapidly the hold of a number of unIslamic social values (like conspicuous consumption and ostentatious ceremonies) that place a heavy pressure on resources and hurt the realisation of the *maqāṣid.* Such values vitiate the social environment and lead to a consumption pattern that hurts development and need fulfilment. Unless the governments throw their full weight behind social reform, and apply Islamic values uniformly to all, irrespective of whether they are rich or poor and high or low, it may not be possible to make people eschew behaviour patterns that hurt the realisation of the *maqāṣid.* Some of the adverse social influences on the people leading to higher consumption and lower saving and investment, and how to remove them, will be discussed in Chapter 9 on economic restructuring.

ABILITY

While socio-economic justice, moral consciousness, and proper social environment are all necessary to motivate people, they are not enough for realising 'efficiency' and 'equity'. Two persons may be equally motivated, yet they may be unable to contribute equally to the realisation of the *maqāṣid.* The difference lies in ability which is not only inborn but also acquired, partly through education and training and partly through access to finance. Expansion of educational and training facilities and access of the poor to finance are hence indispensable.

Education and Training

The invaluable contribution that appropriate education and training can make towards improvement in the quality of human beings, greater socio-economic justice, and faster growth is now universally recognised. Education opens the door to social equality and economic opportunity, and has been rightly considered to be "the great equaliser" of human conditions and the "balance wheel of social machinery".[5] Muslim governments have nevertheless been grossly culpable for their neglect of this important sector in their resource allocation. Even literacy, which is the first step on the path of education, has not become universal in most Muslim countries. Of particular significance is the neglect of female education, on which depends the character, health and ability of both the present and the future generations. Such neglect cannot continue for long without ruining the fabric of Muslim society.

The primary stress of education has to be on creating a 'good' and 'productive' human being. This is what will help mobilise the large pools of zeal and talent that remain untapped in Muslim countries. Every Muslim student should be educated about the qualities of a true Muslim and strongly motivated to create those qualities in himself. But this is not sufficient. It is also necessary to teach him the skills in demand and the most efficient production, management and marketing techniques.

The secularist educational system in Muslim countries, has not only failed to make the students better human beings, enriched by the characteristics of a true Muslim and conscious of their responsibilities towards society, it has also failed to make them more productive by teaching them the skills in demand. While qualified young men are unable to get admission to vocational training institutes and engineering and medical colleges due to shortage of facilities, the universities, following loyally the conventional syllabuses bequeathed to them from their colonial masters, have been producing generations of secularised liberal arts majors for clerical and civil service jobs, which have now become more than fully saturated. There is thus a steep rise in the number of 'educated unemployed' in urban areas in spite of a scarcity of trained manpower in several sectors of the economy. While the rich are easily able to get technical education for their children at home and abroad, the poor, who need it more acutely to raise their income and social status, are unable to do so. This tends to widen the gulf between the rich and the poor, and to condemn the poor to a position of permanent misery. This is a clear indictment of the educational systems for not responding positively to the dictates of the *maqāṣid* and to the changing economic and political realities of Muslim countries.

There is thus need for a substantial change in educational curricula with a view to inculcating Islamic values and imparting the needed technical skills. It is also necessary to establish a widespread network of institutions such that even a poor man's child in a rural area or urban slum has fair access to technical education and training facilities. This is an important way of removing one of the primary sources of inequity and poverty and providing everyone with a chance to push ahead on the basis of his innate ability and the training he has acquired.

Access to Finance

Lack of access of the poor to finance is undoubtedly the most crucial factor in failing to bring about a broad-based ownership of businesses and industries and thereby realising the egalitarian objectives of Islam. Unless effective measures are taken to remove this drawback, a better and widespread educational system will only help raise efficiency and incomes but be ineffective in reducing substantially the inequalities of wealth. This would render meaningless the talk of creating an egalitarian Islamic society. Fortunately, Islam has a clear advantage here over both capitalism and socialism through a financial system which is built into its value system and which provides biting power to its objective of socio-economic justice. This will be discussed in Chapter 10.

Notes and References (Chapter 7)

1 For discussion, see M. U. Chapra, *Objectives of the Islamic Economic Order* (1979), pp. 14–16. See also, Hakim Mohammad Said (ed.), *The Employer and the Employed: Islamic Concept* (1972). See also, Sayyid Abul A'la Mawdudi, *Islām awr Jadīd Ma'āshī Naẓariyyāt* (1959), pp. 155–6.

2 See, J. W. Middendorf II, "Employee Share Ownership: An ESOP's Moral for the Third World", *Financial Times*, 25 March 1987, p. 25.

3 See M. U. Chapra, *Towards a Just Monetary System* (1985), pp. 107–25. See also Mohsin S. Khan and Abbas Mirakhor, *Theoretical Studies In Islamic Banking and Finance* (1987); Muhammad Ariff, *Monetary and Fiscal Economics of Islam* (1982); M Nejatullah Siddiqi, "Rationale of Islamic Banking", in *Issues in Islamic Banking* (1983), pp. 67–96; and Ziauddin Ahmad, *Concepts and Models of Islamic Banking* (1984).

4 For a more detailed discussion of the moral characteristics required of a true Muslim, see Sayyid Abul A'la Mawdudi, *The Islamic Movement: The Dynamics of Values, Power and Change* (1984), in particular pp. 93–132. See also, Marwan Ibrahim al-Kaysi, *Morals and Manners in Islam: A Guide to Islamic Adab* (1986), see particularly the Introduction, pp. 13–53.

5 Julian Le Grand, *The Strategy of Equality* (1982), p. 54.

CHAPTER 8

Reducing Concentration of Wealth

The most serious obstacle to the realisation of *maqāṣid* is the existing concentration in ownership of means of production in Muslim countries, as it is in all market-economy countries. Unless this situation is corrected through the adoption of certain radical measures permissible within the framework of the *Sharī'ah,* it will not be possible to make perceptible progress in realising the egalitarian goals of Islam. The Islamic strategy in this case is in sharp contrast with that of socialism which, in order to remove the distributional injustice of capitalism, reduced human beings to a permanent state of wage slavery and also killed their initiative and enterprise by collectivisation of all means of production and centralisation of decision-making. Proliferation of ownership and decentralisation of decision-making appear to be more in conformity with the dignity, freedom and initiative that are associated with the concept of *khalīfah.* This proliferation must be brought about in rural as well as urban areas, and in agriculture as well as industry and commerce.

LAND REFORMS

In the rural areas of Muslim countries, where a majority of the population lives, a small number of absentee landlords control large tracts of land and an equally small number of moneylenders exercise monopoly power over access to finance. These landlords and moneylenders have become concentrated centres of power and act as overlords over a preponderant part of the farming population, which is either landless or has small, uneconomic holdings. They exercise immense power over all local government institutions, including the police and the judiciary, making them subservient to their whims and dictates. This sets the stage for exploitation of the rural population, killing their incentive, retarding growth of output, and perpetuating poverty and economic inequalities.[1]

The poverty of the rural population prevents them from getting training in more productive farming techniques, buying fertilisers, pesticides, better quality seeds and equipment, and operating micro enterprises to supplement their meagre incomes. This vicious circle freezes them into a state of permanent poverty and deprivation and breeds indolence, dishonesty and apathy. It drives the rural young to urban areas in search of work. There they face unhealthy living conditions and remoteness from their loved ones. Social control declines and, combined with low wages and other frustrations, contributes to a rise in crime and social unrest.

It is not possible to uplift the socio-economic condition of the rural masses or to strengthen the roots of democratic institutions in Muslim countries without diluting the power centres in rural areas. This is bound to be a difficult task, but since no other socio-economic reform is likely to have as far-reaching an effect as this on the realisation of the *maqāṣid,* a determined effort is indispensable. Hence, land and financial reforms should constitute the cornerstone of all economic programmes. Any government in Muslim countries that claims to stand for general well-being but does not give a central place to these reforms in its programme, cannot be considered serious in its claim.

The question of land reforms hovers around the size of landholdings and the terms of tenancy. Unless both these issues are settled in conformity with the demands of socio-economic justice, it will be difficult to make significant headway in realising the *maqāṣid.*

Size of Land Holdings

If land had been acquired through fair means and cultivated either by the owner himself or leased to tenant farmers on just terms, and if the Islamic system of inheritance had also been faithfully applied, landholdings would not have become concentrated in the hands of a few families. However, since land has been acquired for centuries through unfair means and the Islamic law of inheritance has been disregarded, landholdings have become inequitably distributed, subjecting most of the rural population to lives of virtual slavery, poverty and misery. Given this highly unjust situation, it is important to set a ceiling on the maximum size of landholdings and to distribute the surplus equitably among landless peasants.

The *Sharī'ah* does not, in normal circumstances, visualise the setting of such limits on private wealth.[2] This is because, if its own just system is in operation, equity would prevail and such limits would not be needed. However, the problem faced by Muslim countries at present is that of moving from the prevailing excessive concentration to the Islamic norm. The *Sharī'ah* does authorise the state to take all measures that are necessary for realising the *maqāṣid,* provided that such measures have not been specifically prohibited.[3]

Allowing the prevailing concentration to continue will permanently frustrate the goal of removing poverty and realising an equitable distribution of wealth. Hence, it is necessary to break the combined monopolistic and monopsonistic power of landlords by imposing certain reasonable limits on the maximum size of land held by one family. Even the enormity of the present rural population relative to the limited size of total available land necessitates the adoption of such a measure for the realisation of the *maqāṣid.* Accordingly, a number of renowned scholars, including Imam Hasan al-Banna and Mawlana Abul A'la Mawdudi, have argued in favour of such limits to restore an equitable balance in ownership and to safeguard the social interest.[4] Since the *Sharī'ah* requires the payment of 'just' compensation to 'rightful' owners, the land need not be given away to the peasants free. It should rather be given at a fair price, the entire value being realised by the government gradually over a number of years out of the peasants' earnings, and used partly to compensate the 'rightful' (and only the 'rightful') owners and partly to meet some of the costs of rural development.

Terms of Tenancy

In addition to reducing the size of landholdings, it is also important to reform the terms of tenancy. While the objective of establishing justice between the landlord and the tenant remains undisputed by the *fuqahā'* of all schools of Muslim jurisprudence, the nature of land tenancy has been one of the most controversial issues in *fiqh* literature.[5]

A small minority of jurists permit neither share-cropping nor fixed-rent tenancy and requires that a landowner should cultivate himself whatever land he can and grant the use of the balance to someone who can do so.[6] There are others (a greater minority) who allow share-cropping but prohibit fixed-rent tenancy. Their contention is that although initially the Prophet, may the peace and blessings of God be on him, discouraged both share-cropping and fixed-rent tenancy, he later on allowed share-cropping, and this became a widespread practice among the Prophet's companions and their successors.[7]

A predominant majority of the jurists, however, allow both share-cropping and fixed-rent tenancy, this being consistent with the permissibility of both *muḍārabah* and leasing in the *Sharī'ah*. Their rationale is that the poverty of most Muslims in the early Madinan period had led the Prophet, may the peace and blessings of God be on him, to be more demanding on the rich. He hence discouraged both share-cropping and fixed-rent tenancy, and encouraged landlords to allow the peasants to cultivate, without paying any compensation, whatever lands the landlords could not cultivate themselves. However, later on when the economic condition of Muslims improved, he allowed both, and not just share-cropping as is argued by the second group.[8]

Nevertheless, a number of jurists feel that, even though fixed-rent tenancy is allowed, it is *makrūh* (undesirable).[9] According to them share-cropping is preferable because, by requiring both the landlord and the tenant to share in the reward as well as the risk of farming, it is fairer to both of them, in contrast with fixed-rent tenancy, which assures the landlord a fixed return even though the tenant may or may not be able to have any output. To be fair to the jurists who allow fixed-rent tenancy, they have tried to ensure justice to the tenant by laying down a number of conditions for the validity of a land-lease contract. For example, according to Imām Mālik, if the output gets destroyed or the lessee is unable to cultivate the leased land due to circumstances beyond his control (e.g., flood or drought) then the lease contract becomes voidable because of excessive risk and uncertainty *(gharar)*.[10] In spite of this controversy, a number of jurists find it to be within the competence of an Islamic state to prohibit fixed-rent tenancy, at least temporarily, or to regulate it sufficiently, if this is necessary for realising the *maqāṣid* and serving the interest of the people.[11]

Since tenants and landless farmers are weak and powerless and are likely to remain so for some time, in spite of the enforcement of a higher limit on the size of landholdings, fixed-rent leasing of land may continue to be a source of injustice and poverty when rents are high and output continues to be uncertain. It would hence be desirable for Muslim governments to make share-cropping the general basis of land lease and to strive for a just sharing of the output between the landlord and the tenant. This should continue at least until the power base in rural areas has become sufficiently broadened and the exploitative edge of land-holding families has been effectively blunted. The radical practice instituted by the Prophet, peace and blessings of God be on him, in the early Madinan period indicates that the Islamic state has the authority to undertake all measures considered necessary for improving the well-being of the peasants and landless farmers and for reducing concentration of wealth in Muslim societies.

The importance of land reforms for creating the egalitarian and democratic climate that Islam visualises cannot be overstated. Distribution of land is a major determinant of the distribution of income and the incidence of poverty.[12] Countries that have combined economic growth with an equitable distribution of landholdings, like Japan, Taiwan, South Korea, and Costa Rica, have been able to achieve a relatively more equitable distribution of income, while countries which have allowed the concentration of landholdings to continue are suffering from a higher incidence of poverty and a more inequitable distribution of income.[13] The creation of a rural sector of small, independent proprietary farmers would also help provide a great boost to farm incentives, thus raising agricultural output and accelerating development. Combined with the proliferation of SMEs, it would help reduce the migration of farm population to urban areas and the associated urban congestion, crime and violence. Reduction in the inequalities of income and wealth would also allow democratic processes to take firm root in these countries and minimise the political instability that has now become a characteristic of most of them.

Given the flagrant inequities that now exist, land reform is not an option which the governments may or may not consider seriously. If a meaningful land reform is not implemented, it will come ultimately through a violent revolution. Historical experience shows that when such revolutions take place, all ethical values get trampled. Landlords may in this case lose not only their lands through expropriation but also other belongings and indeed their lives. It would hence be in their own larger, long-term interest to strive voluntarily for just land reform.

It is argued by some that land reform may tend to make agriculture inefficient by reducing the size of landholdings. Such a contention is not upheld by a number of empirical studies conducted in different countries. These studies have confirmed that farm size and output per acre are inversely correlated. This implies that small farms are more efficient than large farms.[14] Empirical evidence that is in conflict with this view, has been explained by the tendency of resources (such as better seeds, credit, water supply and fertiliser) to gravitate towards large farms as a result of the ability of big landlords to use their wealth as a collateral to borrow from financial institutions.[15] Even according to the World Bank, "the resilience and productivity of small family farms throughout the world is striking", especially in view of the considerable disadvantages faced by them in terms of limited access to services, markets and productive inputs such as fertilisers.[16] It is important to bear in mind that implementation of land reforms does not necessarily imply that landholdings be reduced below a certain economically viable level.

PROLIFERATION OF SMALL AND MICRO ENTERPRISES (SMEs)

The counterpart of rural land reforms in the industrial and business sectors is the proliferation of efficient SMEs in rural as well as urban areas. This would complement land reforms in reducing the prevailing concentration of wealth and power in Muslim countries. It also has other advantages which occupy a place of high priority in the Islamic value frame.

The proliferation of SMEs would be in sharp contrast to the prevailing situation in the capitalist and socialist worlds. Large businesses dominate the economic and political scene in capitalist countries and the long-term trend seems to be in favour of even bigger businesses and farms. Consequently, competition, which was the predominant form of market relations in the 19th century in the capitalist world, has ceased to occupy that position.[17] To solve this problem, socialism brought about state ownership of all means of production. This has heightened wage slavery and alienation. It has also eliminated competition and reduced incentive and efficiency. It is not yet clear what trend the move towards privatisation of socialist large enterprises will reflect with respect to their size.

While there may be nothing basically wrong in large enterprises if they are more efficient and do not lead to concentration of wealth and power, it seems that the adoption of a policy of generally discouraging large enterprises except where they are inevitable, and of encouraging SMEs, as much as possible, would be more conducive to the realisation of the *maqāṣid*. This would have a number of advantages besides that of reducing concentration of wealth and power. It would be more conducive to social health because ownership of businesses tends to increase the owners' sense of independence, dignity and self-respect. It would induce such owners to innovate and to work harder for the success of their own businesses. It would create a healthier environment for competition and thus contribute to greater efficiency. It would also help expand employment opportunities at a faster rate, as will be discussed in Chapter 9.

WIDER OWNERSHIP AND CONTROL OF CORPORATIONS

Since SMEs may not be feasible for all types of economic activity, it may be preferable to choose the corporate form of business organisation for large enterprises wherever they are necessary. This has the potential of making a positive contribution towards the proliferation of ownership. However, the corporation as it exists in the West is a primary source of concentration of wealth and power.[18] Even though corporations constitute the dominant sector of the economy and exercise an immense power to make basic product, price and investment decisions that affect the entire nation and, in fact, the world,[19] they do not reflect the political democracy of the West in their decision-making.[20] Corporations operate as autocratic institutions; the holding of controlling stock by a few families makes it possible for them to have control over all policies.[21] This is the natural consequence of the Western interest-based financial system, which makes a high gearing ratio possible and leads to the inverted pyramid of corporate power based on a narrow equity base. The leveraged takeovers witnessed in recent years have made the situation even worse.

The Western corporation does not therefore provide a model for Muslim countries. It must be reformed appropriately to reduce the concentration of power. The abolition of interest and a substantial expansion of equity in the capital structure of corporations in accordance with Islamic values would not only minimise the leverage of rich families, but also lead to a wider ownership of corporate shares and a more equitable distribution of power. This may not be enough because most shareholders do not participate in board meetings. Hence other reforms may also be needed to reduce the sweeping powers of directors.

ACTIVATION OF *ZAKĀT* AND INHERITANCE SYSTEMS

The above measures for reducing inequalities of income and wealth would be more successful if they were further strengthened by the activation of Islamic *zakāt* and inheritance systems. Unfortunately, even though the implementation of both these systems is an essential part of a Muslim's religious obligations, they have remained dormant for a long time.

Zakāt: The Social Self-Help Programme

Islam has incorporated in its structure of beliefs an arrangement for social self-help, with everyone contributing in accordance with his ability, to bring to fulfilment its vision of a brotherhood where everyone enjoys dignity and care by virtue of his or her being the *khalīfah* of God and a member of the *ummah.* While it has made it obligatory for every Muslim to earn his livelihood, it has also made it a collective obligation of the Muslim society to satisfy the needs of all those who are unable to help themselves because of some inability over which they have no control. If, in spite of this obligation, there exists poverty alongside of affluence, the society does not deserve to be referred to as truly Muslim. The Prophet, peace and blessings of God be on him, declared that "He is not a true Muslim who eats his fill when his neighbour is hungry."[22] The Prophet also emphasised that a locality where a person has to sleep hungry deprives itself of God's protection.[23] 'Ālī, the fourth Caliph, also emphasised this same idea, in a somewhat different manner: "Allah has made it obligatory upon the rich to pay out of their wealth whatever is sufficient for the poor. If the poor starve, or go unclad, or suffer difficulties, it is because the rich have deprived them. Hence it is proper for God, the Almighty and the Exalted, to bring them to account and to punish them."[24]

One of the ways through which Islam requires Muslims to discharge this obligation is the institution of *zakāt,* which is an inviolable part of Islamic beliefs. The prescription of *zakāt* is a clear and unambiguous signal of the Divine desire to assure that no one suffers because of lack of means to acquire the essential need-fulfilling goods and services. *Zakāt,* which literally means purification *(ṭahārah),* growth, *(namā'),* blessing *(barakah)* and appreciation *(madḥ),*[25] is technically the financial obligation of a Muslim to pay out of his net worth or agricultural output, if these are higher than the threshold of *zakāt (niṣāb),* a specified portion as an indispensable part of his religious duties. It is one of the five pillars of Islam and reflects a determination to purify the society, of the canker of poverty, and the wealth of the well-to-do, of the offence against Islamic teachings committed by the non-fulfilment of everyone's basic needs. It is a way of expressing one's appreciation to God for His bounties and of seeking His blessings, which will be reflected in the growth of wealth and the real well-being of all. It is thus the financial embodiment of an indispensable socio-economic commitment of Muslims to meet the needs of all, without putting the entire burden on the public exchequer which socialism and the secular welfare state have unwittingly done.

The social self-help arrangement which *zakāt* represents is not like a civil obligation to pay a tax. It is an absolutely binding religious obligation imposed by the Creator Himself and is payable out of the wealth which He has provided out of His Benevolence as a trust, to be shared with those who are not so blessed (Qur'ān, 57: 7). It is one of the prescribed forms of worship – which in Islam does not consist mainly of praying, fasting and performing the pilgrimage; it also encompasses the fulfilment of one's obligations towards other human beings, including members of one's nuclear and extended family, friends and neighbours. On the conscientious payment of *zakāt* depends also the acceptance of one's prayers by God and one's well-being in the Hereafter where the neglect of one's obligations towards fellow human beings will be considered a more serious failure than the shortcomings in fulfilling one's obligations towards God.[26] While the avoidance of taxes may remain undetected by the state and hence unpunished, the avoidance of *zakāt* cannot be so. The Almighty sees and knows everything. Hence there is no question of a Muslim avoiding or evading the payment of *zakāt*. If he does so, he hurts his own self-interest.

The payment of *zakāt* by the rich is not a favour to the poor. The rich are not the real owners of their wealth; they are only trustees (Qur'ān, 57: 7). They must spend it in accordance with the terms of the trust, one of the most important of which is fulfilling the needs of the poor. Any attempt on the part of the rich to show it as a favour, thus injuring the feelings of the poor, reflects their insincerity and destroys their reward in the Hereafter (Qur'ān, 2: 261–74). The poor should also not treat the receipt of *zakāt* as a personal disgrace because what they are receiving is only their right ordained by God in the wealth of the rich (Qur'ān, 51: 91 and 70: 25). They are, moreover, free to choose how to spend their receipts of *zakāt*. It is their money and they may spend it in accordance with their own priorities, which would, in a Muslim society, be within the constraints of the *Sharī'ah*. However, anyone who can provide for himself and does not deserve to receive *zakāt* but still does so, will be disgraced on the Day of Judgement because he is in essence guilty of acquiring income wrongfully and of violating the rights of others.[27] There may not, therefore, be any need for an elaborate system of means testing which tends to be demeaning, expensive, time-consuming, and inconvenient. It would nevertheless be wise, at least in the initial phase, to be alert to misuse and indiscriminate handling of funds. The informal social control system present in a morally-charged Muslim society would help weed out violators. By effectively eliminating those who are able to take care of themselves, the system should be able to provide meaningful assistance to those who are really needy.

It may be expected that every Muslim who is made conscious of his religious obligations, will not fail to pay the *zakāt* if he acts rationally to ensure his short- as well as long-term interests – to attract God's blessings on his wealth in this world and to gain His pleasure in the Hereafter. The Prophet indicated that the payment of *zakāt* does not diminish a person's wealth.[28] God's blessings, which *zakāt* attracts will in fact increase his wealth ultimately. The Qur'ān says: "And let not those who stingily withhold (from others) what God has given them through His Grace, think that this is good for them; no, it is bad for them. Whatever they withhold will be clasped around their neck like a collar on the Day of Judgement. To God belongs the heritage of the heavens and the earth; and God is well aware of all that you do" (3: 180). However, in spite of the prospect of this severe punishment, there may be Muslims who do not pay. The Islamic state must use its coercive power to make such people pay. Abū Bakr, the first Caliph, waged war against those who refused to pay *zakāt* after the Prophet's death. It is the general impression of Muslims that with proper education in Islamic values and the creation of a social environment which is conducive to the practice of Islamic teachings, a majority of the Muslims will not try to evade the payment of *zakāt* and will fully cooperate with the government in knowing about those who do not pay and in making them do so.

The differences of opinion among the various schools of *fiqh* on the 'base' of the *zakāt,* the Ḥanafiyyah being the most extensive and the Ẓāhiriyyah being the most narrow, should not make a significant practical difference.[29] This is because most *fuqahā'*, including the Ẓāhiriyyah, have allowed that if the needs of the poor cannot be satisfied from the proceeds of the *zakāt*, then the state enjoys the right to impose extra levies so as to be able to satisfy all the essential needs of the poor. Ibn Ḥazm al-Ẓāhirī, whose base for *zakāt*, as indicated above, is probably the narrowest of all, wrote:

> It is the obligation of the rich in every country to satisfy the needs of their poor and the ruler should compel them to do so if the proceeds from *zakāt* and *fay'* are not sufficient for this purpose. The ruler should fulfil the needs of the poor for food, clothing for summer as well as winter, and housing that not only protects them from rain, heat and sun but also provides them privacy.[30]

It makes little difference whether the rich provide the resources by way of *zakāt* or special levies for need fulfilment. Those who pay it willingly as a part of their religious obligation towards the poor, increase their reward with God, while those who pay it grudgingly part with the amount anyway, but without the compensating reward and blessings from God.

It must also be borne in mind that *zakāt* does not replace the self-financing arrangements made in modern societies to provide social insurance protection for unemployment, accident, old age and health through deductions from the employees' salary as well as the employers' contributions. *Zakāt* also does not replace the budgetary provisions made by governments for relief and welfare payments at times of calamity. *Zakāt* does not even absolve the Islamic state of adopting fiscal measures and schemes for income redistribution and expansion of employment and self-employment opportunities. *Zakāt* is a social self-help measure adopted with full religious backing to support those poor and destitute who are unable to help themselves, in spite of all the above schemes, so as to eliminate misery and poverty from the Muslim society. If the *zakāt* proceeds are not sufficient, it is the unavoidable responsibility of the society to find other ways and means of attaining the desired goal.

Since it is the obligation of a Muslim to earn his own living, it would be desirable to give preference even in *zakāt* disbursements to the objective of enabling the poor to stand on their own feet. *Zakāt* should become a permanent income supplement for only those who cannot be enabled to earn enough through their own effort. For others *zakāt* should be used to provide only temporary relief along with essential resources to acquire training, equipment and materials to enable them to earn sufficiently. If, along with all the measures discussed in Chapter 9 for expanding self-employment, the *zakāt* proceeds are also utilised to enable people to stand on their own feet within a socio-economic environment which encourages SMEs, then there is no reason why *zakāt* cannot succeed in reducing unemployment, poverty and inequalities in Muslim countries.

Zakāt should also have another salutary effect on Muslim countries. It should increase the availability of funds for investment. The levy of *zakāt* on all wealth, including gold and silver and idle balances held in safes, will induce the *zakāt* payers to seek income on their wealth so as to be able to pay the *zakāt* without reducing their wealth. Thus in a society where the Islamic values have been internalised, gold and silver holdings and idle balances would tend to go down leading to a rise in investment, thus contributing to greater prosperity. Will the levy of *zakāt* promote extravagance, to avoid payment of *zakāt*, or sloth, to receive payment? This should not be the case in a society where simple living is the ideal behaviour, where extravagance and status symbols are frowned upon, and where supporting oneself through one's own labour is obligatory. Nevertheless, the Islamic state must play an important role in ensuring the prevalence of Islamic values and in restructuring the socio-economic environment to serve as effective complements for *zakāt* in the realisation of *maqāṣid*.

Inheritance

Islam has instituted a unique inheritance system designed to bring about a more equitable distribution of wealth. The rules for inheritance are defined by the *Sharī'ah* on the basis of its socio-economic objectives. No one can deprive a genuine *Shar'ī* inheritor except when he is an apostate or guilty of murdering the deceased. Again, no one can make a will for more than one-third of his estate. This one-third has to be for charitable objectives or for persons not already entitled to a share in the estate (unless the other heirs agree).

Both the living parents of the deceased are assured of a prescribed share. This not only ensures their welfare but also enables the distribution of the parent's share to the brothers and sisters of the deceased after the parent's death, thus generating a wider distribution of wealth. The wife is also assured of a prescribed share. The balance goes to all (emphasise all) the children of the deceased. Within the Islamic value frame, it is not possible to pass the entire wealth to just one child, thus depriving others of their just share. If there are no children, the wealth is distributed in accordance with prescribed principles and the will of the deceased to ensure a wider and equitable distribution.

In other words, there is a purpose behind the inheritance scheme prescribed by Islam – to bring about a broad-based distribution of the deceased person's wealth. If the Islamic values are enforced and the inheritance system is effectively applied, the distribution of wealth in a Muslim society cannot but become equitable and continue to remain so.[31]

RESTRUCTURING THE FINANCIAL SYSTEM

The interest-based financial system which Muslim countries have borrowed from the capitalist countries is one of the primary sources of concentration of wealth and power.[32] Therefore, even the implementation of the entire matrix of policies suggested in this chapter may not succeed in bringing about, and then sustaining, the desired proliferation of small and micro enterprises, or in reducing economic inequalities, unless the entire financial system is restructured in the light of Islamic teachings. This subject will be discussed later under a separate heading.

Notes and References (Chapter 8)

1 According to Theodore Schultz, "Because of wrong incentives, the real economic potential of agriculture is not being realised." ("Tensions between Economics and Politics in Dealing with Agriculture", in Gerald M. Meier (ed.), *Pioneers in Development, Second Series* (1987), p. 33. While talking of incentives, one should bear in mind not only prices but also a number of other factors which affect the real income of the rural population. These call for a

package of rural reforms, including land-ownership or tenancy on just terms, adequate rural infrastructure (a well-developed irrigation system, roads, markets, rural electrification, better quality inputs), and financing.

2 See 'Abd al-Salām al-'Abbādī, *Al-Milkiyyah fī al-Sharī'ah al-Islāmiyyah* (1974–75), vol. 2, p. 400.

3 'Alī al-Khafīf, *Al-Milkiyyah fī al-Sharī'ah al-Islāmiyyah,* vol. 1, p. 93.

4 See Imam Hasan al-Banna, *Majmū'ah Rasā'il al-Imām al-Shahīd Ḥasan al-Bannā'* (1989), p. 266; Sayyid Abul A'la Mawdudi, who, in his earlier writings, held the opinion that no 'arbitrary' limits can be imposed on land ownership, recanted later and stated that, in the light of the existing unfair distribution of land, the Islamic state should impose certain desired limits as a temporary, but not permanent, measure to remove the inequities (See Mawdudi, *Mas'alah Milkiyyat-e-Zamīn* (1969), p. 111. See also Muhammad Qutb, *Al-Insān Bayna al-Māddiyyah wa al-Islām,* (1965), pp. 160–8 and 200–1; Muṣṭafā al-Sibā'ī, *Ishtirākiyyah al-Islām* (1960), p. 62; and 'Abbādī (1974–75), vol. 2, pp. 398–420; and Rafiq al-Misri, *Uṣūl al-Iqtiṣād al-Islāmī* (1989), pp. 53–4. There are many others who have expressed similar opinions, for example, 'Ali al-Khafīf, Mahmud Abu Sa'ud, Muhammad Yusuf Musa, Wahbah al-Zuhayli, 'Abd al-Hamid Mitwalli, and Muhammad Anis Ibrahim.

5 For a very cogent summary see, Yusuf al-Qaradawi, *Al-Ḥalāl wa al-Ḥarām fī al-Islām* (1974), pp. 290–301; al-'Abbādī (1974–75), vol. 2, pp. 113–28; and M. Anas Zarqa, "Al-Siyāsat al-Iqtiṣādiyyah wa al-Takhṭīṭ fī al-Iqtiṣād al-Islāmī", in Al-Majma' al-Malikī li Buḥūth al-Ḥadārah al-Islāmiyyah, *Al-Idārah al-Māliyyah fī al-Islām* (1990), vol. 3, pp. 1259–63.

6 This opinion is based on a number of *aḥādīth,* one of which, reported by Jābir ibn 'Abdullāh, says: "The Prophet, may the peace and blessings of God be on him, prohibited the taking of rent or share on land" (*Ṣaḥīḥ Muslim* (1955), vol. 3, p. 1186:90). Another *ḥadīth,* also reported by Jābir ibn 'Abdullāh, says: "Whoever has land, let him cultivate it himself; if he does not do so, let him have his brother do so" (*Ṣaḥīḥ Muslim,* p. 1176:88). See also other *aḥādīth* of similar meaning in the sections on lease of land (*kirā' al-arḍ* and grant of land *(al-arḍ tumnaḥ)* on pp. 1176–80 and 1184–5). This point of view was held by a number of jurists, like 'Aṭā', Makḥūl, Mujāhid and Ḥasan Baṣrī, according to a report by Awzā'ī (see Ibn Ḥazm, *al-Muḥallā,* vol. 8, p. 213). See also, Abdul Hamid Abu Sulayman, "The Theory of the Economics of Islam", in *Contemporary Aspects of Economic Thinking in Islam* (1976), pp. 9–12.

7 For a strong case in favour of this contention, see Ibn Ḥazm, *al-Muḥallā,* vol. 8, pp. 210–14; see also Qaradawi (1974), pp. 295–9.

8 For a strong case in its favour, see Abū Yūsuf, *Kitāb al-Kharāj* (1353 A.H.), pp. 88–91; and Ibn Taymiyyah, *Al-Ḥisbah fī al-Islām* (1967), pp. 28–31; see also Mawdudi (1969).

9 'Abbādī (1974–75), vol. 2, p. 127, and Ibn Taymiyyah (1967), p. 30.

10 See the comments of Dr. Anas Zarqa on the paper of Ahmad Mustafa and Hossein Askari, "The Economic Implications of Land Ownership and Land Cultivation in Islam", in Munawar Iqbal (ed.), *Distributive Justice and Need Fulfilment in an Islamic Economy* (1986), pp. 152–3. The reference Dr. Zarqa cites for Imam Malik's view is: Al-Bājī, *Al-Muntaqā Sharḥ al-Muwaṭṭa'*, vol. 5, pp. 146–8.

11 'Abbādī (1974–75), vol. 2, p. 128 and M. Anas Zarqa in M. Iqbal (1986), p. 153. For some of the legal reforms suggested by Mawlana Mawdudi to regulate the relationship between landlords and tenants, see *Islām awr Jadīd Ma'āshī Naẓariyyāt* (Urdu) (1959), pp. 152–4.

12 N. T. Quan and A. Y. C. Koo, "Concentration of Land Holdings: An Explanation of Kuznet's Conjecture", *Journal of Development Economics*, 18 (1985), pp. 101–17.

13 See C. Gonzales-Vega and V. H. Cespedes, *Growth and Equity: Changes in Income Distribution in Costa Rica* (1983); K. Griffin and A. R. Khan, "Poverty in the Third World: Ugly Facts and Fancy Models", *World Development*, 6 (1978), pp. 1271–80; ILO, *Poverty and Landless in Rural Asia* (1977); A. R. Khan and P. D. Weldon, "Income Distribution and Levels of Living in Java, 1963–70", *Economic Development and Cultural Change*, 25 (1985), pp. 699–711; S. R. Osmani and A. Rahman, *Income Distribution in Bangladesh* (1983); E. Lee, "Egalitarian Peasant Farming and Rural Development: The Case of South Korea," *World Development*, 7 (1979), pp. 493–517; D. G. Rao, "Economic Growth and Equity in the Republic of Korea", *World Development*, 6 (1978), pp. 397–409.

14 See R. A. Berry and W. R. Cline, *Agrarian Structure and Productivity in Developing Countries* (1979); Subrata Ghatak, "Agriculture and Economic Development", in Norman Gemmell, *Surveys in Development Economics* (1987), pp. 355–6; and P. A. Yotopoulos and J. B. Nugent, *Economics of Development* (1976), p. 6.

15 Ghatak, in Gemmell (1987), p. 356.

16 See IBRD, *World Development Report 1982*, pp. 81 and 91.

17 See Paul A. Baran and Paul M. Sweezy, *Monopoly Capital: An Essay on the American Economic and Social Order* (1966), p. 6.

18 See C. Wright Mills, *The Power Elite* (1959), p. 117.

19 See Gabriel Kolko, *Wealth and Power in America* (1964), pp. 68 and 127.

20 Andrew Hacker, *et al.*, "Corporation, Business", *The New Encyclopaedia Britannica*, 15th ed., vol. 5, p. 187.

21 One per cent of all tax filers in 1960 owned 48 per cent of all stock held by individuals (Reagan, "What 17 million shareholders share", p. 102, cited by Greenberg, *Serving the Few* (1974), p. 45). "In the 150 companies on the

current Fortune 500 list, controlling ownership rests in the hands of an individual or of the members of a family'' (Robert Sheehan, ''Proprietors in the World of Big Business'', *Fortune*, 15 June 1967, p. 179.

22 Al-Bukhārī, *Al-Adab al-Mufrad* (1379 A.H.), p. 52:112.

23 Al-Nīsābūrī, *Mustadrak al-Ḥākim*, vol. 2, p. 12, from Ibn 'Umar.

24 Abū 'Ubayd, *Kitāb al-Amwāl* (1353 A.H.), p. 784:1909. Al-Mundhirī reports this same from 'Alī as a saying of the Prophet, may the peace and blessings of God be on him, with somewhat different wording. The authority cited is that of al-Ṭabarānī. See al-Mundhirī (1986), vol. 1, p. 538:5.

25 See the root *zakāt* in al-Zubaydī's *Tāj al-'Arūs* and Ibn Manẓūr's *Lisān al-'Arab*.

26 The Prophet, peace and blessings of God be on him, said: ''Whoever prays but does not pay the *zakāt*, his prayers are in vain'' (Abū 'Ubayd, *Kitāb al-Amwāl*, 1353 A.H., p. 492:919, from 'Abdullāh ibn Mas'ūd. See also al-Mundhirī, vol. 1, p. 540:10).

The following *ḥadīth* from Abū Hurayrah indicates the importance of not doing harm to, and of fulfilling one's obligations towards, fellow human beings. The Prophet, may the peace and blessings of God be on him, asked his Companions about who a bankrupt was. The Companions replied that a bankrupt was one who had no money or assets [to discharge his liabilities]. Thereupon, the Prophet, may the peace and blessings of God be on him, said: ''A bankrupt is a person who will come on the Day of Judgement with prayers, fasting and *zakāt* to his credit. He will, however, have abused this one, slandered that one, misappropriated the funds of someone, shed the blood of someone and beat up someone. His virtues will hence be transferred to them. If his virtues get depleted before his liabilities are discharged, their vices will be transferred to him. He will then be thrown into hell''. (Reported from Abū Hurayrah by Muslim, 1955, vol. 4, p. 1997:59, ''Kitāb al-Birr wa al-Ṣilah wa al-Ādāb'', ''Bāb Taḥrīm al-Ẓulm''.)

27 The Prophet, peace and blessings of God be on him, said: ''Anyone of you who continues to beg will be disgraced when he meets the Great and Powerful God'' (reported by al-Bukhārī, Muslim and al-Nasā'ī, from Ibn 'Umar); and that, ''If they knew what begging involves, none of them would go out begging from anyone'' (al-Nasā'ī and al-Ṭabarānī, from 'Ā'idh ibn 'Amr) – both these *aḥādīth* have been quoted from al-Mundhirī (1986), vol. 1, pp. 572:1 and 573:7. See also the other *aḥādīth* on this subject on pp. 572–92.

28 The Prophet, may the peace and blessings of God be on him, said: ''Charity does not reduce anything from wealth; God increases respect for forgiving; and God exalts him who is humble.'' (Reported from Abū Hurayrah by Muslim, 1955, vol. 4, p. 2001:69, ''Kitāb al-Birr wa al-Ṣilah wa al-Ādāb''.)

29 See Yusuf al-Qaradawi, ''Tawsī' Qā'idah Ījāb al-Zakāt'', *Al-Iqtiṣād al-Islāmī*, Feb. 1982, p. 8.

30 Ibn Ḥazm, *al-Muḥallā*, ''Qism al-Ṣadaqāt'', vol. 6, p. 156:725.

31 For a most comprehensive discussion of the Islamic inheritance system, see Muhammad Abu Zahrah, *Aḥkām al-Tarikāt wa al-Mawārīth* (1963). See also M. Anas Zarqa, "Islamic Distributive Schemes", in Munawar Iqbal (1986), pp. 179–80. The reader may also wish to see Kenneth E. Boulding, *A Preface to Grants Economics* (1973), for an analysis of the effects of inheritance on income and wealth redistribution.

32 See M. U. Chapra, *Towards a Just Monetary System* (1985), pp. 110 and 140. See also the more detailed section ahead on financial restructuring.

CHAPTER 9

Economic Restructuring

Given the scarcity of resources and the need to reduce macroeconomic imbalances, realisation of the *maqāṣid* may not be possible unless there is a reduction in total absorption in such a way that there is a maximum possible increase in need-fulfilment, savings and capital formation, and self-employment and employment opportunities. This demands a restructuring of the economy, and particularly of the consumption and investment patterns of both private and public sectors, with the objective of drying up the flow of resources for all uses that do not contribute to goal realisation. Such a restructuring, as already discussed in Chapter 4, cannot be attained by resort to liberalisation within the value-neutral Enlightenment framework. It can be attained only if all constituent elements of the Islamic strategy are brought into play. Some of the relevant aspects of such a restructuring are discussed below.

CHANGING CONSUMER PREFERENCES: A DOUBLE LAYER OF FILTERS

The objective of squeezing consumption to raise savings and capital formation poses a dilemma. The unequivocal Islamic emphasis on brotherhood and social equality requires that a reduction in aggregate consumption be brought about in such a way that the standard of need satisfaction of the poor is not only not worsened but rather improved. If the needs of all are to be met within the constraint of scarce resources, and if this is also to be accompanied by a rise in capital formation, then an offsetting reduction has to be made by holding consumption within the range of what the society can afford. This requires a revolutionary change in the prevailing life-styles, particularly of the rich. Consumption cannot then be allowed to become the sole end of an individual's life as it has become under capitalism.

Muslim countries have for decades been following a consumption pattern copied from Western consumer culture which measures a person's worth by the luxury of his living and the frequency of his purchases. Accordingly, expensive life-styles, which even some of the rich industrial countries can hardly afford, have become a prestige symbol in the poorer Muslim countries. These, along with a number of unIslamic customs and ceremonies, extending from childbirth to marriage and death, have led to an unrealistic consumption pattern which is unwarranted in the light of their values as well as their resources. The victims of this competition are forced to live beyond their means and to resort to corruption and unethical means to cover the shortfall between income and unrealistic spending. Aggregate consumption has accordingly risen, savings have lagged behind, and capital formation based on domestic savings remains inadequate. Moreover, since most luxury goods and services carrying a snob appeal are of foreign origin, the pressure on foreign exchange resources has risen steeply. The resources gap has had to be filled by external borrowings, contributing to a higher debt servicing burden, with further squeezing of resources in the future.

Need for the Moral Filter

The crux of the problem is how to distinguish 'necessary' from 'unnecessary' claims on resources, and then how to induce everyone to abstain from making 'unnecessary' claims. For this purpose a filter mechanism and a motivating system are essential.[1]

The price system operating in a secularist environment cannot provide either an effective mechanism for filtering out unnecessary claims on resources or a complete motivating system. Although the use of prices as a mechanism for reducing imbalances and generating efficiency in the use of resources is indispensable, it is inadequate to realise equity, particularly if the background conditions are not satisfied. Reliance on prices alone enables the rich to buy what they want of the luxuries and status symbols, no matter how high their prices are raised through taxes, tariffs and currency depreciation. If one family has them others consider them indispensable. Those who cannot afford them also try to be with the 'pace-setters' by acquiring them through suppression of need satisfaction or corruption and unscrupulous means. In developing countries, with their inefficient and corrupt tax administration, it is possible to avoid or evade higher tariffs and taxes by means of underinvoicing, bribery and smuggling. In this case the higher prices resulting from such tariffs and taxes yield higher profit margins and promote not only larger imports but also greater domestic production of such goods. This unintentionally distorts the allocation of resources in favour of status symbols and squeezes their availability for need satisfaction, thus making the prices of needs higher than what they would otherwise be, and accentuating the difficulties of the poor.

This does not imply that the discipline imposed by the price mechanism should not be adopted. It does mean however that the effort to check unnecessary consumption merely by using the price filter cannot be effective. It must also be reinforced by changing the preferences of consumers by the use of another filter based on moral values and a motivating system that can induce even the rich to abide by them. If this is done, a substantial range of claims can be eliminated even before they get expressed in the market. A new equilibrium between aggregate supply and aggregate demand on resources can then be established at a lower level of general prices. This should help need-fulfilment and improve the living conditions of the poor.

In a planned economy, the absence of a moral filter as well as consumer 'sovereignty' makes resource allocation subject to the whims and vested interests of the politburo members and other power elite. Moreover, the absence of realistic market-determined prices removes even the secularist motivation for 'efficiency' in the use of resources. However, if realistic prices and consumer 'sovereignty' are adopted along with private ownership of means of production, as is now the aim in many socialist countries, the absence of a moral filter and motivating system may lead to a resource allocation and price structure that are no better than capitalism.

The Three Categories

As long as the Muslim countries continue to use the capitalist and socialist strategies, they will not be able, any more than the capitalist and socialist countries themselves, to prevent the use of scarce resources for inessential purposes. Resources available for need satisfaction will then automatically be squeezed, making it difficult to realise the *maqāṣid* in spite of increased wealth. What the Muslim countries need to do is to distinguish the 'necessary' from the 'unnecessary' by dividing all goods and services into three categories: needs, luxuries and intermediates. The term 'needs' (including necessities and comforts) may be used to refer to all those goods and services which fulfil a need or reduce a hardship and thus make a *real* difference in human well-being. The term 'luxuries' may be used to cover all those goods and services which are wanted mainly for their snob appeal and make no real difference to a person's well-being. The term 'intermediates' may be used for all those goods and services which it is not possible to classify in a clear-cut manner into needs or luxuries, and some flexibility is considered desirable.

It is possible to derive such a classification of goods and services on the basis of Islamic values. There is some intrinsic discussion in the *fiqh* literature about necessities *(ḍarūriyyāt)*, conveniences *(ḥājiyyāt)* and refinements *(taḥsīniyyāt)*. All of these, as defined by the *fuqahā'* (jurists), fall within the range of what have been termed needs above and do not include luxuries or status symbols. Anything that goes beyond needs has been treated by the *fuqahā'* as prodigality and self-indulgence and strongly disapproved.[2] This discussion in the *fiqh* literature could be developed further in the light of the Qur'ān and the *Sunnah* to enable Muslim countries to realise the *maqāṣid* and reduce the prevailing imbalances.

It is important to bear in mind that since Islam is not an ascetic religion, the classification of goods and services in the three categories need not remain inflexible. As Islam allows a person to satisfy all his needs and even to go after such comforts as may increase his efficiency and well-being, and as the classification of goods and services must reflect the wealth and general living standards in any given Muslim country, the perspective on needs is bound to undergo a change over time with the development of technology and the increase in wealth and general standards of living. In fact, most Muslim countries are richer today and can afford a higher standard of need fulfilment than the early Muslim societies. What is indispensable, however, is the satisfaction of all the basic needs of all human beings in a Muslim society in conformity with their status as vicegerents of God. This goal cannot be realised unless the differences in consumption levels, allowed in conformity with the status and income of individuals, do not go beyond what the economy's resources can bear. They should not reflect snobbery or lead to wide social gaps that can but weaken the bonds of Islamic brotherhood. The objective should not be to create a monotonous uniformity and drabness in Muslim society. Simplicity can be attained in life-styles alongside creativity and diversity. The criteria for classification into the three categories should hence be the Islamic consumption norms along with the availability of resources and the impact on brotherhood and social equality. Removal of the prevailing imbalances will also have to be an additional criterion when such imbalances cease to be manageable.

Liberalising Need Fulfilment

'Liberalisation' may hence be construed only within the framework of these three categories. Production, import and distribution of all goods and services falling within the category of needs should be liberalised. Market forces should be allowed to play their constructive role. The government should do all it can to provide the necessary incentives and facilities to increase the supply of goods and services falling within this category. Any indirect tax which it is considered necessary to impose on these goods and services should be at a lower rate and graduated in the reverse order of their priority. The consumption of goods falling within the category of intermediates should be discouraged through moral suasion and relatively higher tariffs and taxes.

It would, however, be necessary not to liberalise the use of resources for goods and services falling within the category of luxuries and status symbols to ensure that the allocation of resources in the economy reflects social and economic priorities. The price system alone, as argued earlier, cannot accomplish this. It is necessary to change consumer preferences through moral reform. If people understand their social obligations and their accountability before God, and realise that their use of the economy's scarce resources for inessential purposes will deprive others of need fulfilment, they will tend to change their behaviour voluntarily. However, even moral exhortation may be ineffective when conspicuous consumption has become a part of the social frame of mind after having been in vogue for a long time. It is necessary to change the social mood. Individuals cannot change the direction of the tide and are constrained to conform. Hence, for greater effectiveness in creating the needed social environment, it would be desirable to have the campaign for simple living accompanied, at least in the early phase and as long as the Islamic values have not become internalised and the imbalances remain a serious problem, by an officially imposed ban on this category of goods and services, including luxury imports, ostentatious ceremonies, unrealistic dowries and the display of status symbols. The key to success will lie in ensuring that no-one, no matter how rich or highly placed, is able to get by. A single exception may become a flood. The elimination of 'unnecessary' claims on resources brought about in this manner, would help keep exchange rates and the prices of needs at a humane level without the use of controls.

Even efforts directed towards reducing corruption are bound to fail unless the governments first strike at one of the major roots of corruption – the ostentatious life-styles now prevailing in Muslim countries. Such life-styles almost force people to resort to unfair means of earning. The acquisitiveness and corruption of many people may tend to decline substantially once they realise that their effort to acquire greater prestige through conspicuous consumption only blemishes their reputation and raises questions about their source of financing.

REFORMING THE PUBLIC FINANCES: DISCIPLINING THE PRODIGAL

Simple living will undoubtedly reduce private sector pressure on resources and raise the savings needed for investment and development. This will, however, not be enough. Governments in Muslim countries, as in other developing countries, are as blameworthy as, if not more blameworthy than, the private sector, for the excessive claims on resources. They have almost lost control over their public finances and have been experiencing unhealthy levels of budgetary deficits. These deficits have been financed by monetary expansion and excessive levels of domestic and external borrowing. These have generated relatively high levels of inflation and debt-servicing burdens which will continue to plague them for a long time.[3]

Priorities in Spending

In spite of their excessive spending, the governments have neither laid down the minimum infrastructure necessary for balanced and accelerated development nor supplied adequately the services indispensable for realising the *maqāṣid.* Rural infrastructure and agricultural extension services, on which the well-being of a preponderant proportion of the population depends, have been neglected. Education, which should constitute the foundation stone of an Islamic society, has failed to respond to the socio-economic needs even in Muslim countries where it has received emphasis in the government budget. Due attention has not been given to character building and educational and vocational training opportunities have not become uniformly available to all sectors of the population. Health expenditure has been concentrated mainly in the major cities, in large capital-intensive hospitals, and on curative medicine. Yet the majority of the population lives in the countryside, needs a network of simple clinics and paramedical personnel, control of epidemic diseases, and, above all, the provision of clean water supplies, sanitary services and eradication of malnutrition.[4] Housing for the poor has received hardly any public sector attention and slum areas without public utilities and sanitation have mushroomed. Development of an efficient public transport system has been grossly neglected causing great hardship to the poor who have no transport facilities of their own. Yet, all the while, considerable lip-service is paid to Islam and its imperative of socio-economic justice. This sorry state of affairs is bound to perpetuate slower growth and economic inequalities, thus accentuating social tensions and unrest. It is therefore necessary for Muslim governments to restructure their spending in a way that enables them not only to reduce their overall spending but also to concentrate more on projects that will help accelerate development and realise the *maqāṣid.*

The absence of a serious effort on the part of governments to utilise their limited resources more efficiently is due to a number of reasons. Firstly, there is a lack of realisation that the resources at their disposal are a trust from God. This failing, along with the expensive life-style of government officials, has contributed to corruption. Only a moral reform of the society along with a restructuring of life-styles can remove this shortcoming. Secondly, the absence of an indigenous development philosophy worked out with sensitivity to the country's own resources and values has led to the absence of well-established priorities. Without the establishment of such priorities it is not possible to set up agreed criteria for judging the 'essential' from the 'inessential', and the 'productive' from the 'wasteful', use of resources. Unless a long-term commitment is made to an Islamic development philosophy, it may not be possible to remove the existing confusion and conflict in policies. Thirdly, the price system has not been used and resources, particularly foreign exchange resources, are acquired or sold by governments and public enterprises at less than their opportunity costs. This contributes to inefficient use of resources. Fourthly, the absence of an elected parliament and a free press deprives the public of a forum for criticism of government policies. This problem cannot be cured without establishing legitimate governments that are accountable to the people.

Principles of Spending

Commitment to Islamic values and the *maqāṣid* should help on all four counts. The *maqāṣid* will in particular help reduce the existing arbitrariness in government spending decisions by providing the criteria for establishing priorities. The *maqāṣid* could be further reinforced by adhering to the following six broad principles adapted from the legal maxims developed over the centuries by Muslim jurists to provide a rational and consistent basis for Islamic jurisprudence.[5]

1. The principal criterion for all expenditure allocations should be the well-being of the people (Article 58).

2. The removal of hardship and injury must take precedence over the provision of comfort (Articles 17, 18, 19, 20, 30, 31 and 32).

3. The larger interest of the majority should take precedence over the narrower interest of a minority (Article 28).

4. A private sacrifice or loss may be inflicted to save a public sacrifice or loss, and a greater sacrifice or loss may be averted by imposing a smaller sacrifice or loss (Articles 26, 27 and 28).

5. Whoever receives the benefit must bear the cost (Articles 87 and 88).

6. Something without which an obligation cannot be fulfilled is also obligatory.[6]

These maxims have an important bearing on taxation and government spending in Muslim countries. To clarify some of their implications for government expenditure programmes, it may be helpful to consider a few examples.

Since general well-being has to be an essential objective of all public spending in accordance with maxim 1, then maxim 6 would require that all physical and social infrastructure projects, which help realise this objective through accelerated economic growth, job creation and need fulfilment, should be given priority over those that do not make such a contribution. Even among the indispensable infrastructure projects, maxim 2 would demand the giving of preference to projects that would help remove the hardship and suffering caused, for example, by the prevalence of malnutrition, illiteracy, homelessness and epidemics, and lack of medical facilities, clean water supply and sewage disposal. Similarly, the development of an efficient public transport system should acquire priority in accordance with maxim 3 because its absence causes hardship to a majority of the urban population, adversely affecting efficiency and development, and leads to an excessive import of cars and petrol. While these cars provide extra comfort to a smaller proportion of the suburban population, a reduction in their imports and diversion of the savings to import of public transport vehicles could be justified on the basis of maxim 4; such a measure would not only reduce the pressure on foreign exchange resources but also provide comfortable transport services to the majority, with lower congestion and pollution on urban roads.

If priority is to be given to serving the interest of the majority in accordance with maxim 3, then the secondary importance given to rural development programmes has no foundation. Since the majority of the population lives in rural areas and the mass uprooting of manpower from their families and society causes socio-economic problems, the development of these areas to raise agricultural productivity, expand self-employment and employment opportunities, and fulfil their needs must take precedence. This will also automatically improve urban life by reducing congestion and strain on services.

If inequalities of income and wealth are to be reduced, it becomes indispensable, in accordance with maxim 6, to raise the ability of the poor to earn more through greater and more convenient access to better educational and training facilities and to finance. This demands the giving of priority in government spending programmes to the establishment of educational and vocational training institutions in rural areas so that everyone who qualifies has an equal access to them. It is also necessary to restructure the financial system to make financing available to a broad spectrum of entrepreneurs in rural as well as urban areas to raise self-employment opportunities and to increase the supply of need-satisfying goods and services.

Where to Cut

Given the unhealthy fiscal deficits, the *maqāṣid* cannot be realised unless there is a reduction in aggregate spending along with a reallocation in accordance with the priorities discussed above. A decision has therefore to be taken about areas where spending must be reduced. Without such a reduction, either the realisation of the *maqāṣid* will have to be compromised or else spending will exceed the limits of available resources and exacerbate macroeconomic and external imbalances. Where can spending be reduced? It is important to identify some of the major areas where savings could be realised.

Corruption, Inefficiency and Waste

The first and the most obvious way to achieve substantial savings is to minimise corruption, inefficiency and waste, which are seriously eroding the governments' ability to utilise their scarce resources efficiently. Tibor Mende wrote in 1955 that: "Probably no other symptom of Pakistani public life has contributed to the demoralisation of the 'common man' more than corruption." Illicit practices had reached such proportions that "their effect is likely to wipe out whatever benefits new economic projects might have secured for him".[7] The absence of any effective measures to reduce corruption is evident from the continued increase in it such that, even after more than two decades since Mende wrote, the Chairman of the Pakistan National Assembly's Public Accounts Committee had to emphasise that "the major part of the development budget is misappropriated". Instances cited by him include: defective buildings collapsing a few years after construction, roads washed away by a single rainstorm, imported railway machinery becoming scrap without being used, imports being sold elsewhere before reaching Pakistan, and big loans extended by nationalised banks to influential people being written off.[8] Such a high level of corruption is prevalent not only in Pakistan but also in practically all other Muslim countries in spite of its being in the most serious conflict with Islamic values. The effort to reduce corruption will not succeed, however, unless accompanied by moral reform, transformation of life-styles and structural changes in the economy.

Subsidies

A second area where substantial savings can be made is subsidies. Even though the welfare of the poor has to be one of the primary considerations of an Islamic state, a number of subsidies provided by Muslim governments (either directly or through public enterprises, and either transparent or opaque) cannot be convincingly supported. Subsidies are usually defended on equity or economic considerations. However, on both these counts they do not stand up to the test of the *maqāṣid* or the maxims of public spending stated above.

If equity is the goal, the subsidy must redistribute income toward the truly needy. It does not. A lower price that does not cover the costs in accordance with maxim 5 tends to benefit the rich more than the poor because of their larger consumption and easier access.[9] This is not defensible in a system committed to socio-economic justice. If value judgements are not an anathema, there is no justification for a lower price or subsidy for the rich or those who can afford to pay. Only those who are unable to pay a realistic price should be helped. Since price discrimination is administratively difficult and since it is desirable to make everyone pay the realistic price, the best way to help the poor is through substantially increased scholarships, relief payments and income supplements paid out of appropriations made for this purpose by the government or social service organisations, *zakāt* funds, and other voluntary or compulsory donations. In this way the government may be able to provide more intensive relief to the needy by using only a proportion of the total amount spent on a general subsidy. The income supplement would give the poor the chance to determine their own priorities and the realistic price would help minimise the wasteful use of goods or services brought about by a general subsidy.

If efficiency is the goal, the subsidy must strengthen incentives for the realisation of the *maqāṣid* and allocate resources more effectively. It does not. Agricultural subsidy has mainly helped the big farmers "who have obtained a disproportionate share of it and have used it to amass land and other assets."[10] The subsidy paid to large-scale urban industries on the basis of the infant industry argument rarely encourages them to cross the threshold of 'infancy'. However, if the subsidy is used to enable small farmers and SMEs to adopt better technology and inputs, and to stand on their own feet, it could be justified on the basis of the *maqāṣid*. But the rural and urban poor "tend to be dispersed, unorganised and politically inarticulate'' compared with the urban and rural elite.[11] Hence they rarely get producers' subsidies of the kind obtained by large-scale industries and influential landlords. The poor nevertheless end up bearing the tax burden of subsidies because the tax systems in these countries are usually regressive.

Public Sector Enterprises

A third important area of saving could be the gradual lifting of patronage provided to public sector enterprises. ''By and large the performance of state-owned businesses in the developing world has been disappointing.''[12] They have typically failed to provide the spur to industrialisation and faster growth that the governments had hoped. Not only have the financial returns often been unimpressive but the social returns have also been poor. This is because they have operated without competition. The governments have also placed little emphasis on efficiency and have rarely been prepared to use the sanction of liquidation. Low profitability limits their ability to self-finance their investments. Consequently, they have often been a cause of large budgetary deficits, monetary expansion, and external debt. In a sample of 27 developing countries in 1976–79, the net budgetary payments to non-financial state-owned companies were more than 3 per cent of the GDP.[13]

Defence

A fourth area where large savings can be made is defence. According to the World Bank, ''evidence increasingly points to high military spending as contributing to fiscal and debt crises, complicating stabilisation and adjustment, and negatively affecting economic growth and development.''[14] Within the framework of the *maqāṣid* and the principles discussed above, the claim of national defence for the lion's share in budgetary appropriations loses its rationale in the absence of a serious threat of external aggression.[15] It is often forgotten that defence spending imposes not only monetary cost but also other costs, including reduced well-being of the poor, leading to social unrest and political instability. Only a few Muslim countries are seriously threatened; most of the others usually make undue fuss about defence on the basis of unrealistic assumptions. Moreover, it is always possible to have better defence with smaller spending if efficiency is ensured in the use of resources, if corruption, which is more rampant in defence than elsewhere, is removed, and if a conciliatory policy is adopted and unnecessary conflicts with neighbouring countries are avoided.

Since the existence of poverty and extreme inequalities, and the absence of adequate educational institutions, hospitals, and public utilities, particularly in rural areas, is subjecting a majority of the population to hardship and economic backwardness, there seems to be little moral or economic justification for spending huge sums on defence hardware. The absence of a real threat prevents the governments from demanding from themselves and the rich the financial and economic sacrifices that defence requires. Countervailing adjustments are accordingly not made in life-styles and government spending, and the needed sacrifice is hence quietly passed on to the urban and rural poor through inflationary financing and the low priority given to the satisfaction of their needs.

High defence spending does not even provide the security which the governments claim it does. The 'real' source of security for the poorer Muslim countries lies in internal strength attained through moral reform, economic development and socio-economic justice. No amount of defence spending can provide security against internal disintegration which is gaining momentum in many Muslim countries. It seems that sometimes even the very objective of defence build up, ensuring national and territorial integrity, is jeopardised by 'excessive' defence spending. This is because, as Paul Kennedy has rightly argued, a strong economic base is more vital to a nation in the long run than military superiority; and nations which stretch themselves militarily beyond what their economies can sustain are looking for a fall.[16]

One of the most important goals of government policy in Muslim countries should hence be to minimise defence spending through policies of conciliation and peaceful coexistence with a view to releasing resources to satisfy the needs of the majority. If the Muslim countries concerned take an initiative, there is bound to be public pressure for reduced defence spending even in the neighbouring countries from which the Muslim countries feel the psychological threat. Everyone will then be better off. The non-availability of borrowed funds due to the Islamic ban on interest should help compel Muslim governments to resort to conciliatory and peaceful coexistence policies. They also need to derive inspiration from the Prophet, the peace and blessings of God be on him, who signed a truce agreement with the Makkans on extremely unfavourable terms to get a period of peace and tranquillity.

Just and Efficient Taxation

While the elimination or squeezing of a number of inessential and low-priority projects may release some of the resources needed for actualising development and socio-economic justice, this will not be enough. It will also be important to increase the flow of resources to the state treasury through other avenues, particularly taxation. The tax system in Muslim countries needs to be restructured in such a way that it enables the governments to get an adequate increase in revenues in a just and efficient manner.

The 'Right' to Tax

The right of the Islamic state to raise resources through taxes in addition to *zakāt* has been defended by a number of jurists representing practically all schools of Islamic jurisprudence.[17] This is because *zakāt* proceeds are to be used primarily for the welfare of the poor whereas the state needs other sources of funds to be able to perform effectively all its allocational, distributional and stabilisation functions. This right is defended by the jurists on the basis of the Prophetic saying that "in your wealth there are also obligations beyond the *zakāt*".[18] It is also defended on the basis of the already stated maxims 4 and 6 of Islamic jurisprudence which state that, "a smaller sacrifice may be imposed to avoid a larger sacrifice" and that "something without which an obligation cannot be discharged is also obligatory." Abū Yūsuf supported the right of the ruler to increase or decrease taxes in accordance with the ability of the people to bear the burden.[19] Marghīnānī contended that if the resources of the state are not sufficient, the state should collect funds from the people to serve the public interest; if the benefit accrues to the people it is their obligation to bear the cost.[20]

Nevertheless, a majority of the jurists have questioned the right of the state to raise resources through taxes in addition to *zakāt*. The reason for this surprising stand, as explained by Dr. Hasan Turabi, is that governments have been "mostly illegitimate"[21] in the Muslim world over a substantial part of its history. The jurists were hence apprehensive that the permission to tax would be misused and become an instrument of oppression. This view does not, however, establish an irrevocable precedent. As Qaradawi has rightly pointed out, "the obligations of the state were limited at that time." Since the responsibilities have increased over time, one may join him in asking: where is the state going to bring the financing from?[22]

Criteria for a Just Tax System

To be fair to those jurists who support taxation, it must be emphasised that they have considered only a 'just' tax system to be in harmony with the spirit of Islam. A tax system has been regarded by them to be just only if it satisfies three criteria. Firstly, taxes are levied to finance what is considered to be absolutely necessary in the interest of realising the *maqāṣid*; secondly, the tax burden is not too exacting as compared with the ability of the people to bear and is distributed equitably among all those who are able to pay; and thirdly, the tax proceeds are spent conscientiously for the purpose for which they are collected. A tax system which does not fulfil these criteria has been declared to be oppressive and unanimously condemned. All of the rightly-guided caliphs, particularly 'Umar, 'Alī, and 'Umar ibn 'Abd al-'Azīz are reported to have stressed that taxes should be collected with justice and leniency, should not be beyond the ability of the people to bear, nor deprive them of the basic necessities of life.[23] Abū Yūsuf argued that a just tax system would not only lead to an increase in revenues but also to the development of the country.[24] Māwardī argued that a just tax system does justice to both the taxpayers and the treasury; taking more is iniquitous with respect to the rights of the people, whereas taking less is unfair with respect to the rights of the public treasury.[25] Ibn Khaldūn genuinely reflected the trend of thinking of Muslim scholars during his time about equitable distribution of the tax burden by quoting from a letter of Ṭāhir ibn al-Ḥusayn to his son, who was the governor of a province:

> So, distribute [taxes] among all people with justice and equity, making them general and not exempting anyone because of his nobility or wealth, and not exempting even your own officials or courtiers or followers. And do not levy on anyone a tax which is beyond his capacity to pay.[26]

In view of the goals of social justice and equitable distribution of income, a progressive tax system seems to be perfectly in harmony with the goals of Islam.[27] It must, however, be emphasised that from the discussion of the jurists, what is relevant for modern times is the right of the Islamic state to tax with justice. It would be unrealistic to argue that taxation by Muslim countries should even now be strictly confined to the taxes discussed by the jurists. Circumstances have changed and there is need to devise a tax system which takes due cognisance of the changed realities, particularly the massive social and physical infrastructural needs of a developing and efficient modern economy and the commitment to realise the *maqāṣid* within their present-day context. While devising such a tax system, it is necessary to bear in mind that it should not only be equitable but should also yield, without adversely affecting the incentive to work, save and invest, sufficient revenue to allow a modern Islamic state to discharge its responsibilities effectively.

Obligation of Taxpayers

Taxpayers in Muslim countries need therefore to bear in mind that by paying taxes they are not doing any favour to the state or to anyone else. They are only fulfilling an obligation to enable the state to perform its functions effectively. They must also realise that most of the taxes they pay are directly or indirectly for services they are getting from the state, including internal and external security, roads, seaports, airports, water supply, street cleaning and sewerage system. While an effort should be made by governments, in accordance with maxim 5, to recover the costs directly from the users on a *quid pro quo* basis, administrative difficulties and equity considerations do not always permit this. Hence, a substantial part of the cost of government services has to be collected in the form of taxes on the basis of ability to pay. Horizontal and vertical equity demands that, in this operation, equals be treated equally and unequals unequally.

Since taxes represent mainly payment for services enjoyed directly or indirectly by the taxpayers, the effort to evade taxes in a Muslim society is not only a legal crime but also a moral offence punishable by God in the Hereafter. Moreover, to the extent to which this behaviour of taxpayers reduces the financial ability of the government to perform its role effectively, it frustrates the realisation of the *maqāṣid.* What could be a greater offence than this in an Islamic society? Hence, while the jurists have urged the state to be just in taxation they have also urged the people to fulfil their obligation. Ibn Taymiyyah forbids evasion even when the taxes are unjust on the grounds that the non-payment of their dues by some taxpayers will lead to the carrying of an unduly greater burden by others.[28]

Thus, it is clear that Islam places a certain obligation on the taxpayers as well as the Islamic state. While it is the moral obligation of the citizens of an Islamic state to pay taxes, it is also imperative that the government satisfies two conditions. Firstly, tax revenues must be treated by the government in the nature of a trust and spent conscientiously and efficiently for realising the objectives of taxation. Secondly, the government must distribute the tax burden equitably among all those who are able to pay taxes. Unless the taxpayers have an assurance that the funds they are providing to the government will be utilised honestly and effectively for realising the *maqāṣid,* they are not likely to cooperate with the government fully in its effort to collect taxes irrespective of how much their moral obligation to pay taxes is emphasised.

Need for Reform

Muslim countries do not in general satisfy these conditions. While the spending machinery is inefficient and corrupt, even the tax system is inefficient, unfair and corrupt. This undermines the ability of the governments to increase tax revenues. Muslim countries are certainly not overtaxed; their tax revenues are relatively low as a percentage of their gross domestic product. They are, however, like other developing countries, badly taxed. Direct taxes contribute only a small proportion of tax revenues, making the tax system regressive. This is because the number of income tax assessees is small and there are a large number of exemptions and deductions. This makes the tax base narrow and the tax system inelastic; tax revenues do not rise in step with the rise in incomes or the governments' financial needs. The narrow tax base also necessitates high tax rates. This induces evasion and generates black money, the main outlets for which are extravagance and capital flight. Tax base, tax rates, evasion and black money are thus parts of a vicious circle. The narrower the tax base, the higher the rate must be to achieve a given amount of revenue. The higher the tax rate the greater the incentive for evasion and the larger the volume of black money. This vicious circle leads not only to a decline in productive investments and lower rates of economic growth but also to greater reliance on regressive indirect taxes. It is well known that "tax evasion by the well-to-do is colossal, and they are anyhow relatively very few, while the poor are many. Taxation becomes forced to rely on regressive indirect taxes."[29]

A thorough reform of the tax system is therefore necessary to increase its equity and elasticity. Unless the number of assessees is enlarged, most of the unnecessary exemptions and deductions eliminated, and tax rates rationalised, the system will not be able to inspire the confidence of the people and contribute adequate revenues to the treasury without hurting incentive. The sooner the Muslim countries undertake this reform to make the system equitable by expanding the tax base substantially and reducing the tax burden on those who are conscientious taxpayers, the better it will be for accelerated development and socio-economic justice. This is certainly a difficult task, but not an impossible one, if there is the political will to carry it out.

Restrained Deficits

Nevertheless, instead of reforming their expenditure programmes and tax systems, Muslim countries have resorted to the easier course of relying on monetary expansion and borrowing. This course of action creates an unwarranted sense of financial ease which cannot be sustained in the long-run. The result is a relatively high rate of inflation and a steep rise in their domestic and foreign debts and debt-servicing burden. This process tends to be self-perpetuating, leading to higher inflation, greater currency depreciation, unsustainable balance of payments deficits, and an even higher debt-servicing burden. These further squeeze resources for development, decelerate growth, and accentuate unemployment and social tensions.

While all Muslim governments have taken refuge behind the conventional wisdom as regards borrowing, some have inexplicably disregarded an accepted principle of the same conventional wisdom that borrowing may be resorted to primarily for financing capital outlays and not current expenditure.[30] They have been borrowing even to finance their current spending.[31] This is not only extremely unhealthy but also highly unjust to posterity who will have to service the debt. Borrowing does not obviate the ultimate need for sacrifice; it only postpones it. Is it just and morally defensible for the present generation to postpone the burden of its current unproductive spending to the future generation?[32]

Financing Deficits Islamically

The prohibition of interest by Islam has a certain important message for Muslim governments: they must minimise their borrowing. This can be done only if they impose a strict discipline on their spending programmes and do not overstretch themselves. They must rely primarily on tax revenues to finance all their recurring and unproductive spending and even a part of their development outlays, particularly outlays not amenable to Islamically permissible alternative modes of financing.

This need not necessarily act as a constraint on their development programmes. It may be possible for them to arrange the financing of almost all of their worthwhile projects in a number of ways acceptable to the *Sharīʿah* other than borrowing.[33] They may resort increasingly to leasing of infrastructure projects financed and implemented by the private sector on a competitive basis in accordance with government specifications. This will contribute to greater efficiency and less corruption and also open up a wider avenue for greater cooperation between the governments and the private sector. They may also find it possible to arrange some of the financing on the bases of instalment, deferred-payment and hire-purchase. They may be able to invite private sector participation in the equity of projects which are commercially viable, but the management of which it is not desirable to leave to the private sector for some overriding reason. This will make the financing subject to a discipline which the relatively easy access to interest-based borrowing by the governments tends to obviate. The burdensome debt-financed white elephant projects and inefficient public enterprises, which proliferate in most Muslim countries (as indeed in other countries), may then be avoided.

Private Philanthropy

The governments should also encourage private philanthropists to construct and run as many as possible of the educational institutions, hospitals, housing schemes for the poor, orphanages and other social service projects. The institution of *awqāf* (charitable trusts) played an important role over the greater part of Muslim history. Its rich potential has, however, remained untapped in the recent past due to a number of reasons including expensive life-styles and unsound tax policies. The revival of this institution should help reduce significantly the government's burden in financing social welfare projects.[34] The reform of the tax system, as discussed earlier, should remove a major obstacle in the revival of this institution. It may also be possible, but to a much smaller degree, for governments to borrow from the central banks to finance social welfare projects. The imperative of maintaining price stability should serve as a constraint.[35]

Impact on Government Role

None of these alternative methods of financing will create the financial ease that borrowing tends to create in the short-term. The governments will therefore be forced to accomplish more with less. They will have to undertake a careful evaluation of the benefits and costs of all projects, minimise the costs of all new projects, and use more effectively all existing facilities. Accordingly, it would be unrealistic for Muslim governments to talk of Islamisation without making a serious effort to introduce greater efficiency and equity in their public finances and reducing their budgetary deficits.

The constraint on interest-based financing need not necessarily limit the important role that the governments can play in the economy. Their success in realising the *maqāṣid* does not depend primarily on excessive spending through heavy taxation and borrowing; it depends rather on the introduction of greater integrity into government machinery, establishment of proper priorities in spending and project selection, adoption of cost-recovery methods in pricing government goods and services, and restructuring of the economy to the extent necessary to realise the *maqāṣid*. It also depends on helping and invigorating the private sector to play a more active role. To avoid an excessive squeeze in the initial stage, governments may apply the prohibition gradually and not at a stroke, provided that they show a determination to reduce borrowing that is reflected in an annual absolute decline in their deficits. In case of emergencies, it may also be possible to resort to refundable taxes (interest-free borrowing). In extremely difficult circumstances, when the spending is considered indispensable in the overall public interest and the financing cannot be raised otherwise, it may be juristically permissible for a Muslim government to resort to conventional borrowing.[36]

Muslim countries have no alternative to reduced budgetary deficits because even an increased reliance on foreign aid is not feasible. Firstly, rates of economic growth in the industrial countries are low and are expected to continue to be low at least in the medium-term. While the rate of unemployment remains high, inflation has once again become a threat. Budgetary constraints are hence likely to persist and the foreign aid purse may not be allowed to expand. It has in fact shrunk in real terms.[37] Secondly, the decline in the Soviet threat and the diversion of substantial aid to Eastern European countries will probably reduce its flow to Muslim countries. Thirdly, it needs to be borne in mind that except for a small proportion of grants, most of the aid comprises loans.[38] Even though these loans are generally at concessionary rates, they have to be repaid with interest. This could be acceptable if there is a rise in the borrowing country's output and ability to service the debt. However, the irony is that a substantial part of foreign aid is not used ultimately to increase the rate of capital accumulation and growth; it is used to finance private consumption, recurrent public expenditure, and the purchase of military hardware.[39]

Some scholars have alleged that the net impact of foreign aid on a country's long-term rate of growth is negligible and may even be negative[40] because aid programmes are intended to promote the political, commercial, and industrial interests of the aid-giving countries, and are generally not intended to eradicate poverty in the periphery. It is also alleged that much foreign aid is used to prop up military regimes and other authoritarian governments which repress the poor.[41] Some see foreign aid as a weapon of foreign policy in the hands of the donor countries.[42] Even the multilateral aid-giving institutions have been alleged to have ulterior motives. Their aim is said to be to integrate Third World countries into the world capitalist system, making poorer countries dependent on the more advanced ones, and to use their financial power for promoting the interest of private, international capital in its expansion to every corner of the Third World.[43]

Whatever the truth behind these allegations, the poorer Muslim countries have no alternative. They need aid and cannot avoid accepting it, particularly because of the serious external imbalances many of them are now facing. However, it would be in the interest of their geopolitical independence to rely as little on aid as feasible and to use effectively whatever aid they are able to get to build the infrastructure they need and to make the desired structural adjustments in their economies. While the desire to make these adjustments gradually is understandable, there is hardly any justification for seeking aid to avoid making the painful adjustments or to support private conspicuous consumption, recurring public expenditure, and military buildup in the absence of a real threat. The *ḥadīth* of the Prophet, the peace and blessings of God be on him, that "the hand that is above is better than the hand that is below", should be applicable to nations even more than it is to individuals.[44]

IMPROVING THE INVESTMENT CLIMATE: REMOVING THE OBSTACLES

One of the important ways of promoting development, need-fulfilment and employment is increased investment. The increase in savings resulting from implementation of Islamic consumption norms, may not necessarily lead to increased capital formation. Experience indicates that a substantial part of even the existing low-level of savings in most developing countries goes into unproductive channels like hoarding (gold, precious stones and jewellery) and capital flight.[45] Capital flight has become a serious problem for most developing countries. During the 11 years to 1985, about $150–200 billion of the total capital outflow of $250 billion from capital importing countries represented capital flight.[46] Capital flight of this magnitude depresses domestic investment and makes sustained growth more difficult to achieve.

Hoarding of savings and capital flight in Muslim countries are certainly not due to the lack of values that would promote productive investment. Productive investment of savings to contribute to the realisation of *maqāṣid* is the social obligation of every Muslim in accordance with already-quoted maxim 6 that "Something without which an obligation cannot be discharged is also obligatory." Such behaviour becomes even more obligatory because the Prophet, the peace and blessings of God be on him, explicitly praised productive effort and investment by saying: "Any Muslim who plants a tree or cultivates a field such that a bird or a human being or an animal eats from it, this deed will be counted as an act of charity."[47] The Prophet, the peace and blessings of God be on him, also discouraged disinvestment by saying: "He who sells a house [without need], but does not invest the proceeds in something similar, God will not bless the proceeds."[48] Caliph 'Umar used to say: "He who has wealth, let him improve (develop) it, and he who has land, let him cultivate it."[49] The induction of these positive values in Muslim societies can help make productive investment take the place of conspicuous consumption as a prestige symbol. The levy of *zakāt* on all net worth, including currency hoardings and gold and silver jewellery, should also prove to be of great help in inducing savers to get into income-earning financial or real assets to offset the impact of *zakāt* on their savings.

Proper Investment Climate

However, the mere existence of such values and an appeal to people's faith or patriotism are not sufficient to promote productive investment. People do not commit funds for long-term productive investments unless they expect to earn a reasonable rate of profit. This necessitates a proper investment climate – a climate that encourages investment decisions, and helps expedite their implementation by removing obstacles and unnecessary risks and by providing facilities. Some of the factors which vitiate the investment climate are lack of adequate social and physical infrastructure, an inequitable tax system, political uncertainties, continuous depreciation in the exchange rate of the country's currency, and an arsenal of unwarranted controls. The first two factors have already been discussed earlier; the remaining three are briefly discussed below.

Political Uncertainties

Political uncertainties generate fears about sudden changes in official policies which may contribute to backbreaking losses. Such uncertainties are due to the absence of democratic processes and the shifting loyalties of the ruling elite to capitalism or socialism in response to the conflicting demands of their own vested interest and international power politics. Shifting loyalties generate confusion and contribute to the absence of a firm direction in policies. Making a serious commitment to Islam and allowing democratic processes to play their full political role would help provide the needed direction to policies, thereby creating a solid foundation for stability.

The *Sharī'ah* clearly defines the rights and limitations of property holders and the legal enforcement of these should help remove the fears of investors about arbitrary seizures and nationalisation. In his address delivered on the occasion of his farewell pilgrimage, the Prophet, the peace and blessings of God be on him, declared: "Your lives and your properties are as sacred as this day of the Ḥajj."[50] Accordingly, the jurists have unanimously ruled against arbitrary confiscation and nationalisation of property by the state. Abū Yūsuf epitomised this ruling in the legal maxim: "The ruler has no right to expropriate anything except by an established and known right."[51] Even if there is need for nationalisation or public use of private property, the *Sharī'ah* requires a 'just' compensation in conformity with the legal maxim: "A public need does not invalidate a private right."[52]

This clear verdict of the *Sharī'ah* should compel Muslim countries to classify legally all those sectors where only public enterprises will be allowed and sectors where private enterprises will have a free role. Such a classification along with the requirement to make 'just' compensation will minimise the possibility of making arbitrary changes with every change in the government. Public enterprises will anyway have to be kept at a minimum because of the prohibition of interest and the inability of governments to raise sufficient financing for such enterprises through taxes or sale of shares. Once such guarantees, made on the basis of the *Sharī'ah,* have become integrated into the country's constitution and legal framework, it would be difficult for any government to disregard them in the interest of its own domestic popularity and international standing.

Currency Depreciation and Exchange Controls

The continuing depreciation of the currencies of most Muslim countries cannot be prevented without reducing claims on resources through a restructuring of private sector consumption and government spending in the manner already discussed. Instead, most Muslim governments place their main reliance on exchange controls (overvalued exchange rates with import licensing), high tariffs, and promotion of import-competing industries.

Exchange controls, as evidence has indicated, have been

largely ineffective.[53] They lead to the creation of a dual market of official and black market exchange rates. The overvalued official rate encourages imports and discourages exports, thus worsening the external imbalance, distorting resource allocation and depressing the rate of economic growth. They contribute to socio-economic injustice by subsidising import license receivers at the expense of consumers and exporters; the consumers normally pay for imports at the opportunity cost of foreign exchange while the exporters receive less for their output. They also promote corruption and inefficiency. The various bonus schemes adopted to promote exports in the absence of a realistic exchange rate only succeed in exacerbating injustice and corruption. The benefit of these schemes does not permeate to the actual producers; consequently, their resources do not increase to enable them to acquire improved inputs and better technology. Their productivity therefore continues to remain low.

Tariffs and Import-Substitution

Higher tariffs, unlike realistic exchange rates, constitute a single-edged weapon. If applied effectively, they can discourage imports, but do not encourage exports. However, when high tariffs are used in developing countries with a weak and corrupt customs administration, and without any moral reform to change the social mood, there is underinvoicing, smuggling and tariff evasion. This raises the relative profitability of highly taxed, but smuggled, luxury goods and distorts resource allocation against need satisfaction. Hence, a more effective strategy would be to ban the import and use of goods and services within the category of luxuries as discussed earlier.

Promotion of import-competing industries may not be as bad as neoclassical economists have tried to show, provided that this policy is not used to create inefficient white elephants at great cost to the tax payer. When all countries around the world have resorted to such a policy, and continue to do so, there is no reason why Muslim countries should not do so; it is necessary not only for promoting employment and growth but also for creating a broader base for export growth. However, the crucial question concerns the industries that may be selected for import-substitution. In the absence of a consistent development philosophy, the selection tends to be arbitrary with no relationship to the realisation of the *maqāṣid* or the rational principles of resource allocation, both of which must be seriously taken into account in a truly Islamic economy.

The arbitrarily selected industries receive maximum government patronage in the form of subsidised financing, high tariff protection, exemption from duties on the import of capital goods and raw materials, and tax holidays. Such industries are usually large-scale and get established in urban areas. Since most of them are capital intensive and use a more sophisticated technology, their contribution to employment is not as much as that of labour-intensive SMEs. The high tariffs imposed to protect them contribute not only to higher prices for consumers but also, along with other privileges, to the unearned enrichment of those who receive licenses to import capital goods and raw materials for such industries and also resort to underinvoicing. More and more of the nation's resources accordingly move into such industries, thereby distorting resource allocation and enriching the urban and rural rich. Furthermore, in highly protected industries there is usually little competition.[54]

Agriculture and SMEs, which should really be the candidates for protection because of their great potential for growth, need-fulfilment and employment creation, are neglected. They suffer from lack of government support, overvalued exchange rates, import subsidies and commodity aid. Since most units operating in these sectors are small, unorganised and inarticulate, they are unable to exert any political pressure. Concentration of landholdings and absence of democratic processes worsens their position even further. The result is the vicious circle of neglect and poverty of these sectors and their inability to finance investments in improved technology. This is undoubtedly in sharp conflict with the *maqāṣid*.

Bureaucratic Controls

Probably the greatest obstacle to investment in Muslim countries, as in other developing countries, is bureaucratic red tape. This springs from the heavy reliance of governments on controls to realise their objectives rather than on moral reform and the creation of a proper enabling environment. Controls lead to waste of time and energy of investors and an unnecessary rise in costs. Unless most of these controls are dismantled, it would be difficult to improve the investment climate. The general spirit of Islamic teachings is freedom of enterprise within the value-frame of Islam. Controls are an inevitable source of corruption and even the Islamisation of morals may not be able to prevent officials from succumbing to temptation. There is, moreover, no justification for controls on the local production or import of need-fulfilling goods and services and the raw materials and capital goods needed for their production. The removal of bureaucratic controls and reform of the tax system may themselves lead to a substantial rise in capital formation by enabling a productive use of hoardings and reducing capital flight.

Foreign Equity Capital

The Islamic ban on interest will make it indispensable for Muslim countries to encourage and facilitate foreign equity investment. This should no doubt be desirable because "equity investment has proved to be beneficial to developing countries" and it should be possible to attract it by creating a favourable climate for it.[55] It would be difficult to defend stipulations against foreign equity investment which does not conflict with Islamic values and helps realise the *maqāṣid*. It has also the advantage that it makes available foreign exchange as well as technology and management which are scarce factors in Muslim countries and are needed to raise productivity. It does lead to foreign exchange outflow at a later stage but only if the investment earns a positive return. Thus, in contrast with borrowing, the risk is shared with the foreign investor instead of being borne entirely by the host country.

The favourable climate that readjustment of economic policies in the light of Islamic teachings will create, should itself constitute a positive factor in attracting foreign equity capital, and no extra measures may need to be adopted. The Islamic emphasis on the fulfilment of all contractual obligations, if articulated legally, should help provide the reassurance that foreign investors need. The removal of exchange controls on all current account transactions falling within the Islamic value frame, including the ease of profit remittances, is what Islam would find desirable under normal peacetime conditions. It would also be necessary to provide assurances about capital repatriation. But how could an Islamic state even consider the idea of preventing an expatriate investor from getting his right as long as the repatriation is in accordance with agreed terms and conditions? According to the World Bank: "Countries that have followed a more open development strategy have had fewer problems with direct investment."[56] However, until such time as the Muslim countries are able to attract more foreign equity investment, it may be unavoidable for them to tolerate conventional borrowings to the extent absolutely necessary to finance productive, self-liquidating projects that are truly needed for realising the *maqāṣid*.[57]

RESHAPING PRODUCTION

Restructuring the investment climate can only help increase the volume of investments. It is necessary to ensure that this increase in investment does not get diverted to the production of luxury and inessential goods and services, but rather to the production of need-fulfilling and exportable goods and services and capital goods and raw materials needed for this purpose. This cannot and should not be accomplished by imposing a host of controls; the preferable and more effective strategy would be to change individual preferences by motivating them morally and socially, to remove obstacles, and to provide incentives and facilities so that the private sector may find such investments attractive for making long-term commitment of funds. All privileges and subsidies, explicit or implicit, which provide an edge to the production and import of luxuries and status symbols must be withdrawn. Emphasis of government fiscal, monetary and commercial policies should also be tilted in favour of need fulfilment, exports and capital formation.

The general tendency to resort to price controls on necessities leads to long-term shortages in their supply by reducing their profitability and hence discouraging investment in their production. This becomes a permanent source of injury to the poor. In contrast, the long-term supply of luxuries rises, thus serving the interests of the well-to-do. Hence the *Sharīʻah* has prohibited price controls under normal circumstances when there is no national emergency (war or famine) or when businesses are not creating an artificial shortage through monopoly, collusion or hoarding.[58] The short-term harm that the removal of price controls on necessities may inflict on the poor should be offset or minimised through the adoption of a gradual approach (not removing the controls on all items at once), and the use of transfer payments and other measures discussed earlier.

The support to agriculture and rural development and to SMEs, as discussed later, will play an important role in encouraging need fulfilment and exports. The restructuring of the banking system along Islamic lines should also be an essential element of the whole reform package.

AGRICULTURAL AND RURAL REFORMS

Land reforms, though indispensable for reducing concentration of wealth, will not by themselves take the Muslim countries very far in realising the *maqāṣid* unless there is a simultaneous effort to remove some of the other disadvantages from which the entire agriculture sector is suffering – disadvantages that reduce efficiency and output in the agricultural sector, aggravate rural unemployment, depress rural incomes, and accentuate inequalities.

Removing Disadvantages

The most serious disadvantage is the absence of the external economies of an efficient infrastructure (irrigation and drainage, extension services, roads, schools, electricity and health facilities), due to neglect of the agricultural sector in government budgetary appropriations. Unlike the rich industrial countries, which encourage farmers through various incentives, including protection from imports, most developing countries discriminate against their farming sectors.[59] They try to offset the inflationary impact of government budgetary deficits through overvalued exchange rates and low administered food prices. Such policies have turned the terms of trade against agriculture and SMEs, lowered agricultural output, increased dependence on imports, reduced exports and depressed rural incomes. The depressed rural incomes, combined with the inequitable land tenure system, do not leave an adequate surplus to enable tenant farmers to undertake necessary investments in agriculture (improved seeds and tools, fertilisers, pesticides and better storage facilities) and SMEs. This accentuates unemployment and underemployment. There is thus a vicious circle of poverty, paucity of investments, lower output and unemployment. The pressure of population in urban areas has also consequently risen, leading to a decline in urban wages and the creation of slums with miserable living conditions. Hence, the nub of the problem in rural areas, as the authors of *Poverty and Hunger* have indicated, is income distribution rather than agricultural technique.[60]

Financing

Another serious disadvantage faced by the agricultural sector is the lack of availability of financing to small farmers and SMEs. Even though financing is essential, only large farmers are generally able to obtain loans from government credit institutions and agricultural banks. Small farmers find access to these institutions difficult and are 'forced' to rely on informal credit sources.[61] They do not therefore have adequate financing to purchase better quality agricultural inputs and to operate SMEs to raise their incomes and to keep themselves and their family members fully occupied. Since "constant indebtedness to traders, informal money lenders, loansharks or relatives perpetuates the poverty of poor people",[62] an equitable distribution of land holdings, although indispensable, would by itself not lead very far unless suitable arrangements are also made to provide adequate financing to farmers to enable them to make investments not only in their farms but also in SMEs to have an additional source of employment and income.[63] This should naturally be done within the framework of the alternative to the interest-based system provided by Islam.[64] This may not be possible unless the governments and commercial banks who have subsidised large urban enterprises for decades through concessionary or prime-rate financing now tilt the balance in favour of agriculture and SMEs. How this may be done will be discussed later.

Socio-Economic Change

The removal of the disadvantages from which the rural sector is suffering and improvement of economic conditions in rural areas should help not only to expand considerably the productivity of the agricultural sector but also to diversify the rural economy, thus providing greater self-employment and employment opportunities to the rural population. This will help reverse the shift of population from rural to urban areas and reduce urban congestion and crime. If this expansion in opportunities is reinforced by a simple life-style, rural prosperity may be fed back into the investment stream to maintain and strengthen the diversification. There is no reason to doubt that farmers would respond positively to economic incentives. It would nevertheless be necessary to bring about a change in attitudes and work habits in rural areas. This may be attained faster if Islam is used as a mechanism for social change and motivation. Enabling the mosques to play their natural role in rural life could help expedite the desired socio-economic change in rural areas.

A NEW DEAL FOR THE UNEMPLOYED AND THE UNDEREMPLOYED

One of the most constructive ways of realising the *maqāṣid* is the efficient and productive use of the manpower resources of Muslim countries in such a way that each individual person is able to use his or her creative and artistic abilities to the fullest extent in the realisation of the *maqāṣid*. This cannot be achieved if the prevailing high level of involuntary unemployment and underemployment continues. The main policy instruments adopted to reduce unemployment and underemployment are expansion of aggregate demand and establishment of capital-intensive large- and medium-scale urban industries.

Limits of Demand Expansion

While the conventional policy of aggregate demand expansion is no doubt necessary, it is not sufficient and needs to be strengthened by other policies. Within the existing scenario of urban bias of government policies, flagrant inequalities of income and wealth, and demonstration effect of Western life-styles, such a policy helps mainly the rich and spills over to a substantial degree into imports of goods and services for conspicuous consumption. Consequently its full benefit does not go to the indigenous craftsmen and artisans. The demand for their products does not rise significantly and the goal of expanding employment hence suffers. However, if this policy were pursued within the perspective of need-fulfilment and promotion of SMEs, the benefit would tend to permeate to a greater proportion of the population.

Potential of SMEs

Large-scale capital intensive enterprises are not able to employ gainfully more than a small proportion of the working population. Since the poorer Muslim countries have a surplus of labour, scarcity of capital and foreign exchange, and lack the educational infrastructure for training in complex technology, it would be desirable for them to expand self-employment opportunities through the proliferation of SMEs. Imam Hasan al-Banna gave cottage industries a prominent place in his discussion of economic reform in the light of Islamic teachings. These, he stressed, would help provide productive employment to all members of poor families, and thus help reduce unemployment and poverty.[65] Dr. Muhammad Yunus emphasised another aspect of SMEs by saying: "Wage employment is not a happy road to the reduction of poverty", and that self-employment "has more potential for improving the asset base of an individual than wage employment has."[66] Since it would be unrealistic to expect self-employment to absorb the entire manpower, wage-employment cannot be avoided. Efforts should hence be made to ensure that, in accordance with Islamic teachings, labourers receive a 'just' wage, are treated respectfully and humanely like brothers, and are not reduced to the position of small cogs in a big machine, unable to give full expression to their creative and artistic potential.[67] The greater the possibility of such employment in SMEs, the greater may be the possibility of realising these humanitarian goals.

There is a growing realisation now that "the large-scale 'modern' industrialisation strategies of the previous decade generally had failed to solve the problems of global underdevelopment and poverty."[68] Studies conducted in a number of countries by the Michigan State University and host country scholars have clearly indicated the rich contribution that SMEs can make to employment and income. They create new jobs not only directly but also indirectly by expanding incomes, demand for goods and services, tools and raw materials, and exports. They are labour-intensive and require less capital and less foreign exchange. They rely primarily on personal savings and retained earnings and need much less access to credit from governments and financial institutions compared with large-scale industries. They invent new products, revive lost skills and help economies move into new kinds of work. They can be more widely disbursed and thus help maintain the link between a person's place of work and his home which large-scale industries and hectic urbanisation have severed to the detriment of social health. Moreover, they are at least as efficient as large-scale industries.[69] A Michigan State University study has concluded that they consistently generate more output per unit of capital than do their large-scale counterparts.[70] Little, Scitovsky and Scott have concluded that "large-scale modern industry is usually much less profitable than the small craft type industries, in addition to being more costly in terms of capital and creating less employment."[71] Some scholars in fact doubt that large-scale industries can be suitable at all under conditions of labour surplus and capital shortage that are typical of most developing countries.[72] SMEs are therefore being widely viewed as "an effective way of fostering the private sector's contribution to both the growth and equity objectives of developing countries."[73]

Even the OECD countries have realised the job-creating potential of small enterprises.[74] Over the last decade they have accounted for a disproportionate share of new jobs, and those industrial countries where they play an important role have had a greater success in achieving lower rates of unemployment.

Hence, a number of these countries have introduced measures to promote them.[75] "No longer are small firms seen as the Cinderella of the business community, rather they are to be courted and encouraged by politicians of all colours."[76] In Italy, artisans often working in family businesses, are a main factor behind the success of Italian jewellery, gold, silver, leather-working, embroidery, glasswork, furniture, pottery, shoemaking, and clothes manufacturing, to mention just a few sectors.[77] In Germany where the family-owned concern has always played a major part in the economy, there is a renewed awareness of the need to create a favourable climate for small enterprises.[78] Japan's export success is largely due to the vigour of internal competition promoted by the producing firms through their sub-contracting of a lot of work to small businesses on a competitive basis.[79] Small firms are very important in Japan even domestically. They account for 50 per cent of Japanese industrial output and 75 per cent of total Japanese employment.[80] A substantial part of retail sales is still made in Japan through speciality retailers and small family-run stores which are protected by law.[81] This, along with the widespread use of the profit-sharing system, may be among the primary reasons for the lowest rate of unemployment in Japan among industrial countries.[82] Even in other developed countries where the small firms sector has traditionally been weak, high levels of unemployment have made governments very receptive to their promotion. There has consequently been a wealth of public and private sector initiatives to boost the small entrepreneur.

The emphasis of policy in Muslim countries on decentralised production with a proliferation of capital-saving SMEs may perhaps be the most effective way of not only occupying gainfully a large part of the rural landless but also the underoccupied members (husband, wife, parents and children) of rural families with small landholding. This policy will serve to complement the agricultural reforms discussed earlier, and support rural development by raising the incomes of the rural population and enhancing their ability to purchase better seeds, fertilisers and technology, thus raising even their agricultural output. Also, by reducing the outflow of population to urban centres, it will help to maintain family solidarity and be more conducive to moral uplift and crime reduction, which are among the important goals of Islam. While many Muslim countries are, like other developing countries, critical of the policies of their colonial masters "who systematically destroyed all the fibres and foundations" of their societies, they have done little after independence to revive the skills and crafts that were destroyed.[83] Everything has in fact been done to stifle SMEs and to patronise large-scale industries and businesses through a high protective wall, liberal import licenses, concessionary financing, subsidised inputs and tax holidays. This is not a judgement against large-scale industry, which will be indispensable in certain sectors of the economy and which should be encouraged and undertaken where necessary, provided that the overall socio-economic benefits exceed the costs and a heavy dose of permanent protection is not needed.

Promoting SMEs

But how to encourage the proliferation of SMEs all over the country? It requires a number of revolutionary changes in the socio-economic environment. Firstly, there must be a change in life-styles away from imported status symbols and in favour of simple domestically-produced products that satisfy needs and utilise labour more abundantly. Secondly, there must be a change in official attitudes and policies towards SMEs such that they are not dismissed as inefficient small fry and anachronistic leftovers of the past, but are rather encouraged and helped to realise fully their rich potential. Thirdly, they must be enabled, through help in acquiring better inputs, appropriate technology, effective marketing techniques, and other extension services to compete in terms of both quality and price with the products of large-scale industries and imports. Fourthly, they must also be enabled to upgrade their skills through better training facilities; this will require a complete overhaul of educational institutions to remove the existing mismatch between the skills in demand and the education offered. Fifthly, they must also be provided access to finance, the lack of which constitutes the most serious obstacle to their development. Finally, it may also be necessary to eliminate, if not reverse the direction of, the existing bias in favour of large-scale industries which is one of the major hindrances to the expansion of SMEs.

The objective of import-substitution and export promotion may not be realised through the SMEs unless they are helped to acquire more efficient technology to enable them to compete effectively. It would however be preferable if such technology is simple, in which case it would have the following advantages. It would require small capital outlay, thus absorbing the growing labour force with a smaller amount of capital. It would minimise the demand for high skills and be thus suitable for Muslim countries with their relatively lower standards of literacy and technical education. It would enable a greater use of locally available materials and reduce the claim on foreign exchange resources. It would be possible to develop and produce it locally, thus helping reduce the dependence on imported technology. It would be possible to introduce it in small towns and rural areas, thus reducing regional income disparities and minimising concentration of population in a few large urban centres, which large-scale enterprise with its capital-intensive and complex technology tends to create. It would thus be what Schumacher calls "technology with a human face."[84] Even such simple and inexpensive technology has the potential of leading to a "fairly rapid increase in productivity in underdeveloped countries."[85] It would therefore not only help raise incomes and standards of living but also help achieve redistribution.

Notes and References (Chapter 9)

1 See also footnote 3 of the Introduction which discusses 'needs' and 'wants', and 'necessary' and 'unnecessary' claims on resources.

Since the economy's resources are scarce, priority must be given to need fulfilment. The question is how to internalise these priorities. This cannot be left to the psychology of the individual, as Maslow would like. (A. Maslow, *Motivation and Personality,* 1970.) If this were done, snobbery may lead individuals, particularly the rich, to use scarce resources for want satisfaction. To minimise the use of resources for want satisfaction, it may be necessary to change consumers' preferences in accordance with social priorities and also to motivate them to behave accordingly. But how to do this without coercion and despotism? This is where a socially-agreed filter mechanism of values and a system to motivate consumers to abide by these values become important. As Dodgson has pointed out, "it is necessary to avoid the false polarity between the proposition on the one hand, that all needs are subjective, and on the other, that needs can be determined by an all-knowing benevolent political party or despot. A dynamic and open-ended conception of need suggests that the institutions determining, evaluating and assessing needs must be flexible and responsible to both individual claims and public debate.'' (Geoffrey Hodgson, *Economics and Institutions* (1988), p. 251.) Such a polarity cannot be avoided within the framework of either liberalism or anti-liberalism. A moral dimension must be injected into the determination and satisfaction of needs. Individuals must pass their claims on resources through the moral filter before they come to the market-place to cast their dollar votes.

2 For the definition of these terms within the perspective of *fiqh,* see al-Shāṭibī, *al-Muwāfaqāt fī Uṣūl al-Sharī'ah,* vol. 2, pp. 8–12; and Anas Zarqa, ''Islamic Economics: An Approach to Human Welfare'', in K. Ahmad, *Studies in Islamic Economics* (Leicester, U.K.: The Islamic Foundation, 1980), pp. 13–15. Ahmad al-Najjar and Anas Zarqa have in fact argued that, in the light of Islamic teachings, nothing that a man uses (as a consumer or as a producer) is morally free, even if it may be economically free. (See Ahmad al-Najjar, *Al-Madkhal ilā al-Naẓariyyah al-Iqtiṣādiyyah fī al-Islām,* (1973), pp. 32 ff; and Anas Zarqa, (1980), p. 13.) See also Imam Hasan al-Banna, *Majmū'ah Rasā'il* (1989), p. 268, and *Ḥadīth al-Thulāthā'* (1985), p. 410; and Sayyid Abul A'la Mawdudi, *Islām awr Jadīd Ma'āshī Naẓariyyāt* (1959), pp. 136–40.

3 See *IMF Survey,* 6 April 1987, pp. 98–9.

4 See Thomas. McKeown, *The Role of Medicine: Dream, Mirage or Nemesis?* (1979), and Alastair Gray, ''Health and Society: Reflections on Policy'', *IDS Bulletin,* October 1983, pp. 3–9.

5 *Majallah al-Aḥkām al-'Adliyyah,* briefly known as the *Majallah,* states 100 maxims of jurisprudence *(al-Qawā'id al-fiqhiyyah)* in its preamble. An English translation of the *Majallah* by C. R. Tyser, *et al.* and entitled *The Mejelle* was published in 1967 by the All Pakistan Legal Decisions, Nabha Road, Lahore. Although the *Majallah* is a Ḥanafī compendium codified during the Ottoman period, the maxims are almost universally used by jurists of all schools of Muslim jurisprudence. See also Mustafa A. al-Zarqa, *Al-Fiqh al-Islamī fī Thawbihī al-Jadīd* (1967), vol. 2, pp. 945–1060; and Ali Ahmad al-Nadwi, *Al-Qawā'id al-Fiqhiyyah* (1986). The numbers given within brackets after each principle refer to the articles of the *Majallah* from which the principle has been derived.

6 See al-Shāṭibī, *Al-Muwāfaqāt,* vol. 2, p. 394; see also Mustafa al-Zarqa (1967), vol. 2, pp. 784 and 1088.

7 Tibor Mende, *South-East Asia between Two Worlds* (1955), p. 227.

8 ''Most of Pak Funds for Development Misused: Ali Shah Details Pak Findings'', Summary of a report published on the authority of Reuters by the *Saudi Gazette,* 21 June 1987, p. 7.

9 In Morocco, only 16 per cent of the subsidy on subsidised foods reached the lowest income group in 1984 (See ''World Bank Presents its Six-Point Approach to Subsidies in Developing Countries'', *BIS Review,* 8 April 1987, p. 5.

10 *Ibid.*, pp. 4–6; see also IBRD, *World Development Report, 1986*, pp. 90–104.

11 IBRD, *World Development Report, 1986*, p. 92.

12 "Privatisation in the Third World", *Financial Times*, 3 September 1987.

13 IBRD, *World Development Report, 1983*, p. 74. The net deficit of a sample of Niger's state-owned enterprises accounted for about 4 per cent of the country's GDP in 1982 (*ibid.*, p. 67). Turkish public enterprises averaged net losses equivalent to 3.9 per cent of GDP during 1977–9 (*ibid.*, p. 74). One study has found that countries in which state-owned enterprises accounted for higher shares of gross domestic investment generally had lower rates of economic growth. (See IBRD, *World Development Report, 1987*, pp. 66–7.)

14 IBRD, *World Development Report, 1988*, p. 106.

15 Although the average defence expenditure of industrial and developing countries was 16.02 per cent and 13.16 per cent respectively of total government expenditure in 1987, the expenditure of some Muslim countries was: Pakistan, 29.48 per cent (1986); Malaysia, 14.38 per cent (1987); Egypt, 19.45 per cent (1987); Oman, 38.16 per cent (1988); and Yemen Arab Republic, 31.21 per cent (1988). See IMF, *Government Financial Statistics Yearbook*, (1989), pp. 58–9.

16 Paul Kennedy, *The Rise and Fall of the Great Powers* (1988).

17 They have however used different terms for taxes, including, *ḍarā'ib, waẓā'if, kharāj, nawā'ib* and *kilaf al-sulṭāniyyah*. Al-Qaradawi gives the views of Ḥanafī, Mālikī, Shāfi'ī and Ḥanbalī jurists on the subject, while al-'Abbādī gives the views of al-Ghazālī, Abū al-Walīd al-Bājī, Abū 'Abdullāh al-Farrā', 'Izz al-Dīn 'Abd al-Salām, al-Nawawī, al-Shāṭibī, al-Māliqī, and al-'Ansī (Zaydī). The interested reader may see al-Qaradawi, *Fiqh al-Zakāt* (1969), vol. 2, pp. 1100–2 and al-'Abbādī (1974–75), vol. 2, pp. 288–97. For a glimpse of the view against taxation, see Monzer Kahf, "Taxation Policy in an Islamic Economy", in Ziauddin Ahmed, *et al.*, *Fiscal Policy and Resource Allocation in an Islamic State* (1983), pp. 145–53. The reader may also wish to see the discussion on pp. 154–61, which shows the near unanimous view of the participants against the idea of restricting the power of an Islamic state to tax fairly to the extent necessary for serving the interests of the *ummah*.

18 Al-Dārimī, *Sunan al-Dārimī* (1349 A.H.), vol. 1, p. 385; and Abū 'Ubayd, *Kitāb al-Amwāl*, p. 495: 926. For an excellent discussion of this *ḥadīth* see, Al-Qaradawi, *Fiqh al-Zakāt* (1969), vol. 2, pp. 963–92.

19 Abū Yūsuf, *Kitāb al-Kharāj* (1353 A.H.), p. 85.

20 Al-Marghīnānī, *Al-Hidāyah* (1965), vol. 4, p. 105.

21 Hasan Turabi, "Principles of Governance, Freedom and Responsibility in Islam", *The American Journal of Islamic Social Sciences*, September 1987, p. 7.

22 Al-Qaradawi, *Fiqh al-Zakāt* (1969), vol. 2, p. 1074.

23 Abū Yūsuf (1353 A.H.), pp. 14, 16 and 86.

24 *Ibid.*, p. 111.

25 Māwardī, *Al-Aḥkām al-Sulṭāniyyah* (1969), p. 209.

26 Ibn Khaldūn, *Muqaddimah*, p. 308.

27 For Imam Hasan al-Banna's support of progressive taxation, see al-Banna, *Majmū'ah Rasā'il* (1989), p. 267. See also, Muhammad Hashim Awad, "Al-Haykal al-Ḍarībī al-Mu'āṣir fī Ḍaw' al-Mabādī' al-Ḍarībiyyah al-Islāmiyyah", in Monzer Kahf (ed.), *Mawārid al-Dawlah al-Māliyyah* (1989), p. 86.

28 Ibn Taymiyyah, *Majmū' Fatāwā* (1383 A.H. = 1963), vol. 30, p. 339.

29 Gunnar Myrdal, "Need for Reforms in Underdeveloped Countries", *Quarterly Economic Journal* (National Bank of Pakistan), January–March 1979, p. 29.

30 See, Richard A. Musgrave, *The Theory of Public Finance* (1959), p. 560.

31 In Pakistan, for example, the Federal Government's current expenditure has exceeded the total revenue from both tax and non-tax sources since 1984/85. In 1987/88, the excess amounted to 8.7 per cent of total revenue and constituted 1.5 per cent of GDP. (Government of Pakistan, Ministry of Finance, *Economic Survey, 1987/88*, p. xxi.)

32 The Prophet, may the peace and blessings of God be on him, discouraged unnecessary borrowing and borrowing without the intention of repaying. He once prayed: "I seek the refuge of God from disbelief *(kufr)* and debt." Someone asked: "Oh Prophet of God! Is debt equivalent to disbelief?" The Prophet replied: "Yes." (Narrated from Abū Sa'īd al-Khudrī by al-Nasā'ī and termed an authentic *ḥadīth*.) The Prophet, may the peace and blessings of God be on him, also said: "Whoever borrows with the intention of repaying, God will help him repay. But whoever borrows without the intention of repaying, God will not bless the money" (reported from Abū Hurayrah by al-Bukhārī and Ibn Mājah). (Both these *aḥādīth* have been reproduced from Al-Mundhirī (1986), vol. 2, pp. 596–7, Nos. 1 and 7. See also other *aḥādīth* in this Chapter on debt, pp. 596–608.) He also said: "Undue delay in repayment by one who is capable of repaying is *ẓulm*" (Al-Tabrīzī, *Mishkāt al-Maṣābīḥ*, 1381 A.H., vol. 2, p. 109:2907).

33 A considerable amount of literature is now available on the alternatives. For example, see M. Anas Zarqa, "Islamic Financing of Mute Social Infrastructure: A Suggested Mode Based on Istisna'," paper presented to the Seminar on Islamic Banking in Bahrain, 26–28 May 1990; Chapra, *Towards a Just Monetary System* (1985), pp. 132–9 and 166–73; and M. Ariff and M. A. Mannan, *Developing a System of Financial Instruments* (1990).

34 See M. Akram Khan's review of J. R. Barnes', *An Introduction to Religious Foundations in the Ottoman Empire* (1986), in the *Muslim World Book Review*, 2/1988, pp. 34–6.

35 See Chapra, *The Islamic Welfare State and its Role in the Economy* (1979), pp. 14–15.

36 This opinion is based on the Qur'ānic verse related to certain specified items which have been prohibited but the use of which has been allowed in extremely dire circumstances. "He has forbidden carrion, blood, pork and that which has been slaughtered in the name of other than God. However, if one is forced by dire necessity without wilful disobedience or transgression of the limit, no sin shall be on him. Certainly God is Forgiving and Kind" (2: 173). There are a number of other verses of this same implication in the Qur'ān (5: 3, 6: 145, 16: 115, 6: 119). This principle is applied by way of analogy to interest paid if there is a dire need for funds and no alternative arrangement is possible, provided that the borrowing is resorted to only to the extent absolutely necessary.

37 Total net financial flows to developing countries fell by about 15 per cent in volume terms in 1986 – (For details see, OECD, *Financing and External Debt of Developing Countries – 1986 Survey*. According to the World Bank, the net flow of foreign capital to most developing countries is likely to be relatively low in the next one or two decades (IBRD, *World Bank Development Report, 1989*, p. 96).

38 See OECD, "Financial Resources for Developing Countries: 1986 and Recent Trends", OECD *Press Release*, 19 June 1987, Table 2, p. 8.

39 Mohammad Anisur Rahman, "The Welfare Economics of Foreign Aid", *Pakistan Development Review*, Summer 1967, pp. 141–59; see also, "Foreign Capital and Domestic Savings: A Test of Haavelmo's Hypothesis with Cross Country Data", *Review of Economics and Statistics*, February 1968, pp. 137–8; Thomas E. Weiscopf, "The Impact of Foreign Capital Inflow on Domestic Savings in Underdeveloped Countries", *Journal of International Economics*, February 1972, pp. 25–38; Keith Griffin, *International Inequality and National Poverty* (1978), and "Doubts about Aid", unpublished paper, Magdalen College, Oxford University, June 1984.

40 Griffin (1978).

41 Dudley Seers, *The Political Economy of Nationalism* (1983).

42 Teresa Hayter, *Aid is Imperialism* (1969).

43 Cheryl Payer, *The Debt Trap: The IMF and the Third World* (1972), and *The World Bank: A Critical Analysis* (1982).

44 Al-Bukhārī, *al-Jāmi' al-Ṣaḥīḥ*, vol. 2, p. 133; al-Nasā'ī, *Sunan al-Nasā'ī al-Mujtabā* (1964), vol. 5, pp. 45–6.

45 Kindleberger defined capital flight in 1937 as "abnormal" flows "propelled from a country . . . by . . . any one or more of a complex list of fears and suspicions." (Charles P. Kindleberger, *International Short-term Capital*

Movements, 1937, p. 158.) More recently, it has been defined by Deppler and Williamson as "the acquisition . . . of a claim on non-residents that is motivated by the owner's concern that the value of his asset would be subject to discrete losses if his claim continued to be held domestically." (Michael Deppler and Martin Williamson, "Capital Flight: Concepts, Measurement, and Issues", in *Staff Studies for the World Economic Outlook* (August 1987), p. 41.

46 See Stephen Fidler, "Third World's Missing Millions", *Financial Times*, 7 September 1987. See also C. L. Ramirez-Rojas, "Monetary Substitution in Developing Countries", *Finance and Development*, June 1986, pp. 35–8. According to J. P. Morgan, a New York banker, assets held abroad by non-bank private sector residents of the 15 big debtor countries amounted to $300 billion at the end of 1987. ("Brady's Fading Plan", *The Economist*, 12 August 1989, p. 18.)

47 Al-Bukhārī, vol. 3, p. 128; Muslim, *Ṣaḥīḥ Muslim* (1955), vol. 3, p. 1189:12; al-Tirmidhī, *al-Jāmi' al-Ṣaḥīḥ* (1956), vol. 3, p. 666:1382.

48 Al-Suyūṭī, *al-Jāmi' al-Ṣaghīr*, vol. 2, p. 167, on the authority of al-Ṭabarānī; the expression within parentheses has been added on the basis of another *ḥadīth* quoted by al-Suyūṭī on the same page; see also al-'Abbādī (1974–75), vol. 2, pp. 96–107.

49 M. H. Haykal, *Al-Fārūq 'Umar* (1964), vol. 2, p. 229.

50 Muslim (1955), vol. 2, p. 889:147; and Ibn Mājah, *Sunan Ibn Mājah* (1952), vol. 2, p. 1297:3931.

51 Abū Yūsuf (1353 A.H.), pp. 65–6. This maxim has been incorporated in the *Majallah* as Article 97 (see note 5).

52 Article 33 of the *Majallah* (see note 5).

53 See Ramirez-Rojas (1986), p. 37.

54 See OECD, *The Costs of Restructuring Imports – The Automobile Industry* (1987).

55 IBRD, *World Development Report, 1985*, p. 125.

56 *Ibid.*, p. 129.

57 The rationale for this opinion is given in note 36.

58 See, Ibn Taymiyyah, *al-Ḥisbah fī al-Islām* (1967), pp. 22–4; al-Marghīnānī (1965), vol. 4, p. 93; al-'Abbādī (1974–75), vol. 2, pp. 301–15; al-Qaraḍāwī, *al-Ḥalāl wa al-Ḥarām* (1974), pp. 266–73); and Chapra, *Objectives of the Islamic Economic Order* (1979), pp. 20–1.

59 IBRD, *World Development Report, 1986*, pp. 85–109.

60 IBRD, *Poverty and Hunger: Issues and Options for Food Security in Developing Countries, 1986*; see also "Can Better Farming Feed the World?", *The Economist*, 5 July 1986, p. 73.

61 IBRD, *World Development Report, 1982*, p. 76.

62 U.S. House of Representatives, *Report of the Select Committee on Hunger* (May 1986), p. 1.

63 In Japan, three out of four farming households now get most of their income from outside agriculture. See "When the Salt of the Earth Loses its Savour", *The Economist,* 20 February 1988, pp. 43–4.

64 The alternative arrangement, in which cooperative societies, commercial and agricultural banks, and government-sponsored financial institutions will have to play an important role, must avoid interest and be based on risk/reward sharing (*muḍārabah* or *mushārakah*), *murābaḥah* (cost-plus financing), leasing or *bay' salam*. *Bay' salam* refers to a sale where full payment is made in advance against an obligation to deliver the specified fungible goods at an agreed future date. This is not the same as a speculative forward sale because full, and not margin, payment is required. Under this arrangement the farmer may be able to secure the needed financing by making an advance sale of only a part of his expected output. This will not get him into delivery problems in case of a fall in output due to unforeseen circumstances. For details on *bay' salam* see 'Abd al-Raḥmān al-Jazīrī, *Kitāb al-Fiqh 'alā al-Madhāhib al-Arba'ah* (1938), vol. 3, pp. 3–20 and vol. 2, pp. 302–18. For other forms of financing, see IRTI, *Khuṭṭah al-Istithmār fī al-Bunūk al-Islāmiyyah* (1990). See also Chapra, *Towards a Just Monetary System* (1985), pp. 71–3, 163–74, 177–8.

65 See al-Banna, *Majmū'ah Rasā'il* (1989), p. 267.

66 Muhammad Yunus, "The Poor as the Engine of Development", reproduced from *The Washington Quarterly,* Autumn 1987, in *Economic Impact,* 2/1988, p. 31.

67 See Chapra, *Objectives of the Islamic Economic Order* (1979), pp. 14–17; and Hakim Mohammad Said (ed.), *The Employer and the Employee – Islamic Concept* (1972).

68 Carl Liedholm and Donald Mead, "Small-Scale Enterprise: A Profile", reproduced from their "Small Scale Industries in Developing Countries: Empirical Evidence and Policy Implications", a Michigan State University Development Paper, in *Economic Impact,* 2/1988, p. 12.

69 An expression of this view appears in International Labour Organisation (ILO), *Employment, Incomes and Equality* (1972).

70 U.S. House of Representatives, *Report of the Select Committee on Hunger* (1986), p. 4.

71 Ian Little, Tibor Scitovsky, and Maurice Scott, *Industry and Trade in Some Developing Countries* (1970), p. 91.

72 See Mariluz Cortes, Albert Berry and Ashfaq Ishaq, *Success in Small and Medium-Scale Enterprises* (1987), p. 2.

73 Liedholm and Mead (1988), p. 12.

74 A number of books have recently been published indicating the strengths of small businesses. See, for example, Graham Gudgin, *Industrial Location Processes and Employment Growth* (1978); David Birch, *The Job Generation Process* (1979); Steven Solomon, *Small Business USA* (1986); David Storey, *et al., The Performance of Small Firms* (1987); David J. Storey and Steven G. Johnson, *Job Creation in Small and Medium Sized Enterprises* (1987); and Paul Burns and Jim Dewhurst, *Small Business in Europe* (1987).

75 OECD, *Employment Outlook* (1986).

76 Burns and Dewhurst (1987), p. 193.

77 See Alan Friedman, ''Italian Small Business: The Backbone of the Economy Explored'', *Financial Times*, 15 September 1987.

78 See ''Small Business'', *Financial Times*, 29 April 1987, Section III, p. I.

79 See ''Worker-Friendly Programmes'', *The Economist*, 27 September 1986, p. 20.

80 Steven Solomon (1986), pp. 283–4.

81 See ''Why Japanese Shoppers are Lost in a Maze'', *The Economist*, 31 January 1987, p. 64.

82 For a discussion of the Japanese profit-sharing system see Martin L. Weitzman, *The Share Economy* (1984). It is surprising that while profit-sharing as applied to labour, has attracted the attention of the West, profit-sharing as applied to capital, has not.

83 Paul Baran, *The Political Economy of Growth* (1957), p. 149.

84 Schumacher, *Small is Beautiful* (1973), p. 18.

85 See the Report by the United Nations' Department of Economic Affairs, *Measures for the Economic Development of Underdeveloped Countries* (1951), p. 29.

CHAPTER 10

Financial Restructuring

Financing is a powerful political, social and economic weapon in the modern world. It plays a prominent role not only in the allocation and distribution of scarce resources but also in the stability and growth of an economy. It also determines the power base, social status and economic condition of an individual in the economy. Hence, no socio-economic reform can be meaningful unless the financial system is also restructured in conformity with the socio-economic goals of the society. The restructuring should be comprehensive enough to enable the financial institutions to make their full contribution towards the removal of imbalances, and towards the equitable as well as efficient intermediation of financial resources.

Since the resources of financial institutions come from deposits placed by a wide cross-section of the population, it is only rational to regard them as a national resource in the same way as water supply coming out of a public reservoir.[1] They must be utilised for the well-being of all sectors of the population and not for the further enrichment of the wealthy and the powerful. However, since financial resources are extremely scarce compared with water, they need to be used with optimum equity and efficiency. This would take place in conformity with the definitions provided in the introduction if they are used to finance: (i) an optimum number of enterprises, and (ii) the production, import and distribution of goods and services needed for the need satisfaction of all members of society.

The conventional interest-based financial system is not capable of helping realise either of these two goals. It leads to both inequity and inefficiency in the use of resources.

Equitable Intermediation

The inequitable allocation of financing in the conventional banking system is now widely recognised. According to Arne Bigsten, "the distribution of capital is even more unequal than that of land" and "the banking system tends to reinforce the unequal distribution of capital."[2] This is not a contingent event, external to the interest-based banking system. It is its natural consequence. In an economy where differences in wealth are substantial and the lender wishes to get a return without sharing in the risks of business, it would be irrational for him "to lend as much to the impecunious as to the richer members of society, or to lend the same amounts on the same terms to each."[3] The established practice of banks is hence to lend mainly to those individuals and firms who have the necessary collateral to offer and who have, as Lester Thurow has observed, "large internal savings, regardless of whether they are earning above average rates of return on their capital investment." The result is that "the winners are, as in a lottery, lucky rather than smart or meritocratic".[4] Even the Morgan Guarantee Trust Company, the sixth largest bank in the U.S., has admitted that the banking system has failed to "finance either maturing smaller companies or venture capitalists", and "though awash with funds, is not encouraged to deliver competitively priced funding to any but the largest, most cash-rich companies."[5] This bodes ominously for society because it leads to the recruitment of entrepreneurs from only one social class and to the failure of society to utilise its total reservoir of entrepreneurial talent.[6]

Financing of SMEs

Given the bitter reality of inequitable distribution of credit, the goal of realising an equitable distribution of income and wealth must remain only a false hope, in spite of land reforms, unless the tendency of the financial system to contribute to concentration of wealth is corrected. Even the proliferation of SMEs in rural and urban areas, to solve the major economic problems of poverty and unemployment, would similarly remain but a fond dream unless arrangements are made for their financing. Lack of financing constitutes the most serious hindrance to the development of small farms and SMEs. The poor are poor not because of their unwillingness to work hard or lack of skill. They in fact work harder than the rich and have more skill than they can use. Their problem is that they do not have access to financial resources necessary for being self-employed, and wage employment either does not utilise their skills optimally or does not pay them adequately to fulfil even their needs, let alone to save for investment. Dr. Muhammad Yunus has hence aptly emphasised that financing for self-employment should "be recognised as a right that plays a critical role in attaining all other human rights."[7]

The Select Committee on Hunger found that "the provision of small amounts of credit to micro enterprises in the informal sector economy of developing countries can significantly raise the living standards of the poor, increase food security, and bring about sustainable improvements in local economies." The Committee also concluded that "making credit available to entry level micro entrepreneurs is one way to help end the cycle of poverty and hunger among urban and rural landless poor in developing countries." However, as the Committee indicated, "formal financial institutions in these countries do not recognise the viability of income generating enterprises owned by the poor."[8] Reform of the financial system should hence constitute one of the key elements of all socio-economic and political reforms.

The adoption of the Islamic financial system could be more conducive to the needed reform. It would enable a Muslim society to harness the pool of entrepreneurial ability among the poor and to bring to fruition the rich contribution that SMEs can make to output, employment and income distribution. The sharing of risks along with rewards by the financial institutions would substantially reduce the precariousness of a small entrepreneur's position – he would save himself from the back-breaking burden of interest in difficult times by his willingness to pay a higher rate of return in good times. The financial institution is well qualified to share the risk, and could do so without denting its financial strength if it builds loss-offsetting reserves in good times.

Removing the Drawbacks

However, even if the financial system is made to operate on a risk/reward sharing basis, it would be necessary to remove two of the primary causes of the failure or inability of commercial banks to finance small farms and SMEs. The first of these is the serious economic disadvantages under which this sector operates, and the second is the greater risk and expense to which the commercial banks are exposed.

The first drawback cannot be removed without eliminating the implicit bias in official policies in favour of large-scale urban enterprises and replacing it by a strong commitment to support small farmers and SMEs. The adoption and implementation of the programme proposed earlier, through appropriate government policies and budgetary support, should help to divert gradually more and more of commercial bank financing to small farmers and SMEs.

The second drawback cannot be removed without reducing the risk and expense of commercial bank lending to such units. The greater risk of financing SMEs leads to a tough and extensive collateral requirement which they are unable to satisfy. This jeopardises their growth and expansion in spite of their greater potential for contribution to employment, output and income distribution. The financing goes mainly to the rich who are subjected to a lower collateral requirement and which they are able to satisfy without any difficulty because of their greater wealth.

It may be expected that, within the Islamic risk/reward sharing framework, banks may tend to be attracted to provide greater financing to smaller firms because of their well-established greater profitability. Small firms have a record of better performance in terms of growth in real per capita profits in industrial countries where small entrepreneurs have been encouraged.[9] Even in developing countries with their extremely difficult environment for SMEs, they have consistently generated, according to a Michigan State University study, more output per unit of capital and are generally more efficient than their large-scale counterparts. Accordingly, the economic profit of smaller firms is consistently larger than that of large firms.[10]

The risk may be reduced by introducing a loan guarantee

scheme underwritten partly by the government and partly by the commercial banks.[11] In the case of Islamic banks, the guarantee scheme could not ensure the repayment of loans with interest as is the case in the conventional system. The scheme would rather cover the 'moral' risk of financing and relieve the bank of the need for collateral from SMEs whose general credentials have been examined and certified by the guarantee scheme. A large number of SMEs would thus be able to get financing from banks without being able to offer the collateral required by the conventional banks. The bank would receive its money back from the guarantee scheme in case of 'moral' failure of the business. In case of market failure and resultant loss, the bank would share the consequences with the business in proportion to the financing provided by it. The scheme would also be made to include some other non-commercial risks that it is desirable to cover, to increase the availability of funds to SMEs.

Apprehensions about the viability of the loan guarantee scheme due to heavy loan losses may be unwarranted. As indicated above, the scheme would not bear the entire risk of loan losses. It would bear only the 'moral' risk, the business risk being borne by both the bank and the borrower. Hence, the scheme would not be as heavily burdened with losses as conventional schemes are. Moreover, the experience of the International Fund for Agricultural Development (IFAD) is that credit provided to the most enterprising of the poor is quickly repaid by them from their higher earnings.[12] The Report of the Select Committee on Hunger also indicates that the "micro enterprise projects have recorded significant and impressive loan repayment rates."[13] Testimony from the Grameen Bank in Bangladesh indicates a constant repayment rate of 99 per cent since the bank's inception.[14] Other SME credit programmes have yielded similar results. Hence there is no reason to be unduly apprehensive about loan losses from such financing.

The additional expense incurred by commercial banks in evaluating and financing SMEs may be partly offset by the government in the interest of realising the *maqāṣid*. Big business has been subsidised by governments for a long time through various ways, including concessionary financing, import licences, overvalued currencies, and subsidised inputs. To offset this undue advantage received in the past, the governments should now turn the tables in favour of small farmers and SMEs. Both the *maqāṣid* and the principles of public spending discussed earlier justify a reasonable allocation of government resources for this purpose. Nevertheless, a part of the increased cost should also be recovered from banks and SMEs to promote greater responsibility and efficiency. It may be expected that once the credentials of SMEs have been established and the system has started operating, the costs to be shared by the government would tend to go down.

Efficient Intermediation

The inefficient allocation of financial resources of the conventional banking system is also a logical consequence of that system. Since credit is extended to the private sector on the basis of collateral and/or a stable source of income to service the debt, and to governments on the assumption of lower sovereign risk, proposals for financing are not subjected to strict evaluation; the end use of credit is only a secondary consideration. Credit becomes available for any purpose, irrespective of whether it is for productive investment or not. The private sector is able to have access to it even for conspicuous consumption and speculation, while the public sector is able to get it for chauvinistic defence buildup and white elephant projects as well. This contributes to excessive monetary expansion and a wasteful and unproductive use of the society's pool of deposits. Thus, there is an unnecessary pressure on scarce resources and a decline in their availability for productive investment and need satisfaction. A resource allocation that does not lead to optimum investment and need satisfaction because of diversion of resources to unproductive uses is essentially inefficient, even though it may be called 'efficient' within a value-free frame of reference.

In the Islamic equity-based and risk/reward sharing system, value judgements as well as strength of the proposal would both play an important role in the allocation of resources. Credit allocation would thus tend to reflect greater efficiency from both the demand and supply sides. On the demand side, the effective implementation of Islamic consumption values along lines discussed earlier in Chapter 9 should help to reduce substantially the demand for financing inessential goods and conspicuous consumption. On the supply side also, the requirement of risk/reward sharing would tend to make banks careful in their evaluation of proposals. Financing would in this way be available to the private sector and the governments mainly for productive projects. The ability to provide the collateral and to pay the interest would not now be the main consideration. Consumer credit would no doubt still exist on the basis of techniques allowed by the *Sharī'ah*, but to a limited extent and to satisfy the need for 'essential' durable goods. The overall flow of credit for unproductive purposes would thus be substantially reduced, making a healthy contribution to the removal of imbalances and the realisation of both equity and efficiency.

The Islamisation of banks may also help bring into their fold the savings of a large proportion of the rural population not yet absorbed by the banking system because of their lack of trust in conventional interest-based banks, and of the apathy of banks towards them. This would help mobilise the idle savings in the economy and generate a higher non-inflationary rate of growth. It may also help reduce the attractiveness of gold as a store of value and release savings for investment.

Notes and References (Chapter 10)

1 The non-corporate sector in developing countries generally accounts for 60–70 per cent of private sector domestic saving. It is the only sector whose saving exceeds its investment (V. V. Bhatt, "Improving the Financial Structure", *Finance and Development,* June 1986, p. 20

2 Arne Bigsten, "Poverty, Inequality and Development", in Gemmell, *Surveys in Development Economics* (1987), p. 156. Stanley Lebergott also considers the "quite rational" supply of credit to wealthy individuals as one of the major reasons for skewed distribution of capital. See, Stanley Lebergott, "The Shape of the Income Distribution", *American Economic Review,* June 1959, pp. 328–47.

3 E. S. Mishan, *Cost Benefit Analysis* (1971), p. 205.

4 Lester Thurow, *Zero-Sum Society* (1980), p. 175.

5 Morgan Guarantee Trust Company of New York, *World Financial Markets,* January 1987, p. 7.

6 See Charles Leadbearer, ''Rags to Riches – Fact or Fiction'', *Financial Times*, 30 December 1986, p. 5.

7 Muhammad Yunus, ''The Poor as the Engine of Growth'', reproduced from *The Washington Quarterly*, Autumn 1987, in *Economic Impact*, 2/1988, p. 31.

8 U.S. House of Representatives, *Banking for the Poor: Alleviating Poverty Through Credit Assistance in Developing Countries, Report of the Select Committee on Hunger* (1986), p. v.

9 See Alan Friedman, ''Italian Small Business: The Backbone of the Economy Explored'', *Financial Times*, 29 April 1987, Section III, p. I.

10 U.S. House of Representatives, *Report of the Select Committee on Hunger* (1986), p. 4 and Chart 2 on p. 5.

11 Loan guarantee schemes exist in practically all industrial countries which, having realised the potential of small firms, have initiated a programme to encourage them. For some relevant details about such schemes in a number of European countries, see Paul Burns and Jim Dewhurst, *Small Business in Europe* (1987), pp. 199–200.

12 See *The Economist*, 16 February 1985, p. 15.

13 U.S. House of Representatives, *Report of the Select Committee on Hunger* (1986), p. 7

14 See M. Yunus, *Group-Based Savings and Credit for the Rural Poor* (1984), p. 12.

CHAPTER 11

Strategic Policy Planning

It will not be possible for Muslim countries to realise the *maqāṣid* within the constraint of their scarce resources unless they take stock of their needs and resources and have a clear understanding of where they are and where they wish to go. It may be possible to do this more effectively if a long-term strategic policy plan is prepared. Such a plan would enable the state to take a realistic account of all the available physical and human resources and to establish, in the light of this, a set of well-defined priorities. This will help provide a clear direction to government policies and expenditure programmes and initiate effective measures to set in motion the required structural and institutional changes to enable both the government and the private sector to make their full contribution.

The plan should not be comprehensive and *dirigiste*, trying to achieve, through a maze of regulatory controls, a balancing of all inputs and outputs and their allocation among micro units of the economy. The plan should also not rely on the government being the principal source of investments and enterprise. This is neither feasible nor necessary. Any move in this direction will make the economy less responsive to changing circumstances and stifle individual initiative and enterprise, and so bury it in the contradictions and insoluble problems that afflicted the socialist and developing countries which resorted to such planning. Indeed, these countries have all been forced to move away from such planning. What is necessary for the Muslim countries to do is to pass all claims on resources through the filter mechanism of Islamic values and to motivate and activate the private sector, through moral and institutional reform as well as economic incentives, to utilise scarce resources with optimum efficiency and equity in order to realise the *maqāṣid*.

The articulation of the Islamic filter mechanism will thus be indispensable. It will help define the goals of the economy in order of priority and specify ways of achieving them. The establishment of priorities within the framework of the *Sharī'ah* will help in an analysis of the existing allocation of resources and in pinpointing the direction of change. It will also be necessary to articulate the Islamic values regarding consumption, savings and investment, and work ethics, and to devise educational programmes to promote them. The plan will also have to classify goods and services into the three categories of needs, luxuries and intermediates, as discussed earlier.

Public and government officials will need to be motivated to act in accordance with Islamic values. While belief in accountability before God is essential, it is not sufficient to motivate them to put in their best and to be more efficient. For this purpose it is necessary to actualise socio-economic justice. Workers, entrepreneurs, investors and savers must all be able to get a due reward for their contribution to output. Of course, prices and wages must be normally determined by market forces, but, in the existing situation, with wealth and power concentrated in a few hands, they reflect monopolistic or monopsonistic characteristics and are hence not 'just'. They therefore tend to suffocate the drive, initiative, creativity and enterprise of a large proportion of the population. The plan must indicate the policies and institutional reforms needed to remove the existing injustices.

The plan must also specify the structural changes required in the economy to fulfil needs, reduce unemployment and raise the growth rate without creating macroeconomic and external imbalances. The plan must also indicate the institutions that must be established or reformed to reduce substantially the inequalities of income and wealth that now exist, and to bring about a broad-based ownership of businesses and income-earning assets. The reform of the banking system in the light of Islamic teachings will require the special attention of planners because of the great contribution it can make to efficient and equitable allocation of resources. A thorough reform of the education system is also necessary to make the students better

Muslims and more productive. In sum, the plan should not concentrate on any single measure or rely unduly on controls; it should rather use a range of policies and incentives to realise the *maqāṣid*. It should reflect a perceptible change in the development philosophy and strategy. All policies – fiscal, monetary, incomes, import and production – should be formulated within the framework of this strategic policy plan.

The production, import, distribution and consumption of what fits into the strategic policy plan should be permitted freely through the operation of the price system without bureaucratic controls. Controls, including those on the use of foreign exchange for current account transactions, should be employed only where, and as long as, indispensable. A general policy of letting social and institutional reform and incentives take the place of controls will help remove inequities in material rewards, harness people's own inner drive for development, and, not only help reduce corruption and attain greater efficiency, but also make innovation and adjustment to changing circumstances easier. However, what does not conform with the plan should not be allowed – irrespective of how rich or resourceful an individual may be. Special consideration should be given to the adverse effect of any policy measure on the poor, and methods should be devised to offset or minimise this.

There should not be changes in policy from quarter to quarter or year to year because the resource perspective, needs and goals of a country do not change that frequently. Frequent tinkering with policies only generates uncertainties, and enriches mainly those having insider's knowledge. But errors which have been made in the preparation of the plan should be rectified with an open mind and without undue delay. Since the resource endowment of different Muslim countries is different, the same strategic policy plan may not be suitable for all, even though the *maqāṣid* are likely in essentials to be the same for all.

It may be unrealistic to expect governments to be willing to formulate and execute a strategic policy plan of this nature unless they derive their inspiration from the *Sharīʻah* and are committed to the well-being of all people rather than any specific group. This is not possible unless they are legitimate governments, that is, have received their mandate from the people and are accountable to them for their success or failure in formulating and executing proper policies. Political reform therefore constitutes the cornerstone of all reform in Muslim countries. Without such reform, the prevailing distance between the ideals of Islam and the reality in the Muslim world may continue. It would, of course, be a further step in the right direction if the democratic processes as they now prevail around the world are also reformed suitably to blunt the edge they provide to wealth and power.

CHAPTER 12

Conclusion

O believers! Respond to God and to His Prophet when he calls you towards that which will give you life.

(Qur'ān, 8: 24)

If the people of the towns had only believed and lived accordingly, We would have opened out to them blessings from the Heaven and the earth.

(Qur'ān, 7: 96)

We are heading into difficult times and there isn't a great deal that can be done about it. . . . such superficial issues as debates about the short-term business cycle or Republican versus Democratic political philosophy or shifts in tax policy can't significantly change the outlook.

Jay Forrester[1]

THE PARADOX

The challenge that the Muslim countries face is to actualise the Islamic vision of *falāḥ* and *ḥayāt ṭayyibah* for every individual in their societies in spite of the resource constraints they face. This demands not only moral uplift but also brotherhood and socio-economic justice, which cannot be realised unless the scarce resources are used to remove poverty, fulfil needs, and minimise inequalities of income and wealth. Instead, most Muslim countries have got themselves engulfed, like most other developing countries, in a maze of difficult macroeconomic and external imbalances without getting any nearer their vision.

This book has argued that this situation is the logical outcome of policies they have been following within the perspective of the secularist strategies of capitalism, socialism and the welfare state. Were it not the case, countries following these systems would have themselves succeeded in ensuring the good life for all their nationals. But they have not. This is the paradox of wealth. "Rich countries are not typically happier than poorer ones", concludes Richard Easterlin after 30 surveys conducted in 19 developed and developing countries.[2] And Dahrendorf justifiably asks: Why are so many citizens of rich societies unhappy after four decades of peace and prosperity, and why is there such hardship – not just lack of money, but anomie and alienation – in the midst of plenty?[3]

Two Reasons

There are two primary reasons for this paradox. Firstly, happiness is not a function of just material possessions and bodily satisfactions that the secularist ideologies of capitalism, socialism and the welfare state overly emphasise. Secondly, given the resource constraint, even the material well-being of all individuals in society cannot be realised, unless the available resources are used both efficiently as well as equitably.

Happiness, as it is now being generally acknowledged, is a reflection of peace of mind (*al-nafs al-muṭma'innah,* in the words of the Qur'ān, 89: 27), which it is possible to attain only if an individual's life is in harmony with his inner nature. This happens when both the spiritual and the material urges of his or her personality are adequately satisfied. Since the material and the spiritual are not separate identities, the desired satisfaction takes place only when a spiritual dimension is injected into all material pursuits to give them meaning and purpose.

It is probably not possible to satisfy the needs of all members of society, given the resource constraints, or to reduce inequalities, unless all wasteful and inessential uses of resources are eliminated or minimised and all socio-economic institutions that promote inequities are corrected. This in turn is not possible if individuals disregard social priorities in resource use and take into account only their own individual preferences and financial ability. Every individual therefore needs to be made aware of the social priorities in resource use and to be motivated to behave in conformity with these priorities. He needs to be made subject to a discipline that will make him concerned about the well-being of others while striving for his own well-being. What could be more conducive to the creation of such a discipline than a moral system given by the Creator of the Universe Himself, combined with accountability before Him. Within the framework of such a discipline, material possessions do not command a value for their own sake. They are of value as long as they fulfil the objective of their creation as defined by the value system. Such an attitude creates a voluntary restraint in the use of scarce resources – a restraint that minimises unnecessary claims and makes it possible to satisfy the needs of all in spite of scarcity, thus meeting the dictates of human brotherhood. Social solidarity thereby strengthens, and social tensions and crime decline.

In the absence of a moral dimension, material possessions and want satisfaction become an end in themselves. Satisfaction then does not remain a function of need fulfilment but of much more than that, of vying with others. Ostentation and getting ahead of the Joneses become the ideal pattern of behaviour. But conspicuous consumption creates only temporary satisfaction. Without any meaning and purpose of life, fashions and models only exchange one kind of emptiness for another. To maintain the buying orgy, everyone is constantly busy acquiring the necessary resources by fair means or foul, leaving little time or desire to fulfil obligations towards family and friends. The pressures on the individual expand beyond his or her ability to bear and peace of mind suffers. The entire machinery of production becomes directly or indirectly directed toward the satisfaction of a maximum amount of wants. If the banking system also acts as an accomplice, it becomes possible for people to live beyond their means. Claims on resources therefore multiply, imbalances increase and those unable to keep pace with this struggle fall behind. Poverty and economic inequalities rise. The goal of need satisfaction suffers more and more. Dissatisfaction and social tensions become exacerbated and symptoms of anomie and alienation become reflected in all aspects of individual and social life.

The Task Ahead

The problem that Muslim countries face is even more difficult than that faced by the industrial countries; resources at their disposal are even scarcer. Removal of their macroeconomic and external imbalances requires a reduction in aggregate demand. Realisation of the *maqāṣid* requires the opposite of this: increased spending for a number of neglected but essential objectives. How to resolve this conflict is the challenge that Muslim countries face. They cannot respond to this challenge successfully by adopting strategies that have failed. A failed strategy cannot but lead to failure.

What the Muslim countries need to do is to develop their own strategy – one that will help them allocate scarce resources efficiently and equitably in accordance with the demands of *ḥayāt ṭayyibah*. This will also help them fulfil their moral obligation of being a *qudwah ḥasanah* (worthy example) for other countries, an example which they may be able to follow to solve their socio-economic problems. The strategy that needs to be developed should consist of all the three ingredients around which the entire discussion in this book has hovered: (a) a socially-agreed filter mechanism to enable them to distinguish the efficient and the equitable use of scarce resources from the inefficient and the inequitable; (b) a motivating system to induce individuals to use these resources in conformity with the dictates of such a filter mechanism; and (c) a socio-economic restructuring that would reinforce the above two elements in bringing about the kind of reallocation and distribution of resources that the *ḥayāt ṭayyibah* demands.

THE UNSUCCESSFUL STRATEGIES

Capitalism

After divorcing itself from the collective force of Judaeo-Christian values, capitalism had no option but to rely primarily on prices and private profit to provide the filter mechanism and the motivating force for balancing aggregate demand and supply, and realising efficiency as well as equity in resource allocation. Market-determined prices, it is argued, not only regulate aggregate demand but also, by affecting the rate of return unevenly, transfer resources away from the relatively less profitable sectors to those more profitable. These adjustments in demand and supply brought about by the interaction of market forces lead, it is claimed, to a new equilibrium with maximum efficiency and equity without any need for value judgements or government intervention.

The use of price mechanism as the only strategy to allocate resources safeguards individual freedom but frustrates the realisation of both efficiency and equity unless certain background conditions, including equal distribution of income and wealth and perfect competition, are fulfilled. Since these conditions are not, and cannot be, fulfilled under normal circumstances, the freedom to satisfy a maximum amount of wants in accordance with individual preferences enables the rich to have a greater say in the use of scarce resources if no mechanism other than prices is used to regulate their claims on resources. The pressure on resources resulting from the struggle to satisfy a maximum amount of wants tends to establish an equilibrium in the economy at relatively higher prices for all goods and services, including those meant for need fulfilment.

While the ability of the rich to pay the price enables them to get whatever they want, the poor get squeezed because their already inadequate income does not normally rise in step with prices. Their ability to pay the market price for need-satisfying goods and services thus declines even more, leading to inadequate satisfaction of their needs. This lowers their efficiency and their incomes even further. They thus get trapped further in the vicious cycle of poverty and deprivation. The greater the income and wealth disparity, the greater the power of the rich to divert resources away from need fulfilment of the poor, if reliance is placed mainly on the price mechanism to allocate resources and to remove the imbalances. This is further exacerbated by the conventional interest-based banking system which diverts the savings of the society mainly to the rich, who have the collateral to offer and who consequently become yet wealthier and more powerful in diverting scarce resources even farther away from need satisfaction.

Any effort to bring about an equitable distribution is bound to hurt the rich in every society where there exists an inequitable distribution of resources. Why would the rich agree to be worse off in a secularist, value-free society committed to the principle of Pareto optimality? To motivate them to be worse off in the interest of the well-being of others, it would be necessary not only to have socially-agreed values to which everyone stands committed, but also a motivating system that would assure them of an attractive reward for the sacrifice they are required to make.

It is not possible to have socially-agreed values if secularism is the reigning philosophy. Secularism does not necessarily mean an absence of values; all societies have values and secularist societies are not an exception. What secularism does is to deprive values of the collective sanction that religion provides. Without such a sanction, it is difficult for a society or a government to arrive at the social consensus necessary for translating goals and values into a scale of social priorities in the use of scarce resources – priorities that people are ready to abide by even if this hurts their self-interest. Moreover, the short-term, this-worldly perspective that secularism provides to self-interest makes wealth accumulation and sensual satisfactions the primary goal of human life. It would not be 'rational' for anyone to agree to be worse off if he cares for nothing other than serving his this-worldly self-interest.

Hence, while capitalism retained the humanitarian goals of religion in the facade, it messed up the strategy. The role of moral values in the allocation and distribution of scarce resources was blunted by undue emphasis on individual preferences and primary reliance on the price mechanism. The blind operation of market forces thus received an unhindered opportunity to create all the inequities that it is capable of creating. The lifting of the Judaeo-Christian stricture against interest further accentuated the inequities. The conflict between goals and strategy thus ushered in social Darwinism in the innocent garb of humanitarian goals.

Thus, while the strategy of the market system is able to promote private initiative and drive, and a higher rate of growth, by permitting individuals to serve their self-interest, it is not able to serve social interest except where self-interest and social interest coincide. This helps explain partly why the market system has failed on the criteria of both efficiency and equity. It has been unable to produce anywhere, on its own strength, either a configuration of goods and services that would satisfy the needs of all or an equitable distribution of income and wealth. One could thus say that the moral vacuum that secularism has introduced will not make it possible for the market system to achieve growth with redistribution unless the use of coercion to create the right background conditions, such as was used by a foreign occupying power in Japan, South Korea and Taiwan, is envisaged. And even in such a case the gains are likely to be short-lived unless reinforced by a strategy that would help sustain them.

Socialism

The performance of the centrally planned economies is not significantly better. The abolition of the profit motive and private property kills individual initiative, drive and creativity in a society with a short this-worldly life perspective. This reduces efficiency and hurts the supply side of the economy. Central planning and collectivisation do not succeed in promoting equity either – they lead rather to concentration of power in the hands of a few politburo members. This is even worse than monopolistic capitalism which, even though it leads to concentration of wealth and power, does not make possible such an intense concentration of power because of the market's generally decentralised decision-making process. Moreover, the socialist system's inherent secularist and amoral outlook deprives it of a socially-agreed value system. In the absence of both moral values and price system, the only filter mechanism left for making decisions about resource allocation is the whim of the powerful politburo members. Hence the rich and highly placed in these systems have been able to enjoy access to everything they want, just as in the capitalist countries, while the poor have had difficulty in satisfying even their basic needs. No wonder the totalitarian systems have caused a great deal of material deprivation and human misery and been overthrown almost everywhere by popular revolt.

Welfare State

The welfare state, realising the limitations of the market system, tried to combine the price mechanism with a number of other tools, particularly welfare spending by the state, to ensure 'equity'. Given the phobia against value judgements and the self-imposed criterion of Pareto optimality, there was no question of discriminating between the necessary and the unnecessary, or of using means testing. The welfare state tried to provide welfare services to all, the rich and the poor alike, through increased spending by the public sector. Initially this generated a euphoria – a feeling that the problems of both allocation and distribution had been ideally solved. They were not; the strategy was inadequate for the task. Since the increased public sector spending was not accompanied by an offsetting reduction in other claims on resources, budgetary deficits swelled in spite of the heavy tax burden. Since the consumer culture also led to a simultaneous rise in private sector spending, there was no offsetting rise in private sector saving. There was rather an excessive monetary expansion in a proportional-reserve banking system that is willing to lend as much as desired to both the private and the public sectors on the basis of collateral and assumed lower sovereign risk, without due regard to the ultimate use of credit. Claims on resources were hence exacerbated, giving rise to internal and external imbalances. The problems of poverty and deprivation nevertheless continued and indeed deepened. Needs remained unfulfilled. Inequalities in fact increased.

The Dilemma

The problem that the welfare state now faces is how to remove the imbalances that it has created. There being no agreed filter mechanism other than prices with the help of which to regulate aggregate demand, primary reliance is being placed on the market mechanism to remove the existing imbalances. This revival of faith in the market, brings back into focus the failures and inequities of the market and the inability of the poor to pay market-related prices. The welfare state is thus faced with a perplexing dilemma. If primary stress is placed on the market and the welfare role of the state is rolled back to remove the imbalances, then the welfare state is back to square one – the square of capitalism from where it started. So what to do now? The only major tool that the welfare state is left with to provide relief to the poor is a high rate of economic growth. But higher growth does not necessarily improve income distribution. As Adelman and Morris have shown on the basis of a cross-section of data, "development is accompanied by an absolute as well as a relative decline in the average income of the poor."[4] Moreover, the prospects for accelerating the rate of growth are not very bright in the near future without rekindling inflation and aggravating other imbalances.

The inevitable conclusion is that the three existing systems cannot serve as models for Muslim countries. Being secularist they are non-starters in providing inner happiness, which demands the satisfaction of both the spiritual and the material needs of human beings. Being value-neutral, they are unable to bring about a reduction in aggregate claims on resources in such a way that not only the needs of all are satisfied but there is also an adequate level of capital formation for promoting higher growth. The sole reliance on market forces cannot simultaneously help remove the existing macroeconomic and external imbalances and bring about the kind of reallocation that the *ḥayāt ṭayyibah* demands. The Muslim countries have thus no alternative but to Islamise their economies.

ISLAMISATION

Islamisation implies a serious implementation of the Islamic strategy to raise the spiritual as well as the material well-being of all people and to establish socio-economic justice, which is the central objective of the Islamic message. On the spiritual side, the peace of mind that is indispensable to inner happiness cannot be attained except by increasing the nearness of the human being to his Creator, which Islam is capable of bringing about but secularism does not even aspire to. On the material side, Islamisation demands the allocation and distribution of all resources, a trust from God, in such an efficient and equitable manner that the *maqāṣid* are realised and the *ḥayāt ṭayyibah* is made possible for all. This necessitates the balanced and effective use of all the constituent elements of the Islamic strategy to hold aggregate claims within the bounds of resource availability and goal-realisation. Islamisation does not thus mean an absence of liberalisation. It does, however, mean a different kind of liberalisation – one in which all public and private sector economic decisions are first passed through the filter of moral values before they are made subject to the discipline of the market.

Balanced Use of All Elements

The moral system, which influences the inner consciousness of the individual, makes him aware of the trust nature of resources and provides the criteria needed for their efficient and equitable allocation and distribution. It also makes the individual conscious of his unavoidable accountability before the All-Knowing God, thus serving as a strong motivating force for not pursuing his personal preferences and self-interest in a way that hurts the realisation of social well-being. This helps prune a substantial part of the demand for goods and services even before it finds an expression in the market place. If the price system with its decentralised decision-making then takes over, the allocation of resources can be more efficient. However, even a moral system may tend to be ineffective if it is not accompanied by socio-economic restructuring. This is because some individuals may tend to disregard values unless the socio-economic environment makes it difficult and unrewarding to do so. Moreover, even individuals who are committed to abide by the value system may not be aware of the social priorities and what the economy, and not just the individuals themselves, can or cannot afford if the *maqāṣid* are to be realised with the scarce resources.

Socio-economic restructuring could be introduced more effectively if the government were to play an enabling role. Strategic policy planning could help in this task by making the government assess the economy's resources and needs and determine the extent of changes needed in consumption and investment patterns of both the private and the public sectors. Social, institutional and structural reforms could then be designed to create a proper climate for enabling the market mechanism to serve private as well as social goals. These reforms should be further reinforced by an effective implementation of the various Islamic redistribution schemes, without which any effort in the direction of reform would be a non-starter. The combined use of all these tools should set the ball rolling for the removal of the inequities and imbalances. The removal of pressure on resources arising from wasteful and unnecessary consumption, and the higher investment and growth that this may make possible, should help contain inflationary pressures and currency depreciation that are currently afflicting many Muslim countries.

Egalitarian policies, if they are followed within the perspective of the Islamic motivating system, are not likely to meet with the same kind of resistance from the rich that they would in a socio-economic system committed to Pareto optimality. They should also help dampen socio-economic unrest and political instability and contribute to higher growth in Muslim countries. A better fed, healthy, and properly educated and motivated population cannot but improve the quality of the work force in countries where serious consumption deficiencies and health and educational impairments are holding down the quality of work.

Greater social equality, by putting to an end the race for status symbols among the rich and the middle classes, is also bound to promote not only brotherhood and social cohesion but also greater savings. Though a part of the potential increase in savings may be offset by increased need-fulfilment of the poor, a significant part may still be available for increased investment and, combined with improvement in the quality of the work force and its motivation, contribute to greater efficiency and higher growth. More equality need not, therefore, mean less growth. If the growth and equality of different economies are compared, there appears to be "no relationship between the amount of inequality that different countries have been willing to tolerate and their economic performance".[5] Accordingly, the argument that limiting movement towards equality promotes growth should be rejected as "a smoke screen, that cannot be backed up with hard economic data."[6] Nevertheless, a considerable body of evidence from a number of countries indicates that the domestic economic and social policies that have been followed in many countries have not only resulted in greater inequality but have also accentuated poverty.[7]

Islamisation would thus help Muslim countries humanise the operation of market forces and realise both efficiency and equity in the use of scarce resources. Moral reform, along with strategic policy planning and economic and financial restructuring, should make the human factor more conscientious in the use of resources, so that private interest is served without trespassing the limits of social interest even where the two interests do not coincide. The reform of public finances in accordance with Islamic teachings should help introduce greater efficiency and equity in public sector taxation and spending and reduce budgetary deficits. Resources will thus be released from wasteful and unproductive uses for need fulfilment and for higher capital formation, exports, and growth.

The recognition of private property and the profit motive, along with equitable material rewards and structural changes in the economy for need fulfilment, will also create the motivation for hard and conscientious work, greater worker efficiency, and increased savings and investment. Land reforms, along with rural development and proliferation of SMEs throughout the country, will help spread ownership of means of production and expand self-employment opportunities. Improving the investment climate and providing incentives for investment and exports should also go a long way towards accelerating development. Restructuring the conventional financial institutions in the light of Islamic teachings will help restrain them from extending credit for wasteful and unproductive spending to both the public and the private sectors and thus enable them to provide more financing for productive investment, particularly to entrepreneurial talent among the poor.

This should not only strengthen the efforts to reduce imbalances but also help materialise the goal of spreading ownership of businesses and industries, and harnessing the energies and creativity of a greater part of the population for accelerated development. The reduction in inflationary pressures, decline in current account deficits, and the containment of the continuing depreciation in exchange rates should also make a positive contribution to growth and well-being. Nevertheless, the interest of those poor who are unable to help themselves should be further attended to, not through a general subsidy, but rather through organised and intensified relief payments and income supplements provided by the government and social organisations out of *zakāt, awqāf,* voluntary donations, and the maximum possible budgetary appropriations. Implementation of the Islamic inheritance system will help sustain the move towards minimising economic inequalities.

Not Neoclassical Adjustment

In contrast with the strategy discussed above, the adjustment programmes suggested within the secularist perspective of neoclassical liberalism to remove macroeconomic imbalances do not involve any socio-economic reconstructing. It is naively felt that liberalisation of the economies will help not only to remove the imbalances but also to realise greater efficiency and equity. The primary adjustments suggested are reduction of budgetary deficits and the correction of price distortions, particularly those in exchange rates and interest rates.[8] There is no doubt that such adjustments are indispensable for removing the imbalances and for even promoting long-run growth. But would these by themselves help promote socio-economic justice? Experience in many countries has shown that the removal of budgetary deficits and the adoption of market-related prices, unless simultaneously accompanied by a strategy to promote justice, tend to put the major burden of adjustment on the poor. The higher prices do not create any significant dent in the demands of the rich; they continue to buy what they want. The poor however get more squeezed. This accentuates poverty and inequalities and leads to social unrest and political instability, and governments are then forced to roll back the measures they have adopted.

The neoclassical adjustment programmes thus encounter problems because, within the liberal value-neutral tradition, they approach the problem from the point of view, primarily, of stabilisation and nominal efficiency, and give only a secondary importance to equity. However, if a stabilisation programme were designed to realise both real efficiency and equity, it would have a greater chance of success. But such a programme cannot be prepared within a value-neutral framework and, if prepared, cannot be implemented without an effective motivating system – a system that would be able to induce the individual to work for his self-interest within the limits of social well-being.

Urgency of the Task

It may be concluded, therefore, that without Islamisation of their economies and societies, it will not be possible for Muslim countries to combine the removal of imbalances with realisation of the kind of development that Islam visualises. The Muslim governments have unfortunately used Islam so far only as a slogan, failing to realise the positive contribution it can make towards the betterment of their societies and economies and towards their own survival. Prof. Khurshid Ahmad has rightly indicated that: "There is no evidence to conclude that, generally speaking, the policy-makers derived any inspiration worth the name from Islam and tried to translate its economic ideals into development policies."[9] Even with a change in attitudes and policies, the task of adjustment and reconstruction is bound to be difficult and time-consuming. The sooner the policy-makers read the signs of the times, the better it will be for them and the *ummah.*

Islamisation is however a more difficult task than mere adjustment within the secular perspective. It requires a greater and more coordinated effort. Nevertheless, the masses seem to be emotionally prepared for it; having faith in its ability to serve their long-term well-being. The governments are themselves the main obstacles, being controlled by vested interests. The socio-economic restructuring that Islamisation stands for threatens their short-term (but not necessarily long-term) interest. This may be one of the reasons why even democracy is not being allowed to take root in these countries. Democracy would force the governments to Islamise.

The vested interests must realise, however, that they cannot long prevent the gravitational pull of Islamic humanitarian ideas from mustering strong public support. The movement for Islamic revival that is gathering momentum in Muslim countries is bound to accelerate and counter all forces of resistance. Vested interests will ultimately be washed away, as the Qur'ān predicts: "As for the scum, it disappears in vain while what benefits mankind remains in the world'' (13: 17). Keynes also, likewise, observed: ''I am sure that the power of vested interests is vastly exaggerated compared with the gradual encroachment of ideas. Not, indeed, immediately, but after a certain interval . . . it is ideas, not vested interests, which are dangerous for good or evil.''[10] It would hence be in the long-term interest of the rich and powerful not only to not resist the strong tide of social reform but rather to go along with it.

Islamisation should not, however, be conceived as an antidote to all the problems of Muslim countries. Some of the problems created by centuries of socio-economic, political and moral degeneration, misguided domestic policies and unhealthy external shocks are bound to persist for a long time. It must also be appreciated that Islamisation is a gradual process. It cannot be achieved instantly through the use of force and regimentation. Wisdom and understanding have to be the pillars of Islamisation, as required by the Qur'ān (16: 125). Even the Prophet, the peace and blessings of God be on him, encouraged gradual transition through his own example.

Unfortunately the quagmire into which most Muslim countries have already fallen, and which has given rise to poverty, inequalities, internal unrest, external imbalances, and a huge foreign debt, does not permit great leeway in terms of time. Even with significant policy initiatives, the underlying inequities and imbalances cannot be reversed immediately. Moreover, the decline in the Soviet threat is likely to reduce the strategic importance of, and hence the flow of aid to, many Muslim countries. This makes it even more imperative for the Muslim governments to attend to socio-economic reform with the urgency it demands and to play a more positive and assertive role. The more sincerely and determinedly they play their roles, and the more active social reform organisations and educational institutions are in bringing about social change, the less will be the time needed for transformation. They must take inspiration from what the Qur'ān says:

> And if they strive in Our Cause, We will certainly guide them to Our Ways, for God is undoubtedly with those who strive for the good (29: 69).

Notes and References (Chapter 12)

1 Jay W. Forrester, cited by Alfred Malabre, Jr., *Beyond Our Means* (1987), p. xii.

2 Richard Easterlin, "Does Money Buy Happiness?" *The Public Interest,* Winter 1973, cited by Robert L. Heilbroner and Lester C. Thurow, in *The Economic Problem* (1975), p. 538.

The real GDP of the US, West Germany and Britain rose 6.0 times, 7.1 times and 3.4 times over the sixty-year period 1928–88, while that of Japan rose 17.8 times over the period 1930–1988. (See "The Next Ages of Man: A Survey", *The Economist,* 24 December 1988, pp. 5–6 of the Survey Section.) The real GDP of the Soviet Union rose 6.5 times over the period 1928–85. (Calculated on the basis of growth rates given for the period 1928–85 in Gur Offer, "Soviet Economic Growth: 1928–1985", *Journal of Economic Literature,* December 1987, Table 1, p. 1778.)

However, in spite of the rise in incomes and wealth, happiness has not grown in any of these countries. In fact, many people would argue, it has gone down.

3 See Ralf Dahrendorf, *The Modern Social Conflict: An Essay on the Politics of Liberty* (1988).

Similar questions have been raised by a number of other writers. Leonard Silk, for example, writes: "If economic growth and a free marketplace are the all-purpose solutions to poverty, economists are starting to ask, why has American poverty worsened in the last two decades." (Leonard Silk, "Dismal Scientists Adopt Kinder, Gentler Stance", *International Herald Tribune,* 31 December 1988, p. 13.

4 I. Adelman and C. T. Morris, *Economic Growth and Social Equity in Developing Countries* (1973), p. 189.

5 Lester C. Thurow, "Equity, Efficiency, Social Justice, and Redistribution", in OECD, *The Welfare State in Crisis* (1981), p. 137.

6 *Ibid.,* p. 140; see also, Gunnar Myrdal, "Need for Reforms in Underdeveloped Countries", *Quarterly Economic Journal* (National Bank of Pakistan), March 1979, p. 29.

7 See Rene Dumont, *False Start in Africa* (1966); IBRD, *World Development Report, 1984*; and ILO, *Poverty and Landless in Rural Africa* (1977).

8 See, IMF, *Theoretical Aspects of the Design of Fund-Supported Adjustment Programs* (Occasional Paper 55, 1987); Said El-Naggar (ed.), *Adjustment Policies and Development Strategies in the Arab World* (1987); Paul Streeten (ed.), *Beyond Adjustment: The Asian Experience* (1988); Vittoria Corbo, *et al.* (eds.), *Growth-Oriented Adjustment Programs* (1987).

9 K. Ahmad, "Economic Development in an Islamic Perspective", in K. Ahmad (ed.), *Studies in Islamic Economics* (1980), p. 173. According to Dr. Amin, even the motive for rapid economic development is weak. He says:

''Rather than showing a general desire for rapid economic development, Arab governments show a surprisingly weak will to achieve it. . . . A much more powerful motive than economic development is the motive to remain in power.'' (Galal A. Amin, ''The Modernization of Poverty'', *Social, Economic and Political Studies of the Middle East* (1980), vol. 8, p. 108.)

10 J. M. Keynes, quoted by Julian Le Grand, *The Strategy of Equality: Redistribution and the Social Services* (1982), p. 139.

Glossary of Arabic Terms

(frequently used in the text)

'Adālah: Justice.

Aḥādīth: Plural of *ḥadīth* (q.v.).

Amānah: Trust.

Amīn: Trustee.

Awqāf: Plural of *waqf* (q.v.).

Falāḥ: Well-being attained by the satisfaction of both the material and the spiritual needs of the human personality. See also *ḥayāt ṭayyibah*.

Farḍ 'ayn: Personal obligation of every Muslim.

Farḍ kifāyah: Collective duty of the Muslim society.

Fasād: Mischief, viciousness and corruption; opposite of *ṣalāḥ*.

Fiqh: Muslim jurisprudence; it covers all aspects of life, religious, political, social or economic. In addition to religious observances (prayer, fasting, *zakāt* (q.v.) and pilgrimage) it covers family law, inheritance, social obligations, commerce, criminal law, constitutional law and international relations, including war. The whole corpus of *fiqh* is based primarily on the Qur'ān and the *Sunnah* and secondarily on *ijmā'* (consensus) and *ijtihād* (effort to derive juristic opinions).

Fuqahā' (singular, *faqīh*): Jurists who give opinion on various issues in the light of the Qur'ān and the *Sunnah* (q.v.) and who have thereby led to the development of *fiqh*.

Ḥadīth (plural, *aḥādīth*): A report of the saying, deed or tacit approval of the Prophet, the peace and blessings of God be on him.

Ḥalāl: Anything permitted by the *Sharī'ah* (q.v.).

Ḥarām: Anything prohibited by the *Sharī'ah* (q.v.).

Ḥayāt ṭayyibah: Good life attained by the balanced satisfaction of both the material and the spiritual needs of the human personality. It does not at all carry the same connotation as 'good life' carries in any culture which overemphasises 'fun' and 'wealth, women and wine'. See also *falāḥ*.

Ḥuqūq al-'ibād: An individual's obligations towards other human beings, i.e., their rights.

'Ibādah: Worship. In its wider sense, it means living in conformity with Islamic teachings.

Imām: The word is used in this book in its most popular meaning of leader of the congregational prayer; the word is, however, also used for the founders of different schools of Muslim jurisprudence or other eminent jurists and reformers, and also for the prominent descendants of 'Alī ibn Abī Ṭālib and distinguished *Shī'ah* theologians. In *aḥādīth* it has also been used to refer to the ruler.

Khalīfah: Vicegerent.

Khilāfah: Vicegerency.

Maqāṣid: Short form for *maqāṣid al-Sharī'ah* (q.v.).

Maqāṣid al-Sharī'ah: Goals of the *Sharī'ah*.

Qudwah ḥasanah: Worthy example.

Qur'ān: The Holy Book of the Muslims consisting of the revelations made by God to the Prophet Muḥammad, the peace and blessings of God be on him, during his Prophethood of about 23 years. The Qur'ān lays down the fundamentals of the Islamic faith, including beliefs and all aspects of the Muslim way of life. These are supplemented or further elaborated by the *Sunnah* (q.v.). In all references to the Qur'ān in the text (e.g., 30: 41), the first number refers to the *sūrah* (or chapter) and the second to the *āyah* (or verse).

Ṣadaqāt: Refers to all kinds of charitable spending by individuals from lawful income.

Sharī'ah: Refers to the divine guidance as given by the Qur'ān and the *Sunnah* and embodies all aspects of the Islamic faith, including beliefs and practices.

Shūrā: Means consultation, but refers technically to the moral obligation of a Muslim government not to formulate and execute policies except in consultation with the people or their representatives.

Sunnah: After the Qur'ān, the *Sunnah* is the most important source of the Islamic faith and refers essentially to the Prophet's example as indicated by his practise of the faith. The most important way to know the *Sunnah* is through the collection of *aḥādīth* (q.v.).

Sūrah: A chapter of the Qur'ān. There are 114 *sūrahs* of varying lengths in the Qur'ān. In all references to the Qur'ān in the text (e.g., 30: 41), the first number refers to the *sūrah* and the second to the *āyah* or verse.

Tawḥīd: Oneness and unity of God.

'Ulamā': Religious scholars. In its wider connotation, it also includes all highly educated persons and professionals.

Ummah: Means a nation and refers technically to the whole Muslim community, irrespective of colour, race, language or nationality, which carry no weight in Islam.

'Ushr: Ten per cent (in some cases five per cent) of agricultural produce payable by a Muslim as a part of his religious obligation, like *zakāt,* mainly for the benefit of the poor and the needy.

Waqf: Assets entrusted to an individual or organisation for a specified charitable purpose.

Zakāt: The amount payable by a Muslim on his net worth as a part of his religious obligations, mainly for the benefit of the poor and the needy. See also *'ushr*.

Ẓulm: A comprehensive Islamic term used to refer to all forms of inequity, injustice, exploitation, oppression and wrongdoing, whereby a person either deprives others of their right or does not fulfil his obligations towards them.

Bibliography

PART I: THE UNSUCCESSFUL SYSTEMS

Abramovitz, Moses, ''Economics of Growth'', in B. F. Haley (1952), vol. 2, pp. 132–82.

Adam, Jan (ed.), *Employment Policies in the Soviet Union and Eastern Europe* (London: Macmillan, 2nd ed., 1987).

Adams, Charles, Paul Fenton and Flemming Larson, ''Differences in Employment Behaviour among Industrial Countries'', IMF, *Staff Studies for the World Economic Outlook,* July 1986.

Adelman, I., ''Development Economics: A Reassessment of Goals'', *American Economic Review,* Papers and Proceedings, 1975.

———, *Redistribution Before Growth* (Leiden: University of Leiden, 1979).

——— and C. T. Morris, *Economic Growth and Social Equity in Developing Countries* (Stanford, California: Stanford University Press, 1973).

——— and Erik Thorbecke (eds.), *Theory and Design of Economic Development* (Baltimore: The Johns Hopkins University Press, 1966).

Aganbegyan, Abel, *The Challenge: Economics of Perestroika* (London: Century Hutchinson, 1988).

———, *Inside Perestroika: The Future of the Soviet Economy* (New York: Harper & Row, 1989).

Armstrong, Philip, *et al., Capitalism Since 1945* (Oxford: Basil Blackwell, 1991).

Arndt, H. W., ''Development Economics before 1945'', in Jagdish Bhagwati and Richard Eckaus, *Development and Planning: Essays in Honour of Paul Rosenstein-Rodan* (Cambridge, Mass.: The MIT Press, 1972), pp. 13–29.

———, *Economic Development: The History of an Idea* (Chicago: University of Chicago Press, 1987).

Arnold, Thurman W., *The Folklore of Capitalism* (New Haven: Yale University Press, 1959).

Arrow, K. J., *Social Choice and Individual Values* (New York: John Wiley, 2nd ed., 1963).

Aslund, Anders, *Gorbachev's Struggle for Economic Reform* (London: Pinter, 1989).

Australian Bureau of Agricultural and Research Economics, *Japanese Agricultural Policies,* Policy Monograph No. 3, Canberra, 1988.

Ayers, Robert L., *Banking on the Poor* (Cambridge, Mass.: MIT Press, 1983).

Balassa, Bela, *et al., Development Strategies in Semi-Industrial Economies* (Baltimore: The Johns Hopkins University Press, 1982).

Bank for International Settlements, *59th Annual Report* – April 1988–March 1989 (Basle: BIS, June 1989).

———, *60th Annual Report,* April 1989–March 1990 (Basle: BIS, June 1990).

Baran, Paul A., "On the Political Economy of Backwardness", *The Manchester School of Economic and Social Studies,* January 1952, pp. 66–84.

———, *The Political Economy of Growth* (New York: Monthly Review Press, 1957).

——— and Paul M. Sweezy, *Monopoly Capital: An Essay on the American Economic and Social Order* (New York: Modern Reader Paperbacks, 1966).

Bardhan, Pranab, "Symposium on the State and Economic Development", *Journal of Economic Perspectives,* Summer 1990, pp. 3–7.

Barnett, Richard J. and Ronald E. Muller, *Global Reach: The Power of the Multinational Corporations* (New York: Guinon & Schuster, 1974).

Barr, N., *The Economy of the Welfare State* (London: Weidenfeld and Nicolson, 1987).

Barzun, Jacques, *Darwin, Marx, Wagner* (New York: Doubleday, 1958).

Batra, Raveendra N., *The Downfall of Capitalism and Communism: A New Study of History* (London: Macmillan, 1978).

Bauer, Peter T. and Basil S. Yamey, *The Economics of Underdeveloped Countries* (Chicago: The University of Chicago Press, 1957).

———, *Dissent on Development* (Cambridge, Mass.: Harvard University Press, 1972).

Baum, Warren C. and Stokes M. Tolbert, *Investing in Development* (Washington, D.C.: The World Bank, 1985).

Bean, Charles, *et al.* (eds.), *The Rise in Unemployment* (Oxford: Basil Blackwell, 1987).

Bell, Daniel, *The Cultural Contradictions of Capitalism* (New York: Basic Books, 1976).

——— and Lester Thurow, *The Deficits: How Big? How Long? How Dangerous?* (New York: New York University Press, 1985).

Benedict, R., *The Chrysanthemum and the Sword* (Boston: Houghton Mifflin, 1946).

Bergson, Abram, "Income Inequality Under Soviet Socialism", *Journal of Economic Literature*, September 1984.

Berle, Adolf A. Jr., *The Twentieth Century Capitalist Revolution* (New York: Harcourt, 1954).

Berry, R. A. and W. R. Cline, *Agrarian Structure and Productivity in Developing Countries* (Baltimore: The Johns Hopkins University Press, 1979).

Beus, J. G. de, *Shall We Make the Year 2000?: The Decisive Challenge to Western Civilisation* (London: Sidgwick & Jackson, 1985).

Bhagwati, J. and A. Kruger, "Exchange Control, Liberalisation and Development", *American Economic Review*, 2/1973, pp. 419–27.

——— and Richard Eckaus, *Development Planning: Essays in Honour of Paul Rosenstein-Rodan* (Cambridge, Mass.: The MIT Press, 1972).

Bhatt, V. V., "Improving the Financial Structure", *Finance and Development*, June 1986.

Birch, David, *The Job Generation Process* (Cambridge, Mass.: MIT, Programme on Neighbourhood and Regional Change, 1979).

Boonekamp, Clemens, "Industrial Policies of Industrial Countries", *Finance and Development*, March 1989.

Boulding, Kenneth E., *Beyond Economics: Essays on Society, Religion and Ethics* (Ann Arbor: University of Michigan Press, 1968).

———, *A Preface to Grants Economics: The Economy of Love and Fear* (New York: Praeger, 1973).

———, *Human Betterment* (London: Sage Publications, 1985).

Bracewell, Milnes, *The Wealth of Giving* (London: The Institute of Economic Affairs, 1989).

Brady, Nicholas E. *et al.*, *Report of the Presidential Task Force on Market Mechanics* (Washington, D.C.: U.S. Government Printing Office, January 1988).

Brandt Commission, *North-South: A Programme for Survival* (Cambridge, Mass.: MIT Press, 1980).

———, *Common Crisis: North-South Cooperation for World Recovery* (Cambridge, Mass.: MIT Press, 1983).

Briggs, Asa, "The Welfare State in Historical Perspective", *Archives Européennes de Sociologie*, 1961.

Brinton, Crane, "Enlightenment", in *Encyclopaedia of Philosophy* (New York: Macmillan and the Free Press, 1967), vol. 2.
Britnell, G. E., "Factors in the Economic Development of Guatemala", *American Economic Review,* May 1953, pp. 104–14.
Brittan, Samuel, *Two Cheers for Self-Interest: Some Moral Prerequisites for a Market Economy* (London: The Institute of Economic Affairs, for the Wincott Foundation, 1985).
———, *The Role and Limits of Government: Essays in Political Economy* (Aldershot, Hampshire: Wildwood House, 2nd Impression, 1987).
Bruce, Maurice, *The Coming of the Welfare State* (London: Batsford, Fourth ed., 1968).
Brunberg, Abraham (ed.), *Russia Under Khruschev* (New York: Praeger, 1962).
Bruton, Henry, *Inflation in a Growing Economy* (Bombay: University of Bombay, 1961).
———, "The Two-gap Approach to Aid and Development", *American Economic Review,* September 1966.
Buck, Trevor and John Cole, *Modern Soviet Economic Performance* (Oxford: Basil Blackwell, 1987).
Burton, John, *Why No Cuts: An Inquiry into the Fiscal Anarchy of Uncontrolled Government Expenditure* (London: The Institute of Economic Affairs, 1985).
Burtt, Edwin A., *The Metaphysical Foundations of Modern Science* (Garden City, N.Y.: Doubleday, 1955).
Chapel, Rothko, *A New Strategy for Development* (New York: Pergamon Press, 1979).
Chenery, Hollis, *Structural Change and Development Policy* (Oxford University Press, for the World Bank, 1970).
——— with A. Strout, "Foreign Assistance and Economic Development", *American Economic Review,* September 1966.
——— *et al., Redistribution with Growth: An Approach to Policy* (Oxford University Press, 1974).
——— and T. N. Srinivasan (eds.), *Handbook of Development Economics* (Amsterdam: North-Holland, vol. 1: 1988, vol. 2: 1989).
Churchill, Winston, *The Hinge of Fate* (Boston: Houghton Mifflin, 1950).
Clark, C. H. D., *Christianity and Bertrand Russell* (London, 1958).
Cline, William R., *Potential Effects of Income Redistribution on Economic Growth* (New York: Praeger, 1973).
Collard, D., R. Lecomber and M. Slater (eds.), *Income Distribution: The Limits to Redistribution* (Bristol: John Wright, 1980).

Colman, D. and F. Nixson, *Economics of Change in Less Developed Countries* (Oxford: Philip Allan, 2nd. ed., 1986).

Commission of the European Communities, *European Economy,* Supplement A on Highlights on Employment and Unemployment, December 1989.

———, "Economic Transformation in Hungary and Poland", *European Economy,* No. 43, March 1990.

———, "Stabilisation, Liberalisation and Devolution: Assessment of the Economic Situation and Reform Process in the Soviet Union", *European Economy,* No. 45, December 1990.

Commons, John R., *Legal Foundations of Capitalism* (Madison: The University of Wisconsin Press, 1968).

Corbo, Vittoria, Morris Goldstein and Mohsin Khan, *Growth-Oriented Adjustment Programmes: Proceedings of a Symposium Held in Washington, D.C., February 25–27, 1987* (Washington, D.C.: IMF/IBRD, 1987).

Coser, Lewis A., "Socialism", *The New Encyclopaedia Britannica,* 15th ed. (1973–4), vol. 16.

Crosland, C. A. R., *Socialism Now* (London: Jonathan Cape, 1974).

———, *The Future of Socialism* (London: Jonathan Cape, 1963 ed. reprinted in 1985).

Dahrendorf, Ralf, *The Modern Social Conflict: An Essay on the Politics of Liberty* (London: Weidenfeld & Nicolson, 1988).

Dalton, George, *Economic System and Society* (Kingsport, Tenn.: Kingsport Press, 1974).

Danziger, S., P. Gottschalk and E. Smolensky, "American Income Inequality: How the Rich have Fared", *American Economic Review,* May 1989, pp. 310–14.

Dasgupta, Partha, "Well-being and the Extent of its Realisation in Poor Countries", *The Economic Journal,* Supplement 1990, pp. 1–32.

Datta, Anindya, *Growth and Equity: A Critique of the Lewis-Kuznets Tradition* (Calcutta: Oxford University Press, 1986).

Datta-Chaudhuri, Mrinal, "Market Failure and Government Failure", *Journal of Economic Perspectives,* Summer 1990, pp. 25–39.

Desai, Padma, *The Soviet Economy in Crisis* (Oxford: Basil Blackwell, 1987).

Development Committee, *Strengthening Efforts to Reduce Poverty* (Washington, D.C.: World Bank, 1989).

Directorate General of Budget, Accounting and Statistics, Republic of Taiwan, *Statistical Yearbook of the Republic of China, 1988.*

Dixon, John, *The Chinese Welfare System, 1949–1979* (New York: Praeger, 1981).

Dobb, Maurice, *Studies in the Development of Capitalism* (London: Routledge & Kegan Paul, 1963).

Dorn, James A. and Wang Xi (eds.), *Economic Reform in China: Problems and Prospects* (Chicago: University of Chicago Press, 1990).

Dosser, Douglas, "General Investment Criteria for Less Developed Countries", *Scottish Journal of Political Economy,* June 1962, pp. 93–8.

Dumas, Lloyd Jeffry, *The Overburdened Economy: Uncovering the Causes of Chronic Unemployment, Inflation and National Decline* (Berkeley, California: University of California Press, 1986).

Durant, Will, *The Story of Civilisation* (New York: Simon & Schuster, 1953).

———, *The Story of Philosophy* (New York: Washington Square Press, 1970).

——— and Ariel, *The Lessons of History* (New York: Simon & Schuster, 1968).

Edgeworth, F. Y., *Mathematical Psychics: An Essay on the Application of Mathematics to the Moral Science* (London: Kegan Paul, 1881).

Edwards, Paul, "Life, Meaning and Value of", *Encyclopaedia of Philosophy* (New York: Macmillan and the Free Press, 1967), vol. 3, pp. 467–77.

Ellis, Howard S., *Economic Development for Latin America* (London: Macmillan, 1961).

Ellman, M., *Planning Problems in the USSR* (Cambridge: Cambridge University Press, 1973).

———, *The USSR in the 1990s: Struggling out of Stagnation* (London: Economist Intelligence Unit, 1990).

Ellsworth, P. T., "Factors in the Economic Development of Ceylon", *American Economic Review,* May 1953, pp. 115–25.

Emmerij, Louis, "The Social Economy of Today's Employment Problem in Industrial Countries", in *Unemployment in Western Countries: Proceedings of a Conference held by the International Economic Association at Bichenberg, France* (London: Macmillan, 1980).

——— (ed.), *Development Policies and the Crisis of the 1980s* (Paris: Development Centre of the OECD, 1987).

Emmott, Bill, *The Sun also Sets: Why Japan will not be Number One* (Hemel Hempstead, U.K.: Simon & Schuster, 1989).

Fairbank, John K., *The Great Chinese Revolution 1800–1985* (New York: Harper & Row, 1986).

Feldt, Kjell-Olof, "The Acceptable Face of Socialism", *Financial Times,* 16 June 1988, Section IV, p. iv.
Feuer, Lewis S., "Marx", *The New Encyclopaedia Britannica* (Chicago: Helen Hamingway Benton), 15th ed. (1973–74), vol. 11.
Fine, Sidney, *Laissez-Faire and the General Welfare State* (Ann Arbor: University of Michigan Press, 1966).
Fishlow, Albert, "The Latin American State", *Journal of Economic Perspectives,* Summer 1990, pp. 61–74.
Friedman, Milton, *Capitalism and Freedom* (Chicago: The University of Chicago Press, 1972).
———, "The Methodology of Positive Economics", in F. Hahn and M. Hollis (1979).
——— and Rose, *Free to Choose* (London: Secker & Warburg, 1980).
Furniss, Norman and Timothy Tilton, *The Case for the Welfare State: From Social Security to Social Equality* (Bloomington, Indiana: International Union Press, 1977).
Galbraith, John K., *The Affluent Society* (Boston: Houghton Mifflin, 1958).
———, *American Capitalism: The Concept of Countervailing Power* (Boston: Houghton Mifflin, 1962).
———, *Economic Development in Perspective* (Cambridge, Mass.: Harvard University Press, 1962).
———, *The New Industrial State* (New York: New American Library, 1972).
———, *Economics and the Public Purpose* (New York: New American Library, 1975). See also the review on this book, "Economics *Sans* Man *Sans* Purpose", by Gaafar Idris in *Impact* (London), 11 July 1974, p. 8.
———, *Economics in Perspective* (Boston: Houghton Mifflin, 1987).
Galenson, W. and H. Leibenstein, "Investment Criteria, Productivity and Economic Development", *Quarterly Journal of Economics,* August 1955, pp. 343–70.
Gemmell, Norman, *Surveys in Development Economics* (Oxford: Basil Blackwell, 1987).
George, Henry, *Progress and Poverty* (New York: Robert Schalkenbach Foundation, 1955).
Geras, Norman, *Marx and Human Nature: Refutation of a Legend* (London: Verso, 1983).
Gersovitz, Diaz, Ranis and Rosenweig (eds.), *The Theory and Experience of Economic Development* (London: Allen & Unwin, 1982).

Gilbert, Neil, *Capitalism and the Welfare State: Dilemmas of Social Benevolence* (New Haven: Yale University Press, 1983).

Girvetz, Harry K., "Welfare State", *International Encyclopaedia of the Social Sciences* (New York: Macmillan and the Free Press, 1968), vol. 16.

Goldman, Marshal I., *U.S.S.R. in Crisis: The Failure of an Economic System* (New York: Norton, 1983).

Gonzales-Vega, C. and V. H. Cespedes, *Growth and Equity: Changes in Income Distribution in Costa Rica* (New York: United Nations, 1983).

Gorbachev, Mikhail, *New Thinking for Our Country and the World* (New York: Harper & Row, 1987).

Gottlieh, Mannuel, *A Theory of Economic Systems* (Orlando: Harcourt Brace, 1984).

Government of India, Planning Commission, *The First Five Year Plan: A Summary* (New Delhi, 1952).

Government of Pakistan, National Planning Board, *The First Five Year Plan 1955–60* (Karachi, December 1957).

———, *The Second Five Year Plan (1960–65)* (Karachi, June 1960).

———, *The Constitution of the Republic of Pakistan* (Karachi, 1962).

Grand, J. and S. Estrin (eds.), *Market Socialism* (Oxford University Press, 1989).

Gray, Alastair, "Health and Society: Reflections on Policy", *IDS Bulletin,* October 1983, pp. 3–9.

Greenberg, Edward S., *Serving the Few: Corporate Capitalism and the Bias of Government Policy* (New York: John Wiley, 1974).

——— and Richard Young, *American Politics Reconsidered* (Belmont, Calif.: Wadsworth, 1973).

Gregory, Paul R. and Robert C. Stuart, *Soviet Economic Structure and Performance* (New York: Harper & Row, 3rd ed., 1986).

Griffin, Keith, *International Inequality and National Poverty* (London: Macmillan, 1978).

——— and A. R. Khan, "Poverty in the Third World: Ugly Facts and Fancy Models", *World Development,* 6/1978, pp. 1271–80.

Gudgin, Graham, *Industrial Location Processes and Employment Growth* (London: Gower, 1978).

Haberler, Gottfried, "Liberal and Illiberal Development Policy", in Meier (1987).

Hacker, Andrew *et al.,* "Corporation, Business", *The New Encyclopaedia Britannica,* 15th ed. (1973–74), vol. 5.

Hagen, E. E., *On the Theory of Social Change* (Homewood, Ill.: Dorsey Press, 1962).

Hahn, Frank and Martin Hollis (eds.), *Philosophy and Economic Theory* (Oxford: Oxford University Press, 1979).

Haley, B. F., *A Survey of Contemporary Economics* (Homewood, Ill.: Richard D. Irwin, 1952).

Hancock, D. Arnold and Gideon Sjoberg, *Politics in the Post Welfare State* (New York: Columbia Press, 1972).

Haq, Mahboobul, *The Strategy of Economic Planning: A Case Study of Pakistan* (Karachi: Oxford University Press, 1963).

——— and Moin Baqai (eds.), *Employment, Distribution, and Basic Needs in Pakistan, Essays in Honour of Jawaid Azfar* (Lahore: Progressive Publishers, 1986).

Harrington, John J. Jr., "Converting from Western to Islamic Banking" (Pakistan), *Journal of South Asian and Middle Eastern Studies* (Villanova, PA), 2/1988, pp. 3–20.

Harrington, Michael, *Twilight of Capitalism* (London: Macmillan, 1977).

Harris, Ralph, *Beyond the Welfare State: An Economic, Political and Moral Critique of Indiscriminate State Welfare and a Review of Alternatives to Dependency* (London: Institute of Economic Affairs, 1988).

Harrison, Alan, *Distribution of Income in Ten Countries*, Background Paper No. 7, Royal Commission on the Distribution of Income and Wealth (London: Her Majesty's Stationery Office, 1979).

Hasan, Parvez, *Korea: Problems and Issues in a Rapidly Growing Economy* (Baltimore: The Johns Hopkins University Press – published for the World Bank, 1976).

Hattersley, Roy, *Economic Priorities for the Labour Government* (London: St. Martin's Press, 1987).

Hayek, F. A. von, *Individualism and Economic Order* (Chicago, 1948).

Hayter, Teresa, *Aid is Imperialism* (Harmondsworth: Penguin Books, 1969).

Heilbroner, Robert L., *The Limits of American Capitalism* (New York: Harper & Row, 1966).

——— and Lester C. Thurow, in *The Economic Problem* (Englewood Cliffs, N.J.: Prentice Hall, 1975).

———, *The Making of Economic Society* (London: Prentice Hall, 6th ed., 1980).

Hemming, Richard and Ali M. Mansoor, *Privatisation and Public Enterprise* (Washington, D.C.: International Monetary Fund, 1988).

Hewett, A. (ed.), *Reforming the Soviet Economy* (Washington, D.C.: The Brookings Institution, 1988).

Hicks, N., "Growth vs. Basic Needs: Is there a Trade-Off?" *World Development*, 7/1979.

——— and P. Streeten, "Indicators of Development: The Search for a Basic Needs Yardstick", *World Development*, 7/1979.

Hirsch, Fred, *Social Limits to Growth* (Cambridge, Mass.: Harvard University Press, 1976).

Hirschman, Albert O., "The Welfare State in Trouble: Systematic Crisis or Growing Pains", *American Economic Review*, May 1980.

———, "The Rise and Decline of Development Economics", in *Essays in Trespassing* (New York: Cambridge University Press, 1981).

Hodgson, Geoffrey, *Economics and Institutions* (Philadelphia: University of Pennsylvania Press, 1988).

Hofstadter, Richard, *Social Darwinism in American Thought*, revised edition (Boston: Beacon Press, 1962).

Hollis, Martin and Edward Nell, *Rational Economic Man: A Philosophical Critique of Neo-Classical Economics* (Cambridge: Cambridge University Press, 1975).

Holmes, Sir Frank (ed.), *Economic Adjustment: Policies and Problems* (Washington, D.C.: IMF, 1987).

Hook, Sidney (ed.), *Determinism and Freedom in the Age of Modern Science* (New York, 1958).

———, "Welfare State – A Debate that Isn't", in C. I. Schottland (ed.), *The Welfare State* (New York: Harper & Row, 1967).

———, *Revolution, Reform and Social Justice: Studies in the Theory and Practice of Marxism* (New York: New York University Press, 1975).

Hoselitz, Bert F., *The Progress of Underdeveloped Areas* (Chicago: University of Chicago Press, 1952).

———, *Sociological Aspects of Economic Growth* (New York: The Free Press, 1960).

——— *et al.*, *Theories of Economic Growth* (Gleneve, Ill.: Free Press, 1960).

Hough, Jerry, *Russia and the West: Gorbachev and the Politics of Reform* (New York: Simon & Schuster, 1988).

Howe, Irving (ed.), *Twenty-Five Years of 'Dissent': An American Tradition* (New York: Methuen, 1979).

IBRD, *The Basis of a Programme for Columbia* (Washington, D.C.: IBRD, 1950).

———, *World Development Report*, for all years since the first issue in 1978.

——, *Poverty and Hunger: Issues and Options for Food Security in Developing Countries, 1986.*

——, *World Debt Tables: External Debt of Developing Countries, 1989–90* and *1990–91.*

ILO, *Employment Objectives in Economic Development: Report of a Meeting of Experts* (Geneva, 1961).

——, *Employment, Incomes and Equality: A Strategy for Increasing Productive Employment in Kenya* (Geneva: ILO, 1972).

——, *Poverty and Landless in Rural Asia* (Geneva: ILO, 1977).

IMF, *Fund-Supported Programmes, Fiscal Policy, and Income Distribution,* Occasional Paper No. 46 (Washington, D.C.: IMF, September 1986).

——, *Staff Studies for the World Economic Outlook* (Washington, D.C.: IMF, August 1987).

——, *Theoretical Aspects of the Design of Fund-Supported Adjustment Programs,* Occasional Paper No. 55 (Washington, D.C.: IMF, 1987).

——, *The Implications of Fund-Supported Adjustment Programmes for Poverty: Experience of Selected Countries,* Occasional Paper No. 58 (Washington, D.C.: IMF, 1988).

——, *Government Financial Statistics Yearbook* 1989 and previous years.

——, *International Financial Statistics.*

——, *World Economic Outlook,* May 1990.

Jameson, Kenneth P. and Charles K. Wilker (eds.), *Directions in Economic Development* (Notre Dame: Notre Dame University Press, 1973).

Jansen, Marius B., "Japan, History of", *The New Encyclopaedia Britannica,* 15th ed. (1973–74), vol. 10.

Japan, Ministry of International Trade and Industry, *Commercial Statistics and White Paper on International Trade* (1988).

Jay, Elizabeth and Richard Jay, *Critics of Capitalism: Victorian Reactions to Political Economy* (Cambridge: Cambridge University Press, 1986).

Jegen, Mary E. and Charles K. Wilbur, *Growth with Equity* (New York: Paulist Press, 1979).

Jevons, W. S., *The Theory of Political Economy* (Reprint of the 1871 edition) (New York: A. M. Kelly, 1965).

Johnson, Elizabeth S. and Harry J. Johnson, *The Shadow of Keynes* (Oxford: Basil Blackwell, 1978).

Johnson, Harry G., *Money, Trade and Economic Growth* (London: George Allen & Unwin, 1962).

Jonas, Paul, *Essays on the Structure and Reform of Centrally Planned Economic Systems* (Boulder: Col.: Social Science Monographs, 1990).

Karen, Michael, "The New Economic System in the GDP: An Obituary", *Social Studies,* April 1973, pp. 554–87.

Keynes, J. M., *The Collected Writings of John Maynard Keynes* (London: Macmillan, for the Royal Economic Society, 1972).

Khan, Jaliluddin Ahmad, *Alternatives for the Destiny of European Civilization* (Karachi: International Islamic Publishers, 1982).

———, *Atheistic Materialism: A Reaction to Orthodox Christianity* (Karachi: International Islamic Publishers, 1982).

Knight, Frank H., "Social Economic Organisation", reprinted from his book, *The Economic Organisation,* pp. 3–30, in W. Breit, *et al., Readings in Macroeconomics* (St. Louis: Times Mirror/ Mosby, 1986).

Kohler, Heinz, *Welfare and Planning: An Analysis of Capitalism Versus Socialism* (New York: Robert E. Kreiger, 2nd ed., 1979).

Kolakowski, *Main Currents of Marxism,* 3 vols., tr. P. S. Fallan (Oxford: Clarendon Press, 1978).

Kolko, Gabriel, *Wealth and Power in America: An Analysis of Social Class and Income Distribution* (New York: Praeger, 1964).

Kontorovich, V. (1986), "Soviet Growth Slowdown: Econometric Versus Direct Evidence", *American Economic Review,* May 1986.

Kornai, Janos, *Economics of Shortage* (Amsterdam: North-Holland, 1980).

———, "The Hungarian Reform Process: Visions, Hopes and Reality", *Journal of Economic Literature,* December 1986, pp. 1687–737.

Krueger, Anne O., "Government Failures in Development", *Journal of Economic Perspectives,* Summer 1990, pp. 9–23.

———, *Economic Policy in Developing Countries* (Oxford: Basil Blackwell, 1991).

Kunio, Yoshihara, *Japanese Economic Development: A Short Introduction* (Tokyo: Oxford University Press, 1979).

Kuznets, Simon, "Economic Growth and Income Inequality", *American Economic Review,* March 1955.

———, "Quantitative Aspects of the Economic Growth of Nations: Distribution of Income by Size", *Economic Development and Cultural Change,* January 1963.

———, *Modern Economic Growth* (New Haven: Yale University Press, 1966).

Lace, Lawrence J. (ed.), *Models of Development: A Comparative Study of Economic Growth in South Korea and Taiwan* (San Francisco: ICS Press, 1986).

Laird, Sam and Alexander Yeats, "Non-tariff Barriers of Developed Countries, 1966–68", *Finance and Development,* March 1989, pp. 12–13.

Lal, Deepak, *The Poverty of Development Economics* (London: Hobart Paperback No. 16, 1984).

Lampman, Robert J., *The Share of Top Wealth-Holders in National Wealth, 1922–1956* – A Study by the National Bureau of Economic Research (Princeton, N.J.: Princeton University Press, 1962).

Lange, Oscar, *Political Economy* (New York: Macmillan, 1963).

Lappe, Frances M. and Joseph Collin, *World Hunger: Twelve Myths* (London: Earthsean, revised ed., 1988).

Layard, Richard, *How to Beat Unemployment* (Oxford: Oxford University Press, 1986).

Lebergott, Stanley, "The Shape of the Income Distribution", *American Economic Review,* June 1959, pp. 328–47.

———, "Income Distribution II (Size)", *International Encyclopaedia of the Social Sciences* (1968), vol. 7.

Lee, E., "Egalitarian Peasant Farming and Rural Development: The Case of South Korea", *World Development,* 7 (1979), pp. 493–517.

Leeman, Wayne A. (ed.), *Capitalism, Market Socialism and Central Planning: Readings in Comparative Economic Systems* (Boston: Houghton Mifflin, 1963).

Le Grand, Julian, "Who Benefits from Public Expenditure?" *New Society,* vol. 45, No. 833, 1978.

———, *The Strategy of Equality: Redistribution and the Social Services* (London: Allen & Unwin, 1982).

Leibenstein, Harvey, *Economic Backwardness and Economic Growth* (New York: John Wiley, 1957).

———, "Notes on Welfare Economics and the Theory of Democracy", *Economic Journal,* June 1962, pp. 299–317.

———, *Beyond Economic Man* (Cambridge, Mass.: Harvard University Press, 1976).

Lekachman, R., *Economists at Bay* (New York: McGraw Hill, 1976).

Lerner, Warren, *A History of Socialism and Communism in Modern Times: Theorists, Activists and Humanists* (Englewood Cliffs, N.J.: Prentice Hall, 1982).

Lewis, Russell, *The Survival of the Capitalist System: Challenge to the Pluralist Societies of the West* (London: Institute for the Study of Conflict, 1977).

Lewis, W. Arthur, *The Theory of Economic Growth* (Homewood, Ill.: Richard D. Irwin, 1955).

———, "A Review of Economic Development", *Manchester School,* May 1965, pp. 1–16.

Lichtheim, George, *Marxism* (New York: Praeger, 1961).

———, *A Short History of Socialism* (Glasgow: Collins, 1978).

Lindemann, Albert S., *A History of European Socialism* (New Haven: Yale University Press, 1983).

Lipton, D. and Sachs, J., "Creating a Market Economy in Eastern Europe: The Case of Poland", *Brookings Papers on Economic Activity,* vol. 1, pp. 75–145.

Little, Ian M. D., *Economic Development: Theory, Policy and International Relations* (New York: Basic Books, 1982).

Lockwood, William W., *The Economic Development of Japan: Growth and Structural Change* (Princeton: Princeton University Press, 1968).

Lovejoy, Arthur, *The Great Chain of Being* (New York: Harper & Brothers, 1960).

Lundberg, Ferdinand, *The Rich and the Super Rich: A Study in the Power of Money Today* (New York: Bantam Books, 1969).

Lutz, M. A. and K. Lux, *The Challenge of Humanistic Economics* (Menlo Park, Calif.: Benjamin/Cummings, 1979).

Luxemburg, Rosa, *Reform or Revolution* (Oxford: Oxford University Press, 1963).

Magdoff, Harry and Paul M. Sweezy, *The Deepening Crisis of U.S. Capitalism* (New York: Monthly Review Press, 1981).

Malabre, Alfred, Jr., *Beyond Our Means* (New York: Random House, 1987).

Malinvaud, E. and Jean-Paul Fitoussi (eds.), *Unemployment in Western Countries* – Proceedings of a Conference held by the International Economic Association at Bischenberg, Franca (London: Macmillan, 1980).

Malthus, T., *An Essay on the Principle of Population* (London: J. Johnson, 2nd ed., 1803).

Mandelbaum, K., *The Industrialisation of Backward Areas* (Oxford: Basil Blackwell, 1945).

Manser, Anthony, *Sartre: A Philosophic Study* (London: Athlone Press, 1966).

Marsh, David, *The Future of the Welfare State* (London: Penguin, 1964).

Marx, Karl, *Selected Writings in Sociology and Social Philosophy,* (tr. T. B. Bottomore) T. B. Bottomore and M. Rubel (eds.), (London: Penguin, 1963).

——— and Friedrich Engels, *The Communist Manifesto* (New York: International Publishers, 1948).

———, ed., Lewis Feuer, *Basic Writings on Politics and Philosophy* (Garden City, N.Y.: Anchor, 1959).

Masai, Yasuo, "Japan", *The New Encyclopaedia Britannica,* 15th ed. (1973–74), vol. 10, p. 49.

Maslow, Abraham, *Motivation and Personality* (New York: Harper & Row, 1970).

Mason, Edward S., "Corporation", *International Encyclopaedia of Social Sciences* (1968), vol. 3.

——— (ed.), *The Corporation in Modern Society* (Cambridge, Mass.: Harvard University Press, 1980).

——— *et al., The Economic and Social Modernisation of the Republic of Korea* (Cambridge: Harvard University Press, 1980).

Mathews, R. C. O. and G. P. Stafford, *The Grants Economy and Collective Consumption* (London: Macmillan, 1982), p. 77.

McInnes, Neil, "Karl Marx", *The Encyclopaedia of Philosophy* (1967), vol. 5.

McKeown, Thomas, *The Role of Medicine: Dream, Mirage or Nemesis?* (Princeton, N.J.: Princeton University Press, 1979).

McKibben, Bill, *The End of Nature* (New York: Viking, 1989).

Meadows, D. H. *et al., The Limits to Growth: A Report for the Club of Rome's Project on the Predicament of Mankind* (London: Pan Books, 1974).

Medvedev, Roy, *Let History Judge,* tr. George Shriver (New York: Columbia University Press, 1989).

Meier, Gerald M., *Leading Issues in Development Economics: Selected Materials and Commentary* (New York: Oxford University Press, 1964).

——— and Dudley Seers (eds.), *Pioneers in Development,* First Series (New York: Oxford University Press, 1984).

———, *Emerging from Poverty: The Economics that Really Matters* (New York: Oxford University Press, 1984).

———, (ed.), *Pioneers in Development,* Second Series (New York: Oxford University Press, 1987).

Miller, George A., *Psychology: The Science of Mental Life* (New York: Harper & Row, 1962).

Millhand, Ralph, *The State in Capitalist Society* (New York: Basic Books, 1969).

Mills, C. Wright, *The Power Elite* (New York: Oxford University Press, 1959).

Mincer, Jacob, "The Distribution of Labour Incomes: A Survey with Special Reference to the Human Capital Approach", *Journal of Economic Literature,* March 1970, pp. 1–26.

Minford, P., *Unemployment, Cause and Cure* (Oxford: Basil Blackwell, 2nd ed., 1985).

Mini, Piero V., *Philosophy and Economics: The Origins and Development of Economic Theory* (Gainsville: The University Presses of Florida, 1974).

Minsky, Hyman P., *Stabilising an Unstable Economy* (New Haven: Yale University Press, 1986).

Mintz, Morton and Jerry S. Cohen, *America, Inc.: Who Owns and Operates the United States* (New York: The Dial Press, 1971).

Mises, Ludwig von, *Socialism: An Economic and Sociological Analysis*, tr. from the German by J. Kahane (London: Jonathan Cape, 1974).

Mishan, E. J., *The Costs of Economic Growth* (Harmondsworth: Penguin Books, 1973).

———, *Cost Benefit Analysis: An Introduction* (New York: Praeger, 1971).

Moore, Barrington, Jr., *Reflections on the Causes of Human Misery and Upon Certain Proposals to Eliminate Them* (London: Allen Lane, the Penguin Press, 1972).

Morawetz, David, *Twenty-five Years of Economic Development: 1950 to 1975* (Washington, D.C.: IBRD, 1977).

Myers, Milton L., *The Soul of Modern Economic Man: Ideas of Self Interest, Thomas Hobbes to Adam Smith* (Chicago: University of Chicago Press, 1983).

Myers, Robert L. (ed.), *The Political Morality of the International Monetary Fund* (New York: Transaction Books, 1987).

Myint, Hla, "Comparative Analysis of Taiwan's Economic Development with Other Countries", *Academic Economic Papers*, March 1982.

Myrdal, Gunnar, *Economic Theory and Underdeveloped Regions* (London: Buckworth, 1957).

———, *Rich Lands and Poor* (New York: Harper & Row, 1957).

———, *Beyond the Welfare State* (New Haven: Yale University Press, 1960).

———, *Asian Drama* (New York: The Twentieth Century Fund, 1968).

———, "Need for Reforms in Underdeveloped Countries", *Quarterly Economic Journal* (National Bank of Pakistan), January–March 1979.

Nakamura, T., tr. J. Kaminski, *The Postwar Japanese Economy: Its Development and Structure* (Tokyo: University of Tokyo Press, 1981).

Nelson, Joan M. (ed.), *Economic Crisis and Policy Choice: The Politics of Adjustment in the Third World* (Princeton, N.J.: Princeton University Press, 1990).

Nikko Research Centre, *Analysis of Japanese Industries for Investors, 1990* (Tokyo: Nikko Research Centre).

Nolan, Peter and Suzanne Paine (eds.), *Rethinking Socialist Economics: New Agenda for Britain* (New York: St. Martin's Press, 1986).

Nordhaus, N. D., "Soviet Economic Reform: The Longest Road", *Brookings Papers on Economic Activity,* 1990, vol. 1, pp. 287–307.

Novak, Michael, *The Spirit of Democratic Capitalism* (New York: Simon & Schuster, 1982).

Nove, Alec, *The Soviet Economic System* (London: George Allen & Unwin, 1977).

———, *The Economics of Feasible Socialism* (London: George Allen & Unwin, 1983).

Nurkse, Ragnar, *Problems of Capital Formation in Underdeveloped Countries* (Oxford: Basil Blackwell, 1953).

———, "The Structuralist Approach to Economic Development", *American Economic Review,* May 1965.

O'Connor, James, *The Fiscal Crisis of the State* (New York: St. Martin's Press, 1973).

OECD, *The Welfare State in Crisis, An Account of the Conference on Social Policies in the 1980s,* Paris, 20–23 October 1980, (Paris: OECD, 1981).

———, *Employment Outlook* (Paris: OECD, 1986).

———, "Financial Resources for Developing Countries: 1986 and Recent Trends", *OECD Press Release,* 19 June 1987.

———, *Financing External Debt of Developing Countries – 1986 Survey* (Paris: OECD, 1987).

———, *The Costs of Restructuring Imports – The Automobile Industry* (Paris: OECD, 1987).

———, *National Policies and Agricultural Trade* (Paris: OECD, 1988).

———, *OECD Economic Outlook* Nos. 44 and 47 (Paris: OECD, 14 December 1988 and 20 June 1990 respectively).

———, *Revenue Statistics of OECD Member Countries, 1965–89* (Paris: OECD, 1990).

———, *A Study of the Soviet Economy,* study undertaken by the IMF, the IBRD, the OECD and the EBRD (Paris: OECD, 1991).

Offer, Gur, "Soviet Economic Growth: 1928–1985", *Journal of Economic Literature,* December 1987.

Offe, Claus, *Contradictions of the Welfare State,* ed. John Keane (London: Hutchinson, 1984).

Okun, Arthur, *Equality and Efficiency: The Big Trade-off* (Washington, D.C.: The Brookings Institution, 1975).

Packard, Vance, *The Hidden Persuaders* (Harlow, Essex: Longman, 1957).
Passmore, John, "Logical Positivism", *Encyclopaedia of Philosophy* (1967), vol. 5.
Payer, Cheryl, *The Debt Trap: The IMF and the Third World* (New York: Monthly Review Press, 1972).
———, *The World Bank: A Critical Analysis* (New York: Monthly Review Press, 1982).
Pechman, Joseph A., "The Rich, the Poor and the Taxes They Pay", *The Public Interest,* Fall 1969.
——— and Benjamin A. Okner, *Who Bears the Tax Burden?* (Washington, D.C.: The Brookings Institution, 1974).
———, *The Rich, the Poor and the Taxes They Pay* (Boulder, Co.: Westview Press, 1986).
———, *World Tax Reform: The Progress Report* (Washington, D.C.: The Brookings Institution, 1988).
Perkins, Dwight H., "Reforming China's Economic System", *Journal of Economic Literature,* June 1988, pp. 601–45.
Plamenatz, John, *Karl Marx's Philosophy of Man* (Oxford: Clarendon Press, 1975).
Polanyi, Karl, *The Great Transformation* (New York: Reinhart, 1944).
Posner, Richard A., *The Economics of Justice* (Cambridge, Mass.: Harvard University Press, 1981).
Qureshi, M. L., *Strategy of Industrial Planning and Development in Pakistan* (Karachi: Government of Pakistan, 1965).
Rafiuddin, M., *The Fallacy of Marxism* (Lahore: Institute of Islamic Culture, 1969).
Ranis, Gustav and Paul T. Schultz (eds.), *The State of Development Economics: Progress and Perspectives* (Oxford: Basil Blackwell, 1988).
Rao, D. G., "Economic Growth and Equity in the Republic of Korea", *World Development,* 6/1978, pp. 397–409.
Rawls, John, "Justice as Fairness", *Philosophical Review,* vol. 67/1958, pp. 164–94.
———, *A Theory of Justice* (Cambridge, Mass.: Harvard University Press, 1973).
Rees, Albert E., *Wage Inflation* (New York: National Industrial Board, 1957).
Rees-Mogg, William, *The Reigning Error: The Crisis of World Inflation* (London: Hamish Hamilton, 1974).
Reich, Michael, "The Evolution of the U.S. Labour Force", *The Capitalist System* (Englewood Cliffs, N.J.: Prentice Hall, 1972).

Reich, Robert, *The Work of Nations: Preparing Ourselves for 21st Century Capitalism* (New York: Knopf, 1988).
Reisman, David, *Galbraith and American Capitalism* (London: Macmillan, 1980).
Reynolds, Bruce L. (ed.), *Chinese Economic Reform: How Far, How Fast?* (London: Academic Press, 1988).
Reynolds, Lloyd G., "The Spread of Economic Growth to the Third World: 1850–1980", *Journal of Economic Literature*, September 1983, pp. 941–80.
Robbins, Lord, *The Theory of Economic Development in the History of Economic Thought* (London: Macmillan, 1968).
Robinson, William F., *The Pattern of Reform in Hungary* (New York: Praeger, 1973).
Rosenstein-Rodan, P. N., "Notes, on the Theory of the 'Big Push' ", in Howard S. Ellis (ed.), *Economic Development for Latin America* (London: Macmillan, 1961).
Rostow, W. W., "Take-off into Self-sustained Economic Growth", *Economic Journal*, March 1986.
Russell, Bertrand, *A Free Man's Worship: Mysticism and Logic* (New York, 1918).
———, *A History of Western Philosophy* (New York: Simon & Schuster, 1945).
———, *The Impact of Science on Society* (New York: Simon & Schuster, 1953).
Sachs, Jeffrey, *Social Conflict and Populist Policies in Latin America* (Cambridge, Mass.: National Bureau of Economic Research, Paper No. 2897).
Samuelson, Paul A., *Economics* (New York: McGraw Hill, 11th ed., 1980).
Sartre, Jean-Paul, *Being and Nothingness*, tr. Hazel Barnes (London: Methuen, 1957).
Saunders, Peter and Friedrich Klau, *The Role of the Public Sector: Causes and Consequences of the Growth of Government* (Paris: OECD, 1985).
Sawhill, Isabell V., "Poverty in the U.S.: Why is it So Persistent?" *Journal of Economic Literature*, September 1988.
Schadwick, Owen, *The Secularization of the European Mind in the Nineteenth Century* (Cambridge: Cambridge University Press, 1975).
Schneider, W., *Adam Smith's Moral and Political Philosophy* (New York, 1948).
Schottland, C. I. (ed.), *The Welfare State* (New York: Harper & Row, 1967).

Schultz, Charles, *The Public Use of Private Purpose* (Washington, D.C.: The Brookings Institution, 1957).
Schumpeter, Joseph, *Capitalism, Socialism and Development* (New York: Harper, 1950).
Scitovsky, Tibor, *The Joyless Economy* (New York: Oxford University Press, 1976).
———, "Economic Development in Taiwan and South Korea", *Food Research Institute Studies,* 1985.
Seers, Dudley, "The Meaning of Development", *International Development Review,* December 1969.
———, *The Political Economy of Nationalism* (Oxford University Press, 1983).
Seligman, Ben, *Main Currents in Modern Economics* (Chicago: Quadrangle paperback, 1971).
Sen, Amartya, *Poverty and Famines: An Essay on Entitlement and Deprivation* (Oxford: Clarendon Press, 1981).
———, *On Ethics and Economics* (Oxford: Basil Blackwell, 1987).
Sheehan, Robert, "Proprietors in the World of Big Business", *Fortune,* 15 June 1967.
Shmelev, N. and V. Propov, *The Turning Point: Revitalising the Soviet Economy* (London: Tauris, 1990).
Short, Peter, *Appraising the Role of Public Enterprises: An International Comparison* (Washington, D.C.: International Monetary Fund Occasional Papers, 1983).
Sidgwick, H., *Outlines of the History of Ethics* (London, 1946).
Silver, Morris, *Foundations of Economic Justice* (Oxford: Basil Blackwell, 1989).
Simons, Henry C., *Personal Income Taxation* (Chicago: University of Chicago Press, 1938).
Sirc, L., *Economic Revolution in Eastern Europe* (Harlow, Essex: Longman, 1969).
Skinner, B. F., *Science and Human Behaviour* (New York: Macmillan, 1953).
Skinner, Quentin (ed.), *The Return of Grand Theory in the Human Sciences* (Cambridge: Cambridge University Press, 1986).
Solo, Robert A. and Charles W. Anderson (eds.), *Value Judgement and Income Distribution* (New York: Praeger, 1981).
Solzhenitsyn, Alexander, *A World Split Apart* (New York: Harper & Row, 1978).
Soule, George, *Ideas of the Great Economists* (New York: Mentor, 1952).
South Korea, *Agriculture in Korea* (Seoul: Ministry of Agriculture and Forestry, 1970).

Spengler, Joseph P., ''IBRD Mission Growth Theory'', *American Economic Review,* May 1954, pp. 586–7.

Staley, Eugene, *The Future of Underdeveloped Countries* (New York, 1954).

Steidlmeier, Paul, *The Paradox of Poverty: A Reappraisal of Economic Development Policy* (Cambridge, Mass.: Ballinger, 1987).

Stepelevich, L. S. (ed.), *The Capitalist Reader* (New York: Arlington House Publishers, 1977).

Stevenson, Leslie, *Seven Theories of Human Nature* (Oxford: Clarendon Press, 1974).

Stewart, Frances, *Basic Needs in Developing Countries* (Baltimore: The Johns Hopkins University Press, 1985).

Stigler, G., *Production and Distribution Theories: The Formative Period* (New York: Macmillan, 1941).

Strayer, Paul J., ''The Individual Income Tax and Income Distribution'', *American Economic Review,* vol. 45, No. 2.

Streeten, Paul, *Development Perspectives* (London: Macmillan, 1981).

——— *et al., First Things First: Meeting Basic Needs in Developing Countries* (Oxford: Oxford University Press, 1981).

———, ''Basic Needs: Some Unsettled Questions'', *World Development,* 1984.

——— (ed.), *Beyond Adjustment: The Asian Experience* (Washington, D.C.: IMF, 1988).

Sumner, William G., *The Challenge of Facts and Other Essays,* ed. Albert G. Keller (New Haven: Yale University Press, 1914).

Sweezy, Paul M., ''Lessons of Soviet Experience'', *Monthly Review,* November 1967, pp. 9–21.

Tawney, R. H., *The Acquisitive Society* (New York: Harcourt Brace, 1948).

Thoenes, Piet, *The Elite in the Welfare State* (London: Faber, 1966).

Thomas, Roy, *Japan: The Blighted Blossom* (London: Tauris, 1989).

Thorp, Willard, ''Some Basic Policy Issues in Economic Development'', *American Economic Review,* May 1951, pp. 407–17.

Thurow, Lester, *Zero-Sum Society* (New York: Basic Books, 1980).

———, ''A Time to Dismantle the World Economy'', *The Economist,* 9 November 1985.

Titmuss, Richard M., *Essays on the Welfare State* (London: Unwin, 1963).

——— *Commitment to Welfare* (London: George Allen & Unwin, 2nd ed., 1976).

Toynbee, Arnold J., *A Study of History*, abridgement by D. C. Somervell (Oxford: Oxford University Press, 1957).

Trotsky, Leon, *The Revolution Betrayed* (New York: Pathfinder Press, 1972), originally published in 1937.

U.S. Congress, Joint Economic Committee, *East European Economies: Slow Growth in the 1980s* (Washington, D.C.: US GPO, 1986).

U.S. Department of Commerce, Bureau of the Census, *Statistical Abstract of the United States, 1986 and 1988.*

United Nations Conference on Trade and Development (UNCTAD), *Trade and Development Report, 1985* (New York: United Nations, 1985).

United Nations, Department of Economic Affairs, *Measures for the Economic Development of Underdeveloped Countries* (New York: United Nations, 1951).

United Nations, ECAFE, "Criteria for Allocating Investment Resources among Various Fields of Development in Underdeveloped Countries", *Economic Bulletin for Asia and the Far East,* June 1961.

Viner, Jacob, *International Trade and Economic Development* (Glencoe, Ill.: The Free Press, 1952).

Ward, Benjamin, *What is Wrong With Economics?* (London: Macmillan, 1972).

———, *The Ideal Worlds of Economics: Liberal, Radical and Conservative Economic Worldviews* (London: Macmillan, 1979).

Wesson, Robert G., *Why Marxism?: The Continuing Success of a Failed Theory* (New York: Basic Books, 1976).

Westphal, Larry E., "Industrial Policy in an Export-Propelled Economy: Lessons from South Korea's Experience", *Journal of Economic Perspectives,* Summer 1990, pp. 41–59.

Wilczynski, J., *The Economics of Socialism* (London: George Allen & Unwin, 3rd ed., 1978).

Wilensky, Harold, *The Welfare State and Equality* (Berkeley, California: University of California Press, 1975).

Wilhelm, Donald, *Creative Alternatives to Communism: Guidelines for Tomorrow's World* (London: Macmillan, 1977).

Williamson, J. G. and P. H. Lindert, *American Inequality: A Macro-Economic History* (New York: Academic Press, 1980).

———, *Did British Capitalism Breed Inequality?* (London: Allen & Unwin, 1985).

———, "The Historical Content of the Classical Labour Surplus Model", *Population and Development Review,* June 1985, pp. 171–91.

———, *Inequality, Poverty, and History* (Oxford: Basil Blackwell, 1991).

Winglee, Peter, "Agricultural Trade Policies of Industrial Countries", *Finance and Development,* March 1989.

Winiecki, Jan, *Economic Prospects, East and West* (London: Centre for Research into Communist Economies, 1987).

———, *The Distorted World of Soviet-Type Economies* (London: Routledge & Kegan Paul, 1988).

Witt, S. F. and G. D. Newbould, "The Impact of Food Subsidies", *National Westminster Bank Quarterly Review,* August 1976, pp. 29–36.

Wolf, T. A., "Economic Stabilisation in Planned Economies", *IMF Staff Papers,* 1/1985, pp. 78–131.

Wolferen, Karel von, *The Enigma of Japanese Power* (London: Macmillan, 1989).

Yamaichi Research Institute of Securities and Economics, *Monthly Digest of Statistics,* January and September 1989 and July 1990.

Yanowitch, Murray, *Social and Economic Inequality in the Soviet Union* (London: Martin Robertson, 1977).

Yotopoulos, P. A. and J. B. Nugent, *Economics of Development* (New York: Harper & Row, 1976).

Young-Kyun, Oh, "Agrarian Reform and Economic Development: A Case Study of Korean Agriculture", *Koreana Quarterly,* 1969.

Zwass, A., *Money, Banking and Credit in the Soviet Union and Eastern Europe* (London: Macmillan, 1984).

PART II: THE ISLAMIC RESPONSE

Qur'ān Commentaries

Al-Jaṣṣāṣ, Abū Bakr, *Aḥkām al-Qur'ān* (Cairo: Maṭba'ah al-Bahiyyah al-Misriyyah, 1347 A.H.).

Ibn Kathīr, Abū al-Fidā' Ismā'īl, *Tafsīr al-Qur'ān al-'Aẓīm* (Cairo: 'Isa al-Babi al-Halabi, n.d.).

Mawdudi, Sayyid Abul A'la, *Tafhīm al-Qur'ān* (Lahore: Maktabah Ta'mīre Insāniyyat, 1967–73).

Quṭb, Sayyid, *Fī Ẓilāl al-Qur'ān* (Jeddah: Dār al-'Ilm, 1986).

Riḍā, Sayyid Muḥammad Rashīd, *Tafsīr al-Manār* (Cairo: Dar al-Manar, 4th ed., 1954).

Ḥadīth Collections

Abū Dāwūd al-Sijistānī, *Sunan Abū Dāwūd* (Cairo: 'Isa al-Babi al-Halabi, 1952).
Al-Bukhārī, Muḥammad ibn Ismā'īl, *Al-Adab al-Mufrad* (Cairo: Quṣay Muḥibb al-Dīn al-Khaṭib, 2nd ed., 1379 A.H.).
———, *Al-Jāmi' al-Ṣaḥīḥ* (Cairo: Muḥammad 'Ali Ṣubayḥ, n.d.).
Al-Dārimī, 'Abdullāh ibn 'Abd al-Raḥmān, *Sunan al-Dārimī* (Damascus: Maṭba'ah al-I'tidāl, 1349 A.H.).
Al-Haythamī, Nūr al-Dīn, *Majma' al-Zawā'id wa Manba' al-Fawā'id* (Cairo: Maktabah al-Qudsi, 1352 A.H.).
Ibn Mājah, *Sunan Ibn Mājah* (Cairo: 'Isa al-Babi al-Halabi, 1952), vol. 2, p. 1297:3931.
Al-Mundhirī, Ibn 'Umar, in *Al-Targhīb wa al-Tarhīb*, ed. Mustafa M. 'Ammārah (Beirut: Dar al-Kutub al-'Ilmiyyah, 1986).
Muslim, *Ṣaḥīḥ Muslim*, ed. Muhammad Fu'ād 'Abd al-Bāqī (Cairo: 'Isa al-Babi al-Halabi, 1955).
Al-Nasā'ī, Abū 'Abd al-Raḥmān ibn Shu'ayb, *Sunan al-Nasā'ī al-Mujtabā* (Cairo: Mustafa al-Babi al-Halabi, 1964).
Al-Nīsābūrī, Abū 'Abdullāh Muḥammad, *Mustadrak al-Ḥākim* (Riyadh: Maktabah wa Maṭābi' al-Naṣr al-Ḥadīthah, n.d.) vol. 2, p. 12 – narrated by Ibn 'Umar.
Al-Suyūṭī, Jalāl al-Dīn, *Al-Jāmi' al-Ṣaghīr* (Cairo: 'Abd al-Ḥamīd Aḥmad Ḥanafi, n.d.) vol. 2, p. 96.
Al-Tabrīzī, Walī al-Dīn, *Mishkāt al-Maṣābīḥ* (Damascus: al-Maktab al-Islamī, 1381 A.H.), ed. M. Nāsīr al-Dīn al-Albānī.
Al-Tirmidhī, Muḥammad ibn 'Isā, *Jāmi' al-Tirmidhī* with commentary, *Tuḥfat al-Aḥwadhī* (Beirut: Dar al-Kitab al-'Arabi, n.d.).

Others

Abāẓah, Ibrāhīm Dusūqī, *Al-Iqtiṣād al-Islāmī: Muqawwimātihī wa Manāhijihī* (Cairo: Al-Ittiḥad al-Duwali li al-Bunūk al-Islāmiyyah, n.d.).
Al-'Abbādī, 'Abd al-Salām, *Al-Milkiyyah fī al-Sharī'ah al-Islāmiyyah* (Amman, Jordan: Maktabah al-Aqsa, 1974–1975).
Abbasi, S. M. Madni, *Lawful Earning in Islam* (Karachi: International Islamic Publishers, 1985).
'Abd al-Rasūl, 'Ali, *Al-Mabādi' al-Iqtiṣādiyyah fī al-Islām wa al-Binā' al-Iqtiṣādī li al-Dawlah al-Islāmiyyah* (Cairo: Dar al-Fikr al-'Arabi, 1968).

'Abduh, 'Isā, *Al-Iqtiṣād al-Islāmī: Madkhal wa Minhāj* (Cairo: Dar al-I'tiṣām, 1973).

'Abdullah, Ahmed, "Islamic Banking", *Journal of Islamic Banking and Finance,* January–March 1987, pp. 31–56.

Abe, T., *A Comparative Study of Islamic Ownership: Conceptual Frameworks of Ownership in Islamic and Western Value Systems* (Niigata: Institute of Middle Eastern Studies, 1987).

Abul-Fadl, Mona, *Paradigms in Politics: Critical Options and Muslim Perspectives* (Herndon, VA.: The International Institute of Islamic Thought, 1989).

Abū Sa'ūd, Mahmud, *Khuṭūṭ Ra'īsiyyah fī al-Iqtiṣād al-Islāmī* (Kuwait: Maktabah al-Manār al-Islāmiyyah, 2nd ed., 1967).

——, *About the Fiqh of Zakat* (Ohio: Zakat and Research Foundation, 1988).

——, *Contemporary Zakat* (Ohio: Zakat and Research Foundation, 1988).

Abū Sulayman, Abdul Hamid, "The Theory of the Economics of Islam", in *Contemporary Aspects of Economic Thinking in Islam* (Bloomington, Indiana: MSA, 1976).

Abū 'Ubayd, Qāsim ibn Sallām, *Kitāb al-Amwāl,* ed. Muḥammad Khālid al-Harrad (Cairo: Al-Maktabah al-Tijāriyyah al-Kubrā, 1353 A.H.).

Abu Wahid, N. M., "A Theoretical Justification of Islamic Banks", *Islamic Quarterly,* 3/1986, pp. 192–300.

Abū Yūsuf, Ya'qūb ibn Ibrāhīm, *Kitāb al-Kharāj* (Cairo: al-Maṭba'ah al-Salafiyyah, 2nd ed., 1353 A.H.). The English translation of this book by Ben Shemesh was published by Brill, Leiden, in 1969.

Abū Zahrah, Muḥammad, *Aḥkām al-Tarikāt wa al-Mawārīth* (Damascus: Dār al-Fikr al-'Arabi, 1963).

——, *Al-Takāful al-Ijtimā'ī fī al-Islām* (Cairo: Dār al-Fikr al-'Arabi, n.d.).

'Afr, M. 'Abd al-Mun'im, *Naḥwa al-Naẓariyyah al-Iqtiṣādiyyah fī al-Islām: Al-Athmān wa al-Aswāq* (Cairo: Matabi' al-Ittiḥād al-Duwali li al-Bunūk al-Islāmiyyah, 1981).

—— and Yusuf Kamāl, *Uṣūl al-Iqtiṣād al-Islāmī* (Jeddah: Dar al-Bayān al-'Arabi, 1985).

Ahmad, 'Abdul Rahman Yusri, *Al-Tanmiyyah al-Iqtiṣādiyyah wa al-Ijtimā'iyyah fī al-Islām* (Alexandria: Mu'assasah Shabāb al-Jāmi'ah, 1401 A.H.).

Ahmad, Afazuddin, "Economic Significance of Zakāt", *Islamic Literature* (Lahore), August 1952, pp. 5–11.

Ahmad, Ausaf, *Development and Problems of Islamic Banks* (Jeddah: IRTI, IDB, 1987).

———, *Income Determination in an Islamic Economy* (Jeddah: Centre for Research in Islamic Economics, King Abdulaziz University, 1987).

Ahmad, Hasan, "Social Justice in Islam", *Islamic Studies* (Islamabad), 3/1971, pp. 209–19.

Ahmad, Khurshid, "Islam and Simple Living", *Criterion* (Karachi), July–August 1970, pp. 5–12.

———, "The Third World's Dilemma of Development", *Nonaligned Third World Annual, 1970*, pp. 3–18.

——— (ed.), *Islam – Its Meaning and Message* (London: Islamic Council of Europe, 1975).

———, *Social Justice in Islam* (Lahore: Institute of Islamic Culture, 1975).

——— and Z. I. Ansari (eds.), *Islamic Perspectives: Studies in Honour of Mawlana Sayyid Abul A'la Mawdūdī* (Leicester, U.K.: The Islamic Foundation, 1979).

——— (ed.), *Studies in Islamic Economics* (Leicester, U.K.: The Islamic Foundation, 1980), p. 173.

Ahmad, Mumtaz (ed.), *State, Politics and Islam* (Indianapolis: American Trust Publications, 1987).

Ahmad, Salahuddin, "Patterns of Consumption and Saving Behaviour in an Islamic Economy", *Thoughts on Economics,* Winter 1966.

——— (ed.), *Thoughts on Economics: Special Issue on Islamic Banking* (Dhaka: Islamic Economics Research Bureau, 2/1987).

——— (ed.), *Thoughts on Economics: Conference Issue on Distribution of Income and Wealth in Islam* (Dhaka: Islamic Economics Research Bureau, 4/1987).

Ahmad, Shaikh Mahmud, *Economics of Islam* (Lahore: Muhammad Ashraf, 1952).

———, *Towards Interest-Free Banking* (Lahore: Institute of Islamic Culture, 1989).

Ahmed, Badar Durrez, "Riba in Islamic Law", *Islamic and Comparative Law Quarterly,* 6/1986, pp. 51–70.

Ahmed, Manzooruddin, *Islamic Political System in the Modern Age – Theory and Practice* (Karachi: Saad Publications, 1983).

Ahmed, Ziauddin, *et al.* (eds.), *Fiscal Policy and Resource Allocation in Islam* (Islamabad: Institute of Policy Studies, 1983).

——— *et al.* (eds.), *Money and Banking in Islam* (Jeddah: International Centre for Research in Islamic Economics, King Abdulaziz University, 1983).

———, *Concepts and Models of Islamic Banking* (Karachi: Institute of Bankers in Pakistan, 1984).

———, "Islam and Fulfilment of Basic Needs", *Islamic Order,* 2/1987, pp. 53–64.

———, "Interest-Free Banking", *Journal of Islamic Banking and Finance,* January–March 1987, pp. 8–30.

———, "Islamic Banking at the Crossroads", *Journal of Islamic Economics* (Kuala Lumpur), 1/1989, pp. 23–44.

Ahsan, A. S. M. Fakhrul, "Some Issues on the Promotion and Mobilization of Savings Through Islamic Banks", *Thoughts on Economics* (Dhaka), 1987, pp. 25–34.

———, "Islamic Banking in Perspective", *Journal of Islamic Banking and Finance* (Karachi), 1/1990, pp. 39–54.

Ahsan, M. Manazir, "Bayt al-Mal and its Role in the Islamic Economy", *Criterion* (Karachi), September 1975, pp. 14–27.

Akkas, S. M. Ali, "Size Distribution of Income and Wealth in an Islamic Economic Framework", *Thoughts on Economics,* 3–4/1987, pp. 68–75.

Alatas, Syed Farid, "An Islamic Common Market and Economic Development", *Islamic Culture,* 1/1987, pp. 28–38.

Alden, A. J., *Free Action* (London, 1961).

Ali, Abdal Kadir, "Land, Property and Land Tenure in Islam", *Islamic Quarterly* (London) April–July 1959, pp. 4–11.

Ali, Ali Abdulla, "How to Reach the Small Farmer?: An Islamic Formula", International Foundation for Development Alternatives, Nyon, Switzerland, January–April 1990, pp. 35–44.

Ali, M. Sultan Abu, "*Al-Mushkilāt al-Iqtiṣādiyyah al-'Ālamiyyah al-Mu'āṣirah wa Ḥalluhā al-Islāmī*", paper presented to the International Centre for Studies in Islamic Economics, Jeddah, 1401 A.H.

Ali, Mahfooz, "*Sharakat* and *Modarabat* as Basis of Interest-Free Banking", *Journal of Islamic Banking and Finance,* July–September 1986, pp. 67–79.

Ali, Muazzam, *Islamic Banks and Strategies of Economic Cooperation* (London: New Century Books, 1982).

Ali, Shamsher, "Structure and Functions of *Sadaqah* and *Zakah* in Islam", *The Australian Minaret* (New South Wales), 3 (1988), pp. 27–30.

Alrai, Mohammad Saeed, "The Concept of Tawhid and Social Welfare in Islam", *Hamdard Islamicus* (Karachi), 4/1988, pp. 73–6.

Amin, Galal A., "The Modernization of Poverty", *Social, Economic and Political Studies of the Middle East* (Leiden: E. J. Brill, 1980), vol. 8.

Al-Amin, Hasan Abdullah, "Al-Istithmār al-Lāribawī fī Niṭāq 'Aqd al-Murābaḥah", *Al-Muslim al-Mu'āṣir,* 1403 A.H.

Amirahmadi, Hooshang and Parvin Manoucher (eds.), *Post-Revolutionary Iran* (Boulder: Westview Press, 1988).

Ansari, Javed Akbar, "The Poverty of Islamic Economics", *The Universal Message* (Karachi), 10:9 and 10:10, 1989, pp. 11–18 and 39–48.

———, "Pakistan's Economic Policy: An Islamic Alternative to the Fund and the Bank", *The Universal Message* (Karachi), 2/1990, pp. 19–25.

Ansari, M. Fazlur Rahman, *The Qur'anic Foundations and Structure of Muslim Society* (Karachi: The World Federation of Muslim Missions, 1973).

Anwar, Muhammad, "Islamic Justice in a Monetary System: A Modest Proposal", *American Journal of Islamic Social Sciences,* September 1987, pp. 135–40.

———, "Reorganization of Islamic Banking: A New Proposal", *The American Journal of Islamic Social Sciences,* 2/1987, pp. 295–304.

———, *Modelling an Interest-Free Economy: A Study in Macro-Economics and Development* (Herndon, VA.: International Institute of Islamic Thought, 1987), 119 pp.

Al-Arabi, M. A., *The Islamic Economy and Contemporary Economy: Proceedings of the First Conference of the Academy of Islamic Research* (Cairo: al-Azhar, 1964).

Ariff, Muhammad, *Monetary and Fiscal Economics of Islam* (Jeddah: International Centre for Research in Islamic Economics, 1982).

———, "Toward the *Sharī'ah* Paradigm of Islamic Economics: The Beginning of a Scientfic Revolution", *The American Journal of Islamic Social Sciences,* July 1985, pp. 79–99.

———, "Islamic Banking", *Asian-Pacific Economic Literature* (Canberra, Australia), 2:2, 1988, pp. 48–64.

——— (ed.), *Islamic Banking in Southeast Asia* (Pasir Panjang, Singapore: Institute of Southeast Asian Studies, 1988), pp. 194–213.

——— and M. A. Mannan, *Developing a System of Financial Instruments* (Jeddah: IRTI, 1990).

Arsalan, Amir Shakib, *Our Decline and its Causes,* tr. M. A. Shakoor (Lahore: S. M. Ashraf, 1962).

Asad, Muhammad, *The Principles of State and Government in Islam* (Gibraltar: Dar al-Andalus, 1981).

El-Ashkar, Ahmad A., "On the Islamic Theory of Consumer Behaviour: An Empirical Inquiry in a Non-Muslim Country", *Arab Banker,* July–August 1986.

——, *The Islamic Business Enterprise* (London: Croom Helm, 1987), 288 pp.

'Assāl, Ahmad and 'Abd al-Karīm Fatḥī, *Al-Niẓām al-Iqtiṣādī fī al-Islām: Mabādi'ihī wa Ahdāfihī* (Cairo: Maktabah Wahbah, 3rd ed., 1980).

Association of Muslim Social Scientists of the USA and Canada, *Outlines of Islamic Economics: Proceedings of the First Symposium on the Economics of Islam in North America*, Indiana, 6–7 March 1977 (Plainfield: American Trust Publications, 1977).

——, *Some Aspects of Zakat: Proceedings of the Conference on Economics of Zakat*, Indiana, 13–14 April 1979 (Plainfield: American Trust Publications, 1980).

Atiyeh, George and Ibrahim M. Oweiss (eds.), *Arab Civilization: Challenges and Responses* (New York: State University of New York Press, 1988).

'Awad, Ahmad Safi al-Din, *Uṣūl 'Ilm al-Iqtiṣād al-Islāmī* (Riyadh: Maktabah al-Rushd, n.d.).

Awad, Muhammad Hashim, "Al-Haykal al-Ḍarībī al-Mu'āṣir fī Ḍaw' al-Mabādi' al-Ḍarībiyyah al-Islāmiyyah", in Kahf (1989).

Awan, Akhtar A., *Equality, Efficiency, and Property Ownership in the Islamic System* (New York: Lanham, for University Press of America, 1983).

'Awdah, 'Abd al-Qādir, *Al-Māl wa al-Ḥukm fī al-Islām* (Jeddah: Dar al-Saudiyyah li al-Nashr wa al-Tawzī', 1389 A.H.).

Al-'Awwah, Muhammad Salim, *Fī al-Niẓām al-Siyāsī li al-Dawlah al-Islāmiyyah* (Alexandria: Al-Maktab al-Misri al-Hadith, 1975).

Azad, Ghulam Murtaza and S. M. Zaman, "The Question of *Milk* (Ownership) in *Waqf*", *The Muslim World League Journal* (Makkah), 11–12/1988, pp. 17–20.

Azam, Khan Muhammad, *Economics and Politics of Development: An Islamic Perspective* (Karachi: Royal Book Co., 1988).

Al-'Azbawi, Hasan M., *Al-Mawārid al-Māliyyah al-Islāmiyyah wa al-Ḍarā'ib al-Mu'āṣirah* (Cairo: 1976).

Azid, Toseef, "Unemployment and its Solution in Islam", *Journal of Rural Development and Administration* (Peshawar), 1/1989, pp. 65–77.

Azmin, Zulfikri Haji Ulul, "Ownership of Land in Islam", *The Law Majallah* (The Law Society, International Islamic University, Malaysia), 1987, pp. 65–80.

Badawi, Jamal, "Concept of Development from Islamic Perspective", *Al-Nahḍah* (Kuala Lumpur), 1/1989, pp. 20–4.

Al-Badoor, Radi, "The Profit Maximization Behaviour of Islamic Banks and Conventional Banks: A Comparative Study", *The Kashmir Economic Review* (Muzaffarabad, Azad Kashmir), 2/1986, pp. 21–40.

———, "Economics of Profit Sharing: Conceptual and Theoretical Issues", paper presented at the Workshop on Investment Strategy in Islamic Banking – Applications, Issues and Problems, held in Amman, Jordan, 18–21 June 1987.

Badr, Gamal Moursi, "Interest on Capital in Islamic Law", *American-Arab Affairs* (Washington, D.C.), Summer 1989, pp. 86–95.

Al-Bājī, *Al-Muntaqā Sharḥ al-Muwaṭṭa* (Beirut: Dar al-Kitab al-'Arabi, 1332 A.H.).

Al-Banna, Imam Hasan, *Ḥadīth al-Thulāthā' li'l Imām Ḥasan al-Bannā* (ed.) Ahmad 'Isa 'Ashur (Cairo: Maktabah al-Qur'ān, 1985).

———, *Majmū'ah Rasā'il al-Imām Ḥasan al-Bannā* (Alexandria: Dar al-Da'wah, 1989).

Barnes, J. R., *An Introduction to Religious Foundations in the Ottoman Empire* (Leiden: E. J. Brill, 1986).

Barnett, A. Doak and Ralph N. Clough (eds.), *Modernising China: Post-Mao Reform and Development* (Boulder: Westview Press, 1986).

Barnett, Tony and Abbas Abdelkarim (eds.), *Sudan: State, Capital and Transformation* (London: Croom Helm, 1988), pp. 121–40.

Basar, Hasmet (ed.), *Management and Development of Awqaf Properties,* proceedings of a Seminar held from 4–16 August, 1984 (Jeddah: IRTI, IDB, 1987).

Bashir, B. A., "Portfolio Management of Islamic Banks: Certainty Model", *Journal of Banking and Finance* (Amsterdam), 1983, pp. 39–54.

Baysan, C., "Agricultural Development Index for the Islamic Countries", *Journal of Economic Cooperation Among Islamic Countries,* 3–4/1988, pp. 27–85.

Burns, Paul and Jim Dewhurst, *Small Business in Europe* (London: Macmillan, 1987).

Chapra, M. Umer, *The Economic System of Islam – A Discussion of its Goals and Nature* (London: The Islamic Culture Centre, 1970). The first two chapters of this have been published separately under the title *Objectives of the Islamic Economic Order* and a revised version of the last chapter has been published under the title *The Islamic Welfare State and its Role in the Economy.*

———, *Objectives of the Islamic Economic Order* (Leicester, U.K.: The Islamic Foundation, 1979).

——, *The Islamic Welfare State and its Role in the Economy* (Leicester, U.K.: The Islamic Foundation, 1979).

——, "Mokhtar M. Metwally: Role of the Stock Exchange in an Islamic Economy" (Comments), *Journal of Research in Islamic Economics,* 1 (1985), pp. 75–82.

——, *Towards a Just Monetary System* (Leicester, U.K.: The Islamic Foundation, 1985).

——, "The Mechanics and Operations of an Islamic Financial Market", *Journal of Islamic Banking and Finance* (Karachi), 3/1988, pp. 31–6.

——, "Towards an Islamic Financial System", *Journal of Islamic Economics* (Malaysia), July 1988, pp. 1–30.

——, "Economic Development in Muslim Countries: A Strategy for Development in the Light of Islamic Teachings", paper presented to the Seminar on Islamic Economics, Cairo, 6–9 September 1988 held under the auspices of the International Institute of Islamic Thought, Washington, D.C. and the Al-Azhar University, Cairo.

——, "The Need for a New Economic System", *Review of Islamic Economics,* 1/1991, pp. 9–47.

——, "Some Pre-requisites for the Establishment of an Islamic Banking System", in Karachi Chamber of Commerce and Industry, *Islamic Economic System and the Position of Income Tax in the Shari'ah: Collection of Articles of Eminent Islamic 'Ulama and Scholars* (Karachi: Chamber of Commerce and Industry, n.d.), pp. 9–58.

Chishti, Salim U., "Relative Stability of Interest-Free Economy", *Journal of Research in Islamic Economics,* Summer 1985, pp. 3–12.

Choudhary, M. Khairat, "Poverty and Income Distribution in Bangladesh", *The Kashmir Economic Review,* July–December 1985, pp. 59–72.

Choudhury, Masudul Alam, "Principles of Islamic Economics", *Middle Eastern Studies,* January 1983, pp. 93–104.

——, *Contributions to Islamic Economic Theory* (New York: Macmillan, 1986).

——, "Micro-Economic Foundations of Islamic Economics", *The American Journal of Islamic Social Sciences,* 2/1986, pp. 231–45.

——, "The Blending of Religious and Social Orders in the Islamic Economic Order", *International Journal of Social Economics,* 4/1986, pp. 60–70.

——, *Islamic Economic Cooperation* (London: Macmillan, 1989).

———, "The Concept of Islamic Socio-Economic Development in Contemporary Perspectives", *The Journal of Development Studies,* 1990, pp. 1–10.

Cizakca, Murat, *Origins and Evolution of Islamic Banks: Research Papers* (Istanbul: Bogazici Universitesi, 1986), 26 pp.

Cockburn, Patrick, "Doubts Over Prices: Soviet Prices Chief Calls for Overhaul", *Financial Times,* 14 July 1987, p. 2.

Commission of the European Communities, *Job Creation in Small and Medium Sized Enterprises,* vol. 1: Main Report by David J. Storey, Steven G. Johnson (Luxembourg: Office for Official Publications of the European Communities, 1987).

Cortes, Mariluz, Albert Berry and Ashfaq Ishaq, *Success in Small and Medium-Scale Enterprises* (Published for the World Bank by Oxford University Press, 1987).

Council of Islamic Ideology, *Report of the Council of Islamic Ideology on the Elimination of Interest from the Economy* (Islamabad: Government of Pakistan, 1980); reproduced in Z. Ahmed, *et al., Money and Banking in Islam* (1983), pp. 103–200; see also the comments on this report by M. Umer Chapra and M. N. Siddiqi, pp. 212–32, as well as the discussion on pp. 233–57.

Dar, Muhammad Ilyas, "Islamic Economic System", *Journal of Islamic Banking and Finance* (Karachi), 3/1988, pp. 37–52.

Davies, Merryl Wyn and Adnan Khalil Pasha (eds.), *Beyond Frontiers: Islam and Contemporary Needs* (London: Mansell, 1989).

Deppler, Michael and Martin Williamson, "Capital Flight: Concepts, Measurement, and Issues", in *Staff Studies for the World Economic Outlook* (Washington, D.C.: IMF, August, 1987).

El-Din, Ahmad Kamal, "Ten Years of Islamic Banking", *Journal of Islamic Banking and Finance,* July–September 1986, pp. 49–66.

Doak, Ervin John, "Islamic Interest-Free Banking and 100 Percent Money", *International Monetary Fund Staff Papers,* 3/1988, pp. 534–6.

Donhue, J. and E. John (eds.), *Islam in Transition* (New York: Oxford University Press, 1982).

Dumont, Rene, *False Start in Africa* (New York: Praeger, 1966).

Dunya, Shawqi Ahmad, *Al-Islām wa al-Tanmiyyah al-Iqtiṣādiyyah* (Cairo: Dar al-Fikr al-'Arabi, 1979).

———, *Durūs Fī al-Iqtiṣād al-Islāmī: Al-Naẓariyyah al-Iqtiṣādiyyah min Manẓur al-Islāmī* (Riyadh: Maktabah al-Khirayji, 1984).

Easterlin, Richard, "Does Money Buy Happiness?" *The Public Interest,* Winter 1973.

Elgari, M. A., "Some Islamic Insights on the Theory of Consumer Behaviour", *Journal of Objective Studies* (Aligarh, India), 1/1990, pp. 1–9.

Esposito, John L., *Islam and Development: Religion and Socio-political Change* (Syracuse, N.Y.: Syracuse University Press, 1982).

Al-Fa'sī, 'Allāl, "Al-Islām wa Mutaṭallibāt al-Tanmiyah fi Mujtama' al-Yawm", a paper presented at a Conference, "Multaqā al-Fikr al-Islāmī", held in Wahran, July 1971.

Al-Fanjari, M. Shawqi, *Al-Madhhab al-Iqtiṣādī fī al-Islām* (Jeddah: Ukkaz li al-Nashr, 1401 A.H.).

Faridi, F. R., "On Wages in an Islamic Economy", *Islamic Thought* (Aligarh, India), April 1960, pp. 61–6.

——, "Fiscal Policy in an Islamic State", *Journal of Research in Islamic Economics,* Summer 1983, pp. 17–35.

Faridi, Hazrat Shahidullah, *Inner Aspects of Faith* (Karachi: Mehfile Zauqia, 1979).

Faruqi, Jalees Ahmad and Shahid Habibullah, *Islamisation of Banking in Pakistan* (Karachi: United Bank Limited, 1984).

Faruqi, Jalees Ahmad, "Pre-requisites and Consequences of Islamization of Banking in Pakistan", *Journal of Islamic Banking and Finance,* 3, 3 (July–September 1986), pp. 43–8.

Faruqi, Kamal A., "Islam and Social Justice", *Criterion* (Karachi), July–August 1972, pp. 34–45.

Ferdinand, Klaus and Mehdi Mozaffari (eds.), *Islam: State and Society* (London: Curzon Press, 1988), pp. 89–102.

Foster, Durwood and Paul Mojzes (eds.), *Society and Original Sin: Ecumenical Essays on the Impact of the Fall* (New York: Paragon House, 1985).

Friedman, Alan, "Italian Small Business: The Backbone of the Economy Explored", *Financial Times,* 29 April 1987 and 15 September 1987.

Gauhar, Altaf, *The Challenge of Islam* (London: Islamic Council of Europe, 1978).

Ghatak, Subrata, "Agriculture and Economic Development", in Norman Gemmell (1987), pp. 355–6.

Al-Ghazālī, Abū Ḥāmid Muḥammad, *al-Mustaṣfā* (Cairo: al-Maktabah al-Tijariyyah al-Kubra, 1937).

——, *Iḥyā' 'Ulūm al-Dīn* (Cairo: Maktabah al-Mashhad al-Husayni, n.d.).

——, *Al-Islām wa al-Awḍā' al-Iqtiṣādiyyah* (Cairo: Dar al-Kutub al-Hadithah, n.d.).

Ghazali, Aidit, *Development: An Islamic Perspective* (Selangor, Malaysia: Pelanduk, 1990).

——— and Syed Omar (eds.), *Readings in the Concept and Methodology of Islamic Economics* (Selangor, Malaysia: Pelanduk, 1989).

Ghifari, Nur Muhammad, *Social Security in Islam* (Lahore: Atiq Publication House, 1989).

Gilani, Shaukat J., "The Qur'ān on Charitable Giving and Contemporary Social Values", *Journal of Research in Islamic Economics,* 1985, pp. 63–74.

Government of Pakistan, Federal Bureau of Statistics, *Survey of Social and Economic Impact of Zakāt and 'Ushr on Individuals and Households* (Karachi, 1988).

Government of Pakistan, Ministry of Finance, *The Zakāt Manual* (Islamabad: Central Zakat Administration, 1982).

———, *Economic Survey, 1987–88* (Islamabad, June 1988).

Gusau, Sule Ahmed, "Some Issues in Islamic Banking", *Thoughts on Economics* (Dhaka), 2/1987, pp. 1–24.

Al-Habshi, Syed Othman, "The Role of Ethics in Economics and Business", *Journal of Islamic Economics* (Malaysia), 1/1987, pp. 1–15.

Haffar, Ahmad R., "Economic Development in Islam in Western Scholarship", *Islam and the Modern Age* (Delhi), May and August 1975.

Al-Hamashri, Mustafa, *Al-Niẓām al-Iqtiṣādī fī al-Islām min 'Aḥd al-Rasūl (SAWS) ilā Nihāyat 'Aṣr Banī Umayyah* (Riyadh: Dar al-'Ulum, 1985).

Hamdulay, Jamaluddin Ahmed, *Islam: The Future Economic System* (Athlone, S.A.: Bookworld Publishers, 1986).

Hamidullah, Muhammad, *The Prophet's Establishing an Islamic State and His Succession* (Hyderabad, India: Habib & Co., 1986).

Hamoud, Sami Hassan, *Islamic Banking* (London: Arabian Information, 1985).

Haniff, Ghulam M., "The Human Resources Path to Development: A Challenge to Muslims", *Islamic Studies,* Summer 1990, pp. 131–42.

Hannan, M. A., "Towards an Appropriate Model of Rural Development by the Islamic Bank in Bangladesh", *Thoughts on Economics* (Dhaka), 2/1987, pp. 73–6.

Haque, Nadeemul and Abbas Mirakhor, "Saving Behaviour in an Economy Without Fixed Interest", *Journal of Islamic Banking and Finance* (Karachi), 3/1989, pp. 24–38.

Hasan, A., "Social Justice in Islam", *Islamic Studies* (Islamabad), September 1971, pp. 209–19.

Hasan, Zubair, ''Determination of Profit and Loss Sharing Ratios in Interest-Free Business Finance'', *Journal of Research in Islamic Economics*, 1/1985, pp. 13–30.

———, ''Comments on Macro Consumption Function in Islamic Framework'', *Journal of Research in Islamic Economics*, 3/1986.

Hasanuzzaman, S. M., *The Economic Functions of the Early Islamic State* (Karachi: International Islamic Publishers, 1981).

Al-Hasb, Fadil 'Abbas, *Fī al-Fikr al-Iqtiṣādī al-Islāmī* (Cairo: Dar al-Nahḍah al-'Arabiyyah, 2nd ed., 1981).

Hassan, Abdullah Alwi Haji, ''The Arabian Commercial Background in Pre-Islamic Times'', *Islamic Culture* (Hyderabad), 2/1988, pp. 70–83.

Hassan, Tariq, ''Interest-Free System of Banking and Finance in Pakistan'', *Journal of Islamic Banking and Finance*, January–March 1986, pp. 7–17.

———, ''Legal Process for Establishing Rules for Murabahah Contracts'', *Journal of Islamic Banking and Finance*, October–December 1987, pp. 71–4.

Hassani Al-Hassani, Bakir, *Iqtisad: The Islamic Alternative for Economics* (Lanham, MD.: Imamia Centre, 1988).

Haykal, M. H., *Al-Fārūq 'Umar* (Cairo: Maktabah al-Nahdah al-Misriyyah, 1964), vol. 2, p. 229.

Holland, Muhtar, *Public Duties in Islam: The Institution of the Hisba* (Leicester, U.K.: The Islamic Foundation, 1982).

Holt, P. M. *et al.* (eds.), *The Cambrige History of Islam* (Cambridge: Cambridge University Press, 1970).

Hosseini, Hamid, ''Islamic Economics in Iran: Is a New Economic Paradigm in the Making?'' *Journal of South Asian and Middle Eastern Studies* (Villanova, PA), 12:2, 1988, pp. 21–44.

Huq, M. Azizul (ed.), *Readings in Islamic Banking* (Dhaka: Bangladesh Islamic Bankers' Association, 1982).

———, ''Islamisation of Domestic Banking of Pakistan'', *Thoughts on Economics*, 3, 1986, pp. 27–54.

———, ''Islamic Banking and Rural Development – A Case Study of Sudanese Islamic Bank (SIB)'', *Thoughts on Economics* (Dhaka), 2/1987, pp. 59–72.

———, ''Some Thoughts on Islamic Framework for Rural Development and Appropriate Banking Model'' (in the Context of Bangladesh), *Thoughts on Economics* (Dhaka), 2, 1987, pp. 48–58.

Husain, Irtiza, ''Need for Accounting Standards for Islamic Banks'', *Journal of Islamic Banking and Finance*, January–March 1988, pp. 154–9.

Husain, Muzaffar, *Motivation for Economic Achievement in Islam* (Lahore: All Pakistan Educational Congress, 1974).
Hussain, Ch. Muhammed, *Development Planning in an Islamic State* (Karachi: Royal Book Co., 1987).
Hussain, M. M., *Islam and Socialism: A Critical Study of Socialism, Capitalism and Fascism as Contrasted with the Qur'anic Concept of a New World Order* (Lahore: Ashraf, 1970).
Hussein, Raef T. A., "The Early Arabian Trade and Marketing", *Islam and the Modern Age,* May–August 1987, pp. 163–72.
Hussein, Tan Sri Datuk Jaffar, "Facing the Challenge of Islamic Finance", *Al-Nahḍah Muslim News and Views,* 4/1987, pp. 23–8.
Ibn Ḥazm, Abū Muḥammad 'Alī, *Al-Muḥallā* (Beirut: Al-Maktab al-Tijari, n.d.).
Ibn Hishām, *al-Sīrah al-Nabawiyyah,* Mustafa al-Saqqa, *et al.* eds., (Cairo: Mustafa al-Babi al-Halabi, 1955).
Ibn Khaldūn, 'Abd al-Raḥmān, *Muqaddimah* (Cairo: al-Maktabah al-Tijariyyah al-Kubra, n.d.). Tr. by Franz Rosenthal (London: Routledge and Kegan Paul, 1958).
Ibn Taymiyyah, *Majmū' Fatāwā Shaykh al-Islām Aḥmad Ibn Taymiyyah* (Riyadh: Matabi' al-Riyadh, 1383 = 1963), ed. 'Abd al-Rahman al-'Asimi.
———, *Al-Siyāsah al-Shar'iyyah fī Iṣlāh al-Rā'ī wa al-Ra'iyyah,* ed. Muhammad al-Mubarak (Beirut: Dar al-Kutub al-'Arabiyyah, 1966).
———, *Al-Ḥisbah fī al-Islām,* ed. 'Abd al-Aziz Rabah (Damascus: Maktabah Dar al-Bayan, 1967), tr. under the title *Public Duties in Islam,* by Muhtar Holland (Leicester, U.K.: The Islamic Foundation, 1982).
Ibrahim, Anwar, "Development, Values and Changing Political Ideas", *Sojourn* (Pasir Panjang, Singapore), 1/1986, pp. 1–7.
Ibrahim, Ibrahim Ahmad, *Niẓām al-Nafaqāt fī al-Sharī'ah al-Islāmiyyah* (Cairo: Al-Matba'ah al-Salafiyyah, 1349 A.H.).
Ibrahim, Sohair Ahmed, "Economics of Education as a Case Study for the Islamization of Knowledge", *Islamic Order,* 1, 1988, pp. 21–39.
Idris, Ja'far Sheikh, "Al-Taṣawwur al-Islāmī li'l Insān: Asās li Falsafat al-Islām al-Tarbawiyyah", paper presented at the First Islamic Educational Conference, Makkah, 31 March–8 April 1977.
———, "Is Man the Vicegerent of God", *Journal of Islamic Studies,* 1/1990, pp. 99–110.
Imam, Zakariyyah Bashir, *Ṭarīq al-Taṭawwur al-Ijtimā'ī al-Islāmī* (Jeddah: Dar al-Shuruq, 1397 A.H.).

Imtiazi, I. A., *et al.* (eds.), *Management of Zakāt in Modern Muslim Society* (Jeddah: IRTI, IDB, 1989).

International Centre for Research in Islamic Economics, *Dirāsāt fī al-Iqtiṣād al-Islāmī: Buḥūth Mukhtārah min al-Mu'tamar al-Duwalī al-Thānī li al-Iqtiṣād al-Islāmī* (Jeddah: King Abdulaziz University, 1985).

International Institute for Labour Studies, *Islam and a New International Economic Order: The Social Dimension* (Geneva: IILS, 1980).

Iqbal, Munawar, "Zakāt, Moderation and Aggregate Consumption in an Islamic Economy", *Journal of Research in Islamic Economics,* Summer 1985, pp. 45–62.

———, *Distributive Justice and Need Fulfilment in an Islamic Economy* (Leicester, U.K.: The Islamic Foundation, 1988).

——— and M. Fahim Khan, *A Survey of Issues and a Programme for Research in Monetary and Fiscal Economics of Islam* (Jeddah: International Centre for Research in Islamic Economics, King Abdulaziz University, 1981).

Iqbal, Zubair and Abbas Mirakhor, "Islamic Banking: Major Issues of Transition", *Journal of Islamic Banking and Finance,* October–December 1987, pp. 47–60.

———, *Islamic Banking,* Occasional Paper 49 (Washington, D.C.: International Monetary Fund, 1987).

IRTI, Islamic Development Bank, *Economic Cooperation and Integration Among Islamic Countries: International Framework and Economic Problems* (Jeddah: Islamic Research and Training Institute, 1986).

———, *Khuṭṭah al-Istithmār fī al-Bunūk al-Islāmiyyah: al-Jawānib al-Taṭbīqiyyah wa al-Qaḍāyā wa al-Mushkilāt,* proceedings of a conference held in Amman, 16–21 June 1987 (Jeddah: IRTI, 1990).

Ishaque, Khalid M., "Islamic Principles of Economic Management", *Al-'Ilm,* January 1987, pp. 14–49.

Islahi, A. Azim, "Ibn Taimiyyah's Concept of Market Mechanism", *Journal of Research in Islamic Economics,* Winter 1985, pp. 55–64.

———, *Economic Concepts of Ibn Taymiyyah* (Leicester, U.K.: The Islamic Foundation, 1988).

Islahi, Amin Ahsan, *Islāmī Riyāsat: Kārkunon kī Dhimmah Dāriyān awr un kay Awṣāf* (Lahore: Maktabah Jama'at Islami, 1950).

Islam, Mohammad Zohurul, *Islamic Economics* (Dhaka: Islamic Foundation Bangladesh, 1987).

Islamic Council of Europe, *The Muslim World and the Future Economic Order* (London: Islamic Council of Europe, 1979).

Islamic Development Bank, *Proceedings of the Islamic Development Bank's Symposium on Agricultural Development and Food Security in OIC Member Countries* (Jeddah: Islamic Development Bank, 1989).

Islamic Economics Research Bureau, *Thoughts on Islamic Economics* (Dhaka: Islamic Economics Research Bureau, 1980).

———, *Thoughts on Islamic Banking: Proceedings of a Seminar on Islamic Banking*, Dhaka, 15–17 December 1980 (Dhaka: Islamic Economics Research Bureau, 1982).

Ismail, Syed Muhammad, *Critical Analysis of Capitalism, Socialism and Islamic Economic Order* (Lahore: Oriental Publications, 1989).

Issawi, Charles A. (ed.), *An Economic History of the Middle East, 1800–1914* (Chicago: University of Chicago Press, 1966).

———, *An Economic History of the Middle East and Africa* (New York: Columbia University Press, 1982).

Jafarey, N. A., ''Islamic Financing: Multi-dimensional Efforts a Must for Worthwhile Results'' (In Pakistan Context), *Journal of Islamic Banking and Finance* (Karachi), 1988, pp. 77–80.

Jaffar, Kamarudin, ''Role of Muslim Youth in National Development'', *Al-Nahḍah Muslim News and Views,* 4/1987, pp. 12–15.

Al-Jamal, M. ʻAbd al-Munʻim, *Mawsūʻah al-Iqtiṣād al-Islāmī* (Cairo: Dar al-Kitab al-Misri, 1400 A.H.).

Jāmiʻah, al-Imām Muḥammad bin Saʻūd al-Islāmiyyah, *Atharu Taṭbīq al-Niẓām al-Iqtiṣādī al-Islāmī: min al-Buḥūth al-Muqadammah li Mu'tamar al-Fiqh al-Islāmī fī al-Riyāḍ, 1396 A.H.* (Riyadh: Imam Muhammad University, 1984).

Al-Jarhi, Mabid Ali M., ''Towards an Islamic Macro Model of Distribution: A Comparative Approach'', *Journal of Research in Islamic Economics,* Winter 1985, pp. 1–29. See the comment on this by K. A. Naqvi, pp. 67–71.

———, ''The Relative Efficiency of Interest-Free Monetary Economies: The Fiat Money Case'', in: Mohsin S. Khan and Abbas Mirakhor (eds.), *Theoretical Studies in Islamic Banking and Finance* (Houston, Texas: The Institute for Research and Islamic Studies, 1987), pp. 37–74.

Al-Jawziyyah, Ibn Qayyim, *I'lām al-Muwaqqiʻīn* (Cairo: al-Maktabah al-Tijariyyah al-Kubra, 1955).

Al-Jazīrī, ʻAbd al-Raḥmān, *Kitāb al-Fiqh ʻalā al-Madhāhib al-Arbaʻah* (Cairo: Al-Maktabah al-Tijāriyyah al-Kubra, 1938).

Johansen, Baber, *The Islamic Law on Land Tax and Rent* (London: Croom Helm, 1987).

Kabbara, A., "The Islamic State and Economic Intervention", *Arab Banker*, 6/1986, pp. 26–31.

Kabbara, Haitham, "Islamic Banks and Industrial Financing", *Finance and Industry* (Kuwait), 9/1988, pp. 27–42.

Kader, Steven Abdul, "In Search of Financial Identity: Financing Our Future", *Islamic Horizons* (Illinois), 3–4/1988, pp. 27–35.

Al-Kaff, Syed Hamed Abdul Rahman, *Al-Murabaha in Theory and Practice* (Karachi: Islamic Research Academy, 1986).

Al-Kafrawi, 'Awf Mahmud, *Siyāsah al-Infāq al-'Ām fī al-Islām* (Alexandria: Mu'assasah Shabab al-Jami'ah, 1402 A.H.).

Kahf, Monzer, *The Islamic Economy: Analytical Study of the Functioning of the Islamic System* (Plainfield, Indiana: The Muslim Students' Association of the United States and Canada, 1978).

——— (ed.), *Mawārid al-Dawlah al-Māliyyah fī al-Mujtama' al-Ḥadīth min Wujhāt al-Naẓar al-Islāmiyyah* (Jeddah: IRTI, 1989).

———, "Zakat: Unresolved Issues in the Contemporary Fiqh", *Journal of Islamic Economics* (Kuala Lumpur), 1/1989, pp. 1–22.

Karim, Rifaat Ahmed Abdel and Amal El-Tigani Ali, "Towards an Understanding of the Use of Financing Mechanism of Islamic Banks", *The Arab Journal of the Social Sciences* (London), 3:1, 1988, pp. 55–67.

Karsten, Ingo, "Islam and Financial Intermediation", *IMF Staff Papers*, March 1982, pp. 108–42.

Al-Kaysi, Marwan Ibrahim, *Morals and Manners in Islam: A Guide to Islamic Adab* (Leicester, U.K.: The Islamic Foundation, 1986).

Kazarian, E. and A. Kokko, *Islamic Banking and Development* (Lund: National Ekonomiska Institutionen vid Lunds Universitet, 1987).

Al-Kazaz, Aziz, "The Islamization of Banking and Finance in Pakistan and its Effects on Savings and Investment", *Economics*, vol. 36 (1987), pp. 61–88.

Kazemi, Farhad and R. D. McChesney (eds.), *A Way Prepared: Essays on Islamic Culture in Honour of Richard Bayley Winder* (New York: New York University Press, 1988).

Kazi, A. G. N., "Islamic Banking in Perspective", *Journal of Islamic Banking and Finance* (Karachi), 1984, pp. 7–21.

Kennedy, Paul, *The Rise and Fall of the Great Powers: Economic Change and Military Conflict, 1500–2000* (New York: Random House, 1988).

Khadduri, Majid, *The Islamic Conception of Justice* (Baltimore: Johns Hopkins University, 1984).

Al-Khafīf, 'Alī, *Al-Milkiyyah fī al-Sharī'ah al-Islāmiyyah,* vol. 1, p. 93.

Khan, A. R. and P. D. Weldon, "Income Distribution and Levels of Living in Java, 1963–70", *Economic Development and Cultural Change* (1985), pp. 699–711.

Khan, Abdul Hamid, "Islamization of System in Agricultural Development Bank of Pakistan", *Journal of Islamic Banking and Finance,* January–March 1986, pp. 60–9.

Khan, Abdul Jabbar, "Elimination of Beggary from Pakistan: Some Suggestions", *The Universal Message,* February 1988, pp. 26–7.

Khan, Ghulam Ishaq, "Islamic Economic Reform as a Vehicle of Social Change" (Inaugural Address to a Conference in Pakistan). *Journal of Islamic Banking and Finance* (Karachi), 1/1989, pp. 7–13.

Khan, M. Akram, "A Survey of Contemporary Islamic Thought on the Institution of Interest", *Islamic Education* (Lahore), July/August 1973.

———, *Inflation and Islam* (Lahore: Islamic Book Centre, 1980).

———, *Islamic Economics: Annotated Sources in English and Urdu* (Vols. 1 and 2) (Leicester, U.K.: The Islamic Foundation, 1983; 1991).

———, *Issues in Islamic Economics* (Lahore: Islamic Publications Ltd., 1983).

———, *Challenge of Islamic Economics* (Lahore: All-Pakistan Islamic Education Congress, 1985).

———, "Role of the Auditor in an Islamic Economy", *Journal of Research in Islamic Economics,* Summer 1985, pp. 31–44.

———, "Commodity Exchange and Stock Exchange in an Islamic Economy", *Journal of Islamic Economics* (Malaysia), July 1988, pp. 31–55. See also the comments on this paper by Syed 'Abdul Jabbar Shahabuddin, pp. 71–6.

———, "A Survey of Critical Literature on Interest-Free Banking", *Journal of Islamic Banking and Finance* (Karachi), 1/1989, pp. 45–61.

———, *Economic Teachings of Prophet Muhammad: A Select Anthology of Hadith Literature on Economics* (Islamabad: International Institute of Islamic Economics, 1989)

———, "Elimination of Poverty in the Islamic Economic Framework", *Islamic Studies,* Summer 1990, pp. 143–62.

———, *Glossary of Islamic Economics* (London: Mansell, 1990).

Khan, M. Fahim, "Macro Consumption Function in an Islamic Framework", *Journal of Research in Islamic Economics,* Winter 1984, pp. 1–24. See also the comments on this paper by Seif E. I. Tagel-Din S. Iqbal Mahdi and Zubair Hasan in the Summer 1984 and Winter 1985 issues of this journal, pp. 57–61, 73–7 and 79–81 respectively.

——— (ed.), *Distribution in Macroeconomic Framework: An Islamic Perspective* (Islamabad: International Institute of Islamic Economics, International Islamic University, 1989), pp. 111–44.

Khan, Mehr Muhammad Nawaz, *Islam and Other Economic Systems* (Lahore: Islamic Book Service, 1988).

Khan, Mohsin S., "Islamic Interest-Free Banking", *Journal of Islamic Banking and Finance,* October–December 1986, pp. 31–53.

——— and Abbas Mirakhor (eds.), *Theoretical Studies in Islamic Banking and Finance* (Houston, Texas: The Institute for Research and Islamic Studies, 1987).

———, "Islamic Banking: Experiences in the Islamic Republic of Iran and Pakistan", *Economic Development and Cultural Change* (Chicago, Ill.), 2/1990, pp. 353–76.

Khan, Shahrukh Rafi, "Political Economy of an Islamic System", *Hamdard Islamicus,* 4/Winter 1985, pp. 3–34.

———, *Profit and Loss Sharing: An Islamic Experiment in Finance and Banking* (Karachi: Oxford University Press, 1987).

———, "Profit and Loss Sharing as a Substitute for Interest in Islamic Banking", *Saving and Development,* 3/1987, pp. 317–27.

———, "The Pakistani Experiment with Islamic (Profit and Loss Sharing) Banking", *The Banking Development Studies* (Dhaka), 15:4, 1987, pp. 131–48.

———, "Henry George and an Alternative Islamic Land Tenure System", *Economic Development and Cultural Change,* 4/1988, pp. 721–30.

Khan, Tariqullah, *Islamic Economics: A Bibliography* (Jeddah: IRTI, IDB, 1984).

Khan, Waqar Masood, *Towards an Interest-Free Islamic Economic System* (Leicester, U.K.: The Islamic Foundation, 1985).

Khawaja, Jamal, "The Concept of Islamic Economic System", *Khuda Bakhsh Library Journal* (Patna, India), No. 46, 1988, pp. 1–38.

Khouri, Rami G., "Islamic Banking: Knotting a New Network", *Aramco World Magazine,* May–June 1987, pp. 14–27.

Kindleberger, C. P., *International Short-term Capital Movements* (New York: Augustus Kelley, 1937).

———, "Review of the Economy of Turkey: The Economic Development of Guatemala; Report on Cuba", *Review of Economics and Statistics,* November, 1952, pp. 391–2.

Kister, M. J., "The Market of the Prophet", *Journal of the Economic and Social History of the Orient* (Leiden), January 1965, pp. 272–6.

Klein, Lawrence R., *The Keynesian Revolution* (New York: Macmillan, 1954).

Kuran, Timur, "The Economic System in Contemporary Islamic Thought: Interpretation and Assessment", *International Journal of Middle Eastern Studies,* 2/1986, p. 135.

Al-Lababidi, *Islamic Economics: A Comparative Study* (Lahore: Islamic Publications, 1980).

Lahsaeizadeh, Abdolali, "Land Reform and Social Change in Rural Iran", *Land Reform* (Land Settlement and Co-operatives), 1–2 (1987), pp. 22–57.

Laliwala, J. H., *An Outline of Islamic Economic and Financial System* (New Delhi: The Indian Institute of Islamic Studies, 1989).

Lecker, M., "On the Markets of Medina (Yathrib) in Pre-Islamic and Early Islamic Times", *Jerusalem Studies in Arabic and Islam,* No. 8, Part 1 (1986), pp. 133–47.

Lewis, H. D., "Guilt", *The Encyclopaedia of Philosophy* (New York: Macmillan and the Free Press, 1967), vol. 3, p. 397.

Liedholm, Carl and Donald Mead, "Small-Scale Enterprise: A Profile", reproduced from their "Small Scale Industries in Developing Countries: Empirical Evidence and Policy Implications", a Michigan State University Development Paper, in *Economic Impact,* 2/1988, p. 12.

Little, Ian M. D., Tibor Scitovsky and Maurice Scott, *Industry and Trade in Some Developing Countries* (London: Oxford University Press, 1970).

Llewellyn, Othman A., "Islamic Jurisprudence and Environmental Planning", *Journal of Research in Islamic Economics,* Winter 1984, pp. 25–49. See also the comments on this paper by A. Safi El-Din Awad and the author's rejoinder in the Summer 1985 issue of this Journal, pp. 83–90.

Mahdi, Syed Iqbal, "Islamic Approach to Model Building in Economics and Other Social Sciences: A Methodological Framework", *Journal of Objective Studies* (Aligarh, India), 1/1990, pp. 83–94.

Majd, Mohammad G., "Land Reform in Iran", *American Journal of Agricultural Economics,* November 1987, pp. 843–8.

Al-Majma' al-Malikī li Buḥūth al-Ḥaḍārah al-Islāmiyyah, *Al-Idārah al-Māliyyah fī al-Islām* (Amman: Mu'assassat Al-Bayt, 1990).

Mālik, Abū 'Abdullah ibn Anas, *Al-Muwaṭṭa'* (Cairo: 'Isa al-Babi al-Halabi, 1951).

Malik, M. Shafi, ''Wages in an Islamic Economy'', *Islamic Thought* (Aligarh), July 1960, pp. 62–7.

Mallat, Chibli (ed.), *Islamic Law and Finance* (London: Centre of Near and Middle Eastern Studies, School of Oriental and African Studies, 1988).

Manisali, Erol (ed.), *The Middle East and Eastern Mediterranean: Recent Economic and Political Developments* (Istanbul: Istanbul University, Middle East Business and Banking, 1987).

Mannan, M. A., *The Making of Islamic Economic Society: Islamic Dimensions in Economic Analysis* (Cairo: International Association of Islamic Banks, 1984).

———, *Islamic Economics: Theory and Practice* (Cambridge, U.K.: Hodder & Stoughton, Islamic Academy, revised ed., 1986).

———, *Economic Development and Social Peace in Islam* (London: Ta-Ha Publishers, 1989).

Manzoor, S. Parvez, ''Islamic State: Between the Mystique of *Khilafa* and the Logic of *Mulk*'' (Review Article), *Muslim World Book Review* (Leicester), 1/1988, pp. 1–13.

Al-Marghīnānī, Abū al-Ḥasan, *Al-Hidāyah* (Cairo: 'Isa al-Babi al-Halabi, 1965), vol. 4, p. 105.

Martan, Sa'īd Sa'd, *Madkhal li al-Fikr al-Iqtiṣādī fī al-Islām* (Beirut: Mu'assasah al-Risalah, 1986).

Al-Māwardī, Abū al-Ḥasan 'Alī ibn Muḥammad, *Al-Aḥkām al-Sulṭāniyyah* (Cairo: 'Isa al-Babi al-Halabi, 1969).

Mawdudi, Sayyid Abul A'la, *Islām awr Jadīd Ma'āshī Naẓariyyāt* (Lahore: Islamic Publications, 1959).

———, ''Economic and Political Teachings of the Qur'ān'', in M. M. Sharif (ed.), *A History of Muslim Philosophy* (Wiesbaden: Otto Harassowitz, 1963), pp. 178–90.

———, *Khilāfat-o-Mulūkiyyat* (Lahhore: Islamic Publications, 1966).

———, *Islamic Law and Constitution* (Lahore: Islamic Publications, 3rd ed., 1967).

———, *Mas'alah Milkiyyat-e-Zamīn* (Lahore: Islamic Publications, 3rd ed., 1969).

———, *Economic Problem of Man and its Islamic Solution* (Lahore: Islamic Publications, 2nd ed., 1970).

———, *Human Rights in Islam* (Leicester, U.K.: The Islamic Foundation, 1976).

———, *Islāmī Riyāsat* (Lahore, Pakistan: Islamic Publications, 1982).

———, *The Islamic Movement: The Dynamics of Values, Power and Change,* tr. and ed. Khurram Murad (Leicester, U.K.: The Islamic Foundation, 1984).

———, *The Islamic Way of Life*, Khurshid Ahmad and Khurram Murad (eds.). (Leicester, U.K.: The Islamic Foundation, 1986).

Al-Maydani, Shaykh Abdul Rahman Hasan, "Mafāhīm Qur'āniyyah Ḥawla al-Nafs al-Insāniyyah wa mā Tashtamilu 'alyahi", paper presented to the First Islamic Educational Conference, Makkah, 31 March–8 April 1977.

———, *Baṣā'ir li'l-Muslim al-Mu'āṣir* (Damascus: Dar al-Qalam, 1988).

Mdaghri, Driss Alaoui, "Towards an Islamic Common Market", *Journal of Islamic Banking and Finance*, January–March 1988, pp. 73–8.

Meenai, S. A., *The Islamic Development Bank: A Case Study of Islamic Cooperation* (London: Kegan Paul, 1989).

Memon, Noor Ahmed, "Leasing – A Flexible Mode of Financing", *Journal of Islamic Banking and Finance* (Karachi), 1/1989, pp. 18–21.

Mende, Tibor, *South-East Asia between Two Worlds* (London: Turnstile Press, 1955).

Metawally, M. M., *Macro-Economic Models of Islamic Doctrines* (London: J. K. Publishers, 1981).

———, "The Role of the Stock Exchange in an Islamic Economy", *Journal of Research in Islamic Economics*, Summer 1984, pp. 21–30. See also the comments on this paper by M. U. Chapra in the Summer 1985 issue of this same Journal (pp. 25–81).

Mika'ilu, A. S., "On the Prohibition of Riba (Interest) and its Implications for Optimum Economic Performance", *Hamdard Islamicus* (Karachi), 12:1, 1989, pp. 57–64.

Mintjes, H., *Social Justice in Islam* (Amsterdam: Institute for the Study of Religion, Free University, 1977).

Mirakhor, Abbas, "Islamization of the Disciplines: Muslim Scholars and the History of Economics", *The American Journal of Islamic Social Sciences*, 2/1987, pp. 245–76.

———, "The Economic System in an Islamic Society", *Middle East Insight*, August–September 1987, pp. 32–45.

Al-Misri, 'Abd al-Samī', *Muqawwimāt al-Iqtiṣād al-Islāmī* (Cairo: Maktabah Wahbah, 1975).

Al-Misri, Rafiq Yunus, *Uṣūl al-Iqtiṣād al-Islāmī* (Damascus: Dar al-Qalam, 1989).

Molla, Rafiqul Islam, *et al.* (eds.), *Frontiers and Mechanics of Islamic Economics* (Sokoto, Nigeria: University of Sokoto, 1986).

Moreland, W. H., *The Agrarian System of Moslem India* (Delhi: Kanti Publications, 1988).

Morgenbesser, Sidney and James Walsh (eds.), *Free Will* (Englewood Cliffs, N.J., 1962).

Moustafa, Saad Moustafa, "Man and Work in Islam", *Al-Azhar Magazine* (Cairo), 6/1988, pp. 679–82.

Mubarak Al-Mubarak, Muhammad, *Niẓām al-Islām: al-Iqtiṣād, Mabādi' wa Qawā'id al-'Āmmah* (Damascus: Dar al-Fikr, 1972).

Mudawi, M. Baqir, "Medium and Long-Term Finance by Islamic Financial Institutions", *Journal of Islamic Banking and Finance,* April–June 1986, pp. 16–35.

Muhammad, Yar, *Cooperation Among the Muslim Countries of the World* (Peshawar, Pakistan: Institute of Development Studies, 1987).

Muhammad, Yusuf Kamal, *Fiqh al-Iqtiṣād al-Islāmī* (Kuwait: Dar al-Qalam, 1988).

Murad, Khurram, *Sacrifice: The Making of a Muslim* (Leicester, U.K.: The Islamic Foundation, 1985).

Muradpuri, Muhammad Akbar, *Conflict between Socialism and Islam* (Lahore: Muhammad Ashraf, 1970).

Musgrave, Richard A., *The Theory of Public Finance: Study in Public Economy* (New York: McGraw Hill, 1959).

Muslehuddin, Muhammad, *Economics and Islam* (Lahore: Islamic Publications, 1974).

Al-Nabhan, M. Faruq, *Abḥāth fī al-Iqtiṣād al-Islāmī* (Beirut: Mu'assasah al-Risalah, 1986).

Nabi, Malik bin, *Al-Muslim fī 'Ālam al-Iqtiṣād* (Cairo: Dar al-Shuruq, 1978).

Al-Nadwi, Abul Hasan Ali, *Mā dhā Khasira al-'Ālam bi Inḥiṭāṭ al-Muslimīn* (Doha: Matabi' Ali bin Ali, 10th ed., 1974).

Nadwi, Ali Ahmad, *Al-Qawā'id al-Fiqhiyyah* (Damascus: Dar al-Qalam, 1986).

El-Naggar, Said (ed.), *Adjustment Policies and Development Strategies in the Arab World* (Washington, D.C.: IMF, 1987).

Al-Najjar, Ahmad, *Al-Madkhal ilā al-Naẓariyyah al-Iqtiṣādiyyah fī al-Islām* (Beirut: Dar al-Fikr, 1973).

Al-Najjār, Zaghlul Raghib, *Qaḍiyyah al-Takhalluf al-'Ilmī wa al-Taqnī fī al-'Ālam al-Islāmī* (Qatar: Ri'asah al-Mahakim al-Shar'iyyah wa al-Shu'un al-Diniyyah, 1409 A.H.).

Najmabadi, Afsaneh, *Land Reform and Social Change in Iran* (Salt Lake City: Utah University Press, 1988).

Naqvi, S. N. H., "Economics of Human Rights: An Islamic Perspective", *Hamdard Islamicus* (Karachi), Summer 1981, pp. 31–51.

———, *Ethics and Economics: An Islamic Synthesis* (Leicester, U.K.: The Islamic Foundation, 1981).

———, ''The Margins of State Intervention in an Islamic Economy'', *Hamdard Islamicus,* Autumn 1983, pp. 47–61.

Naseef, Abdullah Omar (ed.), *Today's Problems, Tomorrow's Solutions* (London: Mansell, 1988).

Nasr, S. H., *Ideals and Realities of Islam* (London: Allen & Unwin, 1966).

———, *Islam and the Plight of Modern Man* (London: Longman, 1975).

Nasr, Seyyed Vali Reza, ''Islamic Economics: Novel Perspectives'', *Middle Eastern Studies* (London), 4/1989, pp. 516–30.

———, ''Towards a Philosophy of Islamic Economics'', *Hamdard Islamicus* (Karachi), 4/1989, pp. 45–60.

Nasser, El-Gharib, ''The Role of Islamic Banks for Initiating an Islamic Common Market'', *Journal of Islamic Banking and Finance,* January–March 1988, pp. 119–38.

Nassief, Nabil, ''Islamic Banking Around the World'', *Journal of Islamic Banking and Finance* (Karachi), 1/1990, pp. 55–64.

National Bank of Pakistan, *Economic System of Islam: Proceedings of a Seminar* (Karachi: National Bank of Pakistan, 1980).

Nienhaus, Volker, *Literature on Islamic Economics in English and German* (Koln: Al-Kitab Verlag, 1982).

———, ''Islamic Economics, Finance and Banking: Theory and Practice'', *Journal of Islamic Banking and Finance,* April–June 1986, pp. 36–54.

———, ''Islamic Banking: Microeconomic Instruments and Macroeconomic Implications'', *Thoughts on Economics* (Dhaka), 1–2/1988, pp. 66–86.

Nisse, Jason, ''No Interest?'' *The Banker* (a *Financial Times* Publication), October 1987, pp. 35–44.

Al-Nowaihi, Muhammad, ''Fundamentals of Economic Justice in Islam'', in *Contemporary Aspects of Economic and Social Thinking in Islam* (Gary, Indiana: MSA, 1973).

Nurbakhsh, Muhsin, ''The Introduction of Usury-Free Banking in Iran'', *Al-Tawhid,* 4/1987, pp. 89–96.

Ogwumike, F. O. and P. K. Odubogun, ''Alleviation of Poverty Through the Provision of Basic Needs in Nigeria'', *The Indian Journal of Economics* (Allahabad), 1989, pp. 257–69.

Okyar, Osman, ''Economic Growth in the Ottoman Empire, 1800–1914'', *Asian and African Studies,* March 1987, pp. 87–118.

Oran, Ahmad, ''Fiscal Policy in an Islamic State'', *Journal of Islamic Banking and Finance* (Karachi), 4/1988, pp. 7–55.

Osman, Muhammad Fathi, *Some Fundamentals of Islamic Political Thought* (Beirut: Muassasah al-Risalat, 1979).

Osmani, S. R. and A. Rahman, *Income Distribution in Bangladesh* (New York: United Nations, 1983).
Ozal, Turgut, "Islam and the West", *Journal of Islamic Banking and Finance,* 3, 3 (July–September 1986), pp. 7–16.
Pal, Izzud-Din, "Pakistan, Islam and Economics", *Journal of Contemporary Asia,* 2/1987, pp. 187–207.
Parker, Mushtak, "Why Islamic Banking is Catching on", *The Middle East* (London), October 1986, pp. 50–5.
Patel, Zainal Abedin, *Small Kindnesses: Islamic Viewpoint on the Cause and Solution of Global Poverty* (Nuneaton, U.K.: Muslim Venture Publications, 1990).
People Against Interest Debt (PAID), *Usury: The Root Cause of the Injustices – Seminar Transcripts* (Norwich: PAID, 1989).
Poliak, A. N., "Classification of Land in Islamic Law and its Technical Terms", *American Journal of Semitic Languages and Literatures,* 1957, pp. 50–62.
Presley, John R. (ed.), *Directory of Islamic Financial Institutions* (London: Croom Helm, 1988).
Pryor, Frederic L., "The Islamic Economic System", *Journal of Comparative Economics,* 1985, pp. 197–223.
Al-Qadi, Wadad, "The Term *Khalifa* in Early Exegetical Literature", *Die Welt Des Islams* (Leiden), vol. 28, 1988, pp. 392–411.
Al-Qaradawi, Yusuf, *Fiqh al-Zakāt* (Beirut: Dar al-Irshad, 1969).
———, *Al-Ḥalāl wa al-Ḥarām fī al-Islām* (Cairo: Dar al-Itisam, 8th ed., 1974).
———, *Mushkilah al-Faqr wa Kayfa 'Ālajahā al-Islām* (Cairo: Maktabah Wahbah, 3rd ed., 1977).
———, *"Tawsī' Qā'idah Ījāb al-Zakāt", Al-Iqtiṣād al-Islāmī,* February 1982, p. 8.
Qasim, Qasim M., "Islamic Banking: New Opportunities for Co-operation Between Western and Islamic Financial Institutions", *Journal of Islamic Banking and Finance,* April–June 1986, pp. 55–61.
Qila'ji, M. Rawwas, *Al-Iḥtirāf wa Āthāruhū fī al-Fiqh al-Islāmī* (Jeddah: International Centre for Research in Islamic Economics, 1984).
Quan, N. T. and A. Y. C. Koo, "Concentration of Land Holdings: An explanation of Kuznet's Conjecture", *Journal of Development Economics,* 18 (1985), pp. 101–17.
Quraishi, Marghoob A., "Investment and Economic Development in Muslim Countries", *Proceedings of the Third Seminar* (Gary, Indiana: Association of Muslim Social Scientists, 1974), pp. 1–8.

Qureshi, D. M. "The Role of Stock Exchange in Islamic System", *Journal of Islamic Banking and Finance* (Karachi), 3/1988, pp. 9–20.

——, "Lease Financing" (Islamic Banking), *Journal of Islamic Banking and Finance* (Karachi), 1/1989, pp. 14–17.

Qurṭubī, Yūsuf Ibn 'Abd al-Barr, *Jāmi' Bayān al-'Ilm wa Faḍlihī* (Madinah: Al-Maktabah al-'Ilmiyyah, n.d.).

Qutb, Muhammad, *Al-Insān Bayn al-Māddiyyah wa al-Islām* (Cairo: 'Isa al-Babi al-Halabi, 4th ed., 1965).

Qutb, Sayyid, *Al-'Adālah al-Ijtimā'iyyah fī al-Islām* (Cairo: 'Isa al-Babi al-Halabi, 1964), tr. John B. Hardie, *Social Justice in Islam* (Washington, D.C.: American Council of Learned Societies, 1970).

Rahman, Afzalur, *Economic Doctrines of Islam* (Lahore: Islamic Publications, 1975).

Rahman, M. Anisur, "The Welfare Economics of Foreign Aid", *Pakistan Development Review,* Summer 1967, pp. 141–59.

——, "Foreign Capital and Domestic Savings: A Test of Haavelmo's Hypothesis with Cross Country Data", *Review of Economics and Statistics,* February 1968, pp. 137–8.

Rajab, Ibrahim A., "Islam and Development", *World Development,* vol. 8, pp. 513–21.

Ramirez-Rojas, C. L., "Monetary Substitution in Developing Countries", *Finance and Development,* June 1986, pp. 35–8.

Rana, Irfan Mahmud, *Economic System Under Omar the Great* (Lahore: Muhammad Ashraf, 1970), 152 pp.

Al-Ras, As'ad Muhammad, *Muqawwimāt al-Niẓām al-Iqtiṣādī al-Islāmī* (Riyadh: King Saud University, 1987).

Rashid, Salim, "Project Evaluation in an Islamic Framework", *Journal of Islamic Banking and Finance,* October–December 1987, pp. 61–9.

——, "Islamic Economics: A Historico-Inductive Approach", *Journal of Islamic Banking and Finance* (Karachi), 1/1989, pp. 33–44.

Rauf, M. A., *The Islamic Economic Doctrine and Contemporary Thought* (Washington, D.C.: American Enterprise Institute for Public Policy Research).

Rehman, Faizan-ur, "The Time Value of Money Concept and its Application to Long-Term Investment and Working Capital Management Policy Decisions: Some Conceptual Problems in an Islamic Perspective", *Journal of Rural Development and Administration,* 2/1988, pp. 9–34.

Rodinson, Maxime, *Islam and Capitalism,* tr. Brian Pearce (Austin, Texas: University of Texas Press, 1978 – original 1966).

Rushdi, Ali Ahmed, "Effects of the Elimination of Riba on Income Distribution", in Munawar Iqbal (1986), pp. 219–28.

———, "Central Banking Policy: An Islamic Perspective", *Thoughts on Economics* (Dhaka), 2/1987, pp. 77–88.

———, "Monopoly in Islam: A Case for Cross Subsidization", *Thoughts on Economics,* Winter 1987, pp. 38–62.

Al-Sibā'ī, Muṣṭafā, *Ishtirākiyyah al-Islām* (Damascus: Mu'assassah al-Matbu'at al-'Arabiyyah, 2nd ed., 1960).

Sadeq, A. H. M., "Distribution of Wealth Through Transfer Payments", *Hamdard Islamicus* (Karachi), 1/1989, pp. 33–44.

———, "Factor Pricing and Income Distribution From an Islamic Perspective", *Journal of Islamic Economics* (Kuala Lumpur), 1/1989, pp. 45–64.

———, *Economic Development in Islam* (Selangor, Malaysia: Pelanduk, 1990).

Al-Sadr, Muhammad Baqir, *Al-Bank al-Lāribawī fī al-Islām* (Beirut: Dar al-Ta'aruf li al-Matbu'at, 7th ed., 1981).

———, *Iqtiṣādunā* (Beirut: Dar al-Ta'aruf li al-Matbu'at, 14th ed., 1981).

———, *Al-Insān al-Mu'āṣir wa al-Mushkilah al-Ijtimā'iyyah* (Najaf: Matba'ah al-Nu'man, 1388 A.H.).

Said, Hakim Muhammad, *The Employer and the Employee: Islamic Concept* (Karachi: Hamdard Academy, 1972).

Salahuddin, Muhammad, "Political Obligation: Its Scope and Limits in Islamic Political Doctrine", *The American Journal of Islamic Social Sciences,* December 1986, pp. 247–64.

Salamah, 'Abdin, "Tawfīr al-Ḥājāt al-Asāsiyyah fi Ẓill al-Dawlah al-Islāmiyyah", *Majallah al-Abḥāth al-Iqtiṣād al-Islāmī,* Winter 1984.

Saleem, Hafiz M., "Comparative Study of Human Nature", *Hamdard Islamicus,* Spring 1989, pp. 75–81.

Saleh, Nabil A., *Unlawful Gain and Legitimate Profit in Islamic Law: Riba, Gharar and Islamic Banking* (Cambridge: Columbia University Press, 1986).

Saqr, Muhammad Ahmad (ed.), *Al-Iqtiṣād al-Islāmī: Buḥūth Mukhtārah min al-Mu'tamar al-'Ālamī al-Awwal li al-Iqtiṣād al-Islāmī* (Jeddah: International Centre for Research in Islamic Economics, 1980).

———, *Qirā'āt fī al-Iqtiṣād al-Islāmī* (Jeddah: King Abdulaziz University, 1987).

Al-Sarakhsī, Shamsuddīn, *Kitāb al-Mabsūṭ* (Beirut: Dar al-Ma'rifah, n.d.), particularly "Kitāb al-Kasb" of al-Shaybānī in vol. 30.

Sardar, Z., *Islamic Futures: The Shape of Ideas to Come* (London: Mansell, 1985).

Sato, H., *Understanding Zakat: An Inquiry into the Methodological Problems of the Science of Economics* (Niigata: Institute of Middle Eastern Studies, 1987).

Sattar, Zaidi, "The Ethics of Profits in the Islamic System", *The Islamic Quarterly* (London), 2/1988, pp. 69–76.

Al-Saud, Mohamed al-Faisal, "Islam and the West: Towards a New International Economic Order", *Journal of Islamic Banking and Finance,* April–June 1986, pp. 8–15.

Saunders, John J., *The Muslim World on the Eve of Europe's Expansion* (Englewood Cliffs, N.J.: Prentice Hall, 1966).

Schirazi, A., *The Problem of Land Reform in the Islamic Republic of Iran: Complications and Consequences of an Islamic Policy* (Berlin: Freie Universitat Berlin, 1987).

Schotta, Charles, "Islamic Banking in the U.S.: Regulatory Issues", *Banking and Trade,* No. 1 (Spring 1987), pp. 39–42.

Schumacher, E. F., *Small is Beautiful* (London: Blond & Briggs, 1973).

Schuon, Frithjof, *Understanding Islam,* tr. D. M. Matheson (London: Allen & Unwin, 1973).

Shafi, Muhammad, *Distribution of Wealth in Islam* (Karachi: Muhammad Ashraf, 1979).

Shah, Nasim Hasan, "Islamic Concept of State", *Hamdard Islamicus,* Autumn 1987, pp. 35–56.

Shahab, Rafiullah, *Islamic State in Modern Age* (Lahore: Accurate Printers, 1988).

Shaikh, Muzaffar A., "Ethics of Decision Making in Islamic and Western Environments", *The American Journal of Islamic Social Sciences* (Chicago), 1/1988, pp. 115–28.

Shakir, A. M. A., *Individuals and Social Responsibility in Islamic Thought* (New York: New York University, 1966).

Shalaby, Ismail, "The Islamic Common Market", *Journal of Islamic Banking and Finance,* January–March 1988, pp. 83–112.

Shaltut, Shaykh Mahmud, *"Al-Ishtirākiyyah wa al-Islām", Al-Jamhūriyyah* (Cairo), 22 December 1961.

Sharif, M. Raihan, *The Concept of Economic Development in Islam* (Dhaka: Islamic Economics Research Bureau, 1986).

Al-Shāṭibī, Abū Isḥāq, *al-Muwāfiqāt fī usūl al-Sharī'ah* (Cairo: al-Maktabah al-Tijariyyah al-Kubra, n.d.).

Shehata, Shawki Ismail, "Islamic Concepts and Principles as Practiced in Islamic Banks: An Analytic Study", *Journal of Objective Studies* (Aligarh, India), 1/1990, pp. 10–31.

Sheikh, Nasir A., *Some Aspects of the Constitution and the Economics of Islam* (Woking: The Woking Mission, 1967).
Siddiqi, M. A. M., "*Ribā* – Usury and Interest, Qur'ān's Verdict is Clear", *Islamic Order* (Karachi), 1980, pp. 40–70.
Siddiqi, M. Nejatullah, *Some Aspects of the Islamic Economy* (Lahore: Islamic Publications, 1970).
——, *The Economic Enterprise in Islam* (Lahore: Islamic Publications, 1972).
——, *Contemporary Literature on Islamic Economics* (Jeddah: International Centre for Research in Islamic Economics, 1981).
——, *Banking Without Interest* (Leicester, U.K.: The Islamic Foundation, 1983).
——, *Issues in Islamic Banking* (Leicester, U.K.: The Islamic Foundation, 1983).
——, *Muslim Economic Thinking: A Survey of Contemporary Literature* (Leicester, U.K.: The Islamic Foundation, 1983).
——, "Public Expenditure in an Islamic State", *Journal of Islamic Banking and Finance,* October and December 1984, pp. 7–34.
——, "An Islamic Approach to Economics", *Al-Tawhid,* December 1986–February 1987, pp. 105–25.
Siddiqi, M. Yasin Mazhar, "Economic Imbalances and the Role of Islam: An Essay in Qur'anic Interpretation", *Hamdard Islamicus,* Summer 1987, pp. 35–46.
——, "Role of Booty in the Economy during the Prophet's Time", *Journal of Islamic Economics,* King Abdulaziz University, vol. 1, 1989, pp. 83–116.
Siddiqi, Muhammad Iqbal, *Model of an Islamic Bank* (New Delhi: Anis Enterprises, 1988).
Siddiqi, S. A., *Public Finance in Islam* (Lahore: Shaikh Muhammad Ashraf, 1975).
Siddiqui, Dilnawaz A., "Human Resource Development: A Muslim World Perspective", *The American Journal of Islamic Social Sciences,* December 1987, pp. 277–94.
Simonsen, J. B., *Studies in the Genesis and Early Development of the Caliphal Taxation System* (Copenhagen: Akademisk Forlag, 1988).
Singer, H. W., "Economic Progress in Developed Countries", *Social Research,* March 1949.
Solomon, Steven, *Small Business USA* (New York: Crown Publishers, 1986).
Spiessbach, Michael F., "Principles of Islamic Investment: A Primer for Western Businessmen", *American-Arab Affairs* (Washington, D.C.), No. 27, 1988–89, pp. 40–50.

Stockhausen, Joachim von, "Islamisation of Banking: What Does it Mean for Agricultural Financing? – The Case of Pakistan", *Law and Politics in Africa, Asia and Latin America,* 1st quarter 1987, pp. 56–69.

Storey, David J. and Steven G. Johnson, *Job Creation in Small and Medium Sized Enterprises* (Luxembourg: Commission of the European Communities, 1987).

——— *et al., The Performance of Small Firms* (London: Croom Helm, 1987).

Al-Suhaybānī, Muhammad Ibrahim, *Athar al-Zakāt 'Alā Tashghīl al-Mawārid al-Iqtiṣādiyyah* (Riyadh, 1990).

Sutcliffe, C. R., "Is Islam an Obstacle to Development?" *The Journal of Development Areas* (University of Illinois), October 1975, pp. 77–81.

Tag El-Din, Seif I., "Moral Hazard and Financial Islamisation Policy", *Review of Islamic Economics,* 1/1991, pp. 49–69.

Taleghani, Ayatullah S. M., *Society and Economics in Islam,* tr. R. Campbell (Berkeley: Mizan Press, 1982).

Al-Tamimi, Younes "Experience of Islamic Banks in the Middle East", *Journal of Islamic Banking and Finance,* April–June 1986, pp. 63–79.

Al-Ṭanṭāwī, 'Alī and Nājī al-Ṭanṭāwī, *Akhbāru 'Umar* (Damascus: Dar al-Fikr, 1959).

Taylor, T. W. and J. W. Evans, "Islamic Banking and the Prohibition of Usury in Western Economic Thought", *National Westminster Bank Quarterly Review,* (November 1987), pp. 15–27.

Tekir, Sabir, "Modelling Interest-Free Economy: A Study in Macro-Economics and Development", *The American Journal of Islamic Social Sciences* (Herndon, VA.), 2/1989, pp. 373–5.

Tendler, Judith, *Inside Foreign Aid* (Baltimore: Johns Hopkins University, 1975).

The Muslim Students' Association of the USA and Canada, *Contemporary Aspects of Economic Thinking in Islam* (Bloomington, Indiana: MSA, 1976).

The Royal Academy for Islamic Civilization Research, *Problems of Research in Islamic Economics* (Amman: Al-Albait Foundation, 1987).

The World Bank: A Critical Analysis (New York: Monthly Review Press, 1982).

Tillich, Paul, *A Complete History of Christian Thought,* Carl Braaten (ed.) (New York: Harper & Row, 1968).

Tomkins, Cyril and Rifat Ahmed Abdel Karim, "The Sharī'ah and its Implications for Islamic Financial Analysis: An Opportunity to

Study Interactions among Society, Organizations and Accounting'', *American Journal of Islamic Social Sciences,* 1 September 1987, pp. 101–16.

Turabi, Hasan, ''Principles of Governance, Freedom, and Responsibility in Islam'', *The American Journal of Islamic Social Sciences,* 1/1987, pp. 1–11.

Turnham, D., *The Employment Problems in Less Developed Countries: A Review of the Evidence* (Paris: OECD, 1971).

Udovitch, Abraham L., ''Labour Partnership in Early Islamic Law'', *Journal of the Economic and Social History of the Orient,* 1/1967, pp. 68–80.

———, *Partnership and Profit in Medieval Islam* (Princeton, N.J.: Princeton University Press, 1970).

———, ''The Constitution of the Traditional Islamic Marketplace: Islamic Law and the Social Context of Exchange'', in S. N. Eisenstadt, *Beyond the West* (London: Pinter, 1987), vol. 2, pp. 150–71.

U.S. House of Representatives, *Banking for the Poor: Alleviating Poverty through Credit Assistance to the Poorest Microentrepreneurs in Developing Countries, Report of the Select Committee on Hunger* (Washington: U.S. Government Printing Office, May 1986).

Usmani, Muhammad Taqi, ''The Role of Religious Boards in Developing Interest-Free Economy'', *Al-Balagh* (Karachi), 3/1990, pp. 19–22.

Uzair, M., *Interest-free Banking* (Karachi: Royal Book Co., 1978).

———, ''Banks and Financial Institutions: Growth Pattern in the 80s'' (Pakistan Banks after Islamisation), *Journal of Islamic Banking and Finance,* 4/1989, pp. 10–18.

Walsh, James (ed.), *Free Will* (Englewood Cliffs, N.J., 1962).

Weiscopf, Thomas E., ''The Impact of Foreign Capital Inflow on Domestic Savings in Underdeveloped Countries'', *Journal of International Economics,* February 1972, pp. 25–38.

Weiss, Anita M. (ed.), *Islamic Reassertion in Pakistan* (Lahore: Vanguard Books, 1987).

Weiss, Dieter, ''The Struggle for a Vital Islamic Economy'', *The Muslim World* (Hartford, Conn.), 1/1989, pp. 46–58.

Weitzman, Martin L., *The Share Economy* (Cambridge, Mass.: Harvard University Press, 1984).

Welch, Claude, *Protestant Thought in the Nineteenth Century* (New Haven: Yale University Press, 1972).

Williamson, John and Donald R. Lessard (eds.), *Capital Flight: The Problem and Policy Responses* (Washington, D.C.: Institute for International Economics, 1987).

Wilson, Rodney, ''Islamic Banking in Jordan'', *Arab Law Quarterly* (London), August 1987, pp. 207–29.

———, ''The Islamic Development Bank's Role as an Aid Agency for Moslem Countries'', *Journal of International Development,* 3/1989, pp. 18–24.

——— (ed.), *Islamic Financial Markets* (London: Routledge, 1990).

Wohlers-Scharf, Traute, *Arab and Islamic Banks* (Paris: OECD, 1984).

Yalcintas, Nevzat, ''Economic Relations between Turkey and Islamic Countries'', *Studies on Turkish-Arab Relations* (1986), pp. 317–26.

Yunus, Muhammad, *Group-Based Savings and Credit for the Rural Poor* (Dhaka: Grameen Bank, January 1984).

———, ''The Poor as the Engine of Development'', reproduced from *The Washington Quarterly,* Autumn 1987.

Yusri, 'Abd al-Rahman, *Al-Tanmiyyah al-Iqtiṣādiyyah wa al-Ijtimā'iyyah fī al-Islām* (Alexandria: Mu'assasah al-Shahab, n.d.).

Yusuf, Ibrahim Yusuf, *Al-Nafaqāt al-'Āmmah fī al-Islām: Dirāsah Muqāranah* (Dar al-Kitab al-Jami'i, 1980).

Yusuf, S. M., *Economic Justice in Islam* (Lahore: Shaikh Muhammad Ashraf, 1971).

Zaid, Abdulaziz Mohammed, *The Islamic Law of Bequest* (London: Scorpion, 1986).

Zaidi, Nawazish Ali, *Eliminating Interest from Banks in Pakistan* (Karachi: Royal Book Co., 1987).

Zaim, Sabahuddin, ''Islamic Economics as a System Based on Human Values'', *Journal of Islamic Banking and Finance* (Karachi), 2/1989, pp. 13–21.

Zaman, M. Raquibuz, *Some Aspects of the Economics of Zakat* (Plainfield, Indiana: The Association of Muslim Social Scientists, 1980).

———, ''Monetary and Fiscal Policies of an Islamic State: The Claims versus Reality'', *International Journal of Islamic and Arabic Studies* (Bloomington, Indiana), 1/1985, pp. 17–32.

———, *Some Administrative Aspects of the Collection and Distribution of Zakah and the Distributive Effects of the Introduction of Zakah into Modern Economics* (Jeddah: King Abdulaziz University, 1987).

Zarabozo, ''A Basic Need Approach is the Islamic Approach to Development'', *Al-Ittihad,* October–December 1980.

Zarqa, M. Anas, ''Islamic Economics: An Approach to Human Welfare'', in K. Ahmad, *Studies in Islamic Economics* (Leicester, U.K.: The Islamic Foundation, 1980), pp. 13–15.

——, "Capital Allocation, Efficiency and Growth in an Interest-free Islamic Economy", *Journal of Economics and Administration* (Jeddah), November 1982.

——, "Stability in an Interest-free Islamic Economy: A Note", *Pakistan Journal of Applied Economics*, Winter 1983, pp. 181–8.

——, "Islamic Distributive Schemes", in Munawar Iqbal, *Distributive Justice and Need Fulfilment in an Islamic Economy* (Leicester, U.K.: The Islamic Foundation, 1988), pp. 179–80.

——, "Al-Siyāsaṭ al-Iqtiṣādiyyah wa al-Takhṭīṭ fī Iqtiṣād Islāmī", in *Al-Idārah al-Māliyyah fī al-Islām* (Amman: al-Majma' al-Maliki li Buḥuth al-Haḍārah al-Islāmiyyah, 1990).

——, "Islamic Financing of Mute Social Infrastructure: A Suggested Mode Based on Istisna' ", paper presented to the Seminar on Islamic Banking in Bahrain, 26–28 May 1990.

Al-Zarqa, Mustafa A., *Al-Fiqh al-Islāmī fī Thawbihī al-Jadīd* (Damascus: Matabi' Alif Ba' al-Adib, 1967).

Ziring, Lawrence, "Constitutionalism and the Qur'an in the Final Decades of the 20th Century", *Hamdard Islamicus*, Autumn 1990, pp. 15–21.

Zubaida, Sami, *Islam, the People and the State: Essays on Political Ideas in the Middle East* (London: Routledge, 1989).

Zubair, A., "Concept and Protection of Labour Under Islamic Law", *Islamic Order* (Karachi), 3/1989, pp. 18–24.

Zuberi, Khalique, "Islamic Trade Financing Facility", *Journal of Islamic Banking and Finance*, July–September 1986, pp. 17–32.

Index

Index

Index

CPSIA information can be obtained
at www.ICGtesting.com
Printed in the USA
LVOW04s1245300916
506871LV00003B/6/P

9 780860 372172